ARCHITECTURAL TYPE AND CHARACTER

Architectural Type and Character provides an alternative perspective to the current role given to history in architecture, reunifying architectural history and architectural design to reform architectural discourse and practice. Historians provide important material for appreciating buildings and guiding those who produce them. In current histories, a building is the product of a time, its form follows its function, irresistible influences produce it, and style, preferably novel, is its most important attribute. This book argues for an alternative.

Through a two-part structure, the book first develops the theoretical foundations for this alternative history of architecture. The second part then provides drawings and interpretations of over one hundred sites from different times and places.

Architectural Type and Character: A Practical Guide to a History of Architecture is an excellent desk reference and studio guide for students and architectures alike to understand, analyze, and create buildings.

Samir Younés is Professor of Architecture at the University of Notre Dame where he was Director of Rome Studies and Director of Graduate Studies. He teaches architectural design and theory. His books include: *The Imperfect City: On Architectural Judgement*; *Architects and Mimetic Rivalry*; *The Intellectual Life of the Architect*; and *Quatremère de Quincy's Historical Dictionary of Architecture: The True, The Fictive, and The Real.*

Carroll William Westfall's PhD in the history of architecture from Columbia University was followed by five decades of teaching before retiring from the University of Notre Dame. His scholarly and general articles run from studies of Pompeii to critiques of current practice. His books are *In This Most Perfect Paradise*, a study of Rome in the 15th c.; *Architectural Principles in the Age of Historicism*, a dialectic exchange with Robert Jan van Pelt, and a review of architectural theory, *Architecture, Liberty, and Civic Order: Architectural Theories from Vitruvius to Jefferson and Beyond.*

ARCHITECTURAL TYPE AND CHARACTER

A Practical Guide to a History of Architecture

Samir Younés and Carroll William Westfall

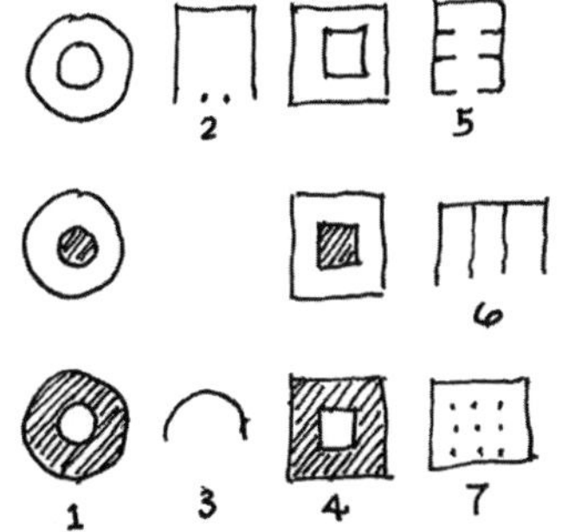

NEW YORK AND LONDON

First published 2022
by Routledge
605 Third Avenue, New York, NY 10158

and by Routledge
2 Park Square, Milton Park, Abingdon, Oxon, OX14 4RN

Routledge is an imprint of the Taylor & Francis Group, an informa business

Library of Congress Cataloging-in-Publication Data
Names: Younés, Samir, author. | Westfall, Carroll William, author.
Title: Architectural type and character : a practical guide to a history of architecture / Samir Younés and Carroll William Westfall.
Description: New York : Routledge, 2022. | Includes bibliographical references and index. |
Identifiers: LCCN 2021037090 (print) | LCCN 2021037091 (ebook) | ISBN 9781138584037 (hardback) | ISBN 9781138584051 (paperback) | ISBN 9780429506260 (ebook)
Subjects: LCSH: Architecture—History. | Architecture—Composition, proportion, etc. | Architecture and society.
Classification: LCC NA203 .Y68 2022 (print) | LCC NA203 (ebook) | DDC 720.9—dc23
LC record available at https://lccn.loc.gov/2021037090
LC ebook record available at https://lccn.loc.gov/2021037091

ISBN: 9781138584037 (hbk)
ISBN: 9781138584051 (pbk)
ISBN: 9780429506260 (ebk)

DOI: 10.4324/9780429506260

Typeset in Bembo
by codeMantra

Printed in the United Kingdom
by Henry Ling Limited

CONTENTS

ILLUSTRATIONS

PREAMBLE

The authors share a fervent commitment to reform the practice of architecture by reforming the ways in which its history is understood. This book results from an exchange of ideas containing many agreements and occasional differences. Here, each author summarizes the complementary reasons that compelled them to write this study.

Samir Younés

Implicit in any historical explanation, as a reconstruction of events, is the linkage drawn by historians between causes that are internal to these events and causes that are external. Histories of architecture reveal the historian's commitment to converge several pursuits, three of which are: writing the history of a given period based on architectural design or composition (causes internal to architecture), an adherence to a certain history of ideas, and a certain philosophy of history (causes external to architecture). One such external cause to the writing of architectural history, is a philosophy of history called Historicism that has deeply marked architectural practice and historical scholarship since the middle of the 19th century. Historicism developed a determinist outlook that included the following ten points:

1 History is qualified by a teleological direction. Time has an arrow.
2 Progress came to be associated with teleology in all fields of human endeavor.
3 The forward or progressive movement of architectural history was evidenced in and assured by stylistic ruptures, and these ruptures were inexorable because the arrow of history itself is inexorable.

4 Architectural and art history was written as a history of ruptures, thereby ignoring continuities.
5 Historians associated ways of slicing time (periodization) with a stylistic understanding of architecture.
6 Historians neglected or ignored the concepts of type and character, and gave overwhelming preference to style.
7 The teleological and progressive argument implied that architecture was moving toward a kind of apotheosis which was embodied by the work of modernist architects and where all previous developments in history additively led to this apotheosis.
8 Since each period was qualified by its own spirit (Zeitgeist) and its own images of the world (*Weltanschauungen*), Modernism was the true expression of that spirit and its images.
9 To be true to the Zeitgeist, the images of the world were to be technologically mediated, indeed technologically determined. This was the only acceptable form of modernity.
10 Therefore, learning from and putting to use the wealth of lessons deriving from multiple traditions is not only anachronistic, it also has no bearing on present concerns. Historicist beliefs prevented architects from putting to use the rich and cumulative lessons of the architectural experience as it stretches over centuries.

With these positions the historicist narrative overstressed the weight of historical forces external to architecture to such a point that architecture appeared as if symptomatic of these forces. More explicitly, this determinist narrative asserted that changes in direction in architecture happened as if by necessity, and that its own recounting of history was a true description of this necessity. Naturally, one of the aims of historians is to convince others of the correctness of their positions, and yet their deterministic arguments are deeply buried within the recesses of their texts and seldom are they expressed on the surface.

Disagreements with historicism abound, and the following ten points are among the most important:

1 Rather than proceeding in one direction, history may be proceeding in multiple directions.
2 Not every linkage of events is necessarily a teleology, and teleology does not inevitably lead to progress, in the sense of improvement.
3 The belief that the same concept of progress applies equally to architecture, the arts, and the sciences is certainly erroneous.
4 There are several modernities, as the concept is in constant flux, and there are therefore multiple images that express these modernities. Architectural Modernism is only one of them.

5 Historians are called to clearly announce their theoretical intentions to their readers. For example, that they hold historicist beliefs which they have brought to bear on their histories, and how do their theoretical intentions differ from other philosophies of history.
6 Historians are called to explain that causation in history is not necessarily determinism in history.
7 Historians and architects are asked to explain how to reconcile their beliefs in the freedom of the individual architect in contrast to the prodigious teleological and supra-personal forces that they believe are operating in history in an inexorable way.
8 An intellectually honest view of history acknowledges both ruptures and continuities. If in expressing their intellectual freedom architects wish to operate a rupture from a certain historical experience, then other architects, also expressing their intellectual freedom, rationalize successful lessons from architectural traditions.
9 Contrary to historicist thinking, a history can argue from the nature of a building to telling its story. This nature is embodied in the concepts of type and character, as we shall see.
10 Type and character, respectively, explain and justify the generative (causative) aspects of architectural form and the expressive qualities of this form. Restoring the vital role of type and character does not negate style, or manner, which has its proper place.

It is possible to write a history that does not follow a grand narrative like historicism. What distinguishes this book is that it presents an integral approach to both architectural design and historical knowledge. *Integral, here, considers architectural design and historical knowledge as one single project and not two separate pursuits.* The concerns of the architect and those of the historian can converge, and this project can potentially reform architectural education and practice at once. Therefore, another view of architectural history is possible, a history that is written for architects who intend on putting to use the durable, successful lessons of history, who intend on improving these lessons in practice, and who pass along to future generations the lessons of their own experience.

Carroll William Westfall

This book responds to the disregard in the discipline of the history of art and architecture of two important characteristics that every building possesses: it is a work of civic art, and the history of architecture can contribute to the education of architects and the laypeople who are engaged in its construction.

Neither of these characteristics was considered important in my education in the history of art and architecture. Nor were they important to me in the years when I taught their history in liberal arts programs and much less when I taught in professional architecture programs. Architecture students found the history of their art to be irrelevant to their professional training that emphasized being creative while learning that buildings in the past were the products of the influences in the past that produced styles belonging only to the past.

My introduction to understanding buildings within the realm of the political life of a nation came through my involvement in historic preservation activities. I expanded my teaching and inquiries into the history of urbanism where I came to appreciate the role buildings play in serving the public, common good. By the time I retired after teaching and being involved with the growing groups involved in modern traditional and classical architecture I had received invaluable mentoring in the role of knowing traditional and classical architecture and urbanism and the means of inventing within them to build beautiful urban places serving the good city, and it continued while working on this book.

In writing it I took the opportunity to explore five additional topics. One is the difference Vitruvius presents between the art of building and the art of architecture. The second, closely related, is the cost of conflating delight with beauty. The third involves restoring beauty to architecture. A fourth is the role that perspective's invention in the early 15th c. has had on the design of buildings and cities. And finally, to consider the three legs supporting architecture, the tectonic, architectural, and urban, both separately and, more importantly, in their unity.

INTRODUCTION

This book is for everyone who encounters a building. We offer ways to recognize its beauty and the role it plays in their lives, with special importance for many people in the culture of architecture who bring them into existence — architects, professors, critics, historians, public officials, political office holders, bankers, officers in major corporate enterprises, private clients, etc.

In Part I, we discuss the general principles about architecture, and in Part II, we provide a Catalogue of 100 buildings, each one presented in free-hand drawings by Samir Younés and a commentary for each, most by Carroll Westfall. Buildings make architecture and architecture makes cities. They belong to one another like hands, arms, and the other parts that make the human body. Our primary focus is on buildings that are skillfully and beautifully made with special attention to their role in building cities where people can prosper and enjoy their full human dignity. This book differs from the usual writing about buildings. In one sense, it is a history of architecture, but it is unlike the presently pervasive treatment of that history that presents individual buildings in a chronological order within a series of styles running from Egypt to the present day and generally neglects their role in urbanism. We cover that chronological range, and we reach across the globe, but we do not follow the usual formula that treats a building as an artifact of the culture that produced it. To say that in another, more professional, academic way, we do not have the *Zeitgeist* operating in a succession of periods produce the influences that induce architects to make buildings that are in the style of their time with each new period leading inevitably to Modernism and its many styles.

In that formula, the architect becomes an automaton commanded by influences that, like influenza, sicken the body, and use the architect to express the culture of the time that is established by a genius such as Michelangelo who

DOI: 10.4324/9780429506260-1

introduces a new style that makes all old things obsolete. Here we recognize that an architect is a person with special talent and knowledge about building and architecture who brings those qualities to the civic forum where others with their own expertise work together to build and maintain a good city. They work together in the aspiration they share with others as they contribute their reason, will, intellect, and special talents to fulfill their human nature's aspiration to do the good with justice, to know the true, and to experience the beautiful.

In that good city, buildings serve purposes that fulfill human nature and are limited in number and universal and enduring. Serving those purposes are functions that are many in number and are discarded and replaced when better ways of doing what they facilitate are found.

In the good city where these human purposes prevail, tradition transmits valuable experience and invention adapts it to changed circumstances. There is no place there for the formula based on relativism of *Zeitgeist* = influence = style. Instead, there is the interaction of type, character, and style, words that are discussed extensively in the text. Those three words play a role in all writings about architecture, but seldom with the same meanings that they carry here. The reader, then, must pay careful attention to their role here, a task assisted by noting that the procedure for designing a building that we present in the next section is the reverse of the one customarily used for interpreting the ones presented here. It is, we hope, a procedure that will assist the builders in making beauty visible and enrich the experience of beauty that good buildings offer.

Buildings within the history of the arts

The current predominant understanding of architecture connects it with the other visual arts within the modern system of the arts that developed in the 18th c. That system allies architecture with painting, sculpture, theater, and music with relatives in literature, poetry, prints, drawings, landscape design, and so on.[1] Their role is to provide a pleasurable experience(s), which is a personal experience that can also come from the taste of good cuisine. The experience is necessarily private but can be shared through language that describes the personal sensations. Others can obtain a *like* experience but not *your* experience; yours is yours, theirs is theirs, and it goes no farther than the sensory organs that transmit the pleasure. Judgments based on that experience are called judgments of taste, and they are not open to reasoned argument or assessment.

This modern role for the arts developed from the claim made by some architects in France in the 17th c. that their new works of art, and especially their new buildings, were superior not only to new Italian ones but also to any that the ancients had built. In antiquity and ever since, judgments about architecture followed universal, objective standards of the beautiful, and beauty was the proper end of the arts. It is quite significant that one of the most important elements of the *Querelle des anciens et des modernes* regarded the reasons for which buildings please: do they please because of inherent objective qualities or because of the observer's subjectivity? Most architects adhered to objective beauty, which resides in qualities that have been willed into a building such as the proportions between the various members. Few architects adhered to the subjectivist view in the 17th c., but this view quickly became dominant since the 18th c. This phenomenon displaced and eventually replaced the assessment based on objective beauty with judgments based on taste or subjective beauty. This opened a gap in the larger framework where beauty was a principal element in philosophy's guidance in assessing achievement in the arts, and the field of aesthetics was developed to fill that gap. But judgments of taste, based as they are on personal experience and evaluation, leave no role for public engagement or significance. They can go no farther than "I like it, you don't,' that's your loss," and never reach "We agree that what we see in this object points outside itself to objective values we share."

This role for taste is a modern concept, and the term modern will occur often in what follows here. We use the word modern to refer to how people today understand the present's relationship to the past. For us, the past is a different time from our present. It holds distinct eras that are both different from one another and from our present. The word itself is modern; that is, there is no equivalent before the 15th c. In the Latin inherited from antiquity there was no way to refer to a modern age as opposed to a past. Instead, people referred to *hodie*, today, or *modo*, just recently, and the past, although marked by distinctive events and individuals, and was not divided into successive eras. We see in the word modern the beginnings of our recent past, which occurred in the 15th c. in Italy, the period we call the Renaissance, the time when individuals whom the historian Jacob Burckhardt more than a century and a half ago identified as the first born of modern man. By then the familiar sequence of historical eras, ancient for the Greeks and Romans, medieval for the age in the middle, and Renaissance as the beginning of the modern, was being solidified into the historical chronicles we read today. It is worth noting that this was the age that developed judgments based on taste and the aesthetic doctrines to discuss them.

The premodern eras saw what we call the past as a continuity marked by dramatic events within an enduring tradition. We see the past, even within the modern age, as a series of notable events that have changed the present with changes being more important in our lives than the continuity of traditions. Within little more than a century the notion has developed that two radical changes have taken root, one called Modernism and the other Postmodernism, with each of these doing to the history that preceded it what the Renaissance modern age had done to the middle ages, which was to separate itself from its immediate past definitively and completely but also, unlike the predecessors of Modernism, from all earlier eras. Central to them is the doctrine in architecture that everything in the past is useless for the present and the general belief that human nature is changeable.

We do not accept the Modernist nullification of the past or the changeability of human nature. Instead, we endorse the modern concept that finds value in and puts to use the successful experience of previous ages. We recognize that the modern age is the present version of that which has always offered enduring value and that, with proper modification, it can continue to serve us as we live our lives as individuals and within communities.

The breadth and depth of past experience offer important material for the need to revise current practices in architecture and urbanism. Among them is restoring the idea of an objective beauty found in nature, and an objective beauty in architecture made in imitation of nature. This idea never disappeared in modern times, even if it was eclipsed by a dominant subjective turn of the mind since the 18th c. If the lessons of the beautiful, the good (and its adjunct the just), and the true have a certain authority, it is the authority of reason in experience, and that makes for their long durability.

This understanding has been severely jolted by ideas hatched in Modernism, but we embrace the recognition that it is human nature to pursue them as we pursue happiness. One name for this way of understanding ourselves and our place in the cosmos is the classical tradition, a term that will be used here. It is, however, not the exclusive possession of the western tradition; similar insights into the world exist in other traditions with their classical existing in the best possible formulations and with their own names for their traditions and their finest achievements.

The western, classical tradition will loom large in what follows here, but only because it is the tradition that is most familiar to us and the one we know best. Our intention here is to provide a makeweight against Modernism and Postmodernism in order to restore and modernize the role that buildings play in our modern present and future. We hope that those who seek to preserve other valued traditions will find guidance here for doing so. And it is our hope that this enterprise will be beneficial to laypeople and all those who are involved in building, understanding, interpreting, and enjoying the world we build.

Appendix 1: How to design a building

The comments here are intended to offer architects and their clients a sequence of steps that allow the material presented in this book to assist in producing a beautiful building that contributes to the common good. The sequence is based on two premises:

1 Design calls for the architect's willful, knowledgeable, and reasoned attention to the purpose the building is to serve and express within the common good.

2 New buildings are made out of other buildings or their parts, with the traditions of a place offering guidance and with inventions used to adapt it to current circumstances.

The first step is to select the **generative type(s)**, that is, the idea type(s), that fit(s) the purpose(s) to be served.

The second step is to gain intimate knowledge of the **traditions** of building and of architectural expression in the realm the building will serve. This knowledge must encompass **tectonic means, expressive character**, and its role in **urbanism**. Next comes the generation of a *parti* from a collection of appropriate **paradigmatic models**; note the plural. After that comes intimate knowledge of the precedents those models offer for adaptation to plan, sections, and interior and exterior elevations. This leads to producing a three-dimensional **configuration**, the **membrature** of the material fabric that will make it visible and enduring, and their **composition** into a serviceable, functional building. Having worked this out in rough drawings that make the building buildable, the design has reached what the art of building or construction requires. This next step elevates the building to architecture. The art of architecture now requires investing the building with the appropriate **expressive character**. This calls for making the **adjustments** and **refinements** to the building's composition, the proportionality of its parts to one another and to the whole, and the addition of any decoration for its expressive character and ornament to honor the membrature. Where we meet the final polishing called **style**, which is the inevitable product of the individual architect and the time and place that burnishes beauty that makes the building a suitable addition to the urban or rural setting it will occupy. Success here gives the building the order, harmony, and proportionality of nature that is the source of the beauty we experience as a counterpart to the good and the service to the justice we seek.

Appendix 2: Notation conventions

Many buildings and cities will be mentioned throughout this book. Part II offers brief comments about many of them along with original, carefully produced drawings, but these can offer only mere suggestions of their formal qualities.

The internet has and increasingly will continue to provide visual material and information, much of it reliable, which the reader is encouraged to consult. The internet's material, like that of most published material, is deficient in plans. These are supplied for many of the examples presented in Part II.

We remind the reader that the best way to know a building is to make its personal acquaintance, sketchbook in hand, for more than a fleeting visit.

Throughout the text buildings WITH ALL CAPS are included in the Catalogue. Material about other buildings **identified in bold** can be found in books and through internet sources with Google Earth being especially useful for seeing its place on the land and in cities. Construction of most buildings stretched over several years; we normally give one date, the earliest likely date when construction began and its design might have been known. We have kept footnotes to a bare minimum; they point to useful sources and acknowledge important contributors. Names of popes and kings are followed by the dates when they occupied the office and sometimes their birth, regnant, and death dates. The names of architects and others are also determined by their birth and death dates. Dates without BCE are in the present age.

Note

1 See Paul Oskar Kristeller, "The Modern System of the Arts," in *Renaissance Thought II: Papers on Humanism and the Arts* (New York, Evanston, and London: Harper Torchbooks, 1965); originally published in *Journal of the History of Ideas*, 12, no. 4 (1951): 496–527, and 13, no. 1 (1952): 17–46; 163–227.

PART I

1

THE HISTORY OF ARCHITECTURE WE HAVE

In 1865, Massachusetts Institute of Technology (MIT) was the first institution of higher learning in the United States to offer instruction in architecture with Columbia in 1881 the first one in a university. To learn their history after 1896 students had a textbook published by a Columbia professor who had studied at the École des Beaux-Arts in Paris.[1] Another history appeared the same year in England with its instruction including now-familiar drawings.[2] In the 1905 edition, Banister Fletcher revised its featured memetic image that ornamented the "Tree of Architecture" whose roots are nourished by "influences" labeled as Geography, Geology, Climate, Religion, Social, and History, putting atop the tree's "MODERN STYLES" the **Flatiron Building, Daniel H. Burnham, New York, 1901–02**.

Fletcher's handbook remains in print without the tree and expanded to an elephantine *omnium gatherum*, but Hamlin's was made obsolete by books based on the urtext of Nikolaus Pevsner (1902–83), a 1934 immigrant to England from Germany published in 1943 titled *An Outline of European Architecture* (London: Penguin Press). He confined himself to Europe, and he scanted everything before Charlemagne. What happened earlier in Greece and Rome is "not part of our Western civilization." It needs some mention only because "it had much influence on the early centuries of Western formation." Constantly expanded and much more inclusive, the historicism it made available now permeates our understanding of the architecture's past and present.

Pevsner's history appeared after the third wave of change had washed over architecture and was now expanding all across the globe. The first wave pervaded the 19th c. when nations, confronted with unsettling, dramatic change, welcomed models for the current practice from earlier, valued eras to associate the present with a past. In France, the models immediately predated the

DOI: 10.4324/9780429506260-3

Revolution and became vehicles to deny the ravages of 1789 and retrieved the grandeur of prerevolutionary France as we see, for example, in the OPÉRA, CHARLES GARNIER, PARIS, 1861–75. Britain reached back to a broader range of earlier eras to feed its 19th c. eclecticism. In the second wave, new building technologies and materials were used for an expanded retrieval from the past as architects labored to adapt traditional styles to modern functions, with the Flatiron Building given the prize atop Fletcher's Tree.

The third wave broke when the Flatiron Building was less than two decades old. It rejected any role for traditional styles, and on the leading edge of progress installed the newly invented Modernist styles serving Modernity, and this change was quickly absorbed into the narrative of the history of architecture.

The narrative that has dominated for the better part of the 20th century has been written under the shadow of a certain philosophy of history known as Historicism. This philosophy rejected beliefs in universal, objective ideas that transcend empirical reality. It asserted the primacy of the particular over the universal. It affirmed the relativism of cultural values that could only be studied according to the unique context and time from which they purportedly emerged. It opposed the beliefs according to which the laws of Nature and human nature changed little and replaced them with the belief that nature and society are in constant change. This change follows some determining patterns, but these patterns did not derive from universal ideas; rather, they are located within the immanently changing values of an incessantly changing culture.

The more forceful exponents of Historicism claimed to have discovered the laws that underlie history and saw historical events as purportedly evolving in a certain direction that was determined by overarching narratives (e.g. the notion of the arrow of time).[3] Accordingly, architectural forms were said to be evolving following determining historical forces, and these forces were in turn evolving in a particular direction – a direction that modernist artists and architects were particularly adept at manifesting. Other concepts, such as that of a *Zeitgeist* (a spirit of a given time frame), of a *Weltanschauung* (a world-view, a world-image), and of teleology and progressivity, merged with Historicism, thus making it a dominant cultural force.

Architectural historians of a historicist bent of mind from Pevsner on applied these general conceptions developed in the philosophy of history and in social science to architectural knowledge. They wrote narratives using stylistic classifications where each period is qualified by its own unique style and each style distinguished by an inexorable break or rupture from previous styles. Such a construct became a vessel for historicist claims in architecture in which stylistic ruptures were assured by determinist forces operating in history. Once teleological thinking came to permeate this construct, historical styles came to be seen as steps leading to the apotheosis of Modernism, as if by necessity.

Historicism carries several notions into the narrative's plot. One is that the many people involved in bringing a building into existence, from architects to building officials and bankers, want what they build to be "of its time." In architecture as in nature that has been untouched by humankind, change has been an evolution that led from slime to humankind and to modern sciences' command of nature. Evolution in nature and in technological progress demonstrates that in progress, there is only forward movement and no looking back. In both, each step was a step "of its time," ape to human, buggy to auto, Greek temple to skyscraper, and so too must the architect's buildings be today.

This historicist narrative treats the traditional historical narrative as obsolete. Traditional narratives presented the cosmos as a stable and dynamic whole with an enduring order, harmony, and proportionality and with unpredictable and inexplicable changes. Things and creatures had fixed natures, with humans uniquely endowed with a nature that includes reason, memory, skill, will, and a moral conscience or soul to use in confronting change and for practicing the social and political arts of living with others to find the happiness that is offered by gaining insight into the good, the true, and the beautiful. The histories written in that world told tales of great events that illustrated those qualities at work, none greater, according to the ancient historian Thucydides, than the Peloponnesian War, "the greatest disturbance in the history of the Hellenes, affecting …I might almost say, the whole of mankind" (Rex Warner trans. ¶1). He explained his purpose:

> It will be enough for me… if these words of mine are judged useful by those who want to understand clearly the events which happened in the past and which (*human nature being what it is*) will, at some time or other and in much the same ways, *be repeated in the future*. My work is not a piece of writing designed to meet the taste of an immediate public, but was done to last forever.
>
> *(¶22; emphasis added)*

Thucydides' narrative presents change occurring within a long-term constancy composed of ups and downs that occur in the nature of things and largely outside our control. There is no arrow pointing upward into inevitable progress. Instead, there is the mythical decline from an age of gold seen in Athens with a different story told in Jerusalem.

The historicist narrative flourished within the growing skepticism and empiricism in the 18th c. and eagerly absorbed the next century's rapidly expanding knowledge of buildings in distant times and places. Historians cataloged this material according to formal, stylistic similarities that slotted buildings into the succession of eras or periods, and by the century's end, they had connected an era's style of buildings to properties of other products of the time to identify the period's common cultural images or *Weltanschauungen*. The extent and longevity of the periods varied from broad and long-lived as in the sequence ancient to gothic to modern revival styles, to slices of whatever span of time stylistic distinctions could support.

This history of architecture that justifies Modernist styles, and the Modernist styles that extend the history of architecture ever farther away from even recently acclaimed buildings now commands the global culture of architecture. It is the possession of those who teach, practice, learn, build, finance, write about, and form the opinions that people have about buildings. It requires a building to be "of its time," and it treats any earlier style or formal property as a threat to Modernity's continued progress.

Assisting this worldwide hegemony has been the validity Modernism has claimed by its absorption of technology into what it calls the evolution of architecture. The theory of evolution has nature do its work without human intervention, and when those forces are put to work in human society, progress is assured. Using the rigor and methods of empiricism that produce demonstrable progress in technology and shaking free of inherited myths and beliefs that saw human society as sequences of ups and downs across an overall average, societies can extend their predestined upward path.

This Modernity rejects traditional beliefs formulated in Athens and Jerusalem, and adapted and interpreted by civil communities ever since. It rejects the position that judgments concerning right and wrong, like those dealing with the presence or absence of the beautiful as the counterpart to the good, are trustworthy, whether held by individuals or by the communities they live within. It dismisses as fancy a body of beliefs and conclusions of reason that have guided actions since their formulation in ancient Athens and Jerusalem with its three fundamental principles.

First, human nature is enduring. Thucydides suggested as much in the passage quoted earlier, and so do the natural law premises of the Declaration of Independence. Each individual has a unique nature, but it is a human nature and not that of some other being. We can enter into a contract with another person but not with a horse or a dog. Socrates was unique as an individual, and he was also unique among humankind.

Second, the individual's human nature seeks fulfillment by doing the good, knowing the truth, and enjoying the beautiful. These are moral qualities that no other species possesses. Each person has a different capacity to fulfill the ideals of each, and every person knows that perfect and complete attainment is impossible in our mortal lives, but every person finds happiness in pursuing them.

Third, people are naturally sociable. Aristotle noted that they assemble into three kinds of groupings, each with a purpose, and that they can be joined by synoecism: individuals into families to assure the perpetuation of the race, families into tribes or villages to exchange expertise and labor to assure their sustenance, and these then into political entities or cities to attain the good life. Humans are equipped to make cities, which do not appear as if by nature's evolution or technology's progress but through the efforts of individuals who work together in communities to achieve the fullness of human nature. To be the good city where each individual can thrive is the aspiration of every community. In it, the members of the city bring their special talents and unique abilities to the common forum to support a common enterprise, including the physician, the lawyer, and the public official. The life available in the good city has been pursued in this way in varied forms across the millennia, and the architect was among those making lasting and conspicuous contributions to that common pursuit, until the radical rupture at the dawn of the 20th c.

With Modernism, the architect placed a higher emphasis on the historicist *Weltanschauung* – understood as the set of images that are proper for production by the technological society – than on the common good architects are called to serve as citizens. Architects and historians recast changes of style as architecture's natural evolution, gave technology the upper hand in serving functions and forms, and applied to architecture and the arts the same idea of progress as understood in science and technology. The architect is uninterested in interrogating the past to find the best way to serve the common good and seek beauty as the counterpart to justice, although that has been the architect's traditional role and method. To that end we present here several propositions that point the way toward their reformulation.

Proposition One: reforming architecture requires loosening the restrictions of historicist determinism and the limitations of stylistic classifications keyed to the *Zeitgeist* and replacing it with a history of architecture that offers architects a wider realm for assisting them in their practice.

The prevailing narrative of the history of architecture dissuades architects from consulting past experience for assistance in designing in the present. Its interest is on the change from period to period and building to building, not in the continuity of the formal properties of buildings serving similar roles in succeeding years and eras.

We argue here that historians and architects can usefully investigate, interpret, and present the wisdom gained by the experience of the minds and hands that have been building throughout centuries and millennia. This body of wisdom and knowledge resides in the buildings and cities we still admire and are lovingly cataloged within stylistic classifications by historians, but they are presented as belonging to the past with nothing to offer the present. We argue that to the contrary, this wisdom can be synthesized and put to use in the present. It must be done judiciously and not indiscriminately, and most emphatically not by the unthinking copying of past forms and for reasons no more profound and important than satisfying an emotional nostalgia for a preferred past age(s). Rather, we emphasize the optimal interaction between imitation and invention – a conceptual couple that has been the driving creative force behind architectural and artistic expressions down to a century ago when it fell into disrepute. A little later we will discuss the inseparability of this couple.

Our contact with the past gives us access to a vast experience with the building mind that rational analysis shows to be successful and can and should be maintained and sustained as well as reveals proven failures that we ought to discontinue. This cumulative experience with the judicious use of the mind theoretical and the mind practical is embodied in the traditions and conventions of the art of building. Conventions (*con venire*: to come together) have developed through repeating and improving successful experiences and discontinuing failed ones, and they provide a major portion of the content of tradition (*traditio*: handing over). Early experiments lead to established experience, and established experience leads to mature expression. There is no stasis.

To build is a natural act whether it be to feather a nest or serve a civil order. It is done to fulfill certain purposes. In human experience, using the conventions transmitted through the art of building necessarily develops in close relationship to existing, local, cultural contexts and experience, and it uses the available building materials and technologies. As conventions become deeply anchored within a context, they endow buildings with distinctive architectural qualities and produce what we call a sense of place coming from the layering of various local conventions over time. Another name for this sense of place is regional architectural character. Distinctive traits of character are not limited to architecture. They are also found in spoken dialects, music, gastronomy, behavior in public, etc., where strands of local conventions mingle with other strands, and over time these mature and expand into identifiable traditions in regions and beyond them to nations. In a nation a people live in a society that is organized with traditions that serve its aspirations.

Traditions inform the architect's intellectual life that is further stimulated and informed by the rational content encapsulated in the millennial architectural experience. This value is in continuity, the continuity of reason. But the value of continuity can be negated when the past is parceled into discrete eras marked by distinctive styles that offer mere trifling encounters with the past, as when the architect extracts only superficial formal aspects from precedents and then proceeds immediately to discard them or applies them superficially in producing a building that is "of our time."

In the alternative history presented here, the architect's mind becomes an instrument that uses enduringly successful architectural, tectonic, and urban forms.

Proposition Two: designing architecture and studying its history are two facets of one single endeavor.

When programs in architecture were introduced in American universities the past of architecture was intimately bound to the instruction and practice of architecture. Old, existing buildings and their parts provided models that guided the designing of new buildings, and the architect's most useful resource was the sketchbook documenting investigations of buildings along with the numerous treatises and books illustrating the work of other architects and only rarely written by non-architects.

The programs' model was that of the École des Beaux-Arts in Paris where history provided images for making new buildings. The introduction of histories of architecture in the universities programs was intended to lift the "programs above the schools of engineering and mines" and their graduates into the professions.[4]

Those Beaux-Arts-based programs were then radically altered after 1937 when Walter Gropius and Joseph Hudnut were called to Harvard and Ludwig Mies van der Rohe to Chicago to institute instruction in Modernism. In 1941, Harvard's press published the first historicist narrative appearing in English: *Space, Time and Architecture: The Growth of a New Tradition* by Siegfried Giedion, two years before Pevsner's *An Outline of European Architecture* that was soon given an "American Postscript." Gropius, Giedion, Pevsner, and their successors down to the present day offer history as a body of knowledge ancillary to practice and presenting the historicist arrow of progress. They run through earlier styles that were "of their time" and culminate in buildings that are "of our time." This disconnection between the past and the present was fine for historians who wanted to investigate "the various significant problems which confront the student of architectural history today," as the mission of the Society of Architectural Historians founded in 1940 puts it. This positivist intention arose in the 18th c. when judgments about beauty were organized as the discipline of aesthetics that Bernard Bosanquet in 1892 defined as "a branch of philosophy … [that] exists for the sake of knowledge and not as a guide to practice."[5]

Students in accredited schools of architecture were now required to gain an "understanding" of history that conveyed major lessons, which are the same that laypeople encounter whenever they read anything about architecture. This understanding has several parts.

First, by responding to influences, architects can be assured that the style of their buildings will be "of their time."

Second, the styles of previous periods that history documents are forbidden in current use.

Third, architects operate independently from their compatriots in the other visual arts except in so far as they too point to progress, reject traditional forms as useful in their work, and introduce new styles befitting the modern age and leading into the future.

And fourth, they are to lead the culture of architecture into the future where people will achieve the security and prosperity that it is human nature to seek.

Embedded in this historicist narrative are three major flaws in language that must be remedied if the deficiencies of the narrative are to be remedied.

Building and architecture

All pickles are cucumbers, but not all cucumbers are pickles; all architecture is buildings, but not all buildings are architecture. A building is the product of the art of building that uses materials to make a structure serving the needs of a patron. Architecture is achieved when the structure serves the common good with beauty, commodity, and propriety.

Lord Henry Wotton in his 17th c. translation of the Augustan theorist Vitruvius wrote that a building "hath three Conditions. Commoditie, Firmenes, and Delight," or as we put it, function, material stability and longevity, and the aesthetic pleasure that a well-built building offers. Every architect and many laypeople know this trilogy, but unlike Vitruvius and Wooten, they do not know that these are not the conditions of good architecture. They are *necessary* for building and architecture but not *sufficient* conditions for architecture. Vitruvius states that architecture requires three other, additional criteria: *symmetria* or proportionality; *eurythmia* or the ability to make their qualities perceptible; and *decorum* or the obvious appropriateness of the role the building plays in the civil order. This differentiation between a building and architecture has parallels in many other fields, for example in the difference between my singing and what can be heard on an opera stage, or a battle group holding the line and one that makes a historic breakthrough, or voting and acquitting oneself well in holding office.

The current historicist narrative uses building and architecture interchangeably, and it substitutes the criterion of being "of its time" for assessing its service to the common good and its embodiment of beauty.

Purpose and function

All purposes are served by functions, which are changeable and therefore unlike purposes, which are enduring and limited in number, but not all functions serve purposes that reach the common good.

Today the words function and purpose are conflated and have been at least since Jean-Nicolas-Louis Durand in the late 18th c. introduced what became the "form follows function" mantra. He taught it in his crash course on design for engineers in the school Napoleon Bonaparte had established, instructing them that in comparison to architecture, "[P]ainting and sculpture, two arts whose productions, made to please not only the eyes but the soul, are also incomparably easier to learn....[I]n consequence, the purpose of architecture cannot be pleasure but utility."[6] In the 19th c., the mantra took hold when technological innovations and social and economic changes demanded new buildings that technological innovation and the expanded production of iron, glass, terra cotta, and other materials made possible. Market halls built with iron and glass then inspired early Modernist architects to use undecorated technology to make buildings serving lowly functions such as manufacturing and social housing, which would make them "of their time" in the modern era and also make old buildings look old fashioned. The "form follows function" mantra then began producing the expressive character of buildings working their way up the spectrum of civil purposes that expected the expression of the efficiency and modernity of their functions.

In our argument, a building's purpose is not limited to giving pleasure or serving utility. Its purpose is to serve a common good, whether it is a public purpose, a private one, or a combination of the two. This purpose depends on functions as means of accomplishing its purpose. A state capitol serves the common good, and the officials working there perform a number of functions to fulfill that purpose. A bank is chartered by a public body to serve specific purposes while rendering services to the public that involve various functions (keeping money safe; lending money) that earn a profit for its owners. The PALAZZO FARNESE in Rome was built for the purpose of allowing a family to exercise its authority in the civil order, but its many functions ran from accommodating family needs to stabling horses.

Purposes are enduring with no change or with only slow changes over time, while functions are constantly revised as new and better ways of serving purposes are introduced. State capitols, banks, and the Palazzo Farnese remain as a potent expression of the purposes of authority in public life even though the chambers and offices inside have moved from using quill pens to digital technology and the Palazzo Farnese, the French embassy in Rome, garages automobiles and not horses. Changes in banking functions may have had a bank abandon its former home, but the building may continue to decorate (a word related to decorum) and grace the city with a changed function, say that of a restaurant.

Using the two words interchangeably reveals a disinterest in the common good, an immunity to instruction from the past, and a commitment to being "of the time." Preservation suffers from this. It selects old buildings that are to be admired but may not be serving useful functions or provide models in current practice. They are to be kept as faithful representatives "of their time," which requires that any alteration must be identifiable as "of their time," even if the results disfigure the old building. Paradoxically, however, the public supports preserving old buildings such as factories or warehouses that requires elevating the status of their roles by adapting them to serve as schools, office buildings, or residences. Understandably motivated by nostalgia for a lost era, the activity is also driven by apprehension about what a new building will look like and "do to" a street's or neighborhood's character that people recognize as a servant to the common good.

Purpose and appeal

In the first words of his 1943 history, Pevsner made a distinction between a *building* and *architecture*: a bicycle shed is a building, and Lincoln Cathedral is a piece of architecture. "[T]he term architecture," he intones, "applies only to buildings designed with a view to aesthetic appeal."

Here Pevsner plants us firmly in what Bernard Bosanquet had identified as the field of knowledge of aesthetics, which abandons judgments made by reasoning from principles of objective beauty and service to the common good and gives the judgment to subjective responses with no particular or authoritative criteria outside an individual's experience.

OFFICER TO LITTLE BOY: "Why did you steal that bicycle?"
LITTLE BOY: "I felt like it; I wanted to ride it."
CRITIC TO STUDENT: "Why did you make that bicycle shed (or cathedral) look like that?"
STUDENT TO CRITIC: "I felt like it; I wanted it to look like that."

The officer can admonish the little boy for committing an unlawful action and instruct him on the principles of justice. What criteria can the critic use for responding to the student?

Nearing the end of his book Pevsner introduced a 1914 building by Walter Gropius for a factory whose status is only a little higher than that of a bicycle shed, declaring that it "was ... completely of today in every detail." Although twenty years old, it "might be misdated by anybody." By 1914, "the leading architects of the younger generation had courageously broken with the past and accepted the machine-age in all its implications: new materials, new processes, new forms, new problems."[7] Neglected in his history and in those that followed are the very many handsome buildings serving similar lowly functions that are not now and never have been "completely of today in every detail." Unlike many newer buildings, preservation is protecting them from demolition by giving them new functions because people want them to continue to grace the street, neighborhood, and city they inhabit. Here form defies function, and character defeats being "of its time."

Proposition Three: The couple of imitation and invention is the essential workhouse in the arts.

We return here to imitation, now surrounded by a minefield laid by the historicist narrative's attempts to banish it and its inseparable partner, invention. Imitation has been the driving force in the arts ever since humankind articulated a rational and reasonable understanding of practices in the arts. Aristotle was not the first to explain that people are naturally imitative. We learn through imitation, which we all use with our own understanding, means, and methods and which separates our imitation from mere copying. Imitation is so deeply embedded in the practice of the arts across the millennia that it largely escapes explicit notice in tradition's theories of art. The historicist narrative in all the arts has dismissed imitation as unworthy of any of the arts, which must respond to current influences and be "of their time." But in earlier ages, it played the role that influence now plays.[8] Buried under the perfidious calumny that reviles imitating as copying, disinterring a proper understanding of the imitation–invention couple is essential for understanding the alternative to the historicist narrative and influence.

Imitation and invention are pervasive in tradition where they play their roles in making a law that seeks to be just, a song that is beautiful to hear, and a building beautiful to see. Justice and beauty possess the harmony, order, proportionality, and what Leon Battista Alberti called concinnity of the order of the cosmos.

The jurist, the singer, and the architect seek those qualities in justice, singing, and architecture by looking through the paradigms and models of good laws and beautiful songs and buildings, paradigms and models that tradition transmits. In them are sought insights into the perfect justice and beauty found in two broad categories of cosmic nature. One is Nature with a capital N to designate the qualities of order, harmony, and proportionality that he or she uses in his or her work; this is *natura naturans*. The other is *natura naturata*, or the natural products or things that embody the order, harmony, and proportionality found in the cosmos. We look through paradigms and models using first our senses, then engaging our intellect to assess and review our judgment of sense, and then seek to discern in them the principles of justice and beauty that inform and guide our labors and govern our inventions by fitting these perfect forms to the possibilities and the contingencies and circumstance in which we are working.

Imitation and invention in the figurative arts

The figurative arts imitate both sources of beauty to present both things Nature has made and what she could make, but both must be consulted to avoid making a near copy and not a full imitation. When *natura naturans* is given the leading role in painting a product of *natura naturata*, it will present an ideal, as we see for example in Antonio Canova's sculpture of *Bonaparte as Mars* in the Brera courtyard in Milan. A greater role for *natura naturata* can make a literal depiction of nature's work within time, as Jean-Baptiste Pigalle did in his sculpture of the actual old *philosophe*, *Nude Voltaire* in the Louvre.

Paintings showing buildings and cities can exhibit similar differences. David Robert's realistic depiction of *Saint Paul's Cathedral and the Thames Docks* (Figure 1.1) shows us *natura naturata* or what we would see with our own eyes (the way things are). We find *natura naturans* at work in William Marlow's capriccio of *Saint Paul's Cathedral on a Venetian Canal* (Figure 1.2) (the way things could be). Here is an ideal or propositional truth but an improbable and in fact false representation; here fiction expresses truth in that the cathedral's character would allow it to occupy that site. The two paintings present different kinds of truth with the one about Venice always being Venice and in the other London always being London.

Modernist works are not concerned with either kind of truth. The artist's vision serves as the content, and invention without imitation is the means of presenting it. We can find the infant steps away from imitation in the late

FIGURE 1.1 David Robert, *Saint Paul's Cathedral and the Thames Docks,* 1863.

FIGURE 1.2 William Marlow, *Saint Paul's Cathedral on a Venetian Canal*, c. 1795.

16th c. when Giorgio Vasari established the first modern art academy. In his Florentine academy instead of using paradigms and models to give access to Nature and nature, the student learned by imitating Raphael and Michelangelo so that they could do as they had done when they produced works that would legitimate the offices of their princely patrons. Here we are in Machiavelli's world where the prince claims obedience because he is great and powerful, not because he is good and just. In the paintings and sculptures validating his claims of legitimacy, beauty was less the issue than the content's allegorical force, but in Modernism, allegorical content was replaced by what Pevsner would later call the "aesthetic appeal." I like it, you don't, too bad.

Imitation in architecture's tectonics

While Nature and nature provide direct sources for imitation in the figurative arts, in architecture they offer something very different in the art's three essential components, the tectonic structure, the formal configuration, and the composition's concinnity. Here we will introduce the tectonic structure.

The building's tectonic structure resists the forces of nature's laws that seek to return materials to their primordial form and place, the former through rot and decay, the latter with the pull of gravity and earthquake. Forfending against rot and decay requires walls and roofs protecting against the intrusion of damp, while stability requires material that can resist nature's seven directions of movement in their numberless combinations and variations – up and down, back and forth, left and right, and circular. Three tectonic types provide the resistance: the wall (with its roof), the post and beam, and the arch. The apparatus of forms that convert the tectonic types into an actual material membrature, or the material assembled into the tectonic structure, are built up from a catalog that tradition transmits and is composed of pieces, elements, and motifs.[9] A **piece** is the smallest material entity in a building's membrature: a brick, an ashlar stone, a sweep of stucco, a marble facing, a timber beam or strut, a voussoir, etc. An **element** is the conventional assemblage of pieces to make a passage of wall, a column, a lintel, an arch, a roof, etc. And a **motif** is the conventional assemblage of elements to make one complete structural unit: a wall with a base, middle, and top; a bay in an arcade or colonnade, a vault, etc. The artifice used to convert nature's raw material into the building materials runs across the range of classes from vernacular in the art of building on up to the best possible in architecture, or the classic.[10]

Artifice is used to produce the apparatus of forms, and different conventions guide the artifice in different traditions, all with great richness in their variations. In the western classical tradition, the apparatus uses the five orders to proportion walls and in assembling motifs such as colonnades, arcades, temple fronts, propylaea, and tabernacle windows, all with their extensive medieval variations. In the Chinese tradition's apparatus, we find bracket assemblies, *dougongs*, and *tialings* within a more rigidly controlled and produced range of configurations.

In every apparatus of forms, the conventional motifs serving the art of architecture occupy a spectrum that runs from vernacular to classic. It most likely developed from rude beginnings in the vernacular to finished classic examples, but other sequences are possible. The classic can also be diluted to vernacular uses. The means to produce the best may not be available, but the highest possible standards serve the most important buildings.

The motifs in any tectonic apparatus must fulfill two roles: they must make clear how they are serving stability and longevity, and they must do so in a manner that invests the building's configuration and composition with concinnity. Here we again meet the important distinction between building and architecture: the art of building will produce the actual stability, while architecture will give the stability its expressive presence. All buildings must have a tectonic order to span openings, to let forces change direction as they descend, and bear increasing loads as forces accumulate in their flight to the earth. These are actual truths, and they must be expressed with convincing perceptible truths that often call on fiction to tell the tale.

The tree becomes the column and the architrave, both of which in turn become a colonnade; the individual stones become the voussoir and the voussoir becomes a dome; the shapes of stone, brick, walls, doors, windows, moldings, cornices, roofs. Working together, they frame openings, enclose interiors, bear loads, and shed water. All these elements, when refined and ennobled, become the art of tectonics. Construction becomes architecture. When composed, these elements become a recognizable and identifiable architectural character that serves with propriety vernacular needs (e.g., the house) and civic needs (e.g., the courthouse). The simple character of vernacular architecture becomes distinguished from the articulated character of civic architecture, each of them being justifiable based on social propriety.

Imitation provides the means of expressing these perceptible truths. *Natura naturata* offers a few paradigmatic models, for example, the human figure with feet, body, and head, and trees with the widened bottom, rising trunk, and bloom on top. This tripartite division has an analogical presence in human life with a beginning, a long maturity, and a final conclusion, and it may properly appear in the tripartition of a wall with a sill, a rise, and a cornice. Medieval buildings often include in their membrature imaginative depictions of things in nature, especially in capitals and moldings. Renaissance architects occasionally made reference to nature as a source, as when a Tuscan column (always the Tuscan, the lowest of the five orders) presented itself as if it is a tree trunk with its branches lobbed off, or in treatises where a nature-man is depicted as a column. And Vitruvius has *natura naturata* give the acanthus leaf the role of ennobling the highest class of order in the classical apparatus of forms, something a young architect did when he saw *natura naturans* sending the weed up alongside the basket of toys at the grave of his beloved maiden and thereby ennobling her. These and other possible beginnings were perfected in practice and transmitted and varied in tradition, with one more, the primitive hut, figuring in various theories and presenting a special problem.

Imitation, *natura naturans,* and modernism

Vitruvius is emphatic that to achieve architecture, the building must imitate the order, harmony, and proportionality of the cosmos, which is embodied in perfect numbers and in the well-formed human figure. Renaissance architects draw the image of the Vitruvian man, with Leonardo da Vinci's being the most familiar, where we see him with his limbs in two positions to touch the encompassing square and circle. This makes him an active person, the very symbol of the laws of Nature (*natura naturans*) occupying the two perfect mathematical geometric forms that stood for the earth and the heavens.

Vitruvius, and theorists from the Renaissance on, made proportionality in numbers and geometry fundamental in the proportionality required for beauty. Alberti stressed the combination of *symmetria* (proportions) and *eurythmia* (the adjustments to make the proportions visible as proportionality) to produce the required concinnity, or the integration of all the parts into a beautiful whole. These propositions run through the treatises, and their principles have two explicit appearances in *The School of Athens* in the Vatican Palace that Raphael painted between 1509 and 1511. A figure said to be Bramante accompanied by young people is shown using dividers to generate a proportional geometric figure. Across the painting, a tetractys (a pyramidal assembly of ten dots) is being shown to an attentive group of older men. This group is clustered on the side where Plato holding the *Timaeus* gestures upward, suggesting that the celestial realm is to be imitated on earth, and the Bramante figure is beneath Aristotle with the geometry guiding the making of things on earth.

In the 18th c. when the received knowledge of the past was under review and revision, the primitive hut took on new life. It began with a little book published in 1753 where the Abbé Marc-Antoine Laugier (1713–69) presented it as a model in *natura naturata* for the architect to imitate directly without fiction's mediating role. In doing so he would have the architect act as if in a natural, uncorrupted state: "by imitating the natural process, art was born. All the splendors of architecture ever conceived have been modeled on the little rustic hut…." It was built by "man in his primitive state without any aid or guidance other than his natural instinct." In it, Laugier claimed, were all the principles and rules of architecture; nothing not in the hut ought to be used in building today, he continued. Vaults, arches, pedestals, attics, niches, pilasters, etc. are hereby forbidden.[11] Today we can claim to find here the slippery slope to reductionism. We will come across this hut again in Chapter 2.

Laugier's book avoids addressing imitation in its traditional role, and in subsequent developments this constrained role for imitation gradually falls into desuetude and then into disrepute, only to sneak back in during the 20th c. with new name tags: reference, simulacrum, allusion, illusion, representation, sign, self-referential sign, etc., terms that find lively lives in Modernism's theories and the historicist narrative supporting it, and without recognizing that all of them are examples of small-bore imitation.

With imitation banned, its necessary partner invention was freed to become the sole actor responding to the influences that would make a building be "of its time." This leaves most architects to assemble buildings using technology's products to serve functions and to present a version of the prevailing style to be "of their time," while a few others are christened as agents whose avant-garde style leads progress into the future.

The reaction of two critics lends insight into these and other claims of Modernist architecture. José Ortega y Gasset offered this telling comment about the avant-garde. It is to allow "the elite to recognize themselves and one another in the drab mass of society and to learn their mission which consists of being few and holding their own against the many."[12] This role became especially prominent in the later decades of the 20th c. when Modernism failed to produce convincing progress in its social programs or for its architecture to gain general acceptance, much less popularity, which left Modernists producing works with an aesthetic appeal that an ever smaller number found appealing.

Léon Krier has enriched our understanding of that aperçu: in Modernism, forms of making (architectural and artistic) are "objects of short-term consumption," while "traditional cultures are concerned with the production of objects of long-term use."[13]

These comments recognize that tradition's value resides in its constant renewal with inventions that are made in one of two different ways. One is through improvements in the way a convention is fulfilling its role in the art of building or of architecture. The other is in a response to a new demand or means of making the membrature or configuration so that it can better answer the building's purpose. To be sure, an invention might begin by operating outside of conventions or even in parallel to conventions, but eventually, it will take its place within tradition among those conventions as it finds validation by the collective approval of many reasoning architects. Is this not the way ancient classicism became the Gothic and the way the Renaissance expanded the catalog of conventions?

Proposition Four: Cities and Buildings are made from other Cities and Buildings and their Parts in order to improve the Urban or Rural Territory the Buildings will inhabit.

The chronological arrangement and emphasis on style in the historicist narrative and in almost everything now being written about architecture give a new building a claim for attention merely because it is new. This is a radical *volte-face* from the earliest days down to the present when buildings and cities have been at once imitatively and inventively composed from other cities and buildings and their parts.

In the art of architecture, to make its necessary adaptations continuity within tradition is vital, as is the perpetual reciprocal relationship between imitation and invention guided by tradition. In this age-old and everywhere practice, cities and their buildings benefitted from a constant updating and modernization of valued traditions to offer continued service to the common aspirations of communities. It acknowledges that anything new must have as its object the improvement of the urban or rural territory that its insertion will inevitably change. The parallels to the civil orders that seek to assure security and sustenance is clear.

This earlier reciprocity between imitation and invention in architecture carries two important characteristics: one internal to architecture, and the other in its outside relationship to the world it inhabits.

The internal characteristic is the interaction among the three legs that support architecture, the tectonic, the architectural, and the urban. The tectonic involves the material qualities of the membrature that produces stability, longevity, and visibility. The architectural concerns the configuration and composition that the tectonic serves and makes visible. And the urban allows the building to join with others in serving and expressing the aspirations of the community that brings the building into existence. The architect must bring these into a satisfying congruence that allows the building to serve its purpose in the civil order.

Its outside relationship is no less important because it provides the control for achieving the synthesis of the three legs, which is in Nature. The happiness individuals seek is found in the best possible fulfillment of the person's unique, and uniquely human, nature. Facilitating that aspiration is the work of the civil order and the urbanism it builds. Here the accumulation of past knowledge and wisdom interacts with present circumstances and contingencies. This interaction allows human nature to connect its human purposes with forms that serve them and that facilitate our pursuit of happiness. Here we find that part of human nature that connects a purpose with a meaning conveyed in a form, whether in speech in a language we know or in a building in a place we live. We are best served when the familiar is made new, and we are frustrated when something new lacks familiarity. In our experience in a place, familiarity leavened by the new provides a refreshing connection of form to purpose, because the familiar is necessary if we are to recognize the human purpose the form serves. In the next chapter, we will take up the meaningful forms that convey human purposes.

In architecture, the ever-reinvigorated familiar is conveyed in the conventions that tradition transmits as architecture's paradigms and models. These incorporate and make available the knowledge gained through the imitation of nature and especially of Nature. As we saw, what *natura naturata* offers must be digested into practice, but now the importance of *natura naturans* becomes prominent. By imitating Nature's order, harmony, and proportionality, the talented and skillful architect can fulfill two necessities of the art of architecture. One purpose is to invest the material pieces, elements, and motifs of its tectonic conventions, the composition within the configuration that they materialize, and the building's role in the civil order and thereby fulfill the tripod, or the tectonic, architectural, and urban legs, which supports architecture with the concinnity that allows it to serve and express the good sought by the civil order that built it and embody beauty as the counterpart to the good. This is a quality of all great buildings. The other purpose is to provide the rapport between the people who encounter and use the building with the moral order of the universe that is the ultimate source of the happiness we pursue.

Here we find the physical, material realm of buildings and cities congruent with other realms we experience where purpose, form, and meaning are synthesized. Whether the form is in a building or a song, its purpose is to convey meaning, and its form must be invested with a familiarity that allows us to interpret it, internalize it, and discern its connection to our understanding and knowledge of ourselves and our unique and common human nature.

> *From this, we must conclude that the act of constructing a building or a city is to construct the meaning it carries. Meaning accompanies the very act of constructing meaning. At the most rudimentary level, the art of building matured across time into the art of architecture as the two arts drew their meaning increasingly from the lessons of Nature and nature as they were being called to serve and express the complementary purposes and activities of communal living and individual aspiration. This conjunction of humankind's natural sociability and the penchant to invest meaning in what we make embeds architecture and city making deep into Nature and nature with their forms serving the purposes that give meaning to human nature.*

Proposition Five: Architecture and Urbanism are Public Arts, which makes them Unique among the Arts.

Here we arrive at the fundamental difference between architecture and the other arts. The current term "the arts" calls to mind the Modern System of the Arts that in the 18th c. came to identify music, poetry, painting, sculpture, and architecture as compeers. Note that while architecture was included, its related necessary aspects of the building arts involving the mechanical and operative arts, draftsmanship, and so on were not.[14] As historical studies developed later in the next century the Fine Arts were linked within the historicist narrative presenting the sequence of styles, and in the first decades of the 20th c. the Modernists, fired with revolutionary avant-garde zeal and anathematizing tradition, clamored for a place in the sequence. After their early divorce from their political allies and their continued failure to deliver on their promised utopia, the arts, architecture prominent among them, devoted themselves to what Pevsner would call their "aesthetic appeal." Giedion's and Pevsner's historicist narratives provided the propagators of Modernist styles with justificatory genealogies that pointed to its inevitability, and popular or not, the arts, with architecture prominent among them, increasingly became the prized possession of the cultural élite whom Ortega y Gasset identified.

In this milieu, architecture weakened two of the most important attributes that differentiated it from its fellow arts: that (1) because it enjoys an indubitable role as a public art, it does so because (2) its form of making is also one of the forms of dwelling in nature and in society. A building, unlike a song, poem, painting, or sculpture, is necessarily a public object in which to dwell; it cannot be obscured from public view. Furthermore, it necessarily occupies a public site, even if the site is privately owned: a public authority allowed it to be private, the civil order guarantees that ownership, and protects it from unwanted incursions. The civil order imposes taxes on its value, and it establishes the restrictions of zoning and building codes and minimum maintenance standards. Although its interiors enjoy the right of privacy, a building, unlike a painting or sculpture, cannot escape from public view. And here we find one of the most fundamental justifications for urbanism: buildings engage each other across public streets and squares just like citizens engage the faces of others across the very same public streets and squares.

In earlier eras, the various arts accepted the duties entailed in their presence in the public realm, and they did so in a way that served their office of contributing to the common good. The historicist narrative is mute about this public role and its opposite, the radical privatization of the art of architecture. Instead, it treats a building as an individualistic artistic expression just as it does the other products of the arts. It acknowledges that a building does have the unique duty to serve a useful function, and it is allowed to do so in a way that is intended to lead the public into an appreciation of an "aesthetic appeal" that is "of its time," if not of the future where the avant-garde is leading it and the public is reluctant to go.

The public character that architecture inevitably carries suggests an analogy between a building and an individual in a civil order. An individual possesses a human nature that is shared universally across time with all other individuals while also possessing one's own unique human nature, and the person binds with others in communities ranging in reach from family to nation to fulfill their individual and common purposes. The same applies to the buildings and city where people live their lives: they have the common and universal end of serving those human purposes with beauty, purposes that as ideals are everywhere and at all times the same but are manifested within distinctive traditions, customs, and conventions. Individuals working within a civil order build the buildings and accumulate them within urban and rural areas so that they may serve and express the aspirations of the civil order and of the individuals in the nation that synoecism constructs from their various communities. Here the role of the architect is the same as every other person, which is to engage with others working to serve a common end. From this we can conclude that the art of architecture and the art of urbanism differ only in the scale of time and place in what they build, which will be "of its time" but also, and more importantly, of all time, past, present, and future.

Proposition Six: Reforming Architecture passes through the Study and Practice of Architecture under the General Categories of Type, Character, and Style.

This discussion is the content of Chapter 2.

Notes

1 A. D. F. Hamlin, *A Text-book of the History of Architecture* (New York, etc.: Longmans, Green, 1896).
2 Banister Fletcher, *A History of Architecture: For the Student, Craftsman, and Amateur being a Comparative View of the Historical Styles from the Earliest Period* (London: B.T. Batsford; New York: Charles Scribner's Sons). Before the 4th, 1901 edition the title page included his father, Banister F[light] Fletcher (1833–99). For more see W. Hanneford-Smith, *The Architectural Work of Sir Banister Fletcher* (London: Batsford, 1934).
3 On Historicism see Benedetto Croce, *Estetica* (1902), (Adelphi, 2005), and *Storia come pensiero e come azione* (1938); Raymond Aron, *Introduction à la philosophie de l'histoire* (1938), (Gallimard 1986); Friedrich Meinecke, *Historicism*, trans. J. E. Anderson (London, 1972); Karl Popper, *The Poverty of Historicism* (1944), (Routledge, 2002); Nikolaus Pevsner, *Studies in Art, Architecture and Design*, Vol. II (New York: Walker & Co, 1968); Peter Reill, *German Enlightenment and the Rise of Historicism* (University of California Press, 1975); David Watkin, *Architecture and Morality* (Oxford, 1977); Michael Podro, *The Critical Historians of Art* (Yale, 1982); Leopold von Ranke, *The Theory and Practice of History*, eds. Georg Iggers and K. von Moltke (New York: Irvington Publishers, 1983); P. Paret, *Art as History: Episodes in the Culture and Politics of Nineteenth-Century Germany* (Princeton, 1988); Alan Colquhoun, *Modernity and the Classical Tradition* (MIT, 1989); H. Aram Veeser, ed., *The New Historicism* (Routledge, 1989); Robert J. van Pelt and Carroll W. Westfall, *Architectural Principles in the Age of Historicism* (Yale, 1991); Samir Younés, *The Imperfect City: On Architectural Judgment*, 2012 (Routledge, 2016).
4 Gwendolyn Wright, "History for Architects," in *The History of History in American Schools of Architecture, 1865–1975*, eds. Wright and Janet Parks (New York: The Temple Hoyne Buell Center for the Study of American Architecture and Princeton Architectural Press, 1990), 13–52, 17.
5 *A History of Aesthetics* (New York: Macmillan, 1932; reprinted as Meridian Books Library Edition, 1957), Preface, p. ix, dated 1892.
6 J.-N.-L. Durand, *Précis of the Lectures on Architecture*, trans. David Britt (Los Angeles, CA: The Getty Research Institute, 2000), p. 133; original published in 1802–05.

7 Quoting here from Gropius, *op. cit.*, 5th ed., 1954, 281.
8 The comparison is that of James S. Ackerman, "Imitation," in *Origins, Imitation, Conventions* (Cambridge, MA and London: MIT Press, 2002), 125–41.
9 The current argot's kit of parts suggests industrially produced components and is agnostic about the formal properties.
10 The word classic used here refers to an achievement, not a style, to the best of a kind of thing, not to ancient architecture and its legacy.
11 Marc-Antoine Laugier, *An Essay on Architecture*, trans. Wolfgang and Anni Herrmann (Los Angeles, CA: Hennessey & Ingalls, 1977), with the 1753 and 1755 texts, 11–13 and ibid.
12 José Ortega y Gasset, "The Unpopularity of the New Art," (1948) in *The Dehumanization of Art and Other Writings on Art and Culture* (Garden City, NY: Doubleday Anchor Books, n.d.), 7.
13 Léon Krier, "Tradition, Modernism, Modernity", in *Archives d'architecture moderne*, N° 35–36, Prix Européen de la Reconstruction de la ville, Belgium, 1987, p. 17.
14 See Kristeller, *op. cit.*

2

THE ALTERNATIVE

Type, character, and style

Introduction

In the previous chapter, we presented a critique of the historicist narrative that organizes buildings according to style and arranges them in a teleological-chronological sequence, and we presented several expansions of the understanding of architecture that the narrative neglects. In that narrative's chronological scheme each sequence begins with a first building that influences its successors just as they influence their successors until the style of a new first building initiates a new sequence. The contact these buildings make with the world around them is through the influences that are in operation in the concomitant sequence of eras.

In this chapter, we present an alternative to that scheme. It has a different organization and a different relationship to the world. Here origins rather than first buildings stand in the forefront of sequences, and the world that the buildings connect to is the world of the busy activities of Nature and the nature it produces. Our purpose in offering this alternative is to reestablish a liaison between the civil order and architecture that exists within Nature and serves humankind.

A common emblem of this relationship is the primitive hut that we encountered in Laugier and which, as we noted, is included in a broad range of theories of architecture including the oldest known, that of Vitruvius, which others followed with greater or lesser fidelity. He placed the beginnings of civilization and architecture in the crude material that people living "like wild animals in forests, caves, and woods" made from what *natura naturans* supplied through nature. He noted that because they "were naturally imitative and quick to learn, they would show each other the results of their building, proud of their

DOI: 10.4324/9780429506260-4

own inventions, and so, sharpening their wits in competition," they developed the primitive hut. Using their "intellectual capacities with powers of reasoning and common sense," they "moved themselves on from their wild, rustic lives to gentle civilization" (II, i, 1–7; here as infra, Schofield trans.). They developed the craftsmanship of the art of building to translate their wooden huts into the refined tectonics of stone construction that made their buildings useful, durable, and delightful. And they engaged their rational and imitative capacities to elevate their buildings to an architecture whose symmetria, eurythmia, and decorum provided a visible imitation of the order, harmony, and proportionality of Nature.[1] "They gave their seal of approval to those things which, explained in rational argument, have the force of truth" (IV, ii, 60).

Vitruvius and classical thought recognize that the principles that bind architecture to the service of civil orders originate in Nature. They are used to seek the highest standards of the art of architecture and the art of governing. The origins of these principles are different from the beginnings of the stream of examples that archeologists and historians chart. However, within those examples there may exist, in parts of wholes, paradigmatic models revealing Nature's standards, but they are not necessarily in a sequence's most recent practices or examples. Nonetheless they, like paradigmatic models more closely allied with a tradition, allow insight into Nature that inventive imitation and adaptation use to address current contingencies and circumstances. They may even be found in models scattered across the past and the globe where the work of imitation and invention have honed useful architectural and civil conventions.

The Renaissance architects who took up the primitive hut worked with a sharper sense of the distinction between Nature and nature than obtained among their predecessors. Leon Battista Alberti endorsed reason and introduced a more sophisticated articulation of civil institutions and the particular building types serving them. He also held out concinnity, the ultimate criterion of beauty in Nature, as the ultimate standard for judgment assessing the relationship between the institutions and the buildings serving them.

These developing, traditional connections between the civil and architectural realms and Nature and nature began to fray in the 17th c. as attention was increasingly focused on material nature and, separately, on the nature of civil and political life. The formulation that has gained an increasing role throughout the world was most forcefully and enduringly enunciated in the words of the American Declaration of Independence. Citing the "Laws of Nature and of Nature's God," the Founders held certain "truths to be self-evident, that all men are ... endowed with certain unalienable Rights," with governments based on "the consent of the governed" holding the "just powers" to secure those rights.

In the tradition of thought from antiquity down to that period, there was always an intimate connection within the triplet of the civil, the architectural, and Nature. The connections would begin to fray in the lead-up into the 18th c.

We see it in full flower in the role the Abbé Laugier gave the primitive hut with a thesis that augers the abandonment of imitation and down the slippery slope of reductionism leading to Modernism. For him, the hut was both a conceptual model and a beginning for a house or a temple even though it could not be measured, excavated, or dated. Nonetheless, he could state emphatically, "nothing not in the hut ought to be used in building today."

For him the hut was an artifact in *natura naturata* made by *natura naturans* that was to be modified without recourse to *natura naturans*: it was a thing in itself (a *Ding an sich*). The forceful limits he put on invention prevented it from being a paradigm giving access to Nature where imitation could complement invention. Only the conventions and configurations within the traditions of the art of architecture and nothing more could lift a building above the art of building. It is not for nothing that Laugier's little book appeared at a time when architects were beginning to limit the range of elements and motifs in their buildings' tectonics.

Natura naturata is not completely absent. He does provide origins for some things that only *natura naturans* can produce – in Chapter 1 he cites trees, the human figure, and the course of life; to them, we can add rustication of stone on a building's lowest levels. These can find their way directly or indirectly into architecture and reveal *natura naturans* at work, but not if they are treated merely as models. They can draw concinnity from *natura naturans* into the work, but if they are not consulted, for example when the orders are based solely on examples in books of the orders, we can see what is missing and identify neoclassicism at work.

So all beginnings have origins, but not all beginnings can serve as paradigmatic models that give imitation access to Nature. Consider a composition using the pycnostyle intercolumniation (1:1.5 or less of the column diameter). The Temple of Venus Genetrix in Rome's Forum of Caesar is this convention's ostensible model.[2] But its origin lay elsewhere, in paradigmatic knowledge of Nature's proportionality that connects the temple to Nature. Its composition is not merely a replica of a predecessor. In more complex configurations and compositions the relationship between origins and beginnings is more complicated. **Palazzo Chiericati, Palladio, Vicenza, 1550** and **Queen's House, Inigo Jones, Greenwich, 1616–35** share a conceptual origin in the primitive hut, but for the proportionality of each, the origin is in Nature. Palladio's building embraces the full maturity of 16th c. experience, and it is the precedent for Jones', while Jones' is the beginning of English Palladianism. Note, however, that both are redolent with what nature offers.

To summarize these remarks: Both origin and beginning occupy causal roles vis-àvis architectural form, but the first is causal on the level of paradigm (a type), while the second is causal on the level of a historical sequence (a particular model or a direct historical precedent). Origin denotes a principle from which, whereas a beginning denotes a point from which, a chain of examples might proceed. The distinction between origin and beginning corresponds to the distinction between justification and discovery. Here we encounter the power of types. They alone can synthesize the relationships between the many, complex components within architecture's tripod, for example in commanding the idea-forms designating purpose and the membrature's types among several buildings serving similar purposes. Another connects architecture's service to the public and private political realms of the civil life. And a third brings multiple combinations of geometries and materials into a building's expressive character.

Putting typology's great strength to work in these relationships allows the practices of statecraft or architecture to accept Nature as the origin for the forms that serve human needs and aspirations. That common parentage makes it possible to establish the tightest possible bond between a civil order and the buildings serving and expressing the purposes of its authoritative institutions and other entities. At the conclusion of the previous chapter, we identified **Proposition Six**, which stated that the practice of architecture presented here is achieved through *the study and practice of architecture under the general categories of type, character, and style.* Here we develop that proposition.

The three words have figural qualities embedded in their etymologies. Type derives from the Greek τύπος: *typos*, and implies a mark, impression, mold, incision, figure, outline, or pattern. We presented type in the previous chapter as an idea-form or a root-form or a building-idea that provides a conceptual framework for fulfilling the human penchant to connect purpose with meaning.

Character comes from the Greek χαρακτήρ: *characteer,* which suggests the form the type takes from an engraving, impress, stamp, reproduction, representation, figure, or letter.

And style alludes to a more material quality that stems from the Greek στύλος: *stylos* that designates a column, pillar, or small rod used to engrave letters on a wax-covered tablet. In the previous chapter, we found the word style serving as the workhorse of a chronologically organized narrative and enjoying greater authority in assessments than character and functional type. Here the order is reversed with the building's purpose taking the place of function and dictating the type with character and style following in serving and expressing the purpose.

All three terms imply that a distinctive mark or form is made for a predetermined reason. In architecture, each belongs to a different, essential, and inseparable aspect of architectural form-making with type being generative, and character and style being expressive. Each gives the architect a rational basis for the origins, transformations, and migrations of architectural form as well as for the distinctive aesthetic qualities of its compositions and the combinations with the past and the site in producing a sense of place.

Before discussing types, two comments are in order.

1 Types are given body within paradigmatic models, the very generative causes of architectural form. These transcend and incorporate precedents

and examples. The word precedent ought never to be used in the singular, and neither should a single precedent be used for a building nor an example be used without understanding its model.

2 Types, as paradigms, possess a universality and connection with Nature while precedents, as beginnings, possess particularities of buildings, traditions, and regions.

Type, or the generative qualities in architecture

Type refers to an originating idea that provides the beginning for generating architectural form. This role for type goes back at least to Vitruvius, but the meaning it now has was articulated during the great overhaul undertaken during the Enlightenment. New interest in historical studies that included comparative histories was organized within the broad epistemological reach of the *encyclopédie*. In newly defined fields such as ethnography, archaeology, linguistics, and so on, new theories raised questions about the distinctions between what we are calling beginnings and origins. In overlappings with the life sciences' elaboration of grand taxonomic classifications, analogies were found for organizing building types across history.[3]

One of these with the deepest penetrations to the present came from the *Receuil et parallèle* (Figure 2.1) of J.-N.-L. Durand (1760–1834), who made a brief appearance in the previous chapter for his "form follows function" mantra.[4] The typological approach he offered is at once classificatory, analytical, and operative. Its classificatory systems were wide-ranging: elementary modes of construction (walls, trabeations, arcuations), what he called horizontal combinations (plans) and vertical combinations (façades, roofs), and finally geometric assemblies (squares, parallelograms, circles). When used for analysis it presents the combinatory geometric possibilities inherent in plans, sections, volumes, and façades. When put to work in the operative sense it provides material for multiple combinatory schemes, which he illustrated for private palaces, palaces of justice, treasuries, schools, museums, libraries, markets, theaters, hospitals, prisons, houses in cities and in the countryside, stairs, and courts. His was nothing less than a standardized procedure for architectural composition that taught his student engineers to generate a multitude of compositions serving a variety of functions with an economy in disposition and distribution. This system found broad use in the rapidly rising industrialized building practices serving an expanded range of functions with a zealous pursuit of efficiency and economy.

Durand included model buildings, but they were not arranged as a succession of historical styles. In his arrangement buildings from any period or culture could provide models for an architect with indifference to the fit of their form to their purpose. For example, he preferred the plan of the Basilica of Constantine to that of the later Saint Peter's Basilica in Rome. Because it would

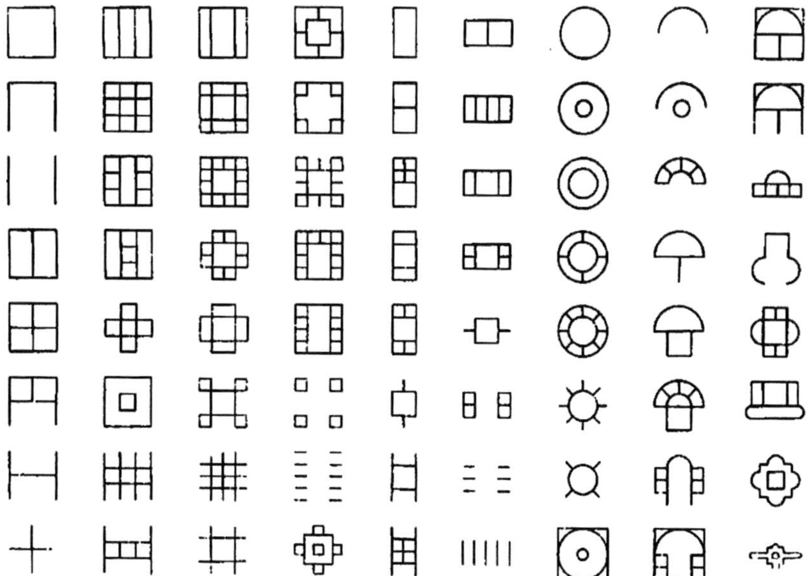

FIGURE 2.1 Types as combinatory geometries, J-.N.-L. Durand, 1802–05.

function more efficiently and be more economical, criteria that had nothing to do with the building's purpose. It did, however, fit as a criticism of the devastating wars waged by/on behalf of the church.

The very different path hewn by his contemporary Antoine Chrysostôme Quatremère de Quincy (1755–1849) has received inadequate attention by historians, but it has played a major role in this book's formulations.[5] Quatremère made a vital distinction between architectural types and models, emphasizing the type as an originating reason accessible to the intellect, and the model as a formal thing, a concrete form that the senses apprehended directly. His types are ideas, conceptual forms, or irreducible images that precede empirical reality (as in the Greek *eidos* or the Latin *idea*), while models are fully differentiated and composite forms (as in the Greek *morphé* or the Latin *forma*). We can say that for Quatremère, Durand offered only models and no types. Quatremère's types are similar to Platonic Forms, that is, *imagistic universals and generative causes that explain the essentialist commonality between similar buildings of varied forms*. Buildings descending from the same type can vary widely in their appearance, that is, their character, but no matter how far away they travel from the type, they always carry with them some indissociable qualities of the type.

Durand had shown a way to organize buildings into functional and compositional typologies that were independent of a chronological narrative. Quatremère's approach suggested how the types could be used to have a building serve and express its role in archetypal human activities that address human purposes and not the mere functions that Durand's scheme serves.

Durand's and Quatremère's fundamental reflections on type were considerably amplified in the 20th century within a rationalist approach to urban morphology and building typology that provided a curative alternative to the repetitive, functionalist standardization of modernist forms.[6] In a 1991 study, C. W. Westfall extended Quatremère's reflections on type by arranging them in an ideogrammatic fashion of "six, or so," architectural types, *tholos, temple, theater, regia, dwelling, shop*, with each serving a purpose in the civil order.[7] To these S. Younés added a seventh, the *hypostyle*, and retained the words "or so" to suggest, as Westfall had, that there may be other, as yet unidentified types.[8]

We must stress that each type serves a particular purpose, which is not the same as a building's use or function. *Uses* and *functions* serve *purposes* in the same way that human activities serve human purposes. They are means to an end, and when other means of achieving the end are developed, the end remains the purpose that the new means serve. Consider the difference between function and purpose in a museum. Its function is to gather, conserve, and display objects. Its purpose is to allow people to engage with authoritative and instructive examples of the kind of objects it contains to contribute to the fullness of one's life that great art offers and to provide prized examples for study by people who would make works of the same kind.

The seven idea-types (or types)

The seven idea-type forms presented here arise directly, enduringly, and globally from what people naturally do when they perform the activity whose purpose the type serves. The congruence of action, purpose, and form makes each type an imitation of Nature (it is in human nature to do the activity) and of nature (when they do so, they naturally do it in a particular way).

These seven or so types are presented here in their undifferentiated state, although types, like human activities, often combine related purposes, which leads to buildings that are collections or composites of types. We provide several examples in Part II. A collection or composite generally has a dominant purpose, which is the one that contributes the greatest good to the common good.

The catalog in Part II presents examples in the sequence used here.

1 The ***tholos*** serves venerating. This purpose is broadly inclusive, tending toward the universal with a formal ideogrammatic character that is circular or polygonal with a hollow center and often with multidirectional *horizontal* approaches but one *vertical* direction or axis.

   People venerate both privately and communally but separately. The root, doughnut form of the *tholos* occurs when people group around a campfire, in the ballerina's pirouette around an axis, and the whirling moves of Turkish dervishes. In buildings it generates the Pantheon in Rome; the Rotunda of the Dome of the Rock in Jerusalem; the Baptistery in Pisa; the Buddhist stupa at Sanchi; and the Hall of Private Audiences, Fatehpur Sikri, India.[9]

2 The ***temple*** is for celebrating. Unlike the *tholos*' multiple horizontal directionalities, the *temple* root-form is an enclosure with definite frontality and an axial approach serving actual or conceptual celebratory processions. Evanescent temples form, for example, when the multitude of fans follow a local team in the open-topped bus down Main Street after winning a championship.

We see examples enclosed within precincts in the Parthenon in Athens; the Temple of Jupiter in Pompeii, the Temple of Trajan in Rome; and the Church of Sant'Ambrogio in Milan.

Others, such as Saint Martin in the Fields in London, are not hedged in.

The ***tholos*** and ***temple*** are often combined in religious rites that involve both veneration and celebration. Prominent examples are the Church of the Holy Sepulcher in Jerusalem, the Cathedral in Chartres, the Basilica of Saint Peter in Rome, and the Church of the Val de Grâce in Paris.

3 The ***theater*** serves participation in imagining. Its shape as a half-circle allows an assembly of people to contemplate and enjoy an improved condition, whether presented in a play or a musical composition or in a public lecture, or interacting within a deliberative assembly engaged in governing, or even as a temporary gathering around an instructor in a piazza. With minimal and temporary modification, a theater configuration can be formed by people around the Reflecting Pool in the Mall in Washington for a seminal event focused on the Lincoln Memorial.

Examples: the theater at Epidaurus in Greece; the Colosseum in Rome; the Chand Baori stepwell in Rajasthan, India; and the La Scala Opera House in Milan.

4 The service of the ***regia*** is in protecting authority with an idea-form of a square doughnut or some variation of it. There are two varieties depending on the character of the authority within its enclosure. One protects authority vested in a political body, an individual, or an institution of government. Examples are legion and varied: The Hall of Supreme Harmony in Beijing; Palazzo Farnese in Rome; Maison Laffitte near Paris; and the Gamble House in Pasadena.

The other serves authority exercised through a civil institution such as a court, school, library, or museum: the modern Capitoline Hill in Rome; the Basilica and its Loggia in Vicenza; the Altes Museum in Berlin; and the Bibliothèque Sainte Geneviève in Paris.

5 The ***dwelling*** offers safety to those whose authority is strictly curtailed or that extends little beyond an immediate or extended family and its

dependents. Imaged as a rectangular enclosure with an open narrow end and interior compartments, examples are generally vernacular and display vast variations. Dwellings can also be assembled within a hypostyle as in modern urban hotels. In most of the world until the modern age, the dwelling provided the background fabric in urbanism and will be discussed more fully elsewhere.

Our examples in Part II illustrate townhouses in the Groot Begijnhof in Leuven and along the Royal Crescent in Bath, and the individual cells of the Hôtel des Invalides in Paris.

6 The ***shop*** serves sustaining life. It provides places for making, storing, trading, and other activities, especially those involved in commerce, and its form is similar to that of the dwelling without the interior compartments and with which it is often combined as a composite. Examples are normally aligned on a street or square or stacked one on another in modern skyscraper hypostyles. Diverse examples include Trajan's Market in Rome; the Souks of Isfahan, Iran; the Galerie Vivienne in Paris; the Galleria Vittorio Emanuele, Milan; Market Square in Lake Forest, Illinois; and the towers in Rockefeller Center, New York.
7 The ***hypostyle*** serves gathering by sheltering people within a volume where a floor and ceiling are separated by a field of supports or its replacement by trusses or vaults. A hypostyle's tectonics often assumes command of its character as it serves a variety of purposes for the gatherings, whether civil, religious, communal, martial, mercantile, familial, recreational, or something else. Among our pre-modern examples are the Basilica Giulia, Rome, used for legal, commercial, and general gathering, the Throne Hall at Persepolis, Iran, performing the service of a regia, and the Great Mosque of Córdoba, Spain, a place for religious worship. In the modern era are the Crystal Palace, London, the Marquette Building in Chicago, and Pennsylvania Station in New York.

Character and style, or the expressive qualities in architecture

Character and style are the completion of type. They are the visible qualities that are materialized from types' generative forms. In Nature as in architecture, the *form* generated from a *type* is intended to fulfill a particular *purpose* with its material possessing visible and perceptible qualities that serve and express that purpose through *character* and *style*.

In a well-made object, whether in nature, the civil order, or architecture, the form of a thing makes its purpose known. Character is the name of that expression of purpose. Among purposes, there is a hierarchy arranged according to the relative importance of the purposes to the aspirations held for them. In the world humans make, this hierarchy is ultimately defined and controlled by the political structure and the operations of the civil order, understanding politics as used here to be the art of participating in the collective elaboration of a community's cultural life to realize the community's ideals.

A building's expressive character signals two aspects of the place it occupies in that hierarchy. One is generated by the type's idea-form that identifies the universal and enduring purpose that a building serves. The other identifies the specific way it does so in the tradition it joins within urbanism, which bears on several expressive qualities. It must be designed from the outside in, that is, as an element in the public realm. This is because as a servant of the civil order, its first obligation is to the public, and so it is to the public that it must present the proper visible expression of its role among the civil order's purposes: this is where political authority resides, justice is administered, education is proffered, cultural narratives are portrayed, dwellings are arranged, commerce is conducted, or where the privacy and security of a private house is available. This calls for the clear distinction in urbanism between buildings serving the public realm (*res publica*, e.g., a courthouse, a library, a theater) and those of the private realm (*res privata*, e.g., a house, a villa, an office, a shop, a factory), with the former given proper prominence for their higher standing in serving the common good. At the most basic level they serve all of the community's members' needs for security and sustenance, and beyond that for living justly and well. We will say more about this in the chapters about the city and its urbanism.

Here we reiterate the important role of tradition in identifying not only the purpose of the building but also the function used to fulfill that purpose. The purpose and function in a city or rural district will be identified by the traditional configuration, composition, and siting of the buildings it will join. For example, a regia type generates a place where authority is protected, and the building's expressive purpose expresses who or what is entrusted with the functions attendant on that purpose. Oligarchic political orders build palaces for the few who govern, while democracies build capitols for the assembly of representatives of the people who live in houses or other private regias.

The PALAZZO FARNESE in Rome was built as the seat of a duke who wielded papal authority, and without change, it could become the seat of the French ambassador in Italy whose authority came from that nation's government. But in Paris, the **Palais Bourbon**, built as a residence for an offspring of Louis XIV, was transformed inside and out to equip it to serve and express the change from monarchic to republican government, from the Council of the 500 during the Directoire, to the Consulate, Revolution, and Empire, to the present **Assemblée Nationale**. No one would mistake either of these buildings for anything other than seats that protect and project authority, which made the Roman palace the appropriate literal model for the **Reform Club, Charles Barry, London, 1837–41**, a private club for Whig leaders.

Dramatic disruptions to traditional expressive character can mark dramatic disruptions in the conduct of traditional purposes. Barry's building for the Whigs who wanted to disrupt the programs of government reached back to an admired period, the Renaissance, whose buildings had disrupted the status quo. When the disruption does not call on formal associations with earlier buildings but instead seeks to challenge them with new forms, confusion about what the message is can ensue unless clarified by signage, as at the **Bauhaus, Walter Gropius, Weimar, 1925–26** where its appearance as a modern industrial factory had to be supplemented by publicity in the press and the word BAUHAUS on the building to assure its identity for what it was, a new school for the arts.

Like individuals, the character of buildings can have additional attributes that are captured by adjectives that are appropriate to their function and their purpose. When properly expressed by the architect, character invites naming (adjectives) on the part of the observer who responds to qualities inherent in the building.

> Buildings may be majestic and sublime like the **pyramids of Giza**; solid and massive like the COLISEUM IN ROME.... They may be weighty and commanding, like the PALAZZO FARNESE AT CAPRAROLA; grand and sublime like the **Duomo in Florence**; modest, like the **farmer's house** in the countryside; imposing like the **Palazzo Pitti in Florence**; ... tenebrous and forbidding like Piranesi's carceri; ... oppressively big like the skyscraper, or oppressively small like the low ceilings within offices in skyscrapers.[10]

Naming also calls forth inherent qualities in a derisive way, e.g., when the **Monument to Vittorio Emanuele in Rome** was referred to as the "wedding cake," or when a proposed extension to the **National Gallery in London** was called a "monstrous carbuncle." Achieving the proper expressive character is perhaps the architect's greatest challenge, difficult because it is produced within the triangular relationship between the exigencies of the civic realm, those of the private realm of a patron, and the architect's inventive and technical skills.

Because it, like all things, comes into being in a particular time within a tradition, it inevitably will portray the style of the time and place it was built, and because it was made by someone, it will also carry the unique expression of that person's personal style. In antiquity and again from the Renaissance on, an architect's notable contribution to the common good was rewarded with fame just as the achievements of generals, statesmen, and authors were. Only later when historicist histories began to be written with time stamps and location labels dominating a chronology driven by the idea of progress did architects begin to gain fame for innovations that disrupted tradition.

Style occupies the last place in the declension of type, character, and style in this study. It identifies the unique talent of an architect, and it assists in recognizing certain repeated or reiterated ways of composing and executing buildings (e.g., Palladianism), and particular times and places (e.g., Italian Renaissance). It is, however, secondary to a building's character that expresses its contribution to the public good.

Character is a building's principal expressive quality. It concerns the ways in which buildings are endowed with their own distinctive physiognomy or identity. It pertains to the ways in which local conventions and larger traditions overlap with other conventions and traditions and thus collectively produces the regional sense of place. It must portray type without ambiguity and with a clarity that allows a person untutored in architecture to identify the purpose being served, not only individually but universally and among other buildings. For people familiar with the traditions and conventions of a place, such as those who live where it is situated and who use it or might do so, it must also individualize its particular service. And it must also provide a decorous ornament to the urban realm as it takes its proper place within the accumulation of different types and multiple architectural characters along a street or square in a city, a region, and a nation. This role is disrupted when style as individual self-expression, or manner, overshadows the regional and national traditions and conventions that make a place people call home.

Expressive means current in the modern era

In our presentation we have identified six aspects that are held in unity within tradition: (1) the root-form or idea-form of a building's membrature and of its configuration; (2) the purposes it serves in the public and private realms of the civic and political life; (3) the unique qualities of the place it occupies; (4) the special conditions or expectation of a civic realm; (5) the unique qualities sought by a public or private patron; and (6) the qualities that the architect contributes to the common good. When practice and theory were based on imitation and invention, these were united, but as that unity frayed and these became separated and displaced, other means of investing or discovering the meanings that a building conveyed were developed. Common to these is the substitution of content from outside architecture or the civic purpose that a building is built to serve, a substitution that banished type and character from their operative roles and elevated personal or period style to supremacy within a historicist narrative.

The implications of this change are profound and warrant a brief discussion.

One major shift came through the linguistic analogy of *l'architecture parlante* (or speaking architecture). Introduced in the 18th c., it argued that the unadorned composition of a building ought to stir the sentiments as language does and thereby identify its function. The "form follows function" mantra is prominent here: A hospital should express something about healing, a bank about securing material wealth, or an art gallery about displaying art. But note: these sentiments belong to the observer and not to the function's role within the purpose that serves the civil order.

Consider the example of an art gallery. What should it express about holding works of Raphael, or of William-Adolphe Bouguereau, or Norman Rockwell, or Jackson Pollock? Should it be the appreciation the visitor has for the artist in question or for the putative style they have in common? Is that expression more important than the expression of an art gallery's purpose, which is to collect, conserve, and display the works to make the authority of their excellence in the art of painting available for appreciation and instruction? So too for other arts, such as music with its many genres from French Baroque compositions, New Orleans Jazz, Brazilian Samba, or Acid Rock. Are these separately to be transparently expressed in the architectural characters of the concert halls that house them, or does their common quality reside in music that provides different expressions of the *harmonia mundi*? Should a museum dedicated to the history of the piano be made in the curving shape of a piano?

The point is while paintings and sculptures express human emotions and sentiments, buildings do not. Buildings express the purposes they serve, and individuals respond to the buildings in ways that they share universally with others and more acutely in deeply personal ways that they develop within the traditions that bind them to the buildings. The LINCOLN MEMORIAL, HENRY BACON, WASHINGTON, 1914, and the MAUSOLEUM OF SUN YET SEN, LǛ YANZHI, NANJING, 1926–29, are examples of the tholos, and that universal type evokes from people a veneration even when they are largely ignorant of the venerable qualities of those statesmen, yet each will surely evoke a deeper and more uniquely personal response from those who know the role the person memorialized therein played in their nation's history.

Consider other examples. **Santa Maria della Salute, Baldassare Longhena, Venice, 1631** was built to fulfill a vow made to the Virgin after a devastating plague of 1630. A tholos with an octagonal plan, an internal ambulatory, and a dome, its paradigmatic models include the **Lateran Baptistery, Rome, 440?,** the **Church of Santa Costanza, Rome, 354?,** and the **Church of San Vitale, Ravenna, 526**. In Venice, the Virgin stands on a crescent moon and wears a crown of twelve stars. Twelve very large scroll-buttresses corresponding to the twelve stars of the Virgin's crown mediate between the lower and upper octagons, and they are adorned with statues of the Apostles. Longhena's text accompanying his competition entry commented that the church's rotund form was "in the shape of a crown, since it is dedicated to the Virgin."

It has been said that the building expresses gratitude to the Virgin for ending the plague and offering health or salvation, which the dedicatory term Salute certainly implies. But these meanings, while understandable responses, are felt by a person and attributed to the building, which misses its point. As a tholos that serves veneration, here veneration of her role in the miracle of relief from the plague, and veneration connects the respondent to the Virgin. The building alone can do this; the statuary, valuable as it is as ancillary decoration and ornament, is unnecessary for the unmistakable votive building's civic-religious purpose.

Nearby the **Zecca, Jacopo Sansovino, Venice**, **1536**, facing the Lagoon among nearly contemporaneous civic buildings has been similarly misinterpreted. Behind a façade with an especially robust membrature involving a pier arcade followed by two stories of trabeation (the upper one Sansovino's later addition) are the foundries, workshops, and various administrative offices involved in minting the city's coins. Although the façade has more openings than wall, it has nonetheless been said to present the expressive character seen in the walls and gates of fortifications such the **Fortifications, Michele Sanmicheli, Verona, 1527**. It has also been said to convey to citizens and foreigners alike the impregnability of Venice's economy, political stability, and military defenses. And yet another sees it expressive of its function as a factory. Fine, but these attributes misinterpret this regia's principal expression, which is the state's authority in controlling precious metal for the common good, a point reinforced by its robust character, its siting, and its scalar relationship to its neighbors. We will say more about the piazza as an example of good urban form in Chapter 4.

Sentiments and attributes are not the only non-architectural content imported into architecture's expressive character. An extreme example is found in the competition-winning design by a Danish architect for the **Opera House, Jørn Utzon, Sydney, 1959**, in Sydney's harbor. It has only very negligible architectural content with white-tiled precast concrete roofs slightly inflected one from the other over its two most important interior volumes, the Concert Hall and the Opera Theatre. It is frequently admired as expressionistic monumental sculpture, or for a "poetic factor" exhibiting cloud canopies of the heavens over its earth-like base, or for referring to the harbor's sails, shells, or swans. A conspicuous landmark, it has been declared a national monument "as representative of Australia as the pyramids are of Egypt and the Colosseum of Rome." How so? It has no analogies in Australia's national architecture, no architectural relationship to concert halls, and no connection to the universal culture of architecture. It is indeed a unique and stunning sight, an intensely personal and an unrepeatable Modernist abstraction identified with the architect, but lacking is architecture's expressive character connecting it to the purposes of the civil order.

Numerous outliers are similarly admired for their distinctive forms, for example the **Second Goetheanum, Rudolf Steiner, Dornach, 1924**; **Notre Dame du Haut, Le Corbusier, Ronchamp, 1953**; and **Guggenheim Museum, Frank Gehry, Bilbao, 1995**. Distinctly estranged from their contexts, they are also unconnected to their civil purposes or even to what their expression points to. Is Goethe's thought embodied in the first, the spiritual qualities of the Virgin in the second, or in the third the character of the Guggenheim's purpose in collecting and displaying works of art? Like the Sydney Opera House, they are deeply subjective formal expressions of their authors, each one offering a stirring "aesthetic appeal".

These comments illustrate the more fully developed form for the sentiments that *l'architecture parlante* authorizes and aesthetics explains. Aesthetics as a field of knowledge allowed lively, emotional sensations rather quickly to overwhelm beauty's role in stirring the deep recesses of the soul. Aesthetics offered the sublime with its terrific pleasure found in the sensation of being freed from the threat of death, and it pushed beauty to the opposite end of the pole where it offered charm. Before long this heightened emotional engagement managed to have romanticism displace judgments based on classical equipoise. Meanwhile, with the rapidly expanding catalogs of past styles belonging to earlier eras, people began to associate the valued qualities of those eras with particular past styles. First this ushered in the age of neo-styles, and then associations were used to recover from the political revolutions in the decades surrounding the year 1800 and return European nations to their roles in the march of progress. By using past styles, they restored their traditional national identities and reaffirmed their unique places in the world. The École des Beaux-Arts used France's pre-Revolution classical styles, and Austrian architects rebuilt their capitals with similarly national evocations. After flirting with the Greeks the Germans rediscovered a role for the Romanesque and the Neo-Gothic. And the English used its national styles, Gothic and others, to produce the buildings now identified as Neo Gothic, eclectic, Victorian, Tudor, Edwardian, etc.

While this was happening the philosophical work of G. W. F. Hegel (1770–1831) was producing the foundations for the discipline of the history of art as a field of study that was unconnected to practice. In the 20th c., Erwin Panofsky (1892–1968) achieved prominence as a medieval historian using iconography and iconology to uncover the meanings of a personage, object, or story that were opaque to us and rendered in an earlier era's style. It allowed us to decipher "symbolic content" as a "cultural symptom" of an era's unique display of "the essential tendencies of the human mind."[11] By extension, the style that is "of our time" renders that service in our era, that of Modernity.

Rudolf Wittkower (1901–71), a specialist in Renaissance and Baroque Italian art and architecture, called attention to the popularity both in the 19th c. and in the 15th and 16th centuries of buildings using styles that "derive from classical antiquity" and were said to be valued because their "pure forms" offer delight and aesthetic pleasure which their predecessors did not supply. These Renaissance buildings, it was said, demonstrated the rejection of medieval religiosity in favor of hedonistic Renaissance humanism. But this raised the question, if each style is "of its time," in what way were these two eras different? In exploring Renaissance theorists, he discovered that "numerous the forms of the Renaissance church have symbolical value … which the pure forms as such do not contain." Renaissance architecture, he continued, "like every great style of the past, was based on a hierarchy of values culminating in the absolute values of sacred architecture."[12] Wittkower said nothing more about the 19th c.

Wittkower's conclusion was congruent with Panofsky's, which allowed the "essential tendencies of the human mind" to take different forms in different periods. Both isolated their study within a particular past era without reference to the larger framework of Nature and nature that holds those "essential tendencies" and "hierarchy of values." But without that connection, there is no way to identify the role a building plays in fulfilling the universal human nature of those who build and use it, no criteria for assessing architecture's beauty as a quality that transcends the forms of particular periods or the expression of particular meanings or beliefs, or any connection between the historian's work and that of the architects.

In the 1960s a generation of architects tutored in the historicist narrative rose to prominence with their buildings sometimes illustrating their theories. One prominent theory used semiotics as an interpretive method to reveal and invest building forms with meaning. It held that buildings, like texts, are generated by culture and use signs and symbols to carry meanings. This method, while novel, and other methods like it, is merely a weak form of imitation. It implies that both language and architecture are systems of signs that carry certain messages through a kind of imitative transparency between the visual and the verbal, with the image and the word acting as if they are interchangeable means of expression. And it makes "culture" the author of influences. In all this theorizing we find yet another distraction that impedes uncovering the important meaning. When applied to practice, the building's civil purposes are subverted, the art of architecture is degraded, and urbanism is disfigured.

In the late 1930s, a few scholars began to call historicism to account, but with little effect. Even robust attacks three decades later hardly made a dent. One such is that of Ernst Gombrich (1909–2001) in 1969 who noted that its Hegelianism bundles together eight fields of human involvement with each determined by the *Zeitgeist's* influence and that together constitute an era's "cultural expression": religion, constitution, morality, law, custom, science, technology, and art. This scheme's foundations, he declared, have "crumbled."[13] Hardly.

Architectural form does convey meaning, but how else might we apprehend and discern it? Until the 18th c. there were any number of variations, some very elaborate, others quite simple such as the one Saint Augustine presents in *On Christian Doctrine* from the tail end of the ancient era that resonates all through our study. He begins with identifying a thing (our example would be a doughnut-plan shrine) that he identifies as a sign that points to a something else (in our case, veneration) that carries symbolic value or something invisible that human nature can embody, such as veneration for what a person acknowledges as "Nature or Nature's god," to use Jefferson's words: thing to sign to symbol. All symbols have signs pointing to them but not all signs point to symbols. Two golden arches are a thing and a sign pointing to hamburgers, but that sign does not point to a symbol because our gut, not our human nature, embodies the hamburger. A beautiful sunset is a thing to admire, a sign that points to an author of the universe and in turn to a symbol of the beauty that its author, whether God or cosmic chance or something else, offers for us so that we can feel embodied in Nature. The U.S. Capitol dome is a conspicuous architectural thing; it is a tholos or sign pointing to the veneration held for a democratic form of government, and a symbol of the purpose of government, which is to assure security, liberty, and justice for all who are united in its community.[14]

Modernism and modernity

Modernism became established as a revolutionary movement allied with political movements after the catastrophe of World War I. Its advocates promised a new world that would improve the condition for humankind that any connection with the past would inhibit. The political movements were resisted in many parts of Europe and the rest of the world, and where they did take hold, Modernist architecture was soon replaced by the traditional styles that would have allied the new regimes with successful, prerevolutionary eras of the past. None of these new regimes survived the 20th c.

That early liaison of revolutionary architecture with revolutionary politics was a marriage of convenience, and when they divorced, avant-garde architects sought other sponsors. In Germany and France, some of the leaders of revolutionary architecture courted fascist patrons, but without success. In the United States, where the Depression made people eager to move into an improved future, the advocates of the revolutionary styles were invited into universities and museums, and in the post-war period they quickly gained command of the culture of architecture that is now dominant throughout the world. Architecture has retained its membership within the Fine Arts club where each art and each artist jealously guards the right of self-expression and exercises the role of leading others into a blessed future. Instruction in universities involves competition to be at the cutting edge of the avant-garde while those practicing architecture occupy one of two interconnected realms. In one, they seek to be "on time, on budget, and get good press reviews," to cite the criteria of a university administrator who hires architects. They use styles that are "of our time," their forms follow their functions, and they are assembled with materials that technology makes available. In the other realm, a rarified group of architects commands high fees as they vie for fame at the forefront of the avant-garde that is establishing what is "of our time."

Occupying the position of being "of our time" in Modernity takes various forms and is often evanescent. It might be portraying tension, stress, anxiety, and unsettledness by conceiving a building as fragments of previous fragments. Or it might intentionally distort and destabilize established conventions and meanings.[15] Another approach exploits digital technologies developed for manufacturing automobiles, aircraft, and arms to produce complex, ambiguous, contorted, and unrelated forms with different tectonic expressions and different textures. Yet another uses complex, non-linear geometries and folded forms as direct representations of the complex socio-cultural conditions of the post-Cold War era. Or one might express the rending of the social fabric, resistance to rampant consumerism, or other social-economic malaises. And still others seek forms void of any meaning and representational value whatsoever for buildings that can be used only once and of short duration and will intentionally subvert their acquiring conventional meanings that might arise from the mutual stimulation between minds within historical experience.

Four concluding observations

1 *In both theory and practice, imitation is incompatible with Modernism.* Modernism posits an unrepairable rupture with prior referents and historical precedence. We noted in the previous chapter that the vacuum Modernism created in practice was filled with evolution and technology, and we have just called attention to the weak roles of imitation. Here we add to that gravamen the pervasive strong form that claims explicit imitation of technology's products, for example, airplanes, trains, ships, electrical power plants, or nuclear reactors, that are external to architecture and are sometimes transferred, *mutatis mutandis,* into architecture. This practice reveals Modernism's end to be that of remaking the world in a *technicist* image (the *Weltanschauung*) that is antithetical to the imitation of Nature.[16]

2 *By excessively exalting invention, Modernism separated it from imitation, thereby harming both concepts.* Properly understood, invention refers to the skilled combination and re-combination of forms, some transmitted by tradition, others new, to shape a new whole when that whole is justified by need. Invention and imitation are inseparable concepts, each one constructing the other and rendering the other intelligible. Neither is ever wholly present in architecture, or in any other field, separate from the other. Instead, they are always fused, working reciprocally in the mind and in the buildings as continuity and change address both site-specific and building-specific requirements. All of this must be considered to understand, evaluate, and judge success.

   In Modernism, the term invention has a very different meaning. It refers to original, never-before-seen forms or their combination, and this asks that something be made out of nothing (*creatio ex nihilo*). This separates imitation from invention and logically requires condemning imitation as copying something already made. Imitation also prevents architects from being "of their time." Banishing imitation leads to a generalized opacity toward preceding architectural experience, and it declares that all forms and combinations of forms must be treated as unrepeatable, even by their original authors. Here the practice of architecture is all invention.

3 *Self-expression has been given a higher value than specifically architectural expressions.* In architecture, decorum as propriety is a governing agent across the full range of buildings from the vernacular to the civic, and it can and does incorporate proper acknowledgment of the architect's personal style.

Decorum, that is, propriety, involves the proper placing of proper buildings in urban or rural realms in analogy to Jonathan Swift's literary statement about "proper words in proper places." Working together across time, the architectural and the urban form an interconnected unity within variety.

For many architects today, the freedom of artistic expression stands as a counterpart to political freedom. They proclaim their art to be reformatory; they will lead and others will follow. But even within the profession, there is more anarchy than commonality. Most architects resent being constrained by outmoded norms of propriety in urban realms. Some disregard, and others exploit for expressive effect, the representation of the membrature's tectonic work. Some demand "honest" expression of materials in the membrature's tectonic order, while others make the working of natural laws in the membrature invisible or magically suspended. Some express, others hide, and yet others ignore the relationship between form and function, although most bristle when they see earlier buildings defying form-follows-function, as at **Sanssouci Park, Friedrich Ludwig Perseus, Potsdam, 1841–45**. A person would reasonably identify his building as a mosque (and wonder why it is in a Christian sovereign's park), but in fact it is a water-pumping station serving the park's fountains with the pump's smokestack disguised as a minaret. And yet those same Modernist architects willingly and willfully flaunt decorum's rules when they produce a museum, school, or church that can be mistaken for an industrial factory. Here we see both traditional and modernist architects falling prey to the confusion of genres: a water-pumping station is not a mosque, and neither is an industrial factory a school or museum.

4 *Modernism has largely deprived painting and sculpture of their previous integrated roles in architecture.* Other than in Modernism, familiar, traditional, conventional compositions in each of the three visual arts guide imitation and provides instant recognition, which allows a work's purpose in serving the good to be understood and provides a means for assessing the artist's talent and inventiveness in achieving beauty. A Madonna and Child had a familiar composition but a unique rendering, and churches and palaces within regional and national traditions had similar configurations that invention fitted to places and particular roles. The familiar is essential, as Alberti in his treatise on painting in 1435 suggested when he noted that the painter could draw attention to his painting by including among its figures someone whom the intended audience could recognize.

When Modernism jettisoned these and other practices in the name of progress to be served by unshackled artistic freedom, the arts had to find other subjects for expression. In the figurative arts of painting and sculpture, Modernists embraced abstraction using various means such as depicting the result of physical movement, the "color" or content of moods, distortions of recognizable forms, or forms lacking outside referents. In architecture, architects have used compositional strategies imitating those of the other visual arts to produce volumetric organization, spatial definitions, spatial transparencies, relations between solids and voids, tensions between context and frame, and so on, and they have largely banished figurative images from their buildings.

If this book offers one lesson it is this: Tradition offers a much richer vein of gold for architecture to mine than the limitation "of the time" and of the architect's solo inventions.

Notes

1 Carroll William Westfall, *Architecture, Liberty and Civic Order: Architectural Theories from Vitruvius to Jefferson and Beyond* (Ashgate: Farnham and Burlington, 2005), 16ff.
2 Pierre Gros, *L' architecture romaine*, Vol. I (Picard, 1996), 140–3.
3 Among the theorists in the 18th and 19th cs. were M.-A. Laugier's, *Essai sur l'architecture*, (Paris, 1753); Ribart de Chamoust's, *L'ordre français trouvé dans la nature* (Paris, 1776); F. Milizia's, *Principii di architettura civile*, 1781 (S. Majocchi, 1847); and Ch.-F. Viel de Saint-Maux, *Lettres sur l'architecture des anciens et des modernes* (1787).
4 J-.N.-L. Durand, *Recueil et parallèle des édifices de tout genre …* (Gille, an IX, 1801), and his *Précis des leçons…* (An X, 1802).
5 A.C. Quatremère de Quincy's, *Dictionnaire d'architecture* in C.-J. Pancouke's, *Encyclopédie méthodique* (1782–1825), and his *Dictionnaire historique d'architecture* (A. Le Clère, 1832). For it see Samir Younés, *The True, the Fictive, and the Real: The Historical Dictionary of Architecture of Quatremère de Quincy* (London: Andreas Papadakis, 1999).
6 For reflections on building typology and urban morphology since the late 19th century, see: C. Daly, *L'Architecture privée au XIXème siècle* (Paris, 1864); C. Sitte, *The Birth of Modern City Planning* (1889) (Rizzoli, 1986); W. Hegemann and E. Peets, *The American Vitruvius: An Architects' Handbook of Civic Art* (1922) (Princeton Architectural Press, 1988); P. Lavedan, *Histoire de l'urbanisme* (H. Laurens, 1926–52); M. Morini, *Atlante storico dell'urbanistica* (Hoepli, 1960); S. Muratori, *Studi per una operante storia urbana di Venezia* (Istituto Poligrafico dello Stato, 1960); G.C. Argan, *Progetto e destino* (Il Saggiatore, 1965); C. Aymonino and A. Rossi, *La città di Padova* (Roma, Officina, 1966); A. Rossi, *L'architettura della città* (Marsilio, Padova, 1966); A. Vidler, "The Third Typology" in *Architecture rationnelle*, ed. M. Culot and L. Krier (Archives d'architecture moderne, Brussels, 1976); J. Castex, J-Ch. Depaule, Ph. Panerai, *Formes urbaines* (Dunod, 1977); J.I. Linazasoro, *Permanencias y arquitectura urbana*, (G. Gili, 1978); R. Moneo, "On Typology", *Oppositions*, 13 (1978); R. Krier, *Urban Space* (Rizzoli, 1979); P. Panerai et al., *Eléments d'analyse urbaine* (Archives d'architecture moderne, Brussels, 1980); Casabella, *I terreni della tipologia*, Gennaio-Febbraio (1985); L. Krier, *The Architectural Tuning of Settlements* (The Prince's Foundation, 2008).
7 R-J. Van Pelt and C.W. Westfall, *op. cit.*, pp. 155–60.
8 S. Younés, *The Imperfect City. On Architectural Judgment* (Ashgate, 2012), Routledge, 2016. Chapter 3.
9 Note that the buildings named in these descriptions are included among the examples in Part II.
10 Samir Younés, *The Imperfect City: On Architectural Judgment* (Farnham, Surrey, and Burlington, Vermont: Ashgate, 2012), 147–8; italics as in the original.

11 Erwin Panofsky, "Iconography and Iconology: An Introduction to the Study of Renaissance Art," *Meaning in the Visual Arts* (Garden City, NY: Doubleday Anchor Books, 1957), 26–54; first published 1939.
12 Rudolf Wittkower, *Architectural Principles in the Age of Humanism*, 3rd ed. (London: Alec Tiranti, 1962), first published 1949. Among his students was Colin Rowe whose role in Modernist architecture is important but beyond our scope. In a remark Westfall cannot document but clearly remembers, Wittkower expressed surprise that his book's discussion of proportions was picked up by architects who brought them into their work in England in the years after World War II.
13 E. H. Gombrich, *In Search of Cultural History* (Oxford: Clarendon Press, 1969), 6; See also David Watkin, *Morality and Architecture* (Oxford: Clarendon Press, 1977) and *Morality and Architecture Revisited* (Chicago, IL: University of Chicago Press, 2001).
14 Vitruvius, at I, i, 2, says something similar when he distinguished between the shadow and the thing (umbram non rem).
15 Jeffrey Kipnis, "Toward a New Architecture", in *Architectural Design* (102, London, 1993).
16 On the effects of the technological mind-set and the resulting *technicist* image, see Jacques Ellul, *The Empire of Non-sense*, Introduction by S. Younés and D. Lovekin (London: Papadakis, 2014); original in French published in 1980.

3

URBANISM

So far we have stressed the role of buildings as public objects and how they serve and express the purposes of the public and private institutions and entities that build and use them. In the following chapters, we turn to urbanism. The present general tendency treats a building not as a public object in an urban setting but as a free-standing entity, the product of the influences "of its time," and as a creative product of an inventive architect who walks in no other architect's shadow. We find this tendency in the common practice of using the terms city and urbanism interchangeably, which obscures the public, civic nature of architecture and of urbanism. The word city is synonymous with civilization; we carry its more than 5,000-year history in our present civilization. To benefit from what that past offers us today we will begin with a snapshot history of the city and its urbanism.

Pre-modern cities and urbanism

The first cities were apparently formed when agriculture gradually replaced hunting and gathering in some parts of the world. It is likely that their residents were united by common ideals of religion that were inseparable from their civil order. The site selected for settling may have been where a divinity had touched the earth or, in the case of the Biblical city of Enoch, as a place to hide from Yahweh after having been driven from the Garden. The community honored its divinity by setting sacred sites apart from its secular activities within protective enclosures. Many new foundations exploited a protective topographic feature such as a rocky outcropping (Athens; Rome) or a protective lagoon (Venice). Others chose a site that offered the convenience of a river ford (London; Paris). Imperial powers would build large, sophisticated cities ex novo as defensive

DOI: 10.4324/9780429506260-5

garrisons (Florence) or as centers for government, usually with some role for the grid (Beijing, Antigua Guatemala, Washington, New Delhi). Grid plans also facilitated the distribution of land as property when newly acquired land was being colonized, as in the American frontier and across Canada.

By living and working together people acquired experience in sustaining themselves, in governing, and in building to provide shelter and security against enemies and Nature. With the experience gained by using nature's materials for supporting, walling, spanning, and roofing, they developed the art of building and eventually the art of architecture that they reserved for their more valued buildings. In some cities, early conversations and deliberations eventually became poetry and philosophy that presented principles that interpreted cosmic Nature's order, and these were interwoven into their history and their valued, traditional knowledge. Their habits and customs of government and the architecture and urbanism they built to serve their ends became the most conspicuous and long-lasting expression of their culture and ethos.

Those origins found particularly fruitful beginnings in Greece in the few centuries following the 7th c. BCE. The classic models that have nourished architecture down to the present were built then, and their tumultuous political life became the subject of rational analysis and deliberation that stimulated Plato's and Aristotle's founding of political theory. Plato imagined the ideal, while as we saw in Chapter 1, Aristotle identified the origin in humankind's natural sociability and the synoecism that formed the polis or city, a political entity necessary to achieve the good life that also retained the distinctiveness of the individual, family, tribal unit, and other subsidiary institutions and entities. Political theory described and gave reasons for change within and between the various forms of political unions or civil orders that ran through autocracy (one person governs), oligarchy (the few govern), and democracy (the people govern), each with beneficial and corrupt forms. The Greek philosophers presented lucid accounts of the causes and results of the changes from one form to another, and historians such as Thucydides chronicled their histories.

These ancient Greek political theories have coursed through the western tradition, and they and subsequent experience continue to be absorbed into the lives of nations and peoples throughout the world. Our presentation will be well served by a few brief remarks about the salient content of that tradition.

At its center are the insights from Jerusalem and Athens touched on in Chapter 1, that all individuals share a common human nature that endows each person with certain rights and duties within a moral order, with each person also a unique individual who benefits from living in society with others. In binding themselves into social communities, individuals seek to live in the good polis or city, the *ev topos* (εὖτόπος), the well-place, the good-place where justice imitates the good and things that are made imitate the beauty of Nature. They equip the place they settle with the buildings that will serve their human needs and common aspirations.

Their methods for governing and building imitated the cosmos with its eternal, orderly, hierarchic arrangement of things and individuals. In the sublunary world, humankind occupies the top position, with some individuals being naturally superior to others. This belief validated investing civil authority unequally within a community with God or the gods having ultimate authority in the sublunary realm.

Over the next two millennia, civil orders were organized within a variety of forms with the most prominent being autocratic monarchies. In Greece for a few centuries, the political history was tumultuous with changes providing the material that philosophers and historians marshaled into the beginnings of philosophical inquiries into the nature of humankind and their civil orders. Athens under the democratic leadership of Pericles (495?–429 BCE) was rebuilt after its destruction by the Persian Empire in 480 BC, and it later became the leader in this literary activity. Even Rome admired Athens.

Ancient cities were built in a spatial void and used surrounding walls to protect the urban order from the external void's chaos. The various institutions and entities constituting the civil order within the urbanism were themselves enclosed within precincts, the most important of which honored the gods.

In Athens, the most important precinct was the Acropolis, the high city. On the processional way leading up to it to honor its gods, a person could see the **Temple of Athena Nike, c. 421 BCE** before passing through the precinct's **Propylaea, Mnesikles, 436–31 BCE** or gateway that offered a full view of the large statue of Athena holding the spear whose tip glistened in the sun and guided sailors to the city. To its left was the Erechtheum, a shrine to Athens' foundation, and beyond it the TEMPLE OF ATHENA (PARTHENON), IKTINOS AND CALLICRATES, ATHENS, 447–36BCE that, like the Erechtheum presented itself with an oblique angle to the entrance and thereby revealed its full character, just as the people did when they gathered in their democratic assemblies.

The cities, after exhausting themselves in the Peloponnesian War, passed into the hands of autocratic tyrants, Alexander the Great being the most famous. A consultive body called a boule assembled in a regia, called a bouleuterion, was to provide stability subordinate to tyrannical authority; it joined urbanism's other types, the temple, tholos, and theater being the most prominent. Miletos and Priene, two Ionian cities in Asia Minor destroyed by the Persians, were rebuilt with a rectangular grid plan that held the precincts where these buildings were located as was a large agora lined by stoas arranged in studied relationships. These proved to be very informative models for the Romans who adapted Greek traditions for their own use.

The Romans extended their stable administrative and legal structures across vast lands where the plundered riches of the conquered provided the wealth for their building campaigns. They adapted Greek models to their own uses and filled Rome and other cities with an expanded range of variations for buildings serving religious and civil institutions from their enclosed precincts. After 313 Christianity began to permeate the empire, and churches began to challenge pagan temples for prominence in Roman urbanism even in these earliest years of decline that culminated in the sack by the Goths in 410. In response, Saint Augustine wrote *The City of God* that would solidify the institution of the Church in civil affairs for a millennium. Augustine identified the Church as the earthly antechamber of the Heavenly City, the *città felice*, located within the city of man where humankind could enjoy God's presence before entering its model in Heaven. The subsequent decline in civilization began to abate around the year 1,000 and, with prosperity returning, people began repairing and expanding the cities that hosted that Heavenly City. Buildings serving secular purposes such as city halls and civic granaries remained subordinate to the surrogate for the Heavenly City, the cathedral, the seat of the bishop or highest religious authority; it was also the city's most complete imitation of the order, harmony, proportionality, and radiant splendor of the Heavenly City.

The imperial legal order of Christian Rome remained the basic structure of civil and canon law. It put landowners in command of those dwelling on the land including those who dwelled within cities. As cities became more populous and prosperous, many found ways to gain authority over their civil affairs, some with democratic civil orders, often transient, that contrived acceptable arrangements with landed feudatory powers and the Roman Church and various reformed confessions that held sway down into the 17th c. in England and later on the continent.

The development of the early modern city

In Italy in a growing swell that began in the mid-13th c. people began to develop a sense of the present as a modern age different from a past, and they came to view their ancient forebears' achievements with ever-greater admiration. Italian cities were winning liberty from feudal lords and defending them with wars of words and sometimes with swords and pikes. Around 1400 the Florentines began finding strong weapons for defending their liberty in hand-me-downs of classical antiquity, especially in ancient Greek and Roman rhetoric and histories. And from Saint Augustine, they learned that the way to turn hearts to the love of God was better done with reasoned arguments and a strong will than with the nurturing intellect as Saint Thomas Aquinas. The will's fiery force of love would stimulate people to do in this world the good that validated their access to the next world.[1] In ancient people portrayed in statues and in ancient literature they found better models than the saints for the force of character that stimulated people to do the good. And in ancient buildings, these willful, active people found powerful and instructive imitations of Nature's order, harmony, proportionality, and concinnity. In 1415, a better text of Vitruvius than any known in previous centuries turned up in Florence. Before long, first in Florence and then elsewhere, ancient achievements in architecture were serving as models as people set about building cities in which their good works would serve their eagerness to be allowed through the Gates of Heaven. Here is the willfulness that is such a conspicuous feature of the modern age.

The modern understanding of spatial composition in urbanism and architecture is another legacy from those Florentines. It is based on the geometric perspective that Filippo Brunelleschi demonstrated in about 1410, and it was quickly absorbed into practice in painting, sculpture, and architecture, which is our concern.[2] As we noted, in pre-modern urbanism the walls separated the city from exurban chaos, and within those walls were precincts holding the buildings serving the civil and religious institutions and other entities. These precincts were separated from one another by streets and squares, some of them ceremonial but most of them simply unorganized while serving movement, markets, etc. To move from one precinct to another, say, from an atrium house to the Forum in Pompeii, required a movement from point A to point B, from B to C, from C to D, with no comprehensible relationship between points A and D or B and D. The buildings were sited and designed to guide a person's movement through the city.[3] This care facilitated point-to-point navigation such as that used on the seas where portolan charts guided navigators before the void was organized with latitudes and longitudes. Using it cannot get you to the moon; without Brunelleschi's invention, there could be no GPS systems in the heavens or on the earth. For that you need a comprehension of homogeneous space rationalized with x–y–z coordinates holding rational geometric relationships, which is what modern spatial understanding offers. Everyone today comprehends that. For moderns, space is not an incomprehensible, chaotic void. Instead, it can be comprehended mentally as homogeneous, continuous, and gridded in three dimensions with everything occupying rationally definable relationships to everything else.

This new spatial order could be reproduced, or originally produced, on a two-dimensional surface. Masaccio used Brunelleschi's geometric perspective in his stunningly innovative paintings that included foreshortened halos; later painters would abandon halos altogether. He put the figures in scalar relationships to buildings that made them congruent with our scalar relationship to our world. And he included shades and shadows cast by a locatable light source that placed the figure in the same sun-filled cosmic order that we inhabit. Vase paintings, frescos, and mosaics prove that ancient artists could not render this coherence between object, space, and light, but their successors were now able to render settings that brought heaven to earth to support a scene's allegorical content.

Brunelleschi demonstrated his invention to the public in Florence with two demonstration panels, subsequently lost, and Leon Battista Alberti explained Brunelleschi's role for the geometric matrix of lines and angles in homogeneous space in an Italian treatise in 1435 and in Latin the next year. In mid-century in his treatise on architecture, Alberti explained how those lines and angles are used in *disegno*, which becomes our verb to design and also means to will. From then on the precincts would be dissolved and the world would be conceived as a homogeneous space holding interactions between solids as buildings and other material things isomorphic within voids defined as the space of streets, squares, and landscape. Urban design becomes as much a matter of the mind as of the eye. The perspectival design makes it possible to preordain the best visual balance between solids and voids in places as small as a building's interior rooms and as large as cities and nations. It also makes it possible for buildings to be isomorphic with one another and with their immediate spatial setting. Finally and most importantly, it provides the means of controlling the architecture and the urbanism of a civil order so that it can serve and express the civil order as a whole and not as several discontinuous institutions and entities hemmed in by a wall that separates the urbanism from the rural district. There is little wonder that it appeared in Florence when the republic was defending its liberty against the imperial claims of feudal barons.

People now began to represent the world differently. In the 23″ × 52″ woodcut **View of Florence with the Chain, Francesco Rosselli, 1480**, the Duomo and Palazzo Vecchio stand out, but the great mass of other buildings are in proper relationship to one another. We also see the city's walls and the landscape beyond them as they appeared from the position of a man seen seated in the foreground. Like the panels and the newest works of painting and relief sculpture, we see perspective at work translating what a person saw into a depiction that we understand he saw with his own eyes.

Perspective quickly became featured in architecture. We will present several examples of perspective design in buildings discussed in Part II. Here we can point to three examples or perspectival urban design from Brunelleschi's Florence. One is the unrealized project that Giorgio Vasari reported about **Santo Spirito, Brunelleschi, Florence, 1428** where he intended to reverse the orientation of the church and open a vista for it to be seen from those traveling on the Arno River. The second, the **Piazza degli Innocenti, Florence**, illustrates the extent to which urbanism is a slow art where, as Edmund Bacon noted, success depends on the "principle of the second architect," the one who recognizes the urban potential in an existing situation and extracts urbanism from it.[4] The **Ospedale degli Innoenti, Brunelleschi, Florence, 1417** was set back from the street away from the axis that aligned with the central axis of the Church of the Annunciation. A century later an eleemosynary institution built an **apartment building, Antonio da Sangallo the Elder**, whose configuration and membrature duplicated the Ospedale it faced. It was a mere dwelling, but its role in urban design validated this higher status because it helped produce a piazza as an ordered urban space from a mere void with the piazza then completed in 1601when a loggia was added on the two sides of the church's existing arched porch.

Even before that final touch, this piazza was the apparent model for the **Piazza Grande, Bernardo Buontalenti, Livorno, 1594**. In 1577 Buontalenti had designed the Medici Duke's new city as Tuscany's seaport with a grid of streets within pentagonal defense bulwarks. The piazza fronted the cathedral and was surrounded by an arcaded portico. English Grand Tourists often first encountered Italy when landing in this city, and this piazza is often cited as the model for the urbanism of SAINT PAUL'S COVENT GARDEN, INIGO JONES, LONDON, 1631.

A final example, PALAZZO MEDICI, MICHELOZZO DI BARTOLOMMEO, FLORENCE, 1444 reveals how Brunelleschi's role for perspectival design was absorbed into architecture. The family palace that Cosimo de' Medici, the first among equals governing the Florentine republic, was sited where an axis from the piazza del Duomo jogs slightly. The palace gained prominence by locating at that jog the corner bay of the 1 × 3 loggia absorbed into the palace block.

Perspective found a home in the first modern treatise on architecture. We saw that Alberti had explained perspective for painters in the 1430s in a Latin and an Italian version. Now in mid-century, he incorporated it into his treatise on architecture. A modernization of Vitruvius' treatise, he revised Vitruvius' formula of *ratiocinatio et fabrica* to *lineamenta* and *perscriptio concepta animo*; that is, the architect makes a design that arranges lines and angles for producing the forms of the material components of buildings.[5] Further, he extends this to the control of the material's assembly to invest a building's three-dimensional configuration and membrature with a proportioned, geometric matrix and concinnity that imitates Nature's beauty. He also extended this role for perspectival design into urbanism and its service to the civil order. In a commonplace, he tells readers "that a well-maintained and well-adorned temple [i.e., church] is obviously the greatest and most important ornament of a city." But then there is this: "The principal ornament to any city lies in the siting, layout, fashioning, and arrangement of its roads, squares, and individual works: each must be properly planned and distributed according to use, importance, and convenience."[6] Earlier descriptions of cities had been lists of buildings in precincts; this is quite different. It surely imagines the dissolution of precincts to make a homogeneous spatial void that is given conceptual and perceptual order with grids in two and three dimensions, a spatial realm with buildings that are isomorphic with the grids.

Perspectival urbanism and architectural design spread quickly, especially where autocratic rulers put it to use to exhibit the authority they exercised in cities. Louis XIV used axial roadways within the hexagon of the French state that he had wrung from fractious nobles. He and other rulers legitimated their autocratic authority with perspectival urbanism in rebuilding or expanding cities equipped with carefully sited tholoi, temples, and regias that were designed to exploit the states' associations with their ancient history and legal order.

The modern city and its urbanism

The modern city, the place where we live today and build for the future, lacks the qualities of its predecessors down through history. The same zeal and common beliefs can lead us to seek the good and the beautiful through the interactions of religious, political, and architectural activities imitating Nature and nature. Our *Weltanschauung*, however, contains a skepticism that assaulted accepted doctrines, and the teachings of religious and secular authorities lost their predominant role in charting our actions in the world, increasingly since the late 18th century. The globe shrank, and production and consumption began their expansion. The unity of Heaven and earth became frayed as the knowledge we sought it was divided into two separate fields, the sciences that concentrated on the behavior of matter that was explicable with mathematics, and the humanities or traditional studia humanitatis covering arts, letters, philosophy, governing, and so on. Meanwhile, people began exercising greater willfulness over their actions, claimed increased roles in governance, and loosened the immaterial ideals that bound people into civil orders ranging from family to nation within ever-increasing populations.

These changes were clearly evident in urbanism. In earlier centuries the most prominent buildings served religion, with the regias of the powerful close behind. As authority drained from autocrats and oligarchs to democratic forms of government, authoritative democratic or quasi-democratic institutions gained prominence. Reforms in Britain made the **Houses of Parliament, Charles Barry and A. W. N. Pugin, London, 1837** second only to **Saint Paul's Cathedral, Christopher Wren, London, 1675,** and in the newly formed nation in America the **Dome of the United States Capitol, Thomas U. Walter, Washington, 1850** provided the model for dominance in innumerable state capitols and courthouses. Later in the century and especially in the United States, new cities were being founded and rapidly expanded, those penetrations of the sky were bested by facilities serving industry and commerce, first grain elevators and factory smokestacks, and then towering business buildings.

Populations were expanding at a rapid rate, and so were urban populations. In the developing western nations in 1750, the ratio of urban to rural was 10:90; in 1950 it had reversed to 90:10 with a similar reversal happening in the rest of the world.

Workers earned low wages, and employment was unsteady. Farms that might offer sustenance in times of need were now far away. The available shelter was in small rooms in buildings either old or new that often lacked running water, heat, and sanitation on land formerly used for urban gardens, which increased urban densities. Social networks providing relief were always overwhelmed, other supportive communities were largely lacking, history offered little guidance for ameliorating conditions, and the civil orders and other powers had little interest in doing so.

An assortment of remedies

Britain was an early leader in industrialization with Manchester a leading sink pit epitomized by the local expression, "Where there's muck there's money." The country's long history of controlling the price of wheat to benefit farmers and assure adequate supplies proved inadequate, and in 1834 its first Poor Law reform came about spurred by Edwin Chadwick's knowledge of London and his native Manchester. In 1844 Friedrich Engels and Karl Marx, in publishing their observations of Manchester and contiguous Salford, provided grist for revolutionary mills internationally.

Beyond deficient sustenance was the miserable housing. From antiquity forward some variety of multiple story residences, descendants of ancient Roman insulae or simple party wall, single-family **terraced housing** had been staples in urbanism, even for very high-class residents, as at the PLACE ROYALE (NOW PLACE DES VOSGES), PARIS, 1605–12, in the rows collected on the landscaped ground in **Regent Park, John Nash, London, 1811**, and in THE CIRCUS AND THE CRESCENT, JOHN WOOD THE ELDER and WOOD THE YOUNGER, BATH, 1754. In Britain's industrial centers, terraced houses rapidly strung along streets were minimal in every way: a front and back room on each of two stories and a stair beside a passage leading back to a kitchen wing. Coal for heating and cooking was brought in from a back alley where trash was deposited with a "honeypot" for toilet waste in front providing sanitation. Many abound today, having been improved to satisfy today's standards.

Prince Albert hoped to provoke reforms by displaying an architect-designed **Model Cottage, Henry Roberts, 1851** at the CRYSTAL PALACE, JOSEPH PAXTON, LONDON, 1851, constructed in brick with an open front stair leading to the pair of apartments on each of two floors, each with a living room, kitchen, three bedrooms, and toilet and, as was usual, no bathroom. Although much visited, it gained little following. Later, various "five percent philanthropy" societies provided improved dwellings while seeking only a modest financial return. Another program from 1862 was instituted by George Peabody, a Massachusetts native engaged in banking in London (J. P. Morgan is a successor firm) the philanthropic Peabody Trust survives today. It built the **Peabody Building, H. A. Darbishire, Spitalfields, London, 1864**, the first of many subsidized dwellings where residents had to observe curfews and high moral standards. Fitting into the existing urban fabric, the point of its V plan presents an elaborate entrance between two wings rising four stories above shops in brownstone bases and stepped gables intersecting their pitched roofs; it is now privately owned.

Things were different but not necessarily better elsewhere. After Manhattan Island's buildings began to reach beyond the original walled town, the state produced a plat for the entire island. The famous **Manhattan Island**

Commissioners' Plan, 1811 has broad north-south avenues and narrow east-west streets with 25 × 100 foot lots and no alleys. Rural and foreign immigrants found shelter in older buildings adapted to their needs, but the surge after the European revolutions of the 1840s brought serious overcrowding and highly inadequate new construction. In 1867 an ordinance set out minimum standards for light and air and required a toilet for every twenty residents, the first of many ever-stricter and inadequate laws in New York.

A typical, legal, early New York dumbbell plan for a five or six-story building had a ground floor shop with apartments above, each having two bedrooms, an additional room as a parlor, and a kitchen with a stove and a hot water boiler, rarely a bath, a light court and gas providing light, and common toilets for two or four dwelling units on each floor. Many were built by immigrants who cobbled together financing, many designed to resemble the Central European cities they had left. Peter Herter spent two decades building a real estate empire of tenements. An 1884 immigrant who had studied briefly in the BAUAKADAMIE, KARL FREDERICK SCHINKEL, BERLIN, 1832, his, like many others, had elaborately ornamented brick or red stone facades that gave lower Manhattan's tenement streets their Central European expressive character.

Other cities such as Boston had done no better, and neither did Chicago that lacked tenements but built inadequate wooden cottages and two to four-story crowded flat buildings that, like the vast stores of wood being shipped, were tinder for the 1871 Fire. An ordinance mandating brick construction was quickly passed and just as quickly ignored. In 1890 Jacob Riis' book *How the Other Half Lives: Studies among the Tenements of New York* caused a sensation, but the 1894 publication in *Scribner's Magazine* of Ernest Flagg's unbuilt tenement house design with a frontage of 100 feet hardly caused a ripple. More effective were revisions to the building codes, in New York in 1901 and other cities later.

In these overcrowded buildings, many residents also did piecework or rented out a room or even only a bed, which was especially common in central Europe's rapidly industrializing centers. In Berlin, the urban plan's large blocks were being filled with *Mietkasernen* (rental barracks), large buildings with small courtyards, and a single entrance locked at night to assure moral behavior. A typical ***Mietkaserne*** from 1875 presented a handsome façade of five stories and a basement to the street with six interior courts connected by a ground-level passage running straight through. It held 257 units, most with a kitchen, a parlor, and a bedroom. Only twelve had toilets; the rest depended on small, ground-level structures in each court; baths and other facilities were in a single structure in a separate wing.

A few industrialists, hoping to increase their workers' efficiency, offered remedies. In 1861 Alfred Krupp began his efforts to make Essen into a company town where employees received generous social and health benefits but with strictly controlled activities including prohibiting participation in politics, a model followed by Bismarck and Hitler. By 1905 the city contained more than 20,000 of his employees, 400 in his dwellings that were rent-free to widows, and 1,000 in boarding houses for single men, all with an expressive character that was hardly different from his factories.

A similar and famous American episode involved **Pullman, Solon Spencer Beman, 1880**, where the Chicago industrialist had the young, well-trained architect collaborate with the landscape specialist Nathan F. Barrett to build a factory and a company town on 4,000 acres south of the city with the town returning a six percent profit on his investment. Five years later it had 1,500 buildings for 8,500 people building railroad cars in his factories. Its 1,717 family residences ranged from seven commodious steam-heated houses nearest the factories to 73 "frame tenements" for single men, all with gas, water, and the still rare amenity of toilets. And the town's amenities included a shopping arcade with an 800-seat theater and public library (but with a $3 per year user's fee), public school (rent paid to Pullman), market hall, technical school, water tower, and sewage works, train depot, landscaped grounds and parks, and a landscaped plaza with a fountain, a hotel, and a church (leased to the Presbyterians for $500 per year), but with no saloons or beer parlors. In 1885, a progressive critic found it "monotonous, and rather wearying to the eye" with a "newness … which suggest the epithet 'machine made'." He continued, "The town-meeting in New England has ever been regarded … as one of the bulwarks of our liberty." In Pullman, the "citizen is surrounded by constant restraint and restriction, and everything is done for him, nothing by him.… It is not the American ideal. It is benevolent, well-wishing feudalism, which desires the happiness of the people, but in such a way as shall please the authorities."[7]

The critic was prescient. The Economic Panic of 1893 reduced Pullman's orders and profits, and he reduced wages but not rents. The workers went out on strike and extended it to Pullman's rail cars to make it the first nationwide strike. In 1904 a previously ignored state statute required that the Pullman Company divest itself of the town; much of it survives as an attractive residential district.

These industrial cities were the opposite of the village-like urbanism of untouched villages beyond industry's reach. **Rothenburg ob der Tauber, Bavaria**, founded in 1170 preserves its old town with defensive walls and wattle and daub dwellings three-stories high with another three attic stories under gable-front pitched tile roofs. Two squares occupy the center, one before the church, the other with its handsome town hall (13th and 16th c.) next to the *Kornhaus*, the storage facility used for assuring the supply of grain and controlling its price. In England **Castle Combe, Wiltshire** presents strings of vernacular stone dwellings along the road running across a watercourse and joining others on a market square with a market cross and church from the 14th and 15th centuries.

Several other industrialists built industrial towns without producing a Manchester neighborhood: **New Lanark, Scotland, 1786** for cotton; **Saltaire, West Yorkshire, 1851** for woolens; **Port Sunlight, Merseyside, 1888** for soap; **Bournville, near Birmingham, 1900**, for chocolate. In the new century, the Garden City Movement allowed prospective residents to build new towns not centered on an industry and not like Manchester. A book launched the movement: **Ebenezer Howard, *Tomorrow: A Peaceful Plan to Real Reform*, revised as *Garden Cities of Tomorrow*, 1902**. The first one, **Letchworth Garden City, Raymond Unwin, and Richard Barry Parker, 1903**, was built through a cooperative venture and connected by rail to London. Another was **Hampstead Garden Suburb, Unwin, London, 1906**, whose central square holds two superb churches, **St. Jude, 1909, and Hampstead Free Church, Edwin Lutyens, 1911**. These garden cities were typically focused on community buildings (public hall, church, school, etc.) with dwellings within a protective "green belt." Their legacy was the ambitious 1946 British government New Town Act that has been extended to the present day with Modernist planning and architecture soon overwhelming village imagery.

Addressing deficiencies

The new industrial cities were producing great wealth and abundance and great deficiencies and miseries, but governments and civil reformers addressed them with ginger steps despite the occasional urban riots of a proletariat seeking reforms. Governments favored the protection of landowners' and corporations' interests and allowed them to do pretty much as they wished except for a few restrictions on building heights and materials in the interest of fire safety and assuring minimal sanitation.

In the United States, land use and building controls were the government's most common interventions. Building height restrictions were imposed in Washington after the **Cairo Apartment Building, T. F. Schneider, Washington, 1894** rose twelve stories and challenged the Capitol dome's prominence. In 1893 Chicagoans protected local developers from outside interference by limiting buildings to 130 feet, "for fire safety," they said. A few years later an ordinance required that a majority of those owning a block's frontage had to consent to allow a new use on their block, which protected them from have a livery stable or brewery as a new neighbor. New York City introduced land use zoning to America in 1916 with the ostensible purpose of preventing very tall buildings from depriving streets of light and air, although actually to assure that the garment industry with its hundreds of immigrant workers did not encroach on posh retail streets. Zoning ordinances quickly proliferated across the country, and in 1926 zoning's control survived a Supreme Court challenge.

Controlling the use of land ran against the American ethos. The cabin in the woods or the little house on the prairie fulfills the manifest destiny of covering the continent with productive individuals and abundant unoccupied land. Of course, well before 1893 when the frontier was declared closed, cities had become urban centers of industry, transportation facilities, victualing, and commerce. As these specialized uses occupied larger portions of urbanism's expansion a common pattern emerged: a specialized commercial district expanded with an industrial area developing around it often within the remnants of deteriorating residential areas falling to Jim Crow restrictions with the newer residential districts with "cabins" and "little houses" being built on the former rural periphery, the farther out the better. The plans of these areas had streets that expanded footpaths that had followed the topography or followed the grids surveyors laid on the land, and they were quickly lined by buildings serving a variety of functions and purposes or those cabins and little houses.

The affluent did better, harnessing steam power to reach idyllic suburbs built in rural districts where they raised their families. Ferry service put **Llewellyn Park, New Jersey**, **Andrew Jackson Davis, 1855**, a gated residential community with wooded, rolling terrain, within commuting range of Manhattan. North of Chicago railroad magnates founded **Lake Forest, Almerin Hotchkiss, 1857** (see MARKET SQUARE, HOWARD CAN DOREN SHAW, LAKE FOREST, 1912), a similar landscape with even larger lots and residences. It was not gated, but two years after Chicago's 1886 Haymarket Riot the protection of Fort Sheridan was added on its southern border.

After 1889 when an electric trolley car system proved commercially successful in Richmond, Virginia, affluent residents did not need to go so far to escape crowded neighborhoods. Two decades later the trollies began to be made obsolescent when automobiles and cheap gasoline allowed even greater outward expansion. Typical of many exclusive, large-lot developments is **Windsor Farms, Richmond, Virginia, Charles Gillette, 1926** that was soon enveloped by later development.

"Make no little plans"

From the 18th c. onward, manufacturing centers and national capitals were altered by a full menu of increases: population, density of land occupancy, number of buildings, diversity of activities, quantity of goods made, sold, and moved, means of transportation, and portage, and all the other things that thrive through proximity. These increases outran the ability of those in charge of maintaining the order, health, and safety of rapidly growing urban areas. National governments seldom involve themselves in urban affairs unless they find it in their interest to do so or in response to the pressure and agitation of the urban masses. When they do, they tend to favor big plans.

In the decades around 1800 and then sporadically through the 19th c., power in the various new civil orders was increasingly in the hands of bankers, industrialists, and others who could find advantage in the changes to be made.

Meanwhile, mobility using more powerful motive forces than shanks mare and animals was making ever-larger urban areas with an increasingly segregated urban pattern of isolated industrial and commercial areas and residential districts. This made urban areas more productive but not necessarily more pleasurable for everyone. Interventions that were beyond the power of individuals or the authority of units of government below the national level often concentrated on changes on public land, that is, roads and streets, with minimal interference with privately held land.

An early instance occurred after Rome had recovered as a major world center and it was improved with **Streets, Pope Sixtus V, 1585–90** with obelisks used as markers assisted pilgrims in reaching holy sites scattered about in still largely uninhabited areas. Napoleon, always anxious to leave his mark, followed the model but without obelisks when he addressed Paris' clogged transportation with the Rue de Rivoli named to commemorate a 1797 victory. It supplied the missing east-west link, arcaded on one side and the Louvre and the Tuileries and Gardens on the other. Napoleon III, President of France in 1848 but emperor after 1852, focused on the city's image and infrastructure with the massive project of **Boulevards, Georges-Eugène Haussmann, 1854–70**, which made Paris the esteemed center for bourgeois middle-class culture. That able administrator, elevated to Baron Hussmann for his success, drove broad routes lined by trees and ground floor shops through insalubrious districts and added and connected new, major urban elements: rail stations; former royal domains made into public parks; a new wholesale market (now wantonly gone) called **Les Halles, Victor Baltard, Paris, 1853–70**; the OPÉRA, CHARLES GARNIER, 1861–75; a hospital; etc. Their cross section included utilities buried beneath paved streets. Above them and behind similar but varied facades of uniform height on new or remodeled buildings were apartments decreasing in size and opulence on each new floor upward. Largely left alone were the old streets and fabric that had absorbed the expanding population in the *maison mixtes*, relatively small, usually owner-occupied multistory buildings with small, rundown apartments and a concierge serving as gatekeeper.

In England George, the Prince Regent used his royal patronage to build **Regent Street, John Nash and James Burton, London, 1811–25**, that threaded through London from St. James Park to Regent Park with the street providing only facades (only a few survive) and some new buildings. A later and more comprehensive improvement transformed the Thames River docks and other riverside maritime facilities into embankments. The most famous, the **Victoria Embankment, Francis W. Shields, architect and Joseph Bazalgette, engineer, London, 1865–70**, remains a pleasant, landscaped walkway with traffic lanes atop a cross section holding a portion of the new underground public transit system as well as utility lines including trunk sewers connected to the system under central London, all directed by the engineer, Bazalgette.

The Hapsburgs responded to urban unrest of 1848 with two actions that produced the **Vienna Ringstrasse**. One was a political adjustment that expanded the municipality's jurisdiction beyond the impressive fortifications and deep glacis that hemmed in the central city; let loose private investments that produced new, multistory dwellings. The other was physical, running from 1857 to 1913, that replaced the outdated fortifications with the ring of broad boulevards flanked by formal parks with imposing, usually free-standing buildings for the institutions of state, Church, and culture.

Italy celebrated its 1870 unification with work in Rome that completed the invaluable transit route of the via Nazionale begun earlier by Pope Pius IX (1846–78) connecting the railroad station to the Vatican via the pedestrian **Ponte Sant'Angelo, Hadrian, 135**. Other projects included a few other streets, embankments for the Tiber, and sadly the disinterment of ancient monuments. Mussolini got into the act with his unfortunate **via della Conciliazione, Marcello Piacentini, 1936** between the Ponte Sant'Angelo and the Vatican.

Earlier than any of these was the grand vision embodied in the design of **Washington, D.C., Pierre Charles L'Enfant et al, 1791** on largely otherwise uninhabited land. Over the course of the next century, romantic imagery overwhelmed its classicism that was restored, modernized, and enlarged after 1902. The impetus for the restoration project goes back to the CRYSTAL PALACE EXPOSITION, JOSEPH PAXTON, LONDON, 1851 that led to more world fairs such as in Paris in 1889 that left the **Tower, Gustav Eiffel, 1889** as a relic. Not to be outdone, opening a year late was the **World's Columbian Exposition, Daniel H. Burnham, et al, Chicago, 1893** that offered a display of organized urbanism and classical architecture to the quarter of the American population that visited. They saw a dazzling contrast to the cities of commerce and industry they traveled from and was in full scale in the host city, famed for its wealth, blackened by soot, and famous for corruption and uncaring about misery.[8] The Fair inspired the City Beautiful Movement that took root in numerous American cities and produced innumerable classical public buildings serving all levels of government, often in settings that integrated them within the city's plan and fabric. Two of them, both directed by Burnham, were the most prominent. The U.S. Senate sponsored the **McMillan Commission Plan of Washington, D.C., 1902**, which gave us that city's present form. The other, the ***Plan of Chicago,*** **Burnham and Edward H. Bennett, 1909**, was financed by local commercial interests, and across a generation was implemented with municipal bonds authorized by citizens' votes. Illustrated with alluring graphics by Jules Guérin, the book showed comprehensive changes in the big picture and extensive details about infrastructure; it paid little attention to the residential neighborhoods, and its civic buildings remained concentrated in one single area, but its future prosperity was guaranteed.

The urbanism surrounding these projects benefited from the role they gave traditional architecture for institutional structures, but they did little to ameliorate the plight of the poor. Depression era projects by national governmental and philanthropic organizations had little effect on existing conditions as the Depression deepened. When economic revival came after the end of World War II the urbanism that emerged had a different texture. In the massive building in the post-war era, zoning put commercial activity along arterial roadways and residences in large tracts with single-family residences carefully separated from apartment buildings. Subdivisions wasted no land on alleys and used street plans resembling dead worms or loops and cul-de-sac lollypops built up with houses with a public front yard and private back yard. Their expressive character usually associated them with the region's earlier houses or with distant regions where the new residents would rather be living. The most impressive example was **Levittown, New York, 1947** built to cater to veterans enjoying government subsidies. The single-family residences were alike, and so were the family incomes with racial minorities excluded and anything other than another house more than an easy walk away. Their profligate consumption of land required automobile mobility and got the larger roads they needed.

As the nation went into the 21st c. the deficiencies and injustices of this urbanism became increasingly clear: it reinforced racial segregation, now by income rather than law: the required automobile was the price of admission, people encountered only others like themselves in the shops and on neighborhood streets where the only walkers were accompanying dogs; the general homogeneity of the urbanism precluded forming connections with distinct neighborhoods, etc. These areas offered nothing interesting, so nonresidents never went there. Providing municipal services was unnecessarily expensive, grocery shopping required an automobile, and low density made well-served public transit impossible. The arterial roadways giving access to these enclaves were increasingly clogged and expensive to build and maintain, and relieving traffic congestion with highway projects provided excuses for razing deteriorated residential areas but without providing new places for displaced residents to move to. In many states, the law left older municipalities landlocked by newer, wealthier towns, cities, and counties eager to protect their prerogatives from incursions by the people in the older districts, and these became fiefdoms with little incentive to cooperate in regional intergovernmental programs or to cede authority over urbanism to the state or the nation.

Alternatives

The alternatives that the 20th century offered were hatched in Europe. They developed while political instability reigned in the immediate post-World War I era, which delayed their testing in practice, and when they were tried, architects and others took notice.

In Vienna when new tax revenues became available the municipality built subsidized dwellings for 220,000 people in stripped-down versions of the prewar four, five, and six-story blocks above shops. The most famous is the **Karl Marx Hof, Karl Ehn, 1927–28** with an expressive character that contrasted as sharply with Vienna's predominant classicism as the new government did from its Hapsburg predecessors. Stretching a kilometer along the Danube were two long parallel strands lacking ornament with a connecting link holding four great arches below tiers of red balconies and towers and flag poles extending above terracotta-colored walls. Its 5,000 residents had units with toilets and cold-water taps, and many also had balconies formerly not thought worthy of workers' dwellings. Residents had access to extensive communal facilities from kindergartens and baths to doctors' offices and gardens in the long interior courts and around the building's exteriors. Damaged during the siege when the residents resisted Hitler's Anschluss, it was subsequently repaired.

In Berlin, in the 1920s Martin Wagner, the powerful city planner who would follow Walter Gropius to Harvard, produced thousands of government-sponsored dwellings. They used prefabricated assemblies that were devoid of ornament or decoration, fulfilled the *Existenzminimum* or the minimum requirements for a living unit by having a kitchen, bath, heat, and openable windows, and lacked connections to traditional design. Others in the "Ring" around Walter Gropius made a demonstration project at **Onkle Toms Hütte, Berlin, 1926**, named for the 1880s huts a beer hall proprietor had built in the forest in suburban Zehlendorf. Built as a classless utopian nonprofit community under the supervision of Bruno Taut, its avant-garde buildings by him, Hugo Häring, and Otto Rudolf Salvisberg placed on its 12 acres had 1,100 multifamily three-story terraced houses and eventually 800 single-family residences, all with gardens, colorful facades, and flat roofs.

Not everyone was thrilled. To manifest a protest, a conservative, nonprofit cooperative built houses **Am Fischtal, Heinrich Tessenow, Berlin, 1928** across the road with spare, flat facades but pitched roofs. The newspapers used catchphrases functionalist and regionalist in playing up the juxtaposition heralded as the Zehlendorf Roof War (*Zehlendorf Dächerkrieg*).

Undeterred, soon thereafter came the well-known project of a private workers cooperative near the Siemens factory that employed 60,000 people. **Siemensstadt, Berlin, 1929**, with Hans Scharoun as master planner and director used several architects including Gropius to design the various rows of units, all with balconies that tout their individuality. The 1,370 units are distributed among 23 rows of (mostly) four-story walk-up buildings spread in a greensward in north-south alignments to catch the light with white stucco over the brick (except for Häring's brick), with a school, 14 shops, and a central heating plant within the complex. A variation was the proposed **Wannsee project, Gropius, 1931** with 660 families in four 11-story buildings set in parallel slanted rows in a green passage along a Berlin lake.

The master of broadcasting radical ideas was the Swiss architect Le Corbusier. In his **grand plans, 1919ff** for urbanism and in architecture he disregarded urbanism as a means a civil order can use to serve the human spirit's aspiration for the good, the just, and the beautiful and instead argued that it was the means of liberating the spirit of man from the constraints of society. His well-known maxim, "A house is a machine for living in," identifies him as a technicist totalitarian. In 1929, he and others of like mind formed the CIAM (Congrès Internationaux d'Architecture Moderne). With Sigfried Giedion as its first secretary-general, it hashed out the **CIAM, Athens Charter, 1933** that offered insightful diagnoses of urban ills and offered technical and formal solutions with dwellings in rows or in towers dispersed in a landscape in an image that was christened "towers in a park."

During the Depression, CIAM members or their kin began to gain command of the culture of architecture, and after the war, the "towers in a park" took their place beside the cabin in the woods as the iconic image of the happy house. In government's hands, there was also the added hope of reforming the character of the residents that had put them in need of subsidy, a position supported by Modernism's belief that human nature was changeable and would flourish in new ways in the modern era with architecture as an instrument of reform.

In the U.S. federal housing projects were built on land cleared of decaying Jim Crow and other neighborhoods and obsolete industrial districts as parts of highways constructed to expedite load-bearing freight transportation and to carry commuters into ever-expanding monoculture sprawl. The towers and strips of construction found a place in the urban planner's toolbox along with other disconnected components whose expressive character came from the technical efficiency and strict economy demanded of them. Absent was consideration of the civil purposes for buildings and urbanism.

Our recent experience makes it clear that if we wish to build the good polis or city, the *città felice*, the *ev topos* (εὖτόπος), the well-place, the good-place, we must be ready with a better understanding of how to build an urbanism that serves and expresses that aspiration.

Notes

1 Charles Trinkaus, *In Our Image and Likeness: Humanity and Divinity in Italian Humanist Thought*, 2 vols. (Chicago, IL: University of Chicago Press, 1970).
2 See Norris Kelly Smith, *Here I Stand: Perspective from another Point of View* (New York: Columbia University Press, 1994).
3 C. W. Westfall, "Urban Planning, Roads, Streets and Neighborhoods," in *The World of Pompeii*, eds. John J. Dobbins and Pedar W. Foss (London and New York: Routledge, 2007), 129–39.
4 *Design of Cities*, revised edition (New York: Viking, 1974).
5 *De re aedificatoria*, ed. and Italian trans., Giovanni Orlandi, 2 vols. (Milan, Polifilo: 1966) at I, ii, 21 using the word *perscriptio* that is translated as *disegno*. In *On the Art*

of Building in Ten Books, trans. J. Rykwert et al. (Cambridge, MA: MIT Press, 1989), the glossary presents *linementa* as design, a noun and not a verb that refers to rational deliberation that was surely Vitruvius' meaning for *ratiocinatio*. Rykwert's translation sets *lineamenta* against *materia* with the implicit suggestion that Vitruvius' *ratiocinatio et fabrica* has become *lineamenta et materia*. In present-day English Vitruvius' *ratiocinatio* would be design, which Alberti sets against *structura*, or Vitruvius' *fabrica*, hence Alberti's modernization of Vitruvius inserts perspective into the architect's design process. See also Westfall, *Architecture, Liberty, op. cit.*, 79–80.

6 Alberti, J. Rykwert et al. trans., *op cit.*, pp. 191, 194.

7 Richard Ely, "Pullman: A Social Study," *Harpers New Monthly Magazine*, 70 (1885): 452–66; 457–8, 464.

8 See for example William Stead, *If Christ Came to Chicago: A Plea for the Union of All Who Love in the Service of All Who Suffer* (London: Review of Reviews, 1894) and often reprinted.

4

THE COMPONENTS AND TYPES OF GOOD URBAN FORM

In Chapter 1, we sketched out the history of architecture and commented on its disinterest in affecting the building of architecture and urbanism, and we introduced the tectonic leg in architecture's tripod. In Chapter 2, we moved to the second leg, the architecture leg, and offered a reformulation for both the study of the past of architecture and its potential role in the present practice of architecture. In Chapter 3, we moved to the third leg, urbanism, and gave a quick review of the history of urbanism. Our conclusion was the dispiriting observation that present knowledge and practices offer little to building the good city.

In our study, we have made it clear that the buildings, the architecture, and the urbanism that is built and remains for the future to use, amend, and extend is the product of a succession of civil orders and that as these change, so have the practices in the arts that built the urbanism. The least successful changes have been the most recent ones, which leads to the inevitable conclusion that present practices must be reformulated if we are to serve humankind's enduring aspirations to build the good city, the *città felice*, the *ev topos* (εὖτόπος), the well-place, the good-place committed to the common good, the good that guarantees security, sustenance, and the right to live honorably, justly, and well for both individuals and groups.

The tools for good urbanism include components that are optional, and generative types that are necessary and will be discussed in this order: (1) dimensions and edges; (2) quarters; (3) the generative urban types of streets, squares, and blocks, and (4) urban sequences. These will be qualified and particularized by (5) regional urban characters. There are also optional ancillary components, a few of which will also be presented. This chapter begins with a few instructive examples of their deployment in earlier, quite different circumstances.

DOI: 10.4324/9780429506260-6

Valuable instruction from the past about continuity

The urbanism that we admire in the past presents numerous examples of these tools at work. They come from the recognition that urbanism is always an alteration of an existing condition, even when something is adding to formerly unoccupied land. When making alterations three qualities must be honored: respect for the traditional character of the place, the proper use of the tool, and attention to improving the whole it will join.

In learning from the past about how to use the tools it is important to remember that our conceptual understanding of space is different from the one that prevailed before the 15th c. Valuable as the architecture of those premodern eras is as instruction for the present, when studying the urbanism this difference must be kept in mind.

Recall from our presentation of Pompeii that the precincts holding its buildings were connected by point-to-point navigation. Romans later used what William L. MacDonald identified as an armature in the empire's outposts. He described how the major, central street, the cardo, was lined by the voids between the solids of public buildings and precincts that made a spine that was "formed gradually, in part by somewhat haphazard accumulation" of a variety of buildings vying for passerby's attention.[1] The same comment pertains to the colonnades surrounding Pompeii's Forum. Temple precincts dominated ancient urbanism, which allowed Roman cities to address their supplications to the gods as they bestowed on them their civil orders' highest honors. Christians did the same when they had churches dominate their urbanism with the bishop's church and palace the most prominent.

When we encountered perspectival urbanism in the early modern period, we saw the retention of the expression, and now with even greater clarity, of the relative ranks of buildings situated within the coherent perspectival spatial matrix that now includes carefully configured and designed open areas. In democratic cities and in the autocratic countryside and cities, lessers flattered superiors by modeling the expressive character of their regias with modifications or dilutions required by decorum to give them their proper lesser place in the urbanism. The ancient Romans had done the same, and in the revitalized Renaissance cities, the hierarchic order was exhibited by inventions based on Roman models. In both cities and countryside, this practice yielded a unity across a civil order and an exhibition of the distinctive expressive characters of the buildings' roles in the urbanism with their styles portraying the differences in times, architects, fashions, and means.

In Chapter 2, we saw that the 19th c. builders in different nations used the associative content of expressive characters to reaffirm the continuity of the state's present with its past while also expressing the building's purpose in the civil order. Across the globe, broader regional differences, say, between

Europe, India, and China, were made clear as buildings honored and drew from traditions that guided their tectonic, architectural forms, and urbanism while also displaying differences between their regions and stylistic preferences.

We can summarize by noting that modern perspectival urbanism made possible the construction of urbanism with buildings isomorphic with perspectival space that coordinates the display of the relative importance and distinctive purpose of the various buildings and components serving the common good. Treasured and well-curated survivors from the early modern period in Venice, Florence, and Charlottesville, Virginia, will provide examples.

Founded in the 5th c. as a refuge during the barbarian invasions, Venice provides a textbook example that was produced through the work of centuries. Here we see the role of Bacon's many second architects who maintained decorum in individualized buildings that absorbed contributions from the eastern Mediterranean and then from Rome to make a place that is unmistakably, inimitably, and indubitably Venice (Figure 4.1).

The oldest prominent building is the **Basilica di San Marco** (1; architectural type: tholos/temple) erected in the 11th and early 13th c. in the midst of vernacular buildings. It faces the **Piazza San Marco** that in the 12th c. was given a two-story arcaded loggia with mercantile shops below public offices (shops). The lagoon entrance was also embellished with two granite **Columns** (2; the present statues replaced earlier ones). In the 14th c., the **Doge's Palace** (3, public regia) began its growth with an expressive character that, like the Basilica, used tectonic means that connected it to its eastern Mediterranean trading partners and colonies but acknowledging Verona, its inland neighbor, with some of its materials. The Turks' capture of Constantinople in 1453 cut the Serenissima off from its former trading partners, but it quickly turned inland, expressing this reorientation with the robust classicism of the triumphal **Arch of the Porta Maggiore, Arsenale, Antonio Gambello?, 1460**.

Modern perspectival urbanism began its work with an axial alignment across the Piazza San Marco between the lagoon's columns and a tall, classicizing **Astronomical Clock Tower, Mauro Cadussi?, 1496** (4; hypostyle; arch) signaling access to the route across the city to reach the commercial district where the surviving crossing of several collapsed predecessors, the **Rialto Bridge, Antonio da Ponte, 1588** (5), remains in service. That axis soon gained a cross axis when construction was begun to replace a dilapidated church, **San Geminiano, façade by Jacopo Sansovino, 1505** (temple). Another primarily political axis was solidified with the **loggia, Sansovino, 1537** (6; hypostyle) beneath the Campanile, the work of five centuries, for nobles to assemble before their ritual procession into the Doge's Palace. Richly ornamented, its 1 × 3 framework with a high attic recalled both triumphal arches and the combination of a wide arch with flanking narrow trabeation that Bramante had introduced in the **Vatican's Cortile del Belvedere, 1505,** (regia)

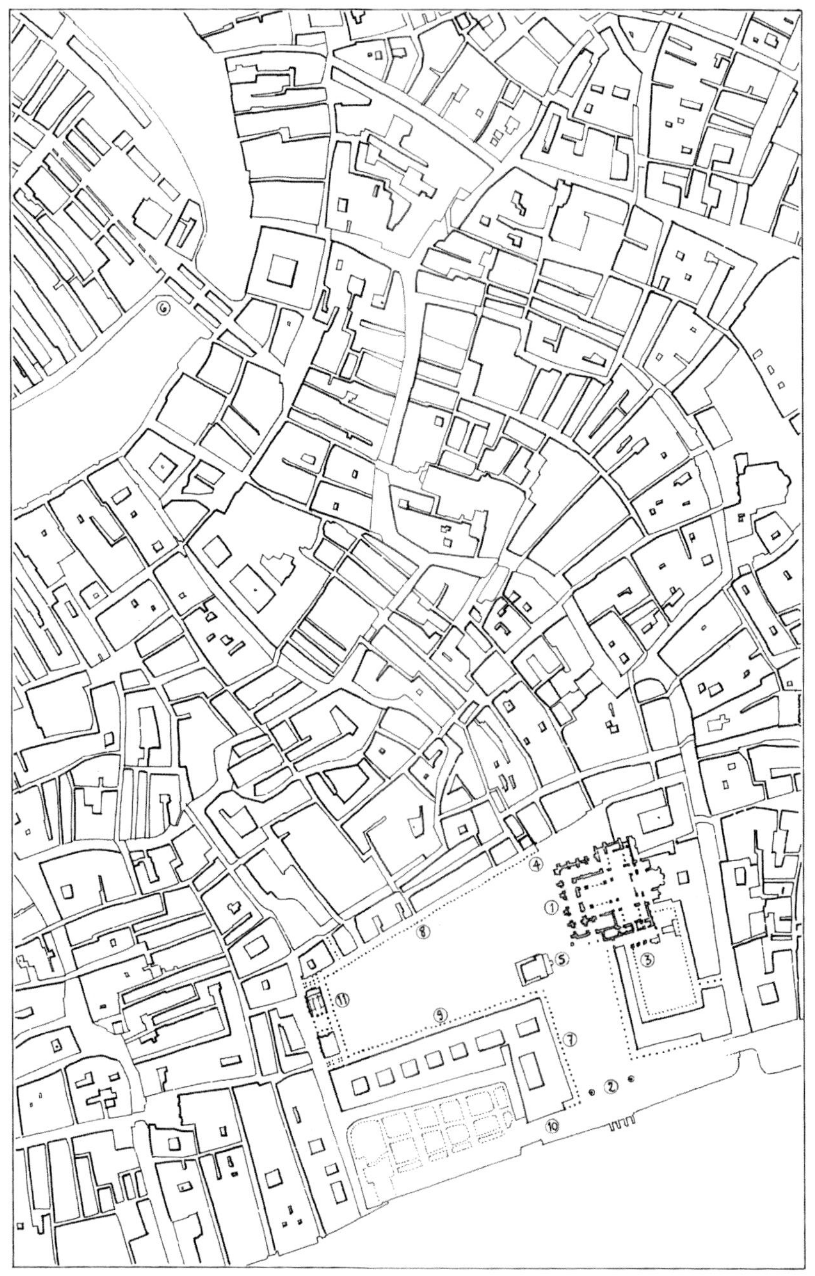

FIGURE 4.1 Venice, between Ponte Rialto and Piazza San Marco.

and would later be called the Veneziana, the Palladiana, or the Serliana. Work had also begun on the two-story **Libreria di San Marco, Sansovino, 1536** (7; regia) facing the Doge's Palace with three end bays enriching the piazza's venerable arcade expressing the higher status of its purpose. Meanwhile, a fire provoked the replacement of the 13th c. **North wing of the piazza, architect unknown, 1512** (8; shop) holding the Astronomical Clock Tower with a pier arcade below two stories of arched windows, two for each lower bay and all quite plane. Across the way, the Library had been set behind the original arcade and now the piazza as enlarged and given a diluted version of the Library facade but elevated to three stories for the new **South wing of the piazza, Vincenzo Scamozzi, 1588** (9; shop), with a century passing before being completed. Behind it had long been granaries except behind the Library and facing the lagoon was the **Zecca, Sansovino, 1536** (10; regia; shop) that we discussed in Chapter 2. The piazza's unifying pavement pattern and grand flagpoles date to 1723.

The Venetian Republic's much-valued independence ended in 1797 when Napoleon incorporated it into Austria, the first of its various subsequent homes. At the narrow end of the piazza, San Geminano and several bays of the flanking loggias were replaced by a ballroom wing, the **Ala Napoleonica, Giovanni Antolini and successor, Giuseppe Soli, 1810** (11; pubic regia) above an arcaded passage giving access to the streets, blocks, and urban sequences within the city's fabric, which completes the ensemble we see today.

Venice flourished as a republic for 1300 years, Florence for a much shorter period (Figure 4.2). As a republic, it benefited from the public mingling of families that were also intense rivals. Five years after becoming a duchy in 1532 the first duke, the young Alessandro de' Medici, resided in the PALAZZO MEDICI, MICHELOZZO, 1444 (1) where a perspective link runs to the cathedral's piazza. (2) Alessandro was assassinated in 1537, and his successor, the more famous Duke Cosimo I, lived there until 1540 when he moved into the **Palazzo Vecchio, Arnolfo di Cambio, 1299**. (3 ; public regia) He governed from there until his death in 1569, but in 1549 he had moved his residence to the more imposing **Palazzo Pitti, Luca Fancelli?, 1458** (domestic regia), across the Arno River. (4) He had the **Uffizi, Giorgio Vasari, completed by Bernardo Buontalenti, 1560** (shop) built to hold government offices with an internal *corridoio* to provide secure passage between the residence and his governing site. (5) The Uffizi presents itself as a civil ornament with two wings with vaulted, colonnaded ground floors followed by two stories of offices, one tall and the other less so. One wing abuts the city's venerable, ceremonial 1 × 3 **Loggia dei Lanzi, 1376–82** (6; hypostyle) facing the **Piazza della Signoria**. The other has a bridge connecting the Palazzo Vecchio to the *corridoio*. (7) It runs through the wings' connection at the Arno River that is formed as a Palladiana and triumphal arch and continues to the **Ponte Vecchio, rebuilt 1345**, with the *corridoio* above the shops. (8) As a duchy Florence gradually declined as a cultural and architectural model.

FIGURE 4.2 Florence, between the Duomo and the Ponte Vecchio.

These two old Italian cities illustrate the expressive character of urbanism achieved over time by a number of actors in the third leg, the leg of urbanism, while drawing on the expressive character of the leg of architecture to engage with what is happening both locally and nationally. A similar achievement is visible at the **University of Virginia, Thomas Jefferson, Charlottesville, 1816–26**, achieved under the supervision of a single designer. His preoccupation and hobby after he had left the presidency and the university's founder through state legislation, he incorporated suggestions from Benjamin Henry Latrobe and William Thornton and included enslaved workers in its construction. The plan planted in the landscape draws on many models from ancient Rome and modern France and England with the role for its greensward from Virginia plantations and the plans for **Williamsburg, Francis Nicholson, 1699** and **Washington, P. C. L'Enfant et al, 1792**. It honors the American tendency to plant buildings in a landscape and to separate private places from public ones. The architecture's expressive character combines the local traditions of tectonics using brick, stucco, and wood for membratures and configurations that evoke classical antiquity. The long, open, public common known as the Lawn is the metaphoric heart on a flattened ridge lined by rows of trees and a colonnaded walkway. At its head stands the Rotunda (tholos), the library modeled on the PANTHEON, HADRIAN WITH APOLLODORUS OF DAMASCUS?, ROME, 117, beneath the dome and classrooms and laboratories (public regias) below the floor. Students live in private, party-wall rooms (dwellings) within the colonnade interrupted by the professors' pavilions that combine residence and classroom (private and public regias) connected by a walkway atop the colonnade. Jefferson intended these variations on temples to provide models of the ancient and modern orders. Gaps between the student rooms lead out to service yards and the wiggly-walled gardens along alleys stretching down the slopes to the threshold at the rural realm. Here, another series of rows of student rooms open to the walkway behind an arcade and punctuated by service buildings (shops). No visible traces remain of the slaves' accommodations in the gardens and elsewhere.

Additions over time left this nucleus untouched except for a theater and classrooms in a large box attached to the Rotunda. Its loss by fire in 1895 provided a vivid illustration of the role a second architect can play in modernizing and expanding an existing architecture and urbanism. The lower, short end of the Lawn was left as a much-valued open vista to the rural countryside, but a faculty vote dictated that it be the site for CABELL, ROUSS, AND McINTIRE HALLS, STANFORD WHITE, 1895. By then Jefferson's complex had already become a model for many other university campuses. An excellent urban version is **Columbia University, New York, McKim, Mead, and White, 1893**, that compressed Jefferson's expansive, open rural scheme to six Manhattan blocks and remains largely intact but damaged by Modernist intrusions.

Having seen the generative urban types (dimensions and edges; quarters; etc.) at work we can now turn to their examination.

1 The city's dimensions and edges

Like any organism, a city's inner workings are surrounded by an outer enclosure. Because urbanism is a creature of a civil order, we would expect that the boundary of its authority would correspond to the urbanism's enclosure, except that along with any one civil authority there are others that are themselves bounded, as for example families at the nuclear scale and the nation at the other extreme. We believe that for urbanism as for governing, the best authority is one composed of people of goodwill engaged in self-governing to achieve a common good. In matters concerning urbanism, that role is generally found at the scale of the municipality or rural county.

The best enclosure is an urban edge that is clearly distinct from the rural countryside and can be experienced from two directions, from within and without the city. Ideally, the enclosure would be a clear morphological meeting between inside and outside like that of the human body's skin. The edge can include a natural feature such as a river (Saint Louis), a lake or other body of water (Chicago; Venice; Hong Kong; Nice), a cliff (in Spain, Arcos de la Frontera, Cuenca, Ronda, Albarracin, and Teruel, or Bozouls in France), or a forest (Saint Cirq Lapopie, France). It can also be an architectural feature such as the threshold arcade at the UNIVERSITY OF VIRGINIA or a visible separation between a built-up area and a restricted green zone as in **Letchworth Garden City** and **Poundbury, Dorchester,** in England. Well into the modern era it was often a defensive wall, but now a civil order's various jurisdictions, especially within built-up areas, overlap, and edges are often marked with a mere roadside sign.

In preindustrial eras, the urban areas and activities easily retained ecological balance with nature, but now they are increasingly invading rural and agricultural zones with inhospitable uses. In Chapter 3 we encountered the ravages that monoculture zoning is spreading on rural lands. To this, we can add the elephantiasis of prosperity's unbounded urbanism spreading across parts of the globe, for example from along the Atlantic Ocean from **Washington to Boston**, across the **Po Valley from Venice to Milan**, along the **Rhine River**, and up the **Yangtze River** from Shanghai to beyond Nanjing. This sprawl normally leaves political boundaries indistinguishable, disrespects the dimensions and edges of cities, and leads to the erosion and often the disappearance of the clear distinction that once existed between the natural and the human-made world to the detriment of the natural world that supports human life.

2 The city's quarters

Within the urban enclosure reside the city's quarters, a name derived from Roman urbanism's sidereal division into four equal parts bisected by the north-south cardo or hinge. Now the quarters are wards, parishes, neighborhoods that

FIGURE 4.3 Street and block in Georgetown, Washington, D.C., U.S.A.

easily acquire names, taken perhaps from early subdivisions or distinctive physical identities, etc. Ideally, it is a political entity holding a community of diverse people animated by a common ideal with nuclear families living along streets in neighborhoods nested within the larger orders of city, state, and nation. A person ought to be able to cross it within a 10-minute walk and find most aspects of urban life—residential, commercial, educational, administrative, religious, recreational, etc.—each accessible by foot or not much more distant. Understanding scale relative to size is important. Note that all of Venice can fit between the Capitol and the Lincoln Memorial in Washington D.C., but within Washington, there are compact neighborhoods of the size discussed here; we provide an example from Georgetown (Figure 4.3). Community cohesiveness, the kind that makes effective neighborhood associations, is encouraged when a quarter has distinct edges or topographic or urban features, or both which might be major streets or avenues that are intersected by a number of smaller streets. And it ought to have at least one main square (center) and other smaller squares offering a hierarchy of urban spaces for gathering, sitting, or strolling, and supplying the vital provision of light and aeration. Pistoia provides a good example of a commanding central square (Figure 4.4).

A small city such as **Pienza** might be a neighborhood or quarter in itself. Large towns have several: **Cefalù; Siena; Dubrovnik**, as do large cities: **Quartier St. Germain, Paris**; **Quartiere degli Spagnoli, Naples**; **The Village, New York**; and **Covent Garden, London**.

Good examples are rarely produced quickly, although suggestions have been offered for making predesigned neighborhoods. The **urban transect theory**

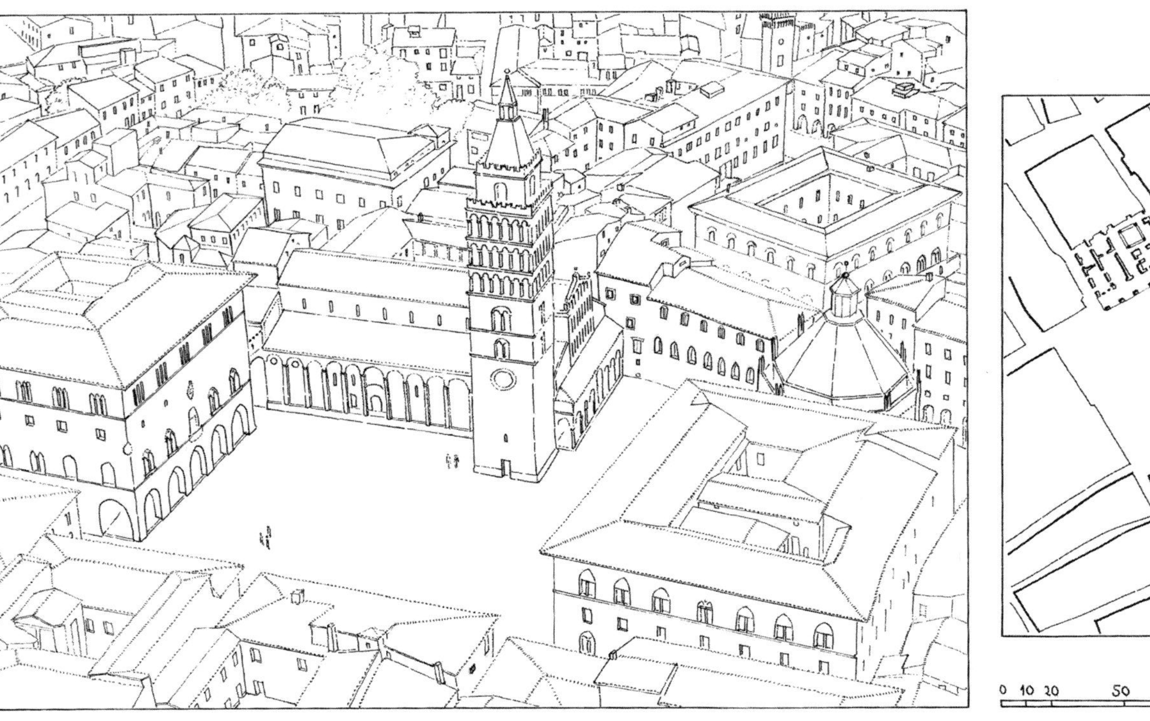

FIGURE 4.4 Square, Piazza del Duomo, Pistoia, Italy.

offers guidance for expanding urbanism with identifiable additions having a gradation from rural to civic or neighborhood center. Two recent built and inhabited examples also offer important suggestions: **Poundbury, Dorchester,** in England, and **Paseo Cayalá, Guatemala City**.

3 The urban types: street, square, and block

The generative urban types of street, square, and block provide the voids and solids in the urban configuration. They compose urbanism's integrated network of routes, open areas, and buildings serving the civil order's various purposes. In Chapter 3, we saw that the network of routes can take both, or either, a regular and irregular urban pattern, and gathering in squares they can provide linear and nodal arrangements for traversing a quarter. They can also produce urban sequences, which are another generative type to be discussed shortly.

Streets and squares (voids) interact with blocks (solids), and blocks with streets and squares, to produce legible urbanism. The buildings dominate, and the streets and squares separate and connect. A hierarchy of streets that assures a gradated connectivity that is integrated with a hierarchy of squares assures the central importance of communal space for the interactions of individuals.

Required for achieving coherence within the streets, squares, and blocks is the proportionate relationship between the width of the space and the height of delimiting and containing buildings; delimiting and containing are two necessary components for defining urban space. Low buildings have difficulty defining wide open spaces even when including sidewalks or other open edges, although containment can be attained with very tall buildings, but this results in dwarfing human scale and makes the alienating environment of an urban canyon. Also problematic is the sparse and distant arrangement of object buildings with considerable setbacks, for this harms both delimiting and containing. Narrow streets or squares delimited and contained by buildings of human-scaled height can also produce an acceptable relationship, but if the voids are too slight and the buildings too high, the result can be excessively restricted and light, aeration, and circulation be too constricted.

Streets have distinctive names that carry with them specific visual and urban qualities. Alleys, mews, lanes, and streets are connectors, and so are boulevards that define a quarter's edge or run through it as a major avenue. Similarly, celebratory avenues and sacred ways approaching sacred precincts, perhaps punctuated by triumphal arches or approached through a propylaeon can, as in a Greek precinct, offer a telling, oblique view of the temple. The many kinds of squares also serve to connect and can also provide important services such as holding markets, cafés, and play areas. Each language has names for them: Arabic, *sahat, maidan*; Chinese, *guangchan*; English, *square, town green, common, park*; Farsi, *maidan*; French, *place*; German, *platz*; Hindi, *Chaupar*; Italian, *piazza, piazzetta, piazzale, largo*; Portuguese, *praça*; Spanish, *plaza, plazuela*; etc.

Premodern city building had little trouble in finding a proper approach for an enclosure or square or finding a pleasing proportion between the size of a void and the height for its enclosure. They are well worth studied attention. Perspective design also offers instructive examples for modern practice with their closer and more disciplined calibration of proportionate control in the relationship between solids and voids expressing the relative status of the several buildings that serve and express their particular roles in the civil order, but that potential is too often ignored or misused.

Blocks: like streets and squares, they also require clear definition, subdivision, and dimensions. Good blocks have buildings with well-defined corners and frontages designed to present a good face to the city's public realm of streets and squares. The contribution to good urban form of a block as an urban type is greatly eroded when building corners are omitted or mistreated and street frontages are ignored.

Inner-block characteristics and *inter*-block connectivity are also important concerns in urban planning and are well served by a variety of interstitial components. These can include a small square, small streets, courts, patios, and light-wells that offer connectivity through the block and provide buildings with secondary entrances, light, and aeration.

Good blocks are rarely superblocks with a single building; instead, they contain several ownership parcels of various sizes that accommodate a variety of requirements. Again here, the location of the building on the property is of critical importance, because buildings relate to each other as edges of blocks and across streets or squares. If all buildings, or even some buildings, occupy the centers of their lot they will be considered isolated objects fulfilling their own exclusive purpose and making it impossible to have a well-defined street. Low buildings fronting open areas such as squares often lack a welcoming sense of enclosure, and even medium height buildings centered in their sites and without connections to the site's edges appear as isolated, even alien, objects, even when surrounded by extensive landscaping. The urbanism in central commercial areas is often rigid `and lifeless and could benefit from having something special such as the skating rink at ROCKEFELLER CENTER, RAYMOND HOOD ET AL, NEW YORK, 1931 (Figure 4.7).

The size of buildings within blocks is also of vital importance. In the 19th c., before artificial illumination and ventilation became available, very large buildings constructed on very large parcels often included very long interior skylit corridors that competed with the streets, depriving them of enlivening pedestrian activity. Now large buildings without connecting corridors are being built with greater heights, dwarfing street life in alienating urban canyons with street fronts seldom softened by enticing design, shop windows, or landscaping. And clearly, the planning of streets, squares, and blocks must seek coherence without banal repetition among their parts.

With their populations exploding, cities sent their urbanism outward into rural surroundings where the land was parceled out into transportation routes and ownership parcels. Little attention was paid to urbanism with a gradation of transitways exhibiting different breadths and cross sections connecting a related gradation of squares and buildings held in a variety of well-coordinated quarters with typological variety among the buildings serving various individual and communal activities. In any urbanism, balance is essential: too few streets make too large blocks and reduce circulatory permeability, and too many streets reduce block sizes and interrupt circulation. Within the quarters of the urban enclosure, having smaller blocks and a greater building density toward the center promotes urban cohesion and retains human scale, while larger blocks and lower density moving toward the periphery eases access to the boundary with the countryside. Within a quarter an important avenue might intersect with a network of smaller streets connecting with smaller squares that, when working together, provide a variety of places for gathering, sitting, and strolling while furnishing natural light and air to buildings' interiors and providing secondary building entrances.

Finally, it is essential that buildings be assembled and crafted with an eye to establishing relationships with one another with streets, squares, and blocks designed from the outside in and not merely with a functionally efficient interior enclosed within a merely adequate face.

4 Urban sequences and secluded sites

In premodern urbanism, point-to-point navigation guided movement without a coherent spatial relationship between the points, even in the armature in imperial Roman urbanism's colonnaded and arcaded streets. With perspectival design, urbanism's spatial realm can be formed with urban sequences that are parts of coherent, comprehensible spatial relationships of elements. The result can be gridded banality, but it can also unify variety into unity with coherent relationships that point-to-point urbanism never could have produced. It allows a comprehension of spatial relationships between a city's elements allowing, consciously or unconsciously, the construction of a mental map that equips a person to move about in previously untraveled routes, for example reaching a bookstore or market by taking a new shortcut or strolling to enjoy the city aesthetically to indulge in its intellectual and sensuous offerings.

There are numerous instructive examples of urban sequences. The most telling and enjoyable urban sequences are often the result of interventions by the "second architect," with modern Rome holding perhaps the richest collection.[2] The CAMPIDOGLIO, ROME, MICHELANGELO, 1538 looks over the ancient Forum and connects to the major processional route where it passes the site that will attract **Il Gesù, Jacopo Barozzi da Vignola and façade by Giacomo della Porta, 1568** (Figure 4.5). A favorite secluded site is the **Piazza Navona, Rome**, an ancient racetrack that became a disheveled open land until it became a market in a secluded site within dense urban fabric. With nine entrances it holds dwellings, shops, palaces, churches, and fountains with perspectival urbanism establishing relationships between some of them. It is the featured element in an urban sequence with several points of great interest (Figure 4.6). Begin at **Santa Maria sopra Minerva, 1280** near the bottom right of the drawing. Saunter alongside the Pantheon and diagonally through the piazza and exit at the far corner. Follow that to the modern Corsia Agonale where a jog to the left brings you to a recently built colonnade. Beyond it, you see the towers of **Sant'Agnese in Agone, G. and C. Rainaldi and Francesco Borromini, 1652**, in spatial juxtaposition with **Fountain of the Four Rivers, Gian Lorenzo Bernini, 1651**. Exiting through the street opposite and moving forward look to the right for the **semicircular portico and facade, Santa Maria della Pace, Pietro da Cortona, 1656** in the little

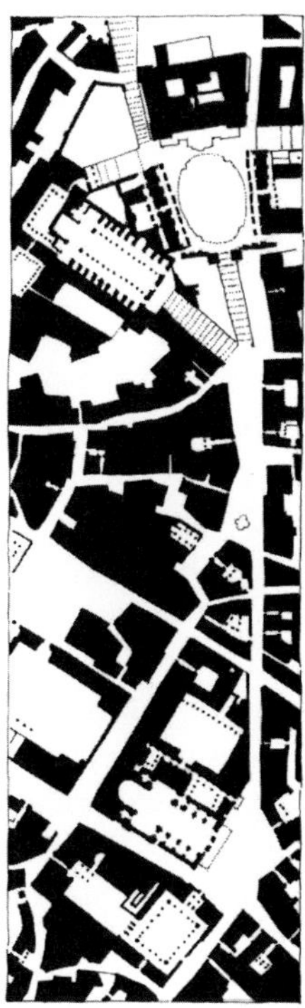

FIGURE 4.5 Rome, urban sequence, from the Campidoglio to Il Gesù

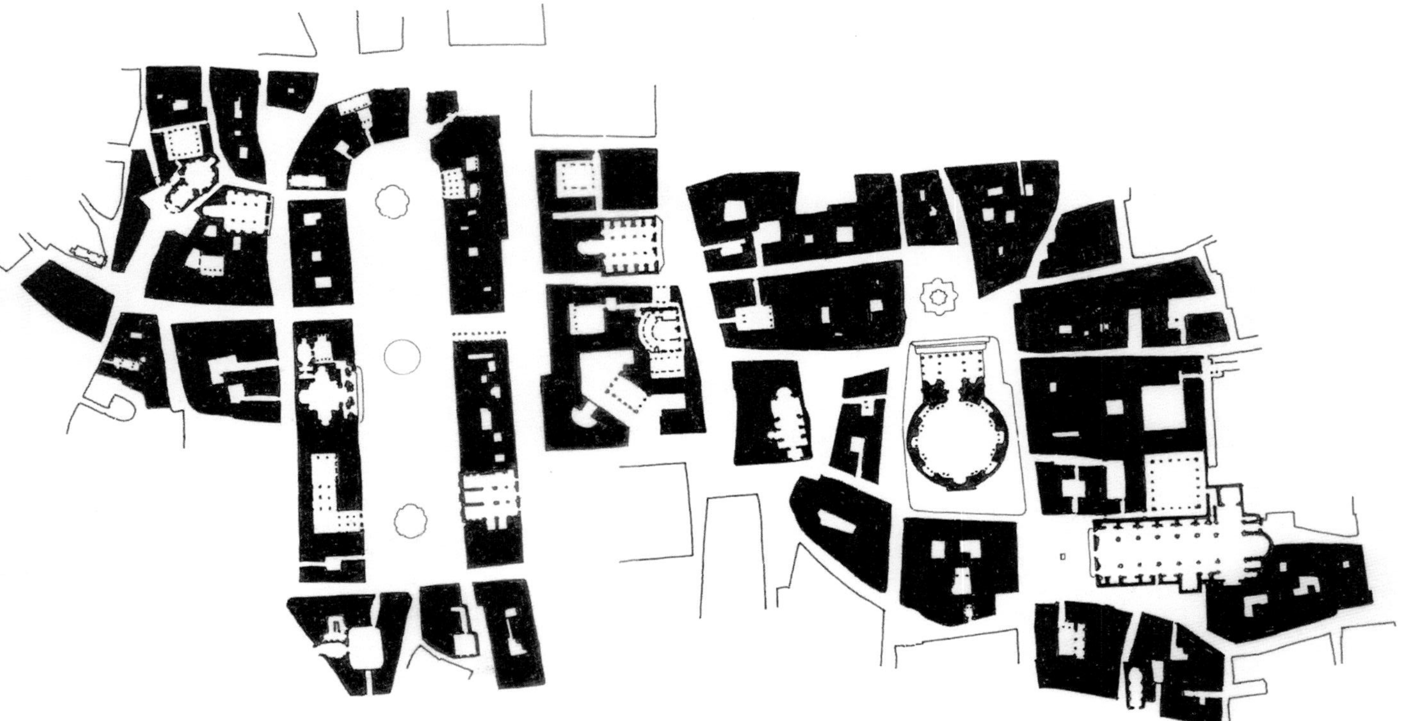

FIGURE 4.6 Rome, urban sequence between Piazza Sta. M. della Pace and Piazza Sta. M. Sopra Minerva.

piazza beyond what the architect called a "teatro." This stroll has indeed been a performance by urbanism.

In urban sequences, proper scaling is fundamental. A banal failure is the **via della Conciliazione, Marcello Piacentini, 1936** leading to the Vatican. It makes Saint Peter's Basilica look like a small and distant goal rather than the impressively large structure it is. Well-equipped but too broad, this street replaced a spine of buildings that obscured the full facade until it was seen embraced by the colonnades of **Piazza di San Pietro, Bernini, 1657**. Unbuilt was the *terzo braccio* (third arm) between the two curved sides that would have enhanced the experience by obscuring the facade until penetrating the colonnades.

A successful urban sequence can include a large building carefully inserted into dense urban fabric. **Les Halles, Louis-Pierre Baltard, Paris, 1853ff**, now gone, that grew into a vast iron and glass central wholesale market allowed transit both through and around it. More spectacular is the transit through the GALLERIA VITTORIO EMANUELE II, GIUSEPPE MENGONI, MILAN, 1865. The centerpiece of an urban enhancement that added a modern commercial center in the city's center, its construction enlarged the Piazza del Duomo and faced it with commercial buildings with two stories and an attic above an arcaded portico. Near the piazza facade's mid-point three bays are altered to produce a grand triumphal arch entrance for the Galleria. Beneath its glass and iron vaults is ornament celebrating Lombardy's 1860 acession into Italy. Intersecting it are cross stubs open to new, four-story commercial blocks. The main trunk exits with a crank to run through a variation of the triumphal arch and graze the front of the City Hall with Luca Beltrami's 1888–92 facade replicating **Palazzo Marino, Galeazzo Alessi, 1557–63** that faces THEATRO ALLA SCALA, GIUSEPPE PIERMARINI 1776.

Secluded places enrich the public realm. The jousting field Henry IV built eventually became the PLACE DES VOSGES, PARIS, 1605. Another is within the various changes made over time to the PALAIS ROYAL, PARIS that now shelters visitors and shoppers beside a *tapis vert* framed by flower beds and pollarded trees. Thomas Jefferson spent leisure hours there and perhaps borrowed some idea from it for his later **University of Virginia, Charlottesville, Thomas Jefferson, 1816–26**. New York City has several stars within its unremitting grid. The **New York Public Library, Carrère and Hastings, 1897** has its stacks tucked under Bryant Park that completes a city block, publicly owned but managed and maintained by its many friends. The privately owned plaza in **Rockefeller Center, Raymond Hood et al., 1931–39** provides a variety of floral and water features, multiple entrances, and changes of level (Figure 4.7). And the campus of **Columbia University, McKim, Mead, and White, 1893** allows public access to the decorous formality of its generous open grounds where children on their tricycles play and scholars engage in disputation.

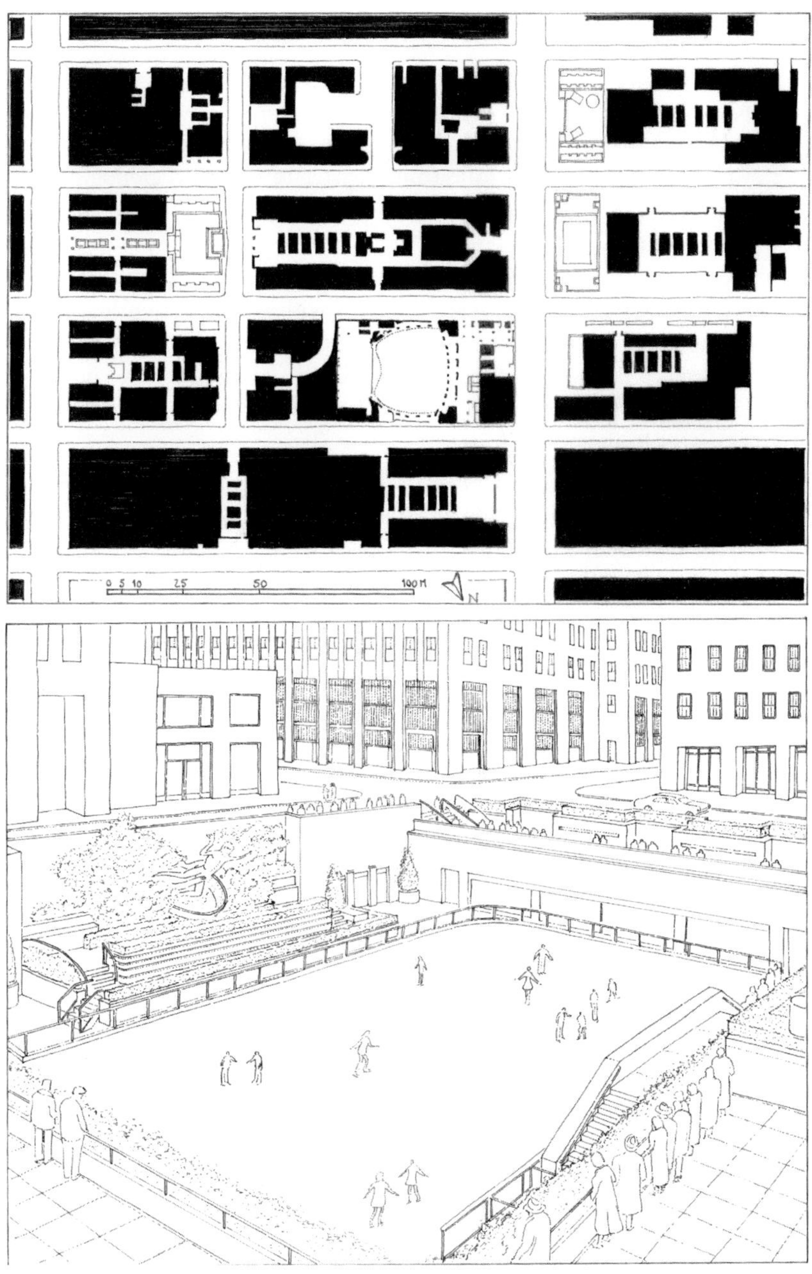

FIGURE 4.7 Rockefeller center, urban plan, and perspective of rink.

5 Regional character

Just as buildings and urban fabric are linked, so too is the expressive character of architecture and urbanism. The faces of streets and squares are made by a variety of individual architectural characters, and this produces a distinctive sense of place at an ascending scale from quarter to city to region and on to the nation. San Francisco does not look like Brooklyn, but both are more like other places in the United States than any place in China or France. A city's urbanism, as we saw in parts of Venice, Florence, and Charlottesville, acquires a distinctive character that effects the observer with the sense of place, a sense that is engendered by the layering over time of the multiple architectural characters of the place. It charms the resident or visitor and supports the civil order with qualities that are missing in places that look newly built, something noted in the review of Pullman in Chapter 3.

Like character in architecture, urban character emerges within the arts of building and architecture in particular cities or nations, but it can also travel and combine with urban or regional characters elsewhere. "Spanish" has been imported and taken root in Santa Barbara and Los Angeles in California, Beaux-Arts academic traditions are found in the massive and smaller public and private buildings in cities, regions, and nations on the European continent and in the United States. Imports are domesticated with distinctive transformations into national expressive character, as in the **Parliament Building, Imre Stiendl, Budapest, 1885**, and post 1902 public buildings in Washington D.C. that lack the pomposity and ornamental richness of their Parisian predecessors. A foreign power routinely builds with its expressive character in its colonies, usually without accounting for the indigenous national architectural character(s), although **New Delhi, India, Edwin Lutyens and Herbert Baker, 1911** did incorporate it, begrudgingly. Across time the importations can come to be considered native or modified when domesticated, as in the Arab, Portuguese, and British architectures that were introduced to Kenya. Any and all of these instances of local, regional, or national expressive character can be erased when standardized building technologies are applied to every country or climate regardless of local architectural characters and material conditions.

Some last words about components and urban types

Using the components within the generative types to build good urbanism requires balance and proportionality among its many parts, a good eye, patience, and a respect for the common good it will serve. There are no formulae, but there are cautions to heed. Repetitiveness as in uniform compositions, heights, cornices, and materials, as in London's and Manchester's housing terraces, produces sameness or uniformity but not unity. In like manner, a frenetic pursuit of variety prevents achieving the coherence needed in properly arranged building configurations and compositions and urban components in the streets, squares, and blocks generated from the urban types.

Urbanism is not a solitary activity. Achieving some place and not just any place takes time and involves the collective reasoning and exchange of ideas among the people who know and live in a place and those who produce and assemble its material components. The builders' goal is a place exhibiting coherence between the political and social decorousness, suitability, or fittingness and the many parts composing its distinctive physical character. In such a place a new thing inserted as a physical intervention elicits delight or revulsion depending on whether or not it suits its purpose with the scale, composition, materials, and general character that contributes to the beauty and concinnity of its setting. Finally, urban character can also be a performance. Because of its analogy with the human character, in particular as manifested in facial expressions, architectural character is "performed" as if the city were a theater and the buildings were the actors in a civic play.

Urbanism's ancillary components

Urbanism includes several physical elements that are not easily comprehended under the term architecture, and they are neither essential components nor urban types, but they enhance and complete urbanism. Their service is as demarcations, ornaments, monuments, parks, and so on, and fall into general categories such as the following in a non-inclusive listing.

Gates

Gates mark transit through walls and sometimes remain after the walls are removed, as was the **Burgtor, Pietro Nobile, Vienna, 1817**, a proud memorial to Austria's victory over the French who had destroyed the gate's predecessor in 1806. It was left when the Ringstrasse, mentioned in Chapter 3, was built. Gates provided access to precincts such as the Acropolis in Athens. In Beijing, they marked transit through the walls enclosing the zones in the axial approach across the city culminating in the HALL OF SUPREME HARMONY, BEIJING, 1406. They were included in the tombs of emperors that were surrogate cities, as at the modern MAUSOLEUM OF SUN YET SEN, LǗ YANZHI, NANJING, 1926.

After technology made fortified walls around cities obsolete, tax walls remained to control the movement of citizens and collect import taxes. Only a few of the **50 gates, Claude Nicholas Ledoux, Paris, 1785 and 1788** remain. Their oppressive proportioning and stark geometric configurations and rugged, squat apparatus of classical forms conveyed their role in enforcing the tax laws that precipitated the Revolution. The **Brandenburg Gate, Carl Langhans, Berlin, 1788–91** served similar functions with an expressive character using forms derived from ancient Greece to claim Germany's roots in ancient Greece; it now serves as a logo for the city. The triumphal arches that were celebratory ornaments in imperial Roman cities were outdone when Napoleon had the huge **Arc de Triomphe, Jean Chalgrin, Paris, 1806** begun to celebrate a victory. Located on a height beyond the broad Boulevard des Champs-Élysées, it was intended to be part of a water works project, but when completed in 1836 it served simply as a boundary marker. The much smaller **Washington Square Arch, Stanford White, New York, 1892–95** at the termination of Fifth Avenue replaced a temporary one celebrating the centenary of Washington's becoming President. **Union Station, Daniel H. Burnham, Washington, 1903–08**, built as part of the city's 1902 renewal, serves travelers with a three-arched version. More modest are gates marking entrances, such as the **Sather Gate, University of California, John Galen Howard, Berkeley, 1910**, and the closeable main gates at Columbia University added in 1970, a gift of George T. Delacorte, Jr.

Tall things, monuments, and memorials

Ancient emperors brought monolithic obelisks from Egypt to Rome to celebrate their control of that ancient civilization. For the **pilgrimage routes, Sixtus V, Rome, 1585–90**, some were re-erected and relocated along routes to guide pilgrims to holy sites and to celebrate the Church's triumph over the pagan empire. The very tall **Washington Monument, Robert Mills, Washington, D.C., 1848** took 40 years to complete with its original intended prominence benefitting from the 1902 McMillan Plan.

Towers perform religious work as minarets that call the faithful to worship or bell towers or campaniles that broadcast sacred time into their parishes' temporal realms. The **Campanile, Venice, finished 1516; collapsed 1902; rebuilt 1912** as the bell tower for the **Basilica di San Marco 11th-13th c.**, has several secular progeny built as memorials for Americans who died in World War I in Europe: the **Sather Tower or Campanile, University of California, John Galen Howard, Berkeley, 1914–16** visible from San Francisco, and the **World War I Memorial Carillon, Ralph Adams Cram, Richmond, Virginia, 1931** marking a boulevard's termination in a park.

Statues of people and events are given prominent places that provoke partisan outrage. A posthumous equestrian statue of **Henri IV, Pietro Tacca, Paris, 1607**, was installed on the **Pont Neuf, 1578** that connected the two parts of Paris. Destroyed during the Revolution, it was replaced with a replica in 1818 at its original site opposite the **Place Dauphine, 1607**. This triangle of ordinary townhouses was built according to the plan the king provided to the man to whom the king had given the land. Its only original surviving buildings face the king at the point of the *place*. Equestrian Confederate generals and a standing statesman prominently installed during Jim Crow on **Monument Avenue, Richmond, Virginia, 1902ff**, were removed in 2021 and are unlikely to be replaced.

Commendable achievements such as supplying a city with healthy water are also memorialized: **Fontana dell'Acqua Paola, Giovanni Fontana and Flaminio Ponzio, Rome, 1612**, visible from the city's center high on a hill is supplied from a restored ancient aqueduct, and the **Bethesda Fountain, Central Park, Calvert Vaux and Jacob Wrey Mould, New York City, 1861,** commemorate the water's arrival from the **Croton Aqueduct, 1837–42.**

Bridges

Bridges can do more than carry streets. We just saw the **Pont Neuf, Paris, 1578** that replaced the two spans of a timber bridge with dwellings on it; the new bridge had no dwellings, but it did have a statue of the king. The axis running from the king through the Place Dauphine to **Notre Dame Cathedral, 1163** at its terminus assisted in making the facilities on the Île de la Cité accessible.

Two ancient crossings of the Tiber survived Rome's decline. We have already encountered **Ponte Sant'Angelo, Hadrian, 135**, equipped in 1669 with the statues of angels holding the instruments of Christ's Passion. The other, a pair of spans flanking the **Tiber Island with Temple of Asclepius, the Pons Fabricius, 62BCE and Pons Cestius, slightly later**, a place still used for healing, survived and kept open access to Rome's trans-Tiber settlements. In Venice, an important thoroughfare connected the Piazza di San Marco to the **Rialto Bridge, Antonio da Ponte, 1581** lined with shops and rising to an open vista point at its peak. The PULTNEY BRIDGE, ROBERT ADAM, BATH, 1770–74, carried on three arches also has shops but with a flat, carriage-friendly roadbed a few blocks away from THE CIRCUS AND THE CRESCENT, JOHN WOOD THE ELDER and WOOD THE YOUNGER, BATH, 1754; 1767.

River embankments can be friendly, as are those along the Ljubljanica River in Ljubljana, Slovenia. To make the **Triple Bridge and later market structure and other improvements, Jože Plečnik,** added a single bridge in 1913 and later improved it with a central roadway and added flanking footbridges fanning out from the old town to transform a mere crossing into an attractive and active urban center.

New technology served and increased traffic, and new bridges sometimes achieved urban-enhancing expressive character. Familiar examples are on each American coast. **Brooklyn Bridge, John Augustus Roebling and his son Augustus, New York, 1867–83** planted two massive celebratory stone towers to support the woven cables carrying the trussed bridge deck. The **Golden**

Gate Bridge, Joseph Strauss, engineer, Irving Morrow, architect, San Francisco, 1933–37 used two steel towers enclosed in steel covers exhibiting the then current simplified classicism of the Art Deco and painted a shade of orange that enhances both sunsets and the colors of the landscape at both ends.

Water

Water, essential for life, enriches urbanism. A fountain occupies a Paradise garden in the final enclosure in the **Cortile del Belvedere, Bramante, Vatican, 1505**. Numerous villas of cardinals in nearly arid Rome celebrate its presence through humankind's control of the natural world, and they give large and small performances both visually and audibly: **Villa d'Este, Pirro Ligorio, Tivoli, 1550–65**; **Villa Lante, Vignola?, Bagnaia, 1566**; and FARNESE VILLA, VIGNOLA, CAPRAROLA, 1559.

Marshy land in France was tortured to control water and enhance a building's setting: CHÂTEAU OF VAUX-LE-VICOMTE, ANDRÉ LE NÔTRE, MOULON, 1657, and even more grandly in the **Gardens, André le Nôtre, Versailles, 1662**. Similar land in China at **Tongli**, the "Venice of the East" in the Yangtze River delta near Shanghai, provided water for the tight, white-walled confines of wealthy Chinese merchants' dwellings. Often rearranged, they presented themes: a miniature world with an ideal landscape, a now-lost past, an improvement on nature, an illustration of literature's poetic images, a calm in a tumultuous world, etc. They invited contemplative meandering along paths through rocks, trees, and plantings with pavilions and half-moon bridges offering carefully composed vantage points.

England's lush, gentle landscape gave rise after the early 18th c. to the informal English garden in rural estates and large urban parks; they continue to model park design worldwide. Ponds, cascades, meandering water courses, bridges, gazeboes, boskets, hills, caves, look-out points, and other elements provide picture-like delights appealing to the romantic sensibilities that replaced the classical garden's rigid, geometric order. Perhaps most complete and famous is the **Garden, Charles Bridgeman, Stowe 1711, continued by William Kent and Capability Brown**.

Parks and landscaping

Architects tend to treat land that their buildings will not occupy as "open space." There is no such thing. Every city occupies a part of the earth's surface, and civil orders, like individuals, always make use of such land for something.

A notable example was the **Academy, Plato, Athens, c387 BCE**, a suburban park, olive grove, and gymnasium sacred to Academus (or Hecademus) for discussions that constituted higher education in the western tradition until it was closed in 529. Medieval courtiers pursued hunting in royal preserves in the countryside, while dwellings and regias had walled gardens with flowers, fruits, and water ornamentation arranged in geometric patterns like those in antiquity, for example the one attached to the ITALIC ATRIUM HOUSE, POMPEII, BEFORE 79 and called the **Praedia of Julia Felix.** The Renaissance became known for their geometric gardens in country villas and chateaux.

The nobility enjoyed recreation in large hunting preserves that later became public parks incorporated into the explosively expanding industrial and commercial centers. Two examples are **Regent's Park at Regent Street**, **John Nash and James Burton, London, 1811–25** and the **Tiergarten Park, Peter Joseph Lenné, Berlin, 1830s**, just outside the **Brandenburg Gate, Carl Langhans, 1788–91**. Other parks are reached by the **Boulevards, Baron Haussmann, Paris, 1854–70**, that included several smaller parks reclaimed from formerly insalubrious sites. His network of boulevards included tree-lined routes like those along the canals in Dutch cities, but they had normally been excluded from important routes within cities and were kept outside, in rural areas, until Rome provided a model. Pope Alexander VII (1655–67), improved the Roman Forum and areas around several gates and within other the uninhabited areas with trees following a **Street plan, Bernini, Rome, 1656** that lined streets with regularly planted trees. When Louis XIV defortified Paris he had the **Boulevards, 1668**, replaced with wide carriageways lined with trees, giving the name to such roadways. Haussmann's work found a home in Chicago just beyond the built-up areas in its 26-mile **Park and Boulevard system, Chicago, south section, Olmsted and Vaux, western section, William LeBaron Jenney, 1869** on land often contributed by landowners who anticipated enhanced value for building sites fronting this improvement; Jenney had spent 1861 in Paris when Baron Haussmann was disrupting it. The southern part of Chicago's new parks and boulevards system had Jackson Park and the Midway Plaisance, the site of the **World Columbian Exposition, Daniel H. Burnham, et al, Chicago, 1893**. In rapidly expanding New York city newspaper publicity stirred up public pressure for reserving a vast tract within previously gridded Manhattan that led to the indispensable romantic landscape in **Central Park, Frederick Law Olmstead and Calvert Vaux, 1857**.

The urbanism in the United States, Britain, and northern Europe, especially in the modern era, is set into, rather than apart from, the land. Natural ponds and water courses within metropolitan areas, when not channelized or put into culverts and pipes, often occupy in public land, and they and carefully designed parks are given informal layouts, places for games and assemblies, equipment for family activities, gazebos, bandstands, toilet facilities, boathouses, or changing rooms. An example is the **Victoria Embankment, Francis W Sheilds architect and Joseph Bazalgette engineer, 1865–70** that replaced the Thames bankside seen in David Robert's *Saint Paul's Cathedral and the Thames Docks* in Chapter 1. Another example is the reworking of the **Hudson River**

along Manhattan, various agencies in various episodes, 20th c., with docks, railroads, expressways, and parks. The **MacMillan Plan of Washington, D.C., 1902** was initiated as a park plan and made extensive improvements to the Potomac River and rustic Rock Creek Park. Landscaped yards at private, single-family residences are nearly normative in America, and a substitute is available to districts with narrow, party-wall units built around the landscaped squares, many in London accessible only to the square's residents. **Newtown, James Craig, Edinburg, 1768**, placed one at each end of George Street that gave distinction to middle-class terraced houses fronting them and perhaps won him the competition. Later and elsewhere, small, public parks and even small, carefully landscaped "pocket parks" have been carved out of dense urban fabric. In the United States, low rise apartment buildings are normally sited in landscaped grounds, and even high-rise apartment buildings in denser urbanism often have at least pots with shrubs flanking the entrance.

In America, except in dense urban centers and even there when possible, the more important the building's purpose, the greater the extent of landscape it commands. County courthouses and state capitals such as the VIRGINIA CAPITOL, THOMAS JEFFERSON, RICHMOND, 1785 illustrates the point. These open capitol and courthouse squares attract fountains, memorials, and free-standing monuments commemorating events and statues of individuals. These also find places in other squares, parks, or even street roundabouts and within trees, turf, and floral displays in the medians of boulevards, for example, **Monument Avenue, Richmond, Virginia, 1902ff** mentioned above.

Postscript

The buildings, architecture, and urbanism scattered throughout this book present many instances of attempts to provide the security, sustenance, and justice that are the rightful possession of each person. In the recent past, the aspiration to achieve that through the participation of all people in their civil order has expanded even as the world is rapidly being urbanized with practices that intrude. Here we offer some examples that provide an optimistic outlook for the future.

In the **Netherlands**, people for millennia have been urbanizing land claimed from the sea. Within homogeneous space they have produced crafted, intensive, multi-use urbanism interlaced with roadways, rail lines, and canals bordered by tree-lined pedestrian and bicycle paths in urban areas built with low-scale modest brick commercial and residential buildings. Newer purposes that demand larger buildings such as airports and hospitals are placed at the nodes of an extensive network of cheap, efficient, public transportation.[3]

Venice, another place won from the sea, provides a counterexample that also proves what a magnet good, compact urbanism is. More than half of its residents have converted their residences to hotels and commute from neighboring

Mestre, a 20th c. industrial district incorporated into the municipality. Mestre's urbanism is also compact but lacks the well-designed examples of the urban types and ancillary elements we presented in Chapter 4. Its residents are there out of necessity, not by choice, while Venice continues to attract visitors from throughout the world.

From the earliest times, cities have expanded by building new towns. After the year 1000 when merchants were not welcomed within a city protective of its civil order, whether Paris, Florence, New York, or elsewhere, they set up their shops and residences outside the town gates. These grew into villages and were eventually incorporated into the enlarged town's governance. Some cities sponsored expansion, as in **Newtown, James Craig, Edinburg, 1768** or did not interfere, as in the several offspring of the Garden City Movement. More recent are the examples are various New Urbanism projects first tested with the resort of **Seaside, Florida, Andrés Duany, Elizabeth Plater-Zyberk, and Léon Krier, 1978**. We conclude with two new towns, the construction of which is still under way within the slow pace required for building the good city in today's business-as-usual world.

In England Charles, Prince of Wales, a long-time advocate of traditional architecture, began collaborating with Krier in 1988 to build a complete model village on his land in the Duchy of Cornwall. **Poundbury, Dorset**, which began in 1993 is scheduled for completion in 2025. Politically and urbanistically an extension of the city of Dorchester, with 150 acres devoted to allotment gardens, playfields, and parkland and 250 acres for the village. Government functions were promised during early planning, but that promise has been withdrawn.

Its coverage of 15–20 dwelling units per acre is nearly double what is usual in current developments. Also unusual is that more than a third of its dwelling units are for low-income residents in social housing or in units owned by charitable trusts with other financial arrangements for the up-and-coming. In developing the plan, Krier studied traditional villages and consulted **Camille Sitte, *City Planning According to Artistic Principles*, 1904**. The village privileges pedestrians over autos, includes access to the full range of modern wants and needs, and includes or will include enough employment opportunities in factories, offices, and shops for nearly all of its projected 6,000 residents. Its buildings by several prominent British architects fit into the regional architecture with inventions especially prominent in the conspicuous community hall and market building in market square's BROWNSWORD HALL-POUNDSBURY VILLAGE HALL, JOHN SIMPSON, 2000.

In contrast to England's valued rural tranquility, the privately administered entity of **Cayalá** in Guatemala offers security and active social engagement to the young who normally reside in rural estates. In contrast is Guatemala City with a population of four million and unsafe streets, administrative crime, and conspicuous private armed guards. Begun in the 1980s on the outer edge of the ever-expanding urban sprawl, in 2003 it adopted a New Urbanism vision to provide a model for future urban transformations and urban quarters. To succeed it must provide personal security offered with plain-clothed armed guards and extensive, largely hidden surveillance cameras, and, importantly, the constant, animated presence of trusted, and trusting, neighbors, acquaintances, and familiar faces.

Its eventual 570 acres is intended to reach 50,000–60,000 people with a density nearly five times higher than Guatemala City's average and offering all the necessities of life. The first of its eight villages, 34-acre **Paseo Cayalá**, designed through charrettes involving Krier and two young Guatemalans, María Fernanda Sanchez and Pedro Pablo Godoy whose Estudio Urbano is carrying it to completion. The buildings serve modern needs such as parking garages and supermarkets with an expressive character based on invention within the country's Spanish-Mayan tradition with stucco over brick, framed openings, wooden or wrought iron balconies, and various flourishes set within an urban plan exhibiting the generative types we have delineated. An Athenaeum, the **Azaria Civic Hall, Richard Economakis, 2011** is down the street from the central plaza surrounded by restaurants and shops below apartments with other residential units and intermixed with other uses.

The range of prices for residential units reaches very far down, but there is no custom in Guatemala of providing subsidies for housing. A neighboring barrio where the builders and the city are now underwriting some educational and cultural initiatives for their residents will be incorporated into the larger project. The central plaza is open and easily accessible to nonresidents, and a wide diversity of people will certainly be drawn to the services of the dominating, domed, pedimented **Santa María Reina de la Familia, Sanchez and Godoy, consecrated in 2021**.

Notes

1 William L. MacDonald, *The Architecture of the Roman Empire II: An Urban Appraisal* (New Haven, CT and London: Yale University Press, 1986), 3.
2 An invaluable and rich source is the map by Giambatista Nolli from 1748 available on the internet.
3 For more about the urbanism of the Netherlands, see Charles Duff, *The North Atlantic Cities* (Liverpool: Bluecoat, 2019) with many useful observations about cities and their dwellings.

PART II

The Catalogue

The Catalogue of drawings accompanied by descriptions has seven chapters, one for each building type with a few including variations within the chapter and normally in chronological order. They are intended to accompany the text in Part I and not to illustrate a narrative whose arrow points to the future. Both the descriptions and the drawings are minimal with the recognition that electronic media can provide more verbal and visual information.

DOI: 10.4324/9780429506260-7

5

THE THOLOS

The ***tholos*** serves venerating what a community holds in the highest regard and occupies the highest rank among buildings.

Variation 1: the tholos alone

The most refined of the nine remaining Bronze Age beehive tombs or *tholoi* in Mycenae, Greece, Heinrich Schliemann, the early excavator of Troy, gave this site this name; an equally specious name is the Tomb of Agamemnon (Figure 5.1). Its interior stone diameter is 14 ½ m and rises upward

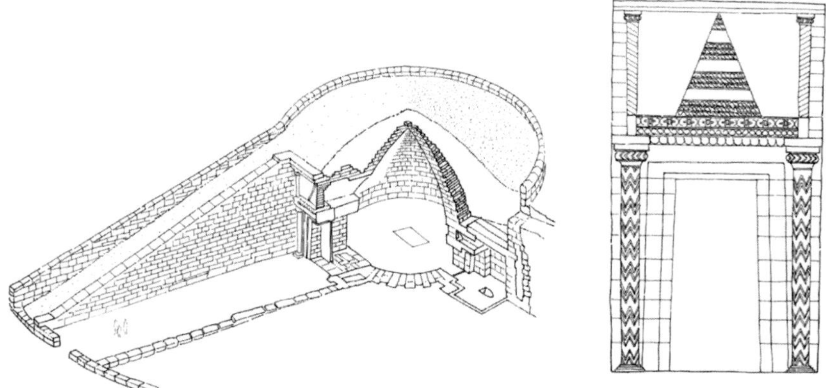

FIGURE 5.1 Treasury of Atreus, Mycenae, Greece, c. 1250 BCE.

DOI: 10.4324/9780429506260-8

13 ½ m through 34 courses to the apex of the conical corbelled dome. A slightly inclined processional east-west causeway (*dromos*) 6 m wide flanked by cyclopean retaining walls, dry-laid like the cone, runs 36 m to the single entrance through an enormous stone lintel supported by the massive walls. The recessed, battered entrance beneath was dressed with green limestone half-columns that tapered downward like Crete's Minoan columns, now in museums in London and Berlin, with zig-zag motifs. Above the lintel, the weight-relieving triangular corbelled void was originally screened with a decorated stone slab. Originally bronze panels lined the entrance doors and the tomb's relatively smooth interior. The nearly cubical room extending north from the rotunda is the actual burial chamber that held the bodies of the prince or chieftain and members of his family and servants along with military and ceremonial implements.

The expressive character of the exterior commemorating or venerating whomever it held was that of a mounded precinct. Some scholars suggest that following the ceremonial burial the *dromos* may have been filled. Here the inhabitant's enduring memory was assured by the durable materials of a partially excavated chamber beneath an earthen mound that weather eventually washes away. A similar tholos with subterranean chambers is the MAUSOLEUM OF SUN YET SEN, LŰ YANZHI, NANJING, 1926–29, which shares the long axial approach and controlled earthen covering. Roman mausolea were not dissimilar: the **Tomb of Hadrian, Rome, 134–9**, connected to Rome by a bridge that survived to connect Rome to the Vatican while the tomb was refitted as the Castel Sant'Angelo, a defensive fortress. Perhaps related is an unwalled tholos, **Stonehenge, Wilts., England, 3000–2000 BCE**, that surely included an axial orientation to serve celestial observations and rituals throughout the year.

Despite their many cult rituals involving the gods, the ancients had few interiors where their votaries assembled. A rare example held extremely important initiation rites at Eleusis near Athens, important since about 800 BCE and sacred to the chthonic goddess Persephone and her mother Demeter, goddess of grain and the harvest. The Persians destroyed it in 480–79 BCE, and Pericles had it reconstructed by Iktinos while working at the TEMPLE OF ATHENA (PARTHENON), ATHENS, with CALLICRATES, 447–36 BCE (Figure 5.2). A marble-paved hypostyle, pairs of entrances on three sides led into eight tiers of seats for as many as 3,000 celebrants seated along its four interior walls with those opposite the front cut into the stone hillside. A 6 × 7 column field held a roof with circular openings (*opaia*; we do not show them) and a mechanical device to open them for light and ventilation. A rectangular shrine, or *anaktoron*, holding the sacred objects running back to the earliest times, was placed on the entrance wall.

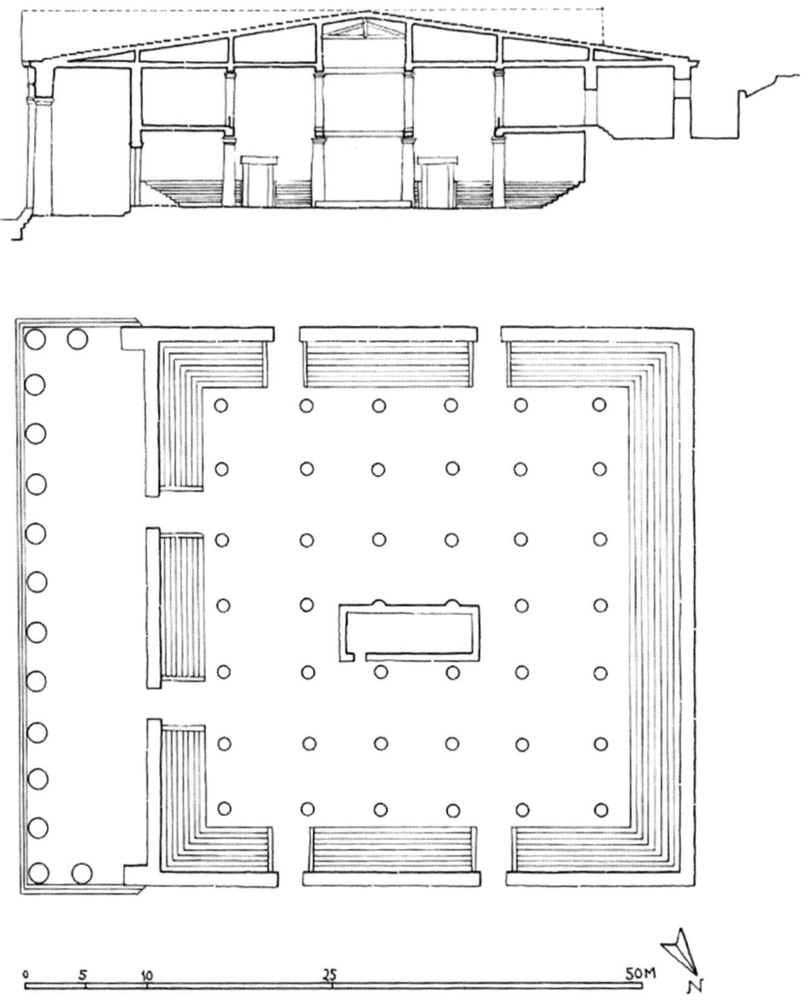

FIGURE 5.2 Telesterion, Eleusis, Iktinos, 435, and Philon, Greece, c. 318 (colonnade).

In about 318 BCE, Philon, who built Athens' famous Arsenal, added a 12-column Doric colonnade with another column set before the side walls' antae to make the stoa porch we show. Over time facilities accrued here for games and rituals. Its popularity with the Romans kept it in repair and even added more facilities, including inserting a *propylaeum* into the precinct's wall. The Visigoths finally reduced it to ruin in 396.

A similar telesterion in Megalopolis in our other drawing was built in about 371 BCE after the Arcadian League united cities as a defense against Sparta (Figure 5.3). Its columns were arrayed to focus on the *anaktoron* on the entrance wall where its

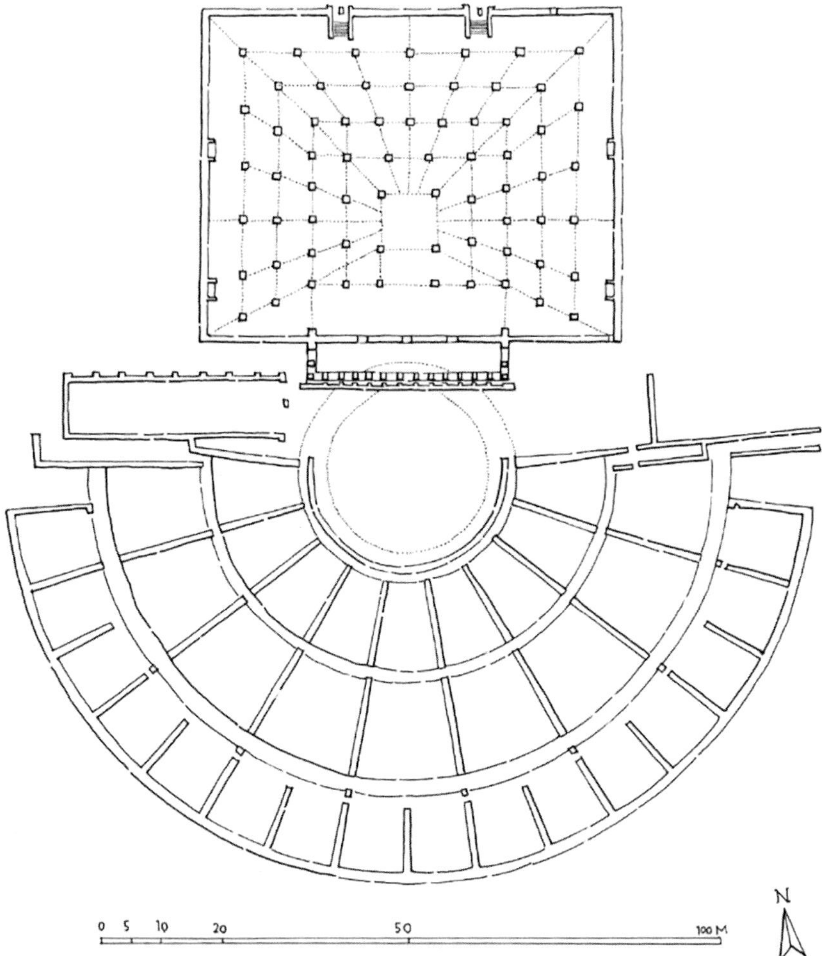

FIGURE 5.3 Thersilion at Megalopolis, Greece, c. 371 BCE.

colonnaded entrance served as the skene for the theater holding 20,000 people (Figure 5.4).

The focus of veneration in Buddhism, a stupa is mound-like, contains the remains of venerable Buddhist monks or nuns or other holy relics, and is often included within a *chaitya*, a temple, or prayer hall. The faithful circumvallate it ritually along a *pradakhshina*. At its crown, a *chhatri* or parasol-like structure proclaims its importance.

The emperor Ashoka the Great (r. c. 268–c. 232 BCE) commissioned this stupa to hold relics of the Buddha. One of the oldest stone structures in India, it included an Ashokan Pillar with the emperor's edicts beneath a lion capital (fragments survive). After being wantonly damaged in the mid-2nd c. BCE it

FIGURE 5.4 The Great Stupa of Sanchi, Madhya Pradesh, India, c. 260 BCE–5th c. After Satish Grover.

was extensively enlarged and reconstructed with its brick core augmented by a sandstone carapace, steps to reach the *pradakhshina*, and a porch to attain its present large size, 37 m wide and 17 m high. Further work that included adding four statues of the Buddha came sometime before 450, but sometime after the 12th c. Sanchi was abandoned. The stupa was rediscovered and reconstructed in the 19th c. to the condition in our drawing, shown with some of the numerous other shrines in the district.

In its final form, a ground-level *pradakhshina* was defined by a railing given an entrance through the eastern *toranas*, one of four on the cardinal axes from the 1st c. BCE (reconstructed in the 19th c.). The masonry's tectonic character in this stupa and elsewhere was clearly modeled on timber construction. This site's importance made these *toranas* models for similar gateways in other eastern religious sites. These have very elaborate ornamentation on their uprights and three cross pieces elucidating the Buddha's life, the stupa's history, and the richness of the world. They anchor the stupa's symbolism in which the enclosure represents the mountains and the dome shows that the Earth supports Heaven and Heaven covers Earth. On top within a square railing is the *chhatri* whose three tiers represent the Buddha, doctrine, and community. The circumambulation of the faithful completes the cosmic symbolism.

The stupa is the forerunner of the pagoda. Miniaturized, it becomes a reliquary when made of crystal, gold, silver, or other precious metals (Figure 5.5).

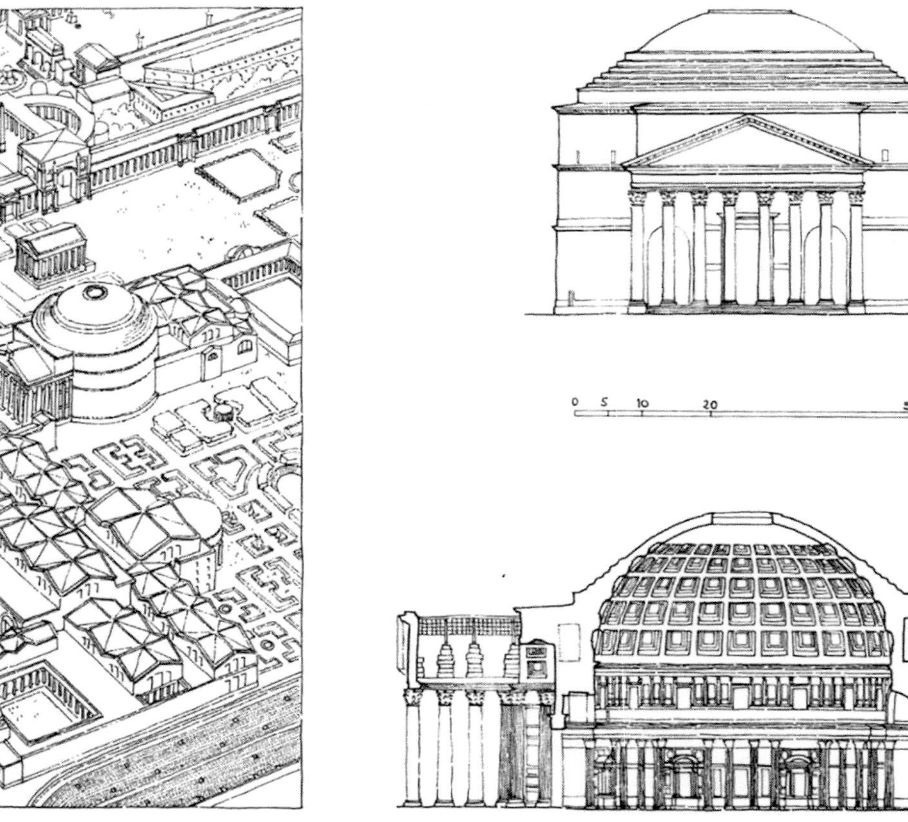

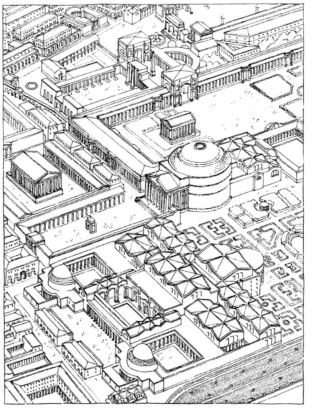

FIGURE 5.5 Pantheon, Hadrian with Apollodorus of Damascus? Rome, Italy, 117–26. After Gilles Chaillet and Mark Wilson Jones.

This world-famous building replaced Agrippa's twice-burned shrine celebrating the victory in 31 BCE that made Augustus emperor. Perhaps designed by the architect of Trajan's Forum (THE TEMPLE OF TRAJAN, APOLLODORUS OF DAMASCUS, 106–13, ROME), it faces north to the Campus Martius where soldiers drilled and Augustus' mausoleum stood. The best-preserved interior from antiquity, it survived because in 609 it was consecrated as a church dedicated to Saint Mary of the Martyrs. It now holds tombs including those of two Renaissance painter-architects, Raphael and Baldassare Peruzzi, and the imposing sarcophagi of the first two Italian kings and a Queen.

A model of the cosmos, the dome's oculus provides a single light source (some does filter through the entrance). Its beam moves in a regular and predictable path across the geometric shapes of the veneered walls and the slightly domed floor; on the equinox, it reaches the pronaos. Roman custom limited a temple to one god, but the name pantheon suggests that many gods were venerated here. Their statues, long ago lost, could have occupied the several niches ringing the circle, the largest opposite the entrance (for the emperor's seat?), six lesser distyle niches with alternating flat or semicircular plans, and eight whose tabernacle frames, with alternating pediments and segmental arches, have served as models for innumerable later variations down to the present around niches, windows, and doors.

The five layers of the concrete dome's coffers, their facias canted to stress the dome's rise and originally equipped with stars and color, diminish in size before reaching a blank field around the oculus.

The register immediately below the dome is from 1747 except for one stretch where the original was restored; we used it for that level in our sectional drawing. Its tightly spaced groups of four pilaster alternating with rectangular niches enlarge the grandeur of the marble veneering below it and of the dome rising above. Note that nothing in this or the other register aligns with other elements or with the coffers; perspective to impose geometry on a void was lacking.

The other, lowest register reaches an entablature with a porphyry frieze; it completes the fictive membrature of the wall's marble veneering and the columns free-standing before the three niches on each side and the embedded piers framing them. The entablature is replaced by an arch at the vaulted entrance and in the hemicycle niche opposite where an arch stands behind the *ressaults* of the free-standing columns acting as sentinels at its sides.

We conjecture a precinct (see Chapter 3) with an axial approach up broad stairs (surviving below the modern pavement) where the pediment. Within it, the done, (originally) bronze-covered, would have been hidden from view. The octastyle temple front, whose width is that of a square inscribed inside the building, now has "40-footer" granite columns; we show it with the intended 50 footers whose pediment is the ghost visible on the wall above the 40-footers' pediment. The marble covering the brick exterior is long gone, as is the pediment's bronze sculpture, that perhaps included a large eagle and references to Agrippa. The original Corinthian capitals have been badly eroded (by rocks thrown in play for a millennium by small boys?) and would have looked like the 17th c. replacements that the Barberini pope installed with the three rose-colored shafts when market stalls were removed. The same pope made cannons from the porch's bronze ceiling, which led to the popular taunt, "What the barbarians did not do the Barberini did" (Figure 5.6).

On a site towering over Jerusalem and sacred to Abrahamic religions were THE JEWISH HOUSE OF THE LORD (TEMPLE) or SOLOMON'S TEMPLE, 833BCE and the SECOND TEMPLE, 535BCE. After its destruction came Hadrian's **Temple of Jupiter, c. 130**, no longer extant, and finally this building, the DOME OF THE ROCK or Qubbat al-Sakhra dominating Mount Moriah's vast esplanade above the surrounding urban quarters. A monumental tholos, a shrine and not a mosque, this early Islamic shrine ranks with the **Kaaba, Mecca, often rebuilt**, and the **Tomb of the Prophet Muhammad, Medina, c. 570–632**. Within is the rock (*sakhra*) marked with the Prophet's footprint or the hoof of Buraq, his winged horse with a human head, whom the archangel Gabriel guided on a spiritual journey (*Miraj*) from the depth of hell to the throne of God, or from the Mosque in Mecca to the Mount's **Al-Aqsa or "Faraway Mosque" (705–09)** 200 meters south. Its composition, proportions, and richness of materials bear a comparison to other monuments in Jerusalem.

Its configuration has numerous parallels with many early Christian structures, now best known through archaeology and scholarship and testifying to Islam's early associations with Christianity. Examples include the very large complex of **Dayr Sim'an al Amoudi (Church of Saint Simeon Stylites), near Aleppo, 475**, where a timber domed octagon enclosed Saint Simeon Stylite's column, and another domed octagon, the **Cathedral of Bora, Syria, 573.**[1] The closest parallel is the Constantinian **Church of the Resurrection (Church of the Holy Sepulcher; Anastasis), Jerusalem, before 350**, a tholos sheltering a rock with Jesus' footprint adjacent to Christ's tomb, freshly rebuilt in 630.

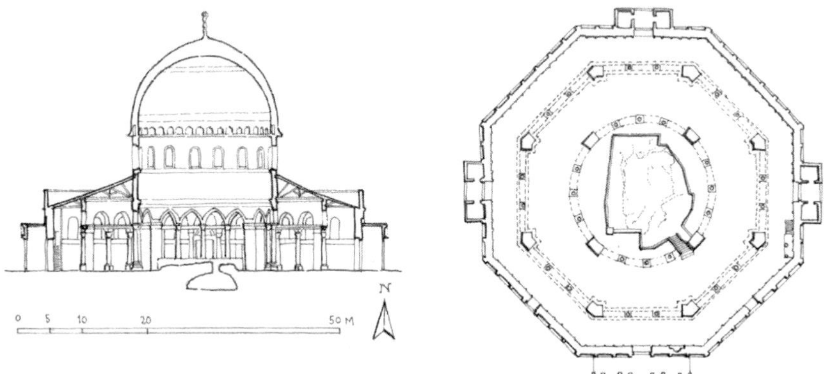

FIGURE 5.6 Dome of the Rock, Raja' Ibn Hayweh and Yazid Ibn Salam, Jerusalem, 687–92.

Apparently, Abd-al-Malik (646–705), the Umayyad Caliph of Damascus, put no limit on costs for Raja' Ibn Hayweh and Yazid Ibn Salam who directed Syrian and Byzantine Christian builders and artisans.[2] A portal on each cardinal axis has a pair of columns carrying an axial vault with four pairs added for the southern porch. Beneath the drum and double-shelled dome (initially wood; its copper exterior gilded since 1994) rests the *sakhra* surrounded by an arcade using spolia serving the circumambulatory rites like those of the Kaaba in Mecca. The inner one is circular with twelve columns and four pillars, the outer one octagonal with sixteen columns and eight pillars and lintels beneath the arches that, like all arches here, are slightly pointed. Constantinopolitan mosaicists certainly executed the lavish polychromies' geometric patterns of natural forms.

Each exterior face has seven arched bays running up through two registers with windows in four upper-level bays and 16 in the drum, all admitting subdued light through intricate geometric screens. Above the white marble lower register the detailed polychromatic patterning, mostly blue, reaches the tall frieze's refined Quranic calligraphy and continues into the drum, an exterior movement from white to blue to dome apparently provided by the Ottoman Sultan Suleyman the Magnificent (1520–66); Figure 5.7).

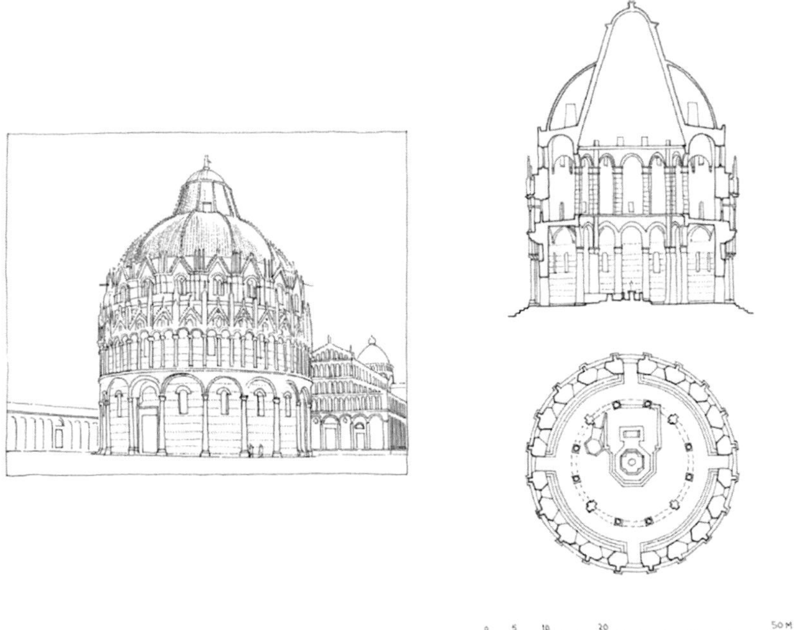

FIGURE 5.7 Baptistery, Nicola Pisano, Pisa, Italy, Diotisalvi, 1153–363.

The tholos serves the veneration of rebirth, through baptism and through resurrection, and in a sense parallels the tholos-as-womb in other faiths. An Italian baptistery is normally free-standing near the cathedral that here joins a precinct including a campanile and cemetery. Important predecessors are the Constantinian **Church of the Resurrection (Anastasis), Jerusalem, before 350,** the **Baptistery at San Giovanni in Laterano, Rome, 324ff,** which is Constantine's putative (but impossible) baptism site, and **Santa Costanza, Rome, c. 350,** with the porphyry sarcophagus of Constantine's daughter Constantina.

Diotisalvi built only the lowest level. After a long hiatus Nicola Pisano, whose famous pulpit is here, and his son Giovanni completed it using the newly popular small-scale membrature and sculpture. The circular plan's two-story interior presents four sets of three bays each. The lower level's stilted arches rise from pairs of monolithic porphyry columns framing the four entrances alternating with pilaster-faced piers; this membrature carries an ambulatory's groin vaults. Above them, an annular vault is carried on the stunted arches of the arcade with pilaster piers that, like the walls and arches below, are built with bichromatic white and green courses with broad and narrow courses visible on the outside as well. A conical dome closes the interior.

The portal on the cathedral's axis displays Mary, John, Apostles, and other subjects. The exterior's ground floor membrature begins with a simple, attached, 24 bay arcade. Next up comes a 28 bay arcade with pairs of bays sharing a tall pediment ornamented with saints with randomly spaced windows behind. In the tall attic zone windows beneath tall pediments align with the ground floor windows. The swelling covering above has twelve crocketed ribs running up the dome's extrados and continuing up the cone's penetration, finally ending in a small domical termination carrying John the Baptist.

Figure 5.8. This small tholos offers veneration at the putative site of Saint Peter's crucifixion. Its vigorously ancient expressive character memorializes the First Pope's death in Rome with its initial construction by the royal house of Spain, an ancient Roman province, with probable sponsorship by the Spanish Pope Alexander VI Borgia (1492–03). Nicholas V (1447–55) initiated a recrudescence of antiquity that Julius II (1503–13) fulfilled with the BASILICA OF SAINT PETER, VATICAN, 1506–1614ff, another Bramante project.

We show the dome's original spring line and delete the escutcheon, two alterations from 1602, but do show the 1638 stairs in the back that gave pilgrims access to the crypt where Peter's cross had stood in the Earth.

A three-step stylobate supports a colonnade of sixteen Roman Doric column shafts, doubtless spolia, with the canonic order's ornament displaying not ancient motifs but Eucharistic instruments. The double bottle balusters' wide spacing suggests that balustrade blocks are missing.

The relationship between the interior and exterior and both to the colonnade reveal Bramante contribution of providing revealing interior-exterior

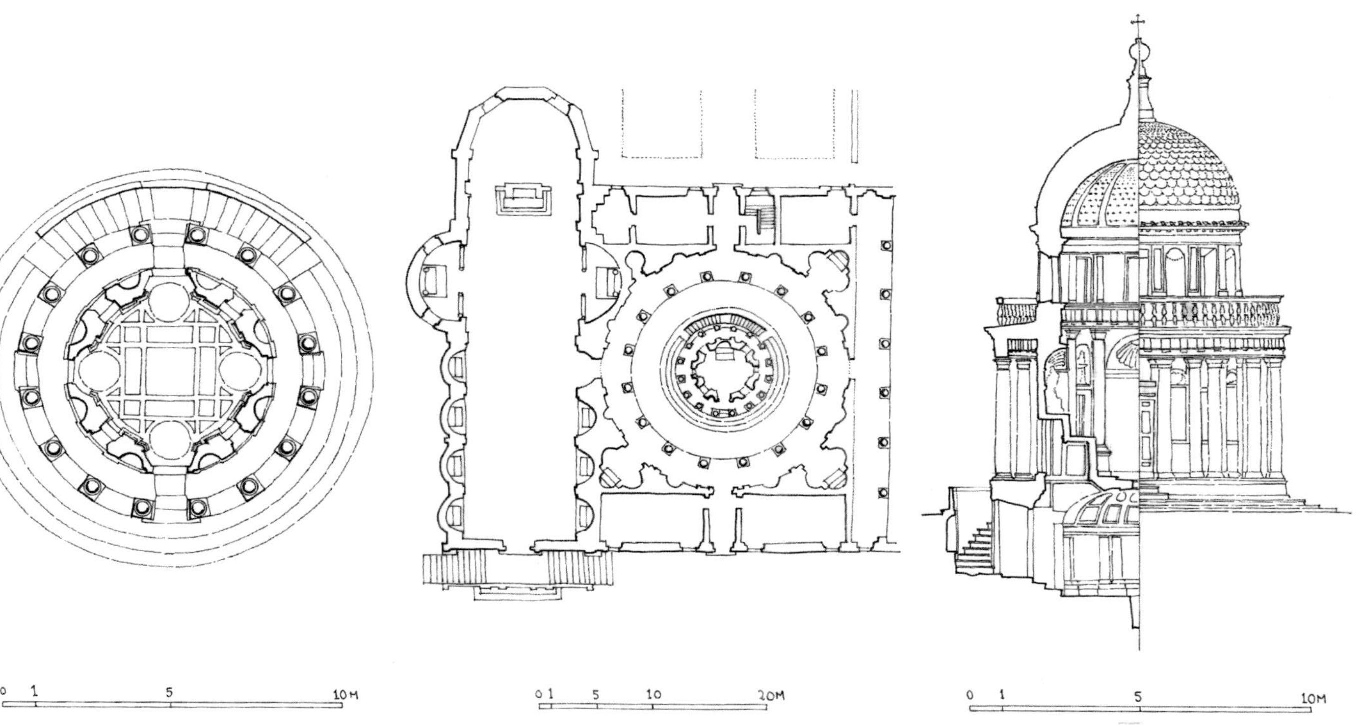

FIGURE 5.8 Tempietto di San Pietro in Montorio, Donato Bramante, Rome, Italy, 1502? 1505–06?

three-dimensional relationships in the fabric. On the two-story cella's face, the columns become pilasters. Between them, windows, some made to red with some made blind, alternate with niches; the upper level's are equipped with shell heads like those found in some ancient buildings. Inside we see a Cosmati floor, and on both levels, we see the exterior's A-B-A alternation of pilasters and niches or windows.

Sebastiano Serlio's 1540 treatise, which explains how to apply perspective to architectural masses, presented four images, placing them among the "ancient buildings in Rome" with images of other recent buildings and called "modern things." Placing it between the PANTHEON, HADRIAN, ROME, 117–26 and the Mausoleum of Romulus, two tholos temples fronted by temple fronts and in a courtyard, perhaps suggest that his colonnade replaces their temple fronts and accounts for his courtyard drawing, although the dimensions of its courtyard would not have allowed it to have been built as shown. That drawing's intent was perhaps to reinforce Bramante's three-dimensionality, with the tholos' niches repeated on the periphery and the window panels becoming deep quatrefoil corner chapels. Furthermore, Mark Wilson Jones' measurements reveal, the design's proportionality is based on the surfaces of the orders and not the walls; that is, the orders are the basis of the design and not merely attached to walls. He further noted that the building's geometric proportionality is founded on "ancient and contemporary written texts, inherited medieval practices, and architects' measurements of ancient buildings. In using dimensions based on 10s and 6s Bramante was distilling the perfect numbers according to theory and precedent and binding the plan into a satisfying rational scheme."[3] It thereby imitated the *harmonia mundi* of the cosmos and illustrates Vitruvius's *symmetria* in Book III, chapter 1 (Figure 5.9).

Suleiman I (1494–1566), known in Turkey as The Legislator and in the West as The Magnificent, had a long reign (1520–66) during its golden age governing from Constantinople, the capital since 1453. This mosque is the most opulent among his many grand public works among hundreds throughout the empire including palaces, fortresses, roads and bridges, courts, caravanserais, mosques, baths, hospitals, markets, aqueducts, tunnels, fountains, etc. Its architect, Sinan (1488–89, or 1490–1588) was born to an Armenian or Greek family and drafted at an early age into the Janissary system where he rose rapidly within the large imperial military and construction bureaucracy, serving 50 years as Court Architect or *Hassa Mimar* (a Turkish corruption of the Arabic *Muammer*: builder).

Built on Beyazit Hill, one of the seven hills of Istanbul overlooking the Golden Horn, the towering mosque and minarets display its prime importance. The mosque dominates the vast religious complex (*külliye*) with madrasas, a hospital, baths, kitchens, shops, Sinan's house and residences for other staff, and a cemetery; only a portion is shown here. In the forecourt on the entrance axis stands the octagonal mausoleum for Suleiman and Roxana followed by the

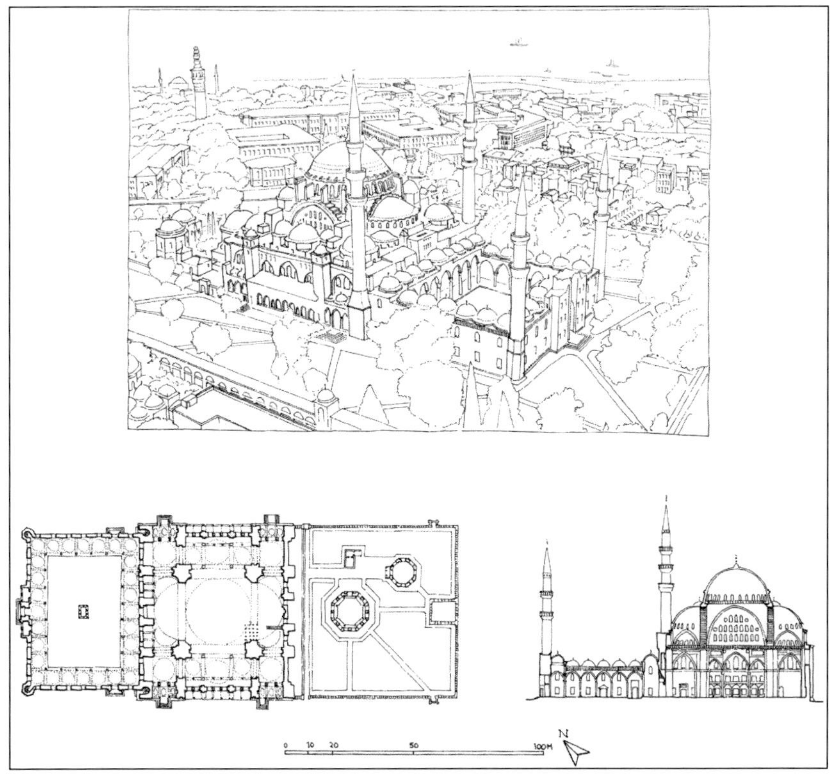

FIGURE 5.9 Suleymanie Mosque, Sinan, Istanbul, Turkey, 1550–57.

mosque and a final courtyard. Two short, fluted minarets flank the courtyard, and two taller ones rise from within the mosque's entrance wall. The obligatory ablution fountain, used in the purificatory rites that precede prayers, stands free within the arcaded courtyard, nine bays by seven, each bay with four slightly pointed arches carrying domes on pendentives.

Outside and in, the mosque owes obvious debts to Justinian's **Hagia Sophia, Isidore of Miletus and Anthemius of Tralles, 532–7, dome later heightened** built in Constantine's new Rome. After 1453 it became a mosque and prototype for many mosques, with the agglomeration of domes producing a quite compact "pyramidal" configuration. The two structure's principal domes have similar dimensions, here a 28 m diameter and 53 m height vs. 31 and 55. Unlike other mosques, two half domes here are added to the axis from the entrance to the *qibla* wall. The slightly pointed arches have bichromatic voussoirs.

The subdued interior decoration that includes brilliant *isnik* tiles culminates in the dome's apex. Light is diffused through the greater number of openings and intensified by the smooth stereotomy and wall surfaces. Monolithic porphyry column shafts stand before the cross-axial bays and inside the entrance to the courtyard. *Muqarnas* form the pendentives of the interior's lower domes and are used for most column capitals, while a few others carry exquisite Turkish triangle capitals (Figure 5.10).

FIGURE 5.10 Hall of Private Audiences (or Diwan-el-Khas), Fatehpur Sikri, India, 1571–85.

This odd tholos served the curious purpose of a wise ruler who venerated the wisdom of religious belief and sought synchronism between various beliefs through discussions with professors of Hinduism, Buddhism, Zoroastrianism, Christianity, Sunni Islam, and in particular, the Sufi tradition in Shia Islam. They squabbled for years, he dismissed them, and he then composed his own synthesis, the *Din-al-Ilahi* (The Religion Divine, 1582). He also established Hindustani as a blend of Urdu, Persian, and Arabic. And he expanded and established centralized imperial rule within the Indian subcontinent's Mughal Empire, the first to do so since Ashoka (268–232 BCE).

This enlightened emperor was Abul-Fath Jalal-ud-din Muhammad Akbar the Great (1542–1605), the third with that title. A descendent of Tamerlane and Genghis Khan, he ascended the throne at age 13. In 1569, he founded a capital, Fatehpur Sikri (Sikri, the town of victory), but with an inadequate water supply and insecure military conditions; he relocated his capital northward to Delhi in 1586.

In the Hall of Private Audiences in Sikri, Akbar conducted philosophical and religious debates with invited religious scholars while enthroned at the center of a cube beneath a quadripartite domed ceiling. His platform stands on a circular array of 36 brackets fanning out, like the branches of a tree, around the upper half of a central monolithic column whose shaft moves from a double cube to octagonal to round. His perch is reached by walkways from corners of the circumvallating balcony carried on brackets with large clusters in the corners and reached by stairs in two opposite corners. All this is equipped with low, perforated sidewalls.

The Hall was located near his private quarters in one of the city's several large courts. A free-standing, two-story cube 15 m on a side has a tall *chhatri* ("canopy" or "umbrella") on each corner. Made of local red sandstone like most of the city, it conveys its high status by being free-standing and much more ornate. Raised on a short base, the facades on both stories have five bays of recessed panels with a single entrance below three upper-story central windows. Bracket clusters carry a peripheral balcony; brackets lesser in size and quantity carry the projecting eaves below a parapet. The planned internal cupola was never built. The solid appearance of the walls and brackets is somewhat softened by the balcony railing's delicate pattern and the *chhatris'* light and elongated silhouettes (Figure 5.11).

Jules Hardouin-Mansart built this great tholos for Louis XIV as his burial place among his troops, who were accommodated in the great *hôtel* he built to lodge 4,000 veterans. Louis later chose to join the other French kings at Saint-Denis, and in 1840, King Louis Phillipe prepared it for Napoleon (not shown).

The veterans' *hôtel's* two stories of pier arcades in its many courtyards include their cubicles and support facilities. Their residents were required to attend a service every day in the basilical Cathedral of Saint-Louis-des-Invalides at the base of the Cour d'Honneur. Commanding the configuration here is an axis, like the

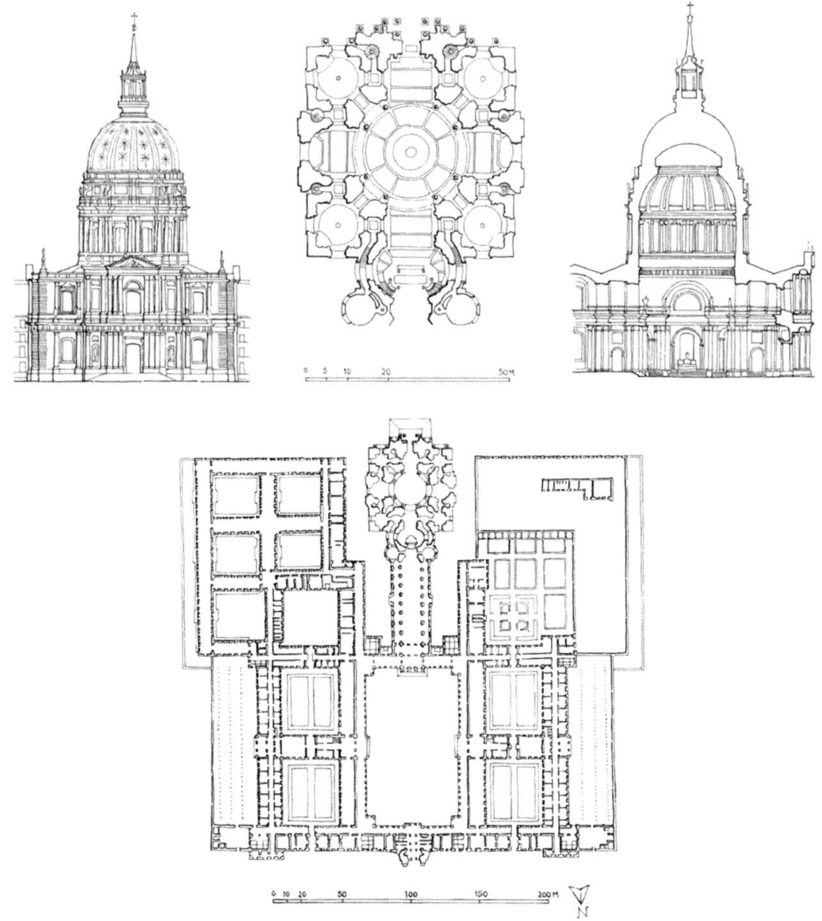

FIGURE 5.11 (a) Dôme des Invalides, Jules Hardouin-Mansart, c. 1677–79 and (b) Hôtel des Invalides, Libéral Bruant, Paris, France, 1670–76.

one from the Louvre into the Tuileries and beyond, this one running from the river's 196 m front through an esplanade, court, and basilica to reach the DÔME DES INVALIDES, which had its own, later forecourt (not shown).

The **Dôme** rises to 107 m from a corpus based on the unbuilt **Francois Mansart, Bourbon Mausoleum, Saint-Denis** using a French, diagonal-axis *parti* found at the **Chapel, Philibert de l'Orme, Anet, 1547–52** and Gian Lorenzo Bernini's (unbuilt) variation on the TEMPIETTO, BRAMANTE, ROME, 1502. Large chapels on the diagonal axes and a larger pair on the cross axes fill a square. The interior's surfaces are richly decorated, ornamented, gilded, and frescoed, and the high altar chapel is shared with the basilica's high altar chapel. Free-standing Corinthian columns following the interior's circle stand free supporting the engaged entablature beneath pendentives. Abundant light streams in through the tall drum followed by a dome whose wide oculus reveals *The Apotheosis of Saint Louis* lit by the attic's invisible light source.

Its 107 m height still stands proud in Paris' skyline. Its flat front presents a wall that is the normative basis for French membrature. It begins at the corners and moves inward with three projections, each with pairs of orders, Doric below Corinthian, with the outer pair becoming pilasters on the upper level where the central, foremost pairs carry a pediment. All this is radically abbreviated on the sides.

The tall superstructure above the wall's middle section begins with a tall drum acting as a third story. Composed with an A-B-A sequence, the As on the diagonal axes are given a solitary window framed by pairs of Composite columns engaged to pier buttresses, and the Bs given a pair of windows separated by a pair of pilasters. The pier buttresses have volutes rising between the attic's windows that alternate with pilasters. ***Pots-de-feu*** ring the dome's spring where gilded ribs reach a tall gilded metallic square lantern with column clusters on the major axes and finally a spire, ball, and cross (Figure 5.12).

After Bavaria freed itself from Napoleon's France in 1807, the Crown Prince and later King Ludwig I (r. 1825–68), spurred by beliefs about Germany's roots in ancient Greece, set about to make Munich a "German Athens." Earlier, this belief about the Greeks had produced the Greek basis for the **Brandenburg**

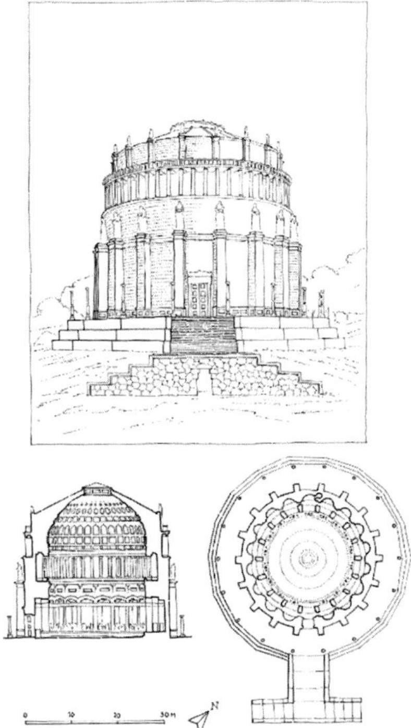

FIGURE 5.12 Befreigunshalle, After Leo Von Klenze, Near Kelheim, Bavaria, 1842.

Gate, Carl Langhans, Berlin, 1788–91. Now, the centerpiece of Munich would be **Karl von Fischer and Leo von Klenze, Königsplatz, 1815** with buildings on three sides, with delayed construction: **von Klenze, Glypothek, 1816**, Ionic; facing **Antiquities collection, Georg Friedrich Ziebland, 1869**, Corinthian; and **von Klenze, Propylaea, Munich, 1846–60**, Doric. Ludwig would also commission three structures to celebrate important Germans: the collection of pan-German notables at the **Walhalla, von Klenze, near Regensburg, 1830** but conceived in 1807; the **Ruhmeshalle, von Klenze, Munich, 1843, Munich**, conceived in 1813 for great Bavarians; and the **Befreiungshalle, Friedrich von Gärtner and, after his death, von Klenze, Kelheim, 1842**. After Bavaria assisted the Greeks in gaining independence from the Ottoman Empire, the Greek connection was solidified when Ludwig's second son Otto was made King of Greece, and Bavaria helped pay for the **Gärtner, Royal Palace, Athens, 1836**.

The BEFREIUINGUSHALLE celebrates Napoleon's defeat in the 1813–15 wars that assured Bavaria's independence. Von Klenze's richly polychromatic design comes from the recent discovery of color in ancient Greek buildings, which, during his apprenticeship under C. Percier and P-F-L. Fontaine in Paris was a topic of extensive debate among that pair, A-C. Quatremère de Quincy, J-I. Hittorff, and others. This round, yellow, stone building perched above the Danube rises three registers from a polygonal base. The first, very tall one has eighteen wall buttresses capped by tall statues representing various Germanic tribes. Above its cornice, a peripheral gray stone Doric colonnade with a triglyph frieze stands before a graceful walkway. The concluding attic features deep pilasters supporting suits of armor breaking the silhouette. Visible only from a great distance is a shallow metal conical dome with an oculus.

A double-ramp stair and single broad stair with the date 1863, the liberation's 50th anniversary, leads to the single framed entrance where the stark exterior gives way to the interior's solemn yet celebratory character. Here as in ancient temples, the only illumination is from above. Counterparts to the exterior's eighteen bays are semicircular niches with segmental heads. On the dais, before each stands a pair of goddesses of victory by Ludwig Schwanthaler, most made of Carrara marble, hand in hand in front of each niche's gilded shields, ostensibly made from melted weapons.

The interior polychromy includes a marble *opere di commessi* floor and red-walled niches whose fronts have gray piers holding segmental arches. A peach-colored marble frieze with placards follows an ambulatory behind a Tuscan colonnade of rose columns beneath the hemispherical dome springing from the level of the exterior colonnade's base. Its intrados rises through seven layers of coffers, each tier different, and some gilded (Figure 5.13a and 5.13b).

This tomb of modern China's founder stresses the new nation's continuity with dynastic China and its connection with the west. In 1912, the medical doctor Sun Yat-sen (1866–1925), attempting to unify and reform a fractious nation, briefly became the first "provisional president" of Nationalist China. Lü Yanzhi

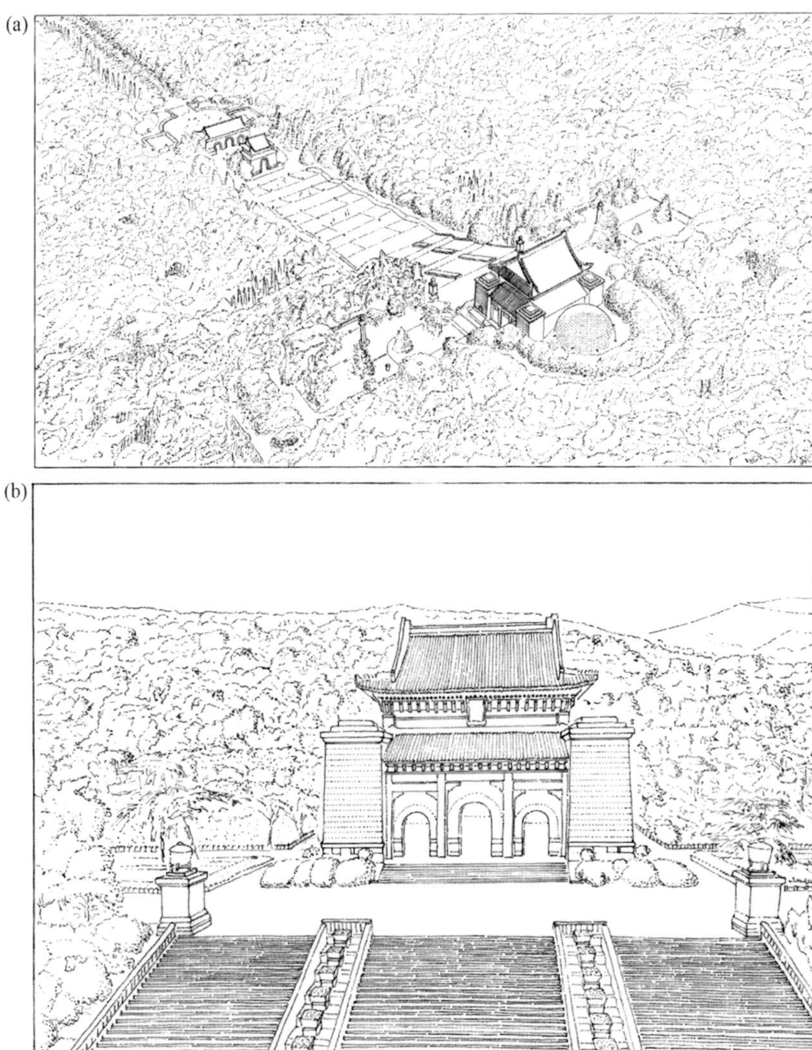

FIGURE 5.13 Mausoleum of Sun Yat-Sen, Lü Yanzhi, Nanjing, China, 1926.

(1894–1929) won the design competition for his tomb. With a mechanical engineering degree from Cornell, in 1918 Lü began working in the New York office of Henry K. Murphy and Henry R. Dana, where an "Oriental Department" handled Murphy's expanding work in Asia. In late 1920 or 1921, he moved to the firm's Shanghai office, and Lü established his independent practice in 1921.

His mausoleum competition entry for the Mount Zijin site wedded traditional Ming tombs, instituted by the first Ming emperor (1368–98), with the LINCOLN MEMORIAL, HENRY BACON, WASHINGTON, 1914–22 and its setting in the **McMillan plan, Daniel H. Burnham et al, Washington, 1902**. It acknowledged Sun's admiration for Lincoln and Washington and to traditional Chinese urbanism that modeled the cosmos while positioning Sun's body like that of an emperor's on the tholos-tomb on the tholos throne in the HALL OF SUPREME HARMONY, BEIJING, 1406.

It occupies a wooded site near the base of Mount Zijin, beginning at a large plaza with a memorial linteled gateway (*torana*) initiating a 350 m path that eventually enters our drawing. A broad range of steps leads up to the memorial plaza whose original design would have been shaped like a ritual bell, but a rectilinear plan with curved corners was substituted. Here we meet a gateway structure with firm corner piers and an attached *torana* on the front beneath a blue-tiled two-step flared-eave roof with heavenly messengers. Close beyond comes the obligatory Tablet Pavilion with a single arch on each face and a roof like the entrance arch's, a square tholos holding specially made traditional characters memorializing the achievements of the interred.

From here steps, 392 of them, move 300 m up the hill in three parallel streams lined by forest rather than the traditional Ming tomb's kneeling officials or animals. After rising slowly and spreading out, the steps eventually gathered more closely in three flights climbing the steeper slope and, like those at the HALL OF SUPREME HARMONY, have two narrow inaccessible runs and the other three, unlike those in Beijing, open to all.

They reach the summit's square with a Ceremonial Hall that we picture with massive corner towers again enclosing *torana* framing arches (Lü called it a "fortress") and covered by a tall, blue-tile two-tiered, flared-eave roof. In its capacious interior hall is a seated statue of Sun and inscriptions declaiming his achievements, a design which evokes the LINCOLN MEMORIAL, while its diluted masonry calls to mind the imperial HALL OF SUPREME HARMONY, but with the star representing post-Qing China rather than the *Xuanyuan Jing* seen in the ceiling in Beijing. Immediately beyond the statue is Sun's sarcophagus, with his recumbent effigy on its top beneath the star of China visible from a parapet at the dome's spring within the small, low dome of the Mortuary Chamber tholos, partially sunken into the Earth.

Variation 2: the composite of tholos and temple

A complex dedicated to the oracle of Apollo in Ionian Didyma was under the protection of Miletus (Figure 5.14). Two predecessors were destroyed before Alexander the Great freed the region from the Persians in 334 BCE and began this marble replacement. (See THRONE HALL OF 100 COLUMNS, PERSEPOLIS, 518–460 BCE). Still incomplete when imperial Rome incorporated the territory, temples and other buildings were built near it.

The most complex, and among the largest, temples in ancient Greece, ten Ionic columns in two-deep rows across the front and 21 down each side support

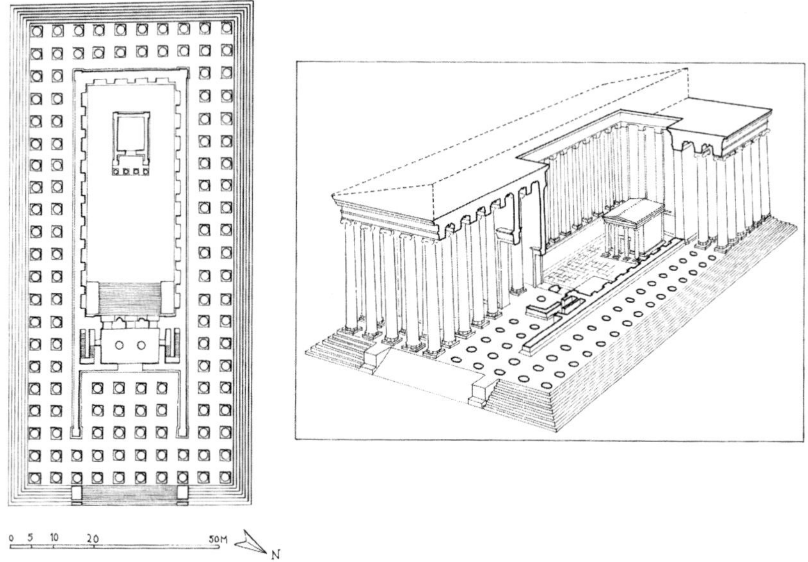

FIGURE 5.14 Tholos and Temple of Apollo, Didyma, in Turkey, 334 BCE.

a flat roof (with dots we suggest a conjectural pitched roof). They rise from a seven-step crepidoma with twice that number carved into its central section to reach its pronaos beyond the second row of columns where antae enclose a 4 × 3 column field. Decoration includes medusa heads in the frieze and meander, guilloche, laurel, gods, etc. carved in the bases of some columns.

The wall beyond the column field has only one opening, placed high up, perhaps to make visible a ritual on a platform seen against the open sky. Tunnels in the antae walls' thickness begin a downward slope that either bypass or lead into a rectangular chamber at the crepedomo level beneath a platform supported on a pair of Corinthian columns, with another pair of half-columns on a wall fragment facing the court. From the crepidoma's surface, fourteen steps lead down into the court or unroofed cella. Enclosed by walls rising 46 feet, it is lined with pilasters whose capitals are elaborately decorated with griffins and flowers and are aligned not with the exterior's columns but with their intercolumniations. Within the court were a spring, a laurel tree, ramps, stairs, and other elements, and at the far end a small temple, a tholos shrine with a cult statue of Apollo. Only conjecture now relates how the cult rituals were performed here (Figure 5.15).

After his conversion to Christianity, Emperor Constantine drew on the full catalog of Roman architecture to serve this religion. In Jerusalem, the Holy Sepulcher (*Anastasis*) and Rock of Calvary were discovered beneath the pagan temple built by Hadrian, and in 335 Constantine built this *martyrium* precinct there for celebration and veneration. We present a hypothetical reconstruction

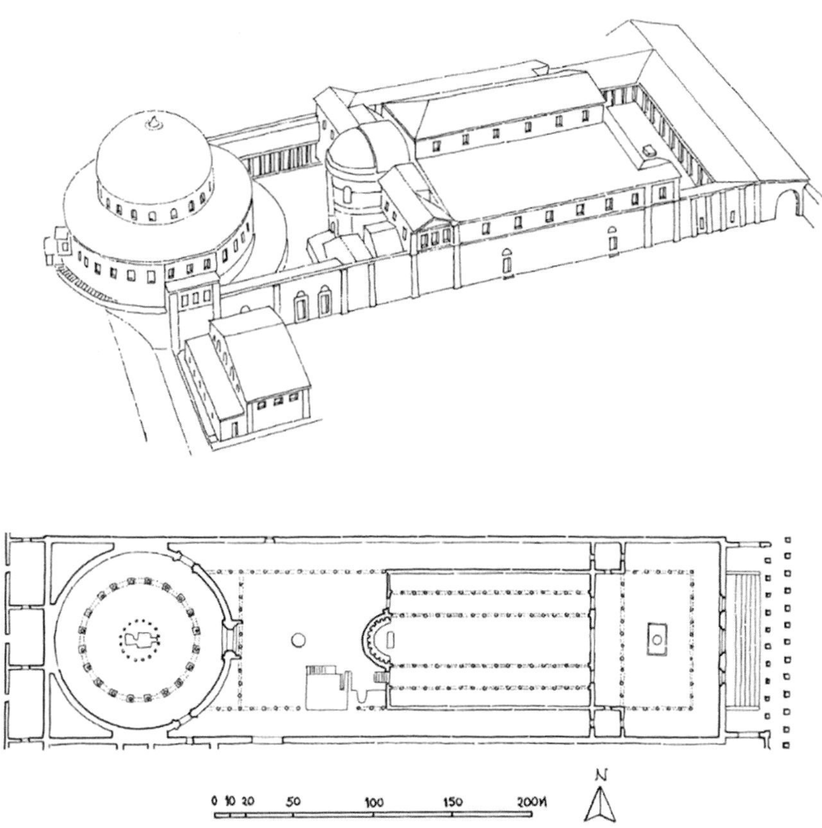

FIGURE 5.15 Church of the Holy Sepulchre, Jerusalem, 326–35.

of what the Persians destroyed with fire in 614. In 630, Heraclius rebuilt it; subsequently, major damage by nature and man and the competition for control by various Christian groups have left little of the original fabric. Its present state is largely the result of an extensive reconstruction in 1811.

While pagans gathered for various activities in a hypostyle, Christians converted the basilica configuration to a temple type, seen here serving carefully choreographed, ritual celebratory events organized along an axis, and still used today.

Beyond a two-deep colonnaded entrance and a few steps stands a colonnaded atrium 130 feet wide. Pavilions in its far corners open to passages leading along the basilica's exterior. Between them stretches the narthex with a colonnade front and three portals giving access to the five-aisle basilica with galleries and a wider, higher nave. The nave's cross section is reduced slightly for transept arms, with the nave extending beyond them to the semicircular apse beneath a semi-dome with seats for the presiders. Lavish interior decoration and ornament included marble columns, gilded capitals with silver capitals in the crossing, and coffered ceilings painted in gold, while the exterior's marble walls were polished, and the roof's bronze tiles were gilded.

The exterior's side passages extend into colonnades beside a square courtyard, perhaps with a colonnade across its back wall. The courtyard is also accessible from the basilica's inner side aisles. The courtyard presents the major entrance to this important site; another entrance is in each colonnade. Within this tholos' massive walls the Tomb and Site of the Resurrection (*Anastasis*) were available for veneration. Twenty columns surrounded it, and twenty more with a second story form an ambulatory and carry a low drum with windows and a dome, constituting a very large baldacchino for this most holy site (Figure 5.16).

This is the best-preserved and most striking structure within a precinct in Karnataka (formerly Mysore) with seven shrines and ancillary structures devoted to related gods. Called the Durga Temple, it offered protection and fortification (*Druga*) for a temple dedicated to either Vishnu (protector of the cosmos) or Shiva (soul of the universe) or both.

Built between the 6th and 8th centuries when experimentation with plans and stone construction was occurring, it stands on a high base with a parapet of the peristyle walkway that is reached by opposed stairs serving the ritual

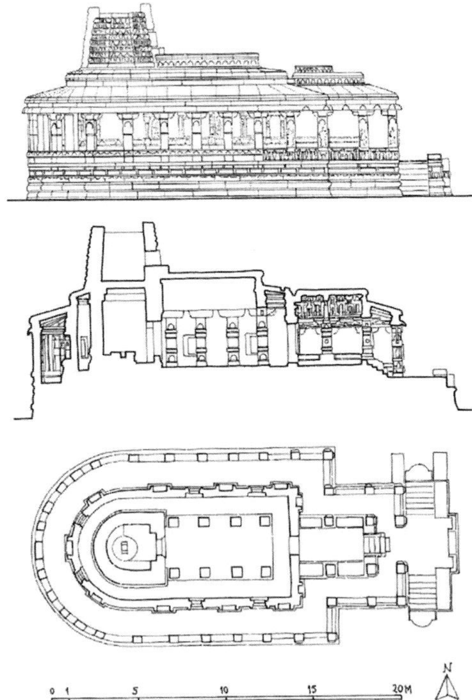

FIGURE 5.16 Durga Temple, Aihiole, India, 6th c.–8th c.

clockwise circumambulation that is part of individual worship. A few steps lead up to the four-column temple pronaos that, like one pier at the back, the inner wall of the peristyle, the porch before it, the entrance within it, and the temple's interior, is profuse with the sculpture of Hindu gods and goddesses.

The hall's ceiling vault is carried on a pier colonnade with an interior ambulatory beyond it with four grilled openings admitting light. The interior terminates in an apsidal tholos familiar from the *chaitya* of later Buddhist rock-cut temples but was an earlier indigenous Hindu feature. It is now bereft of the cult image, but here it is combined with a now truncated feature of Hindu temples, the richly ornamented *shikhara* (mountain peak) tower. We do not show the *amalaka*, the segmented, notched, terminal disk, intact on the ground but lacking its *kalasam* (finial).

With every surface important in worship supercharged with sculpture, this temple's expressive character resides there rather than in stone's exhibition of the arts of building and of architecture except for some incised moldings and forms of capitals and bases (Figure 5.17).

Nara had been made Japan's first permanent imperial seat in 710 (it served until 794), and when the Emperor Shōmu (r. 724–49) was shifting his authority from a warlike to a religious basis he commissioned eight temples and the "Cosmic Buddha," the largest bronze Buddha statue in the world, still extant with various repairs. The eighth temple was built within a large precinct with a pair of 100 m tall pagodas (no longer extant) south of the Great South Gateway (rebuilt with Chinese *Daibutsuyō* construction, rare in Japan, after its destruction in 1199 by a hurricane). Immediately it became a large administrative center for religion and education. The temple was twice destroyed by fire; we show the present one from 1709 that is seven by seven bays, until recently the largest wooden building in the world, even though smaller than the original eleven by eleven bay building.

The temple's grid of 60 columns in three squares places the Buddha statue where four columns have been deleted behind a low circular railing extending on each side into squares where Buddha's two fierce protectors stand guard in smaller circles. The eight columns within Buddha's circle are nearly 5 feet in diameter and 100 feet tall.

In traditional Japanese post-and-lintel tectonics, the expressive character hardly distinguishes between interior and exterior, although here the structural members inside are cinnabar red while those outside are timber colored. The posts support lintels that are supplemented by projecting brackets notched into them and carry additional cross pieces, as many as seven directly above the statue, before reaching flat ceilings. At two levels some beams extend as rafters for the blue-tile double-pitch curved-eave roof, with the ridges of scalloped tiles ending in cast *onigawara* displaying low relief decoration. The tectonic system's redundancy and the work of the joints offer earthquake resistance and a combined tectonic and formal clarity.

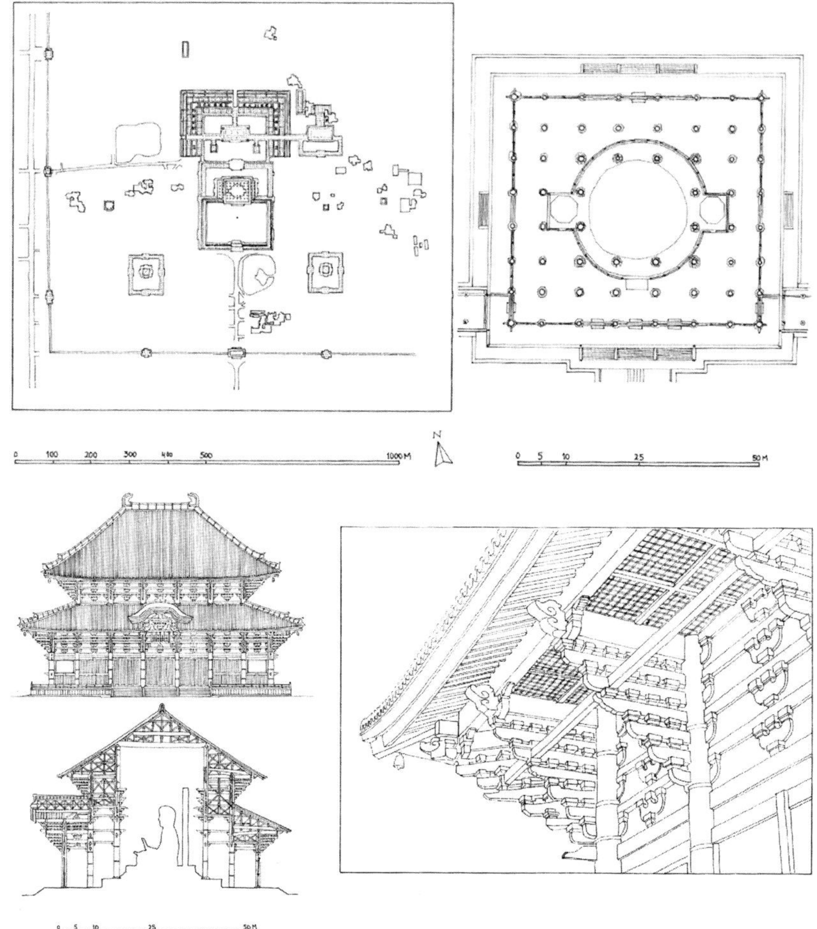

FIGURE 5.17 Todai-Ji Temple, Nara, Japan, 743–52.

Three groups of stairs in the center of the platform's south and north faces lead to the three entrances, while the other two have single stairs and entrances. A canopy above the central, southern portal extends into the roof (the ridge horns are later). The entrances have doors while the other bays have white quadrated panels set within the intercolumniations; above, within the cross beams and bracket edges, are white panels.

The bracket sets rise and push out to reach the roof and extended corners, but note that the beams intersecting at the corners where the roof eaves lift upward are thicker than the same beams over the central portal. This gives the bracket system's upward-lifting eaves an added tensile character, and it clearly indicates that in the expressive character of Japanese architecture, the system is an idealization of a tree's branch network and of tents. Something similar is in Chinese and Korean architecture (Figure 5.18).

FIGURE 5.18 Cathedral of our Lady of Chartres, Chartres, 1134–1270; 1507.

This church, which occupies iconic status within Gothic architecture, has housed an important Marian relic since the 9th c. that has led devoted pilgrims to finance its many reconstructions. The double-towered west end with the *Portail royal* was begun in 1134; it survived a fire in 1194 with the present enlarged building begun then, still without the planned transept towers and spire over the crossing. A lightning strike damaged the liturgical south tower, and it was simplified when rebuilt in 1507–13.

The nave and transept entrance porches introduce the interior's splendor. Each has a triumphal arch with deep jambs holding hosts of Old Testament figures and tympanums with New Testament content in the tympanums, all intended to provide an entry into this earthly substitute for the heavenly City of God. Thee, along with some pier buttresses equipped with pedimented aedicules holding figures, the exterior is a mere container for the interior, its membrature including three tiers of flying buttress with stout, columnar arcades connecting the lower pair.

The radiant interior features the famed colored glass (most from 1205–49) portraying Biblical stories and ordinary people at work. The nave's rose shows Christ as Judge, and the transept roses show Mary and Christ. A two-bay tholos labyrinth for pilgrims is in the nave's pavement. The important cathedral school here stressed the symbolic content of proportionality and light, components of the beauty here satisfy the criteria of Thomas Aquinas (1225–74): integrity or perfection of the thing; proper proportion or harmony; and "clarity – thus things which have glowing color are said to be beautiful."

The plan merges the temple of a basilical church with a tholos in the crossing with the altar within the enclosed choir (no longer extant and not shown). The usual three-aisle basilica is enlarged to five aisles beyond the crossing, making the radiating, half-circular chapels easily accessible for pilgrimages. Each transept projects one additional bay, and two additional western bays serve as vestibules. Nave and transept bays are 1 × 2 rectangles with square half bays in the aisles. Beyond the four choir bays, the seven bays in the semicircular choir follow a half circle and open to chapels, all with cross vaults using the complicated geometry that pointed ribs make buildable.

Elsewhere the vaults are quadripartite with pointed ribs rising from colonnettes. The diagonal ribs start at the tops of the nave arcade's stout piers while the cross ribs and the nave arcades' larger ones rise from the floor. The piers' cross sections show a round core with octagonal colonnettes alternating with octagonal core and round colonnettes, perhaps intended to recall earlier square-bay schemes. The colonnettes rise through the triforium and clerestory without the usual gallery, making an elevation that is higher and has larger clerestory windows. The colonnettes are pinned to the sills by a thin, rounded string course giving a horizontal stress, while the membrature provides a clear scansion of ratios: a single nave bay supports four triforium arches, and the clerestory holds two arches each with a single, eight-lobe circular window; in the aisles, a bay holds a single lancet (Figure 5.19).

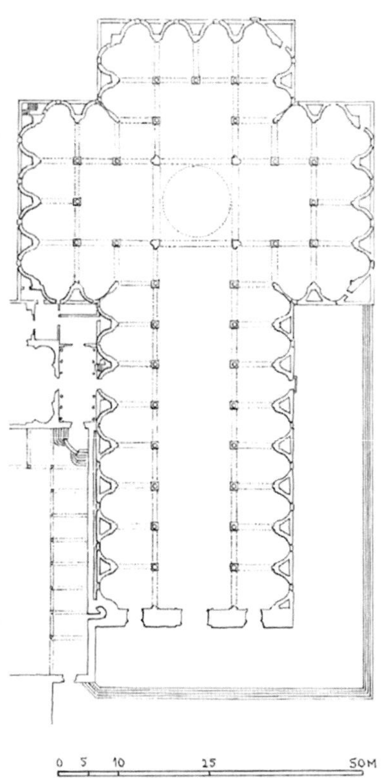

FIGURE 5.19 Santo Spirito, Filippo Brunelleschi, Florence, Italy, 1428? 1434?

In his earlier, three-aisle transeptal church, **San Lorenzo, Florence, 1419**, Filippo Brunelleschi (1377–46) was completing the work of others. Here he was working *ex novo* to replace an Augustinian church, the center of one of Florence's four quarters, that fire had destroyed. He died before it was finished, but it is accepted as his with few changes.

He made it an enlarged version of **Santi Apostoli, Florence, 11th c.**, a miniaturized, early Christian basilica, using the membrature he had explored in Rome and was visible at two 11th c. Florentine buildings that were thought to be ancient, the **Baptistery** and **San Miniato al Monte, 11th c.** Using perspectival design, he integrated their classical apparatus of forms into a coherent tectonic structure that made visible the otherwise invisible order, harmony, and proportionality of God's creation.

Above the nave arcade with fluted Corinthian columns and above similar, higher piers run a high entablature that at the crossing carries arches with pendentives and an umbrella dome. (The building's 1601 baldachin is excluded from our drawing.) The arcade produces tall 1 × 2 bays with pairs extending axially from the crossing, making a centralized, Greek cross tholos. Five liturgical western bays lead to an additional one that would have been two aisle bays serving as a vestibule, but an uncanonical central column and door apparently prevented its being built (we do not show it).

The side aisles are covered by sail vaults (handkerchief domes), with the arcade reproduced on the enclosing wall with engaged columns. Between them are the half-circular frames for the hemi domed chapels. Light enters here through a small window above each chapel's altarpiece (most of the smaller originals have been replaced by later, larger ones), arched like the chapel's entrance and like the clerestory's frames admitting light to the nave and Greek cross.

The clerestory's height from the ceiling down to the frieze topping the arcade is half the distance from there to the floor. Further interlocking proportioning is presented in the floor's tile pavement, where strips of the membrature's darker stone run down the nave's center and across to opposite columns. Five rows of coffers, each with a rosette, complete the ceiling.

Brunelleschi's chapels produced scalloped exteriors, but the indentations collected trash and worse, and were filled with only the swelling window frames remaining visible. His intentions for the west façade are unknown, but it is well known that he proposed reversing the church's orientation to face a piazza open down to the river, and it would surely have had a façade (Figure 5.20).

Leon Battista Alberti (1404–72) began this church in 1470 for Ludovico III Gonzaga, a condottiere ennobled by the Holy Roman Emperor. Ecclesiastically a Minor Basilica, it shelters the Blood Christ lost during the Crucifixion that was collected by the Roman soldier Saint Longinus and deposited in Mantua. The massive configuration has its parentage in the **Basilica of Maxentius and Constantine, 301–12, Rome**, and its composition with the ancient motifs of triumphal arch, temple front, and barrel vault successfully evoke antiquity. The nave was largely complete by 1500, but Alberti's intentions for the rest are not beyond dispute. We show the probable transepts and half-domed apse but not the likely drumless done or the great **Drum and Dome, Filippo Juvarra, 1732**.

Mantua, rich in clay, poor in stone, and marshy, traditionally built with the stucco and terra cotta with stucco still lacking on one exterior transept façade; the interior's surfaces are not original.

Crimping the porch's width is an earlier Benedictine monastery's campanile. The porch's face in low relief terra cotta limning synthesizing a Corinthian temple front and a triumphal arch: the temple front's entablature and pediment are carried by pilasters elevated on plinths, and the triumphal arch's A-B-A sequence uses a tall arch carried on piers with three-story, single-bay flankers with low, square-framed openings below two stacked, arched niches. The central arch springs from an entablature that runs across the wall with modified canonic parts: the frieze cants in to let the cornice stand proud and keep it behind the temple front's pilasters. From the porch runs a vault to the marble-framed portal with transverse vaults lower down.

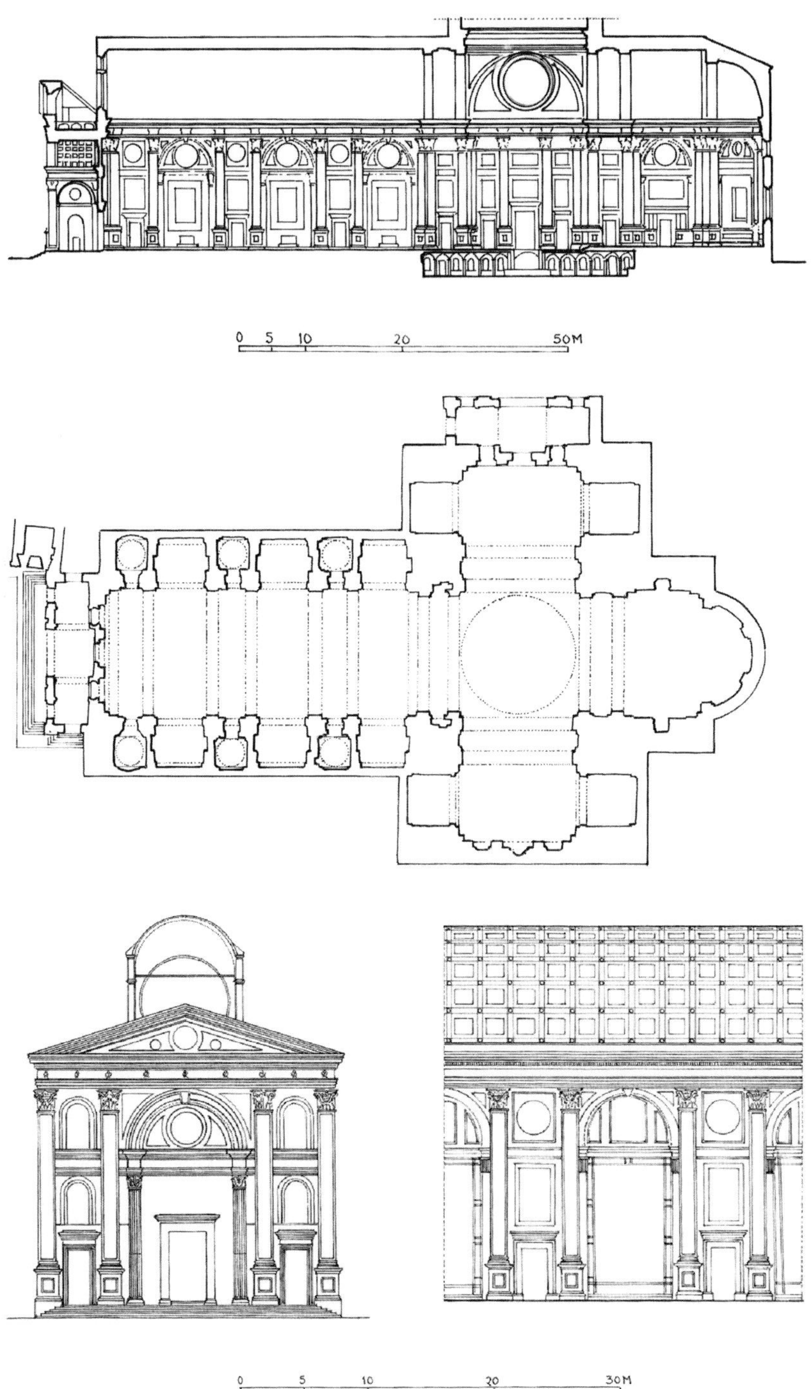

FIGURE 5.20 Sant'Andrea, Leon Battista Alberti, Mantova, Italy, 1470.

The faces of the cavernous nave repeat the façade's A-B-A sequence three times, without overlapping As. The large B arches open to barrel-vaulted chapels, and the linteled As to a lower, domed chapel, with a round window above it letting light directly into the nave. At the crossing, four massive piers repeat the nave's final A on each face, with transepts using a B but no companion A. The stilted barrel vault with fictive coffers is strengthened by buttresses rising between the low chapels.

Conspicuous geometric ratios include the façade fitting in a square; the 3:4 façade ratio without the pediment, the 3 × 3 cross section, the 3:2 vault crown-to-nave height, etc. They resonate within the three-dimensional perspectival composition that further unifies the interior and exterior, with the facades' composition used inside and a common entablature height inside and out.

Stairs in the fabric (not shown) down to the crypt below the crossing facilitate veneration at the Holy Blood that on special festivals is displayed up above (beneath, we suppose, a drumless dome), the spot given the brightest light by shielding the nave's rose with the large, vaulted hood (in our elevation but not our section; note that others give other roles for this curious component; Figure 5.21).

In Milan, briefly the capital of the Christian Roman Empire, Donato Bramante built a small tholos-and-temple transeptal basilica whose perspectival composition produces an impressive ancient expressive character that extends the Romanism seen at SANT'ANDREA ALBERTI, MANTUA, 1470.

It began in 1478 as a parish church attachment to the tiny, 9th century tholos dedicated to Saint Ambrose's brother (see SANT'AMBROGIO, MILAN, 624) on a tight site with a cupola block and three bays on each side. While under construction the project was enlarged with the newly built section becoming transepts, the cupola enlarged to make the present tambour and dome carried by enlarged corner piers, and the addition of a four-bay barrel-vaulted nave with coffers and cross ribs and the fornix motif without pedestals along the sides. Along the nave's sides are aisles with ribbed quadripartite vaults and cross ribs, with another, similar aisle along the newly built transept's liturgical west side. The six-bay transept's east side is rendered in trompe-l'œil with chapels flanking entrances, appearing as the three-bay choir but actually perspectival rendering in stucco and paint less than a meter deep.

The interior originally had white walls with membrature and pendentives frescoed, sculpted, and gilded to make a dazzling display of saints, Evangelists, and Apostles brilliantly lit by many windows, many of them now blinded or reduced in size.

The west façade is from 1871, while the only other visible exterior, the east end's, shows the 400 fabric's brick, granite, terra cotta, and stucco displaying the three-dimensional structural integrity that Bramante would develop more fully in Rome. The two entrances use granite to frame their Tuscan columnar aedicules, while the granite base supports a brick wall with Corinthian pilasters suggesting the corresponding interior bays, and doubled and given *ressaults*

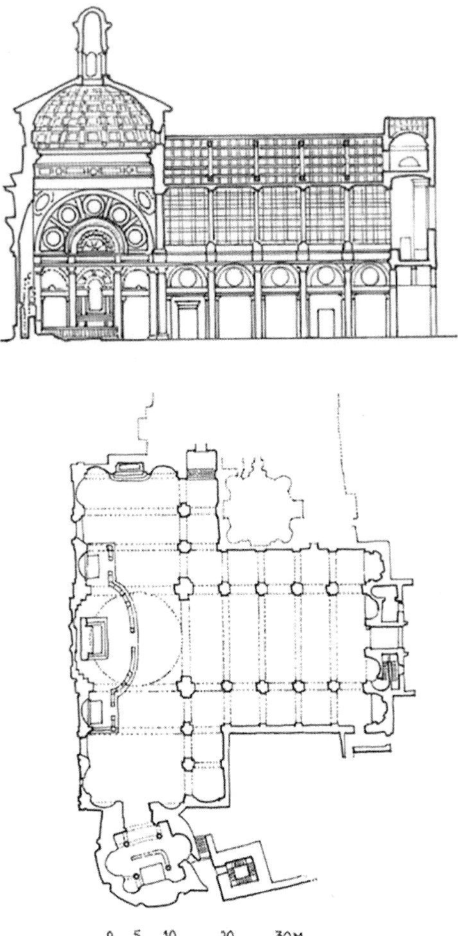

FIGURE 5.21 Santa Maria presso San Satiro, Donato Bramante, Milan, Italy, 1478.

at the ends. Their entablature carries a low attic below a hipped roof while the interior's fictive apse is contained within a slightly projecting pedimented section. Framing it are the crossing's robust piers reaching the properly sized entablature with the tambour with pilasters rising to a conical roof with a tall lantern characteristic of Lombardy.

San Celso was also restored with a distinctively Lombard role for terra cotta and stucco (Figure 5.22).

When in 1420 the papacy returned to Rome from its Babylonian Captivity, the city had become a desolate place with about 17,000 people. Nicholas V (1447–55) initiated a building campaign at the Vatican to present the Church

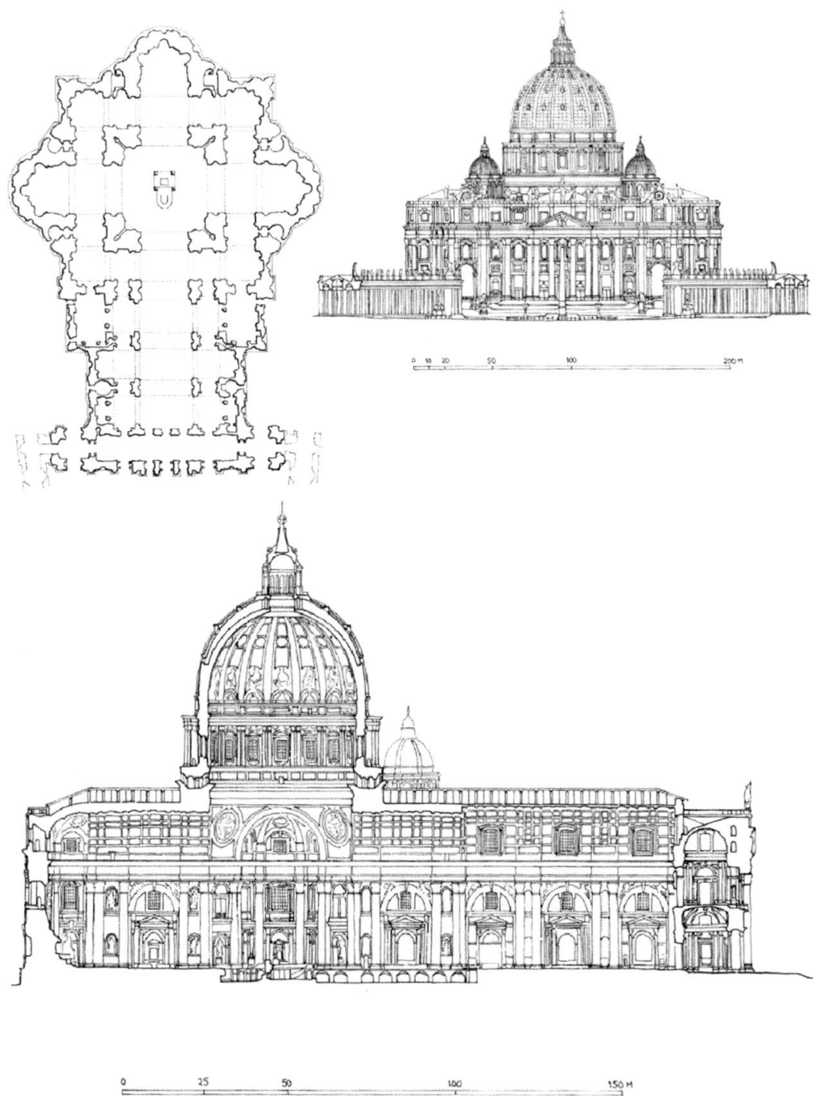

FIGURE 5.22 Saint Peter's Basilica, Alberti? 1447, Bramante, 1503; others: Michelangelo, 1546, Maderno, 1607, Rome, Italy. After Paul Letarouilly.

Universal as the successor to the ancient pagan empire and the Pope as head of the Church. He began rebuilding the Vatican Palace and the tottering **Early Christian Basilica of Constantine, c. 318** with the Tomb of the First Pope, in a project apparently involving Leon Battista Alberti intended to produce a tholos-temple whose expressive character would distinctly link the papacy to the ancient pagan empire it had superseded.

Little had emerged from the ground before Nicholas' death, and work lagged until Julius II (1503–13) had Donato Bramante (1444–1514) undertake an enlarged project. To be financed by selling indulgences, their doctrinal justification was challenged by the Augustinian monk Martin Luther. Julius's successors were not dissuaded, and like the period's energetic kings who were consolidating their holds on the emerging nation states, they staked their claim for autocratic governance.

Bramante's choir would use Nicholas' foundations, and the COLOSSEUM, 70 would supply the travertine just as it had done for centuries in Rome. For his great tholos, Julius had Michelangelo sculpt his tomb to be placed above Peter's, centered below a dome based on the **Pantheon, 117** atop a Greek cross whose arms were derived from the **Basilica of Maxentius and Constantine, 312**. Bramante had carried the work up through the great tholos' crossing arches, but the deaths of Julius and then Bramante were followed by the Reformation and the loss of Germany and England, making the Church not quite so Universal as before. But in 1546 Paul III Farnese (1534–49) threw caution and doubt to the wind and provided clear guidance to the aged Michelangelo for a renewed building campaign (Julius' tomb went elsewhere).

Michelangelo aggrandized Bramante's great tholos, simplifying its plan and consolidating his canted crossing piers to carry its columnar drum and dome, now ribbed, that Giacomo della Porta completed in 1590. Michelangelo had planned a pedimented tetrastyla façade before a row of ten columns. When Pope Paul V Borghese (1605–21) took up the project in 1607, he had Carlo Maderno (1556–1629) complete the covering of the sacred ground within Constantine's Basilica and the later atrium with a three-bay, three-aisle nave with membrature based on the Bramante-Michelangelo crossing piers. His narthex and façade, but not his towers, were completed in 1614 with the pope's family name, PAVLVS BVRGHESIVS ROMANUS above the portal. Still in the future were the two great works of **Gianlorenzo Bernini**, the **Baldachino, 1623** over the Tomb and altar, and the **Piazza di San Pietro, 1657**; its section is shown in our exterior elevation (Figure 5.23).

After 23 years Louis XIII's Queen, a Habsburg raised in Spain but known as Anne of Austria, conceived a son at a Benedictine convent, and in celebration of his birth, he commissioned an expanded convent with this church. France had only recently absorbed lessons from Italian architecture, and the commission went to François Mansart (1598–1666), France's most inventive classical architect. His difficult personality, runaway costs, and court intrigues led to his being cashiered with only the foundations in place, and with Cardinal Richelieu's architect, Jacques Lemercier (1585–1654), replacing him. He honored Mansart's design except for simplifying the vaults, dome, and façade; others would complete the work in 1682 but without Mansart's elaborate forecourt shown in our section.

French construction exploits the limestone's capacity for elaborate stereotomy within tectonics based on walls rather than columns, but here, elaborate

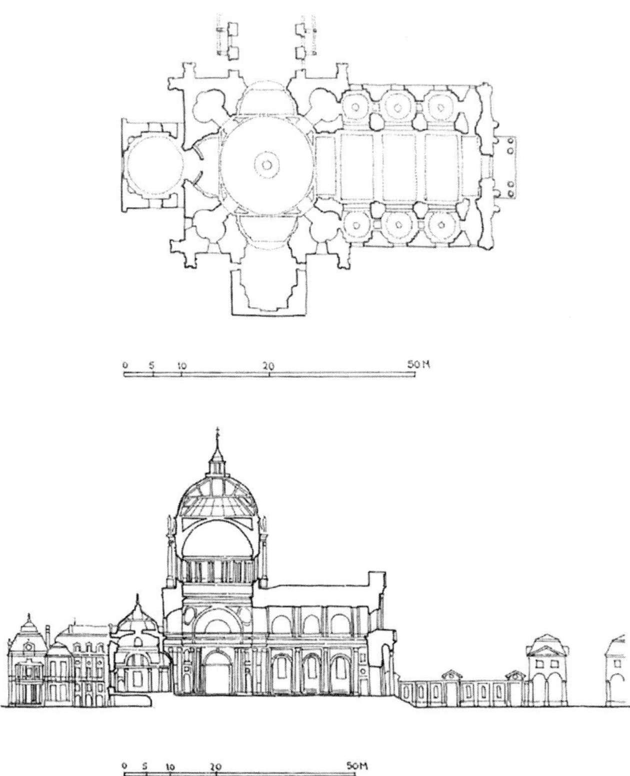

FIGURE 5.23 Church of the Val-de-Grâce, François Mansart, 1645; Jacques Lemercier, 1646ff, Paris, France.

as it is, Mansart's intended display is only hinted at in the finished work. His plan draws on Italian tholos and temple syntheses, e.g., at **Il Gesù, Vignola, Rome, 1568**; in Venice at **S. Giorgio Maggiore, 1566**, and **Il Redentore, 1577, both Palladio**; and SAINT PETER'S BASILICA, ROME. A brief vestibule precedes the temple's three-bay vaulted and coffered nave with carved out arched windows, flanked not with aisles but with centralized tholos chapels. The east end with the tholos and diagonal chapels beyond the grill is raised three steps. Chapels within the canted crossing piers rising into blunted pendentives are entered through arches facing diagonally across the crossing in the manner the **Chapel at Anet, Philibert de l'Orme, 1547–52** had introduced. The transepts and choir beyond three-dimensional arches are semicircular, the one with the high altar with a baldacchino (not shown) projecting into the crossing, another for the nun's choir reached from the convent, and the third for the Saint Anne votive chapel. The drum's twelve pilaster-framed windows, Corinthian as everywhere, carry the hemispherical dome with elaborate falsework for its high extrados.

The wall's supremacy in this all-white interior with low bas relief ornament has the surface shaved back to frame the chapels. Pilasters separating the chapels pay deference to the wall, being doubled where they enter the tholos, folded when they move to the crossing's cant, and appearing again on the curved faces of the large chapel openings.

Lemercier's simplification of Mansart's façade is visible in recession in three planes: in front is a temple front with paired, fully rounded columns; next is a two-second story wall with its upper story presenting immured, paired, three-quarter columns flanking a niche and holding a pediment; then comes with the second story's central section recessed beneath a broken entablature carried on pilasters and a central, segmental tabernacle window and, at the sides, volutes above the outer bay's parapet with a let-in panel with a niche below a small window and ending in a pilaster corner. The dome's exterior is a tour-de-force with deep piers between pedimented windows, an attic, and a ribbed dome extending to a lantern, all elaborated with elongated *pots-de-feu*. At the crossing's corners, onion-domed sentry boxes allude to Anne of Austria's home (Figure 5.24).

The expressive character of this memorial honoring the sixteenth president of the United States draws on the finest achievements of ancient and modern classical architecture, a complement to the classical content of the political and civic culture of the nation he helped preserve. It has been the setting for some of the seminal events in the nation's history, especially those confronting racism.

Its site was suggested for a memorial in the **1902 McMillan Commission Plan**. The formerly swampy land at the opposite end of the Mall from the Capitol is at a pivot on the route to Arlington National Cemetery, whose first internees were Civil War Union dead. The design competition winner Henry Bacon (1866–1924) had worked for McKim, Mead and White since 1884 except for two years of study in Europe before going into private practice in 1897, and he had long been developing ideas for a memorial to a fellow Illinois native.

Bacon's marble tholos-temple cenotaph lacks a pediment and makes its side its front. It occupies a tight, low-walled rectangular precinct within a large circular reservation beyond the Mall's reflecting pool (our plan goes only to the recent World War II memorial). The broad steps entering the precinct recur at the three-stage access to the crepidoma with distyle columns before the square tholos. Skylit, its central, interior square is defined on each side by rows of four fluted Ionic columns on attic bases open to chambers presenting inscriptions of two of Lincoln's addresses below murals by Jules Guerin. The centerpiece is Daniel Chester French's very large marble statue of Lincoln, seated and facing toward the Capitol beyond the baseless, fluted Greek Doric columns of the 8 × 12 peripteral colonnade. Like those at the PARTHENON, CALLICRATES, ATHENS, 447–36 BCE, they include the slight inward lean that eurythmia calls for. In the frieze rather than triglyphs and metopes are the names of the 36 states in the Union at the time of Lincoln's death with the date in joining

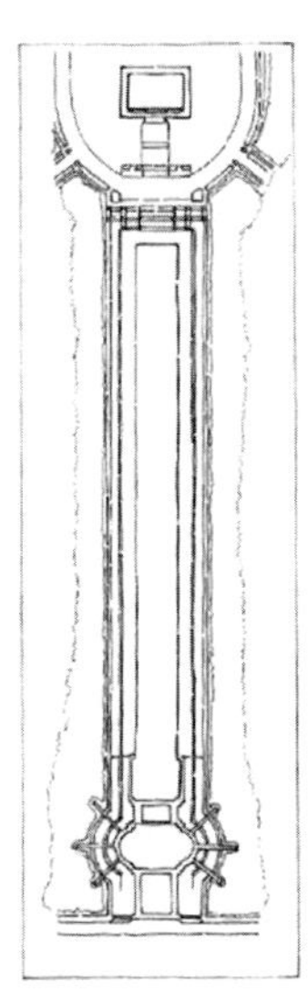

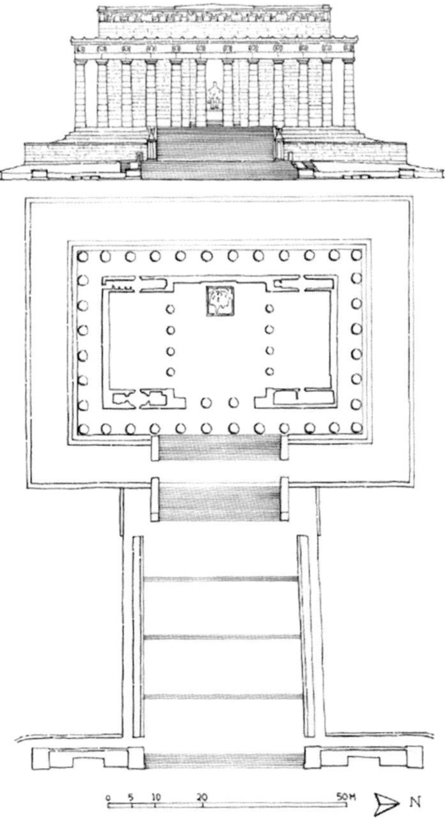

FIGURE 5.24 Lincoln Memorial, Henry Bacon, Washington, D.C., U.S.A., 1914–22.

the union, separated by conjoined wreaths of northern pine and southern laurel above each column. The cella's low attic has eagles holding palm garlands above the names and dates of admission of the 48 states at the time of its dedication.

Notes

1 See Keppel Creswell, *Early Muslim Architecture*, Vol. 1 (London: Oxford University Press, 1969); Henry Duckworth, *The Church of the Holy Sepulchre* (London: Hodder and Stoughton, 1922); A. Elad, "Why did Abd Al-Malik Build the Dome of the Rock? A Re-Examination of the Muslim Sources," in *Bayt Al-Maqdis*, eds. J. Raby and J. Johns (London: Oxford University Press, 1992), 33–58.

2 See Abu Bakr al Wasiti, *Fada'il al Bayt al Muquaddas*, ed. E. Hasson (Jerusalem, 1979); Nasser Rabbat, "The Meaning of the Umayyad Dome of the Rock," in *Muqarnas*, ed. Oleg Grabar, Vol. 6 (Leiden: E.J. Brill, 1989), 14.

3 "The Tempietto and the Roots of Coincidence," *Architectural History*, 33 (1990): 1–28.

6

THE TEMPLE

The *temple* acknowledges divinity by serving celebration. In earlier eras, it was enclosed within a sacred precinct.

Variation 1: The temple for communal celebration

Egypt was already 1,600 years old when the 19th dynasty (1292–1189 BCE), the second in the New Kingdom (1550–1070 BCE), when it, as new dynasties normally did, produced major reforms in government and religion (Figure 6.1). This included expanding this Temple of Amun, making it second only to the pyramids in extent, and connected to the earlier religious nexus at Thebes and Luxor. Another connection came when Ramses II, the dynasty's third pharaoh, restored the third dynasty funerary complex at Saqqara by Imhotep, the first architect to make an organized precinct with cut stone.

In a large precinct at Karnack, this temple is the principal element. The axial approach with ram-headed sphinxes from the Nile to the entrance to this temple complex. During flood stage, Nile water reaches the point where our plan begins. It shows the precinct's four major parts, each entered through pylons built at different times. First is the Great Court entrance to a temple of Ramses III on the side and a vestibule in the pylon before the Great Hypostyle Hall. That Hall's farther wall incorporates the pylon for the thin court that follows. This pylon had been built in the previous dynasty, reportedly with gold plating and turquoise, jasper, lapis lazuli, and amber, and with a silver floor. The court was the repository for the sacred barque that carried Amun on processions and provided the access point for the axis running through a series of pylons to the temple complex at Thebes and Luxor. One of it its two

DOI: 10.4324/9780429506260-9

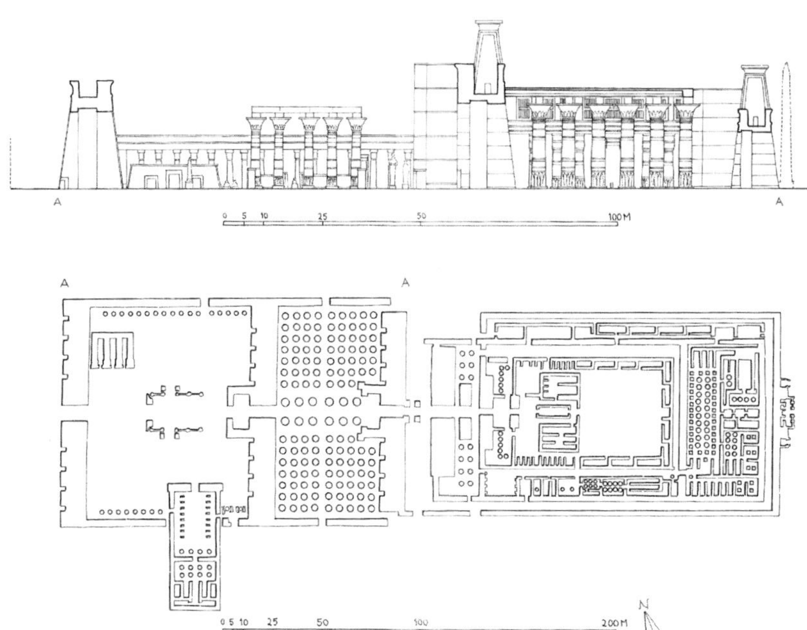

FIGURE 6.1 Temple of Amun, Karnak, Egypt, 1305–1205 BCE.

obelisks is now in Rome. The final court was itself a very large earlier precinct with various shrines, temples, and other sacred elements, now with reduced importance.

Our section, at twice the scale of the plan, shows only the first half of this great complex. The complex's grandest achievement, the Great Hypostyle Hall, is 103 m wide and 52 m deep, with 134 columns, all with papyrus cluster-bud capitals, most of them 12.8 m tall and 3 m in diameter, with twelve more in two rows along the axis rising 21 m with high diameters of 3.7 m. Their greater height is used to produce a central clerestory. The smaller columns are evenly spaced except for the slightly wider median cross aisle leading to side entrances. All the surfaces in this giant trabeated hall are richly painted to extoll the pharaohs' achievements in a complex whose definitive expressive character epitomizes that of ancient Egyptian architecture (Figure 6.2).

In 480 BCE, the Persians destroyed Athens and the predecessor temple of its principal goddess, Athena. Pericles, the leader of democratic Athens, then formed the Delian League to defend Greece, and built its successor using its funds and storing the residue in its rear (western) chamber.

The temple was the focus and Athens' yearly celebration of Athena, the Panathenaic Festival. Its route began outside the city, traversed the agora (central market and government center), and moved up and into the acropolis where the buildings shown in our sketch were built: the small **Temple of Athena**

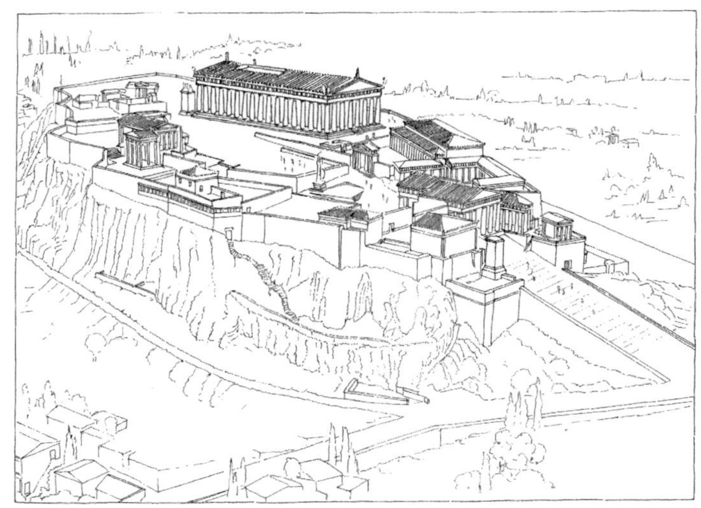

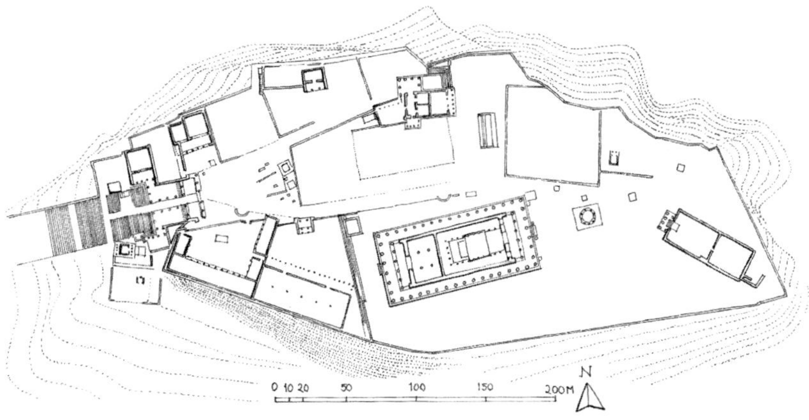

FIGURE 6.2 Temple of Athena (Parthenon), Iktinos and Callicrates, Athens, Greece, 447–36 BCE. After Manolis Korres.

Nike, c. 421; the **Propylaea, Mnesicles, 436–31 BCE**, a pedimented gateway with a side gallery; the Ionic **Erechtheum, Mnesicles, 421–06 BCE** with shrines for various gods; the large statue of Athena; and other lesser buildings. The peplos that Athenian maidens had spent nine months weaving was blessed and placed on the Palladium, the wooden *Athena Poliás* in the cella, the "carving that fell from Heaven," that protected the city. Also, there was the great statue of Athena Phidias had executed, the sculptor also of the frieze high atop the exterior walls portraying the procession, and the gods in its pediments and metope whose reliefs portrayed the gods' involvement in Athens' history (much of this is now in the British Museum).

Built of Pentelic marble and originally richly colored and waxed to glisten in the strong Attic light, the temple's stylobate with the canonic three-step crepidoma supports fluted Doric columns following the canonic eight across the front and seventeen along the sides [A: (2A + 1)] and triglyph and metope entablature.

Now seen in a ruined and reconstructed state, this large building enjoys iconic status within architecture. It exhibits the qualities of symmetria (proportionality congruent with the order of the cosmos) and eurythmia (adjustments to make symmetria visible) that Vitruvius later discussed. Here are four instances: the stylobate balloons slightly toward the center to counter any appearance of sinking; the corner columns are thickened to prevent their looking thinner against the open sky; the columns lean slightly inward; and their entasis reinforces their visible ability to carry their load (Figure 6.3).

The provincial seaside town of Pompeii was badly damaged by an earthquake in 62, then buried in 79 by little stones thrown out of Mount Vesuvius, plundered for building material and accessible artifacts, and then forgotten until 1748 when excavations began.

Samnites, not Greeks, founded it in 7th or 6th c. BCE using a largely regular grid for parceling rectangular house lots, reserving a precinct for a market and others for a temple to Apollo and a basilica based on Rome's. Conquered by the Romans in 80 BCE and incorporated into their civil order a decade later, the native Samnites were largely replaced with army veterans and others. Over time, richer Romans expanded the Samnite dwellings that were largely similar to one another at the expense of poorer neighbors to produce the varied layouts seen in our plan. Throughout the city they added the public works that Romans considered necessities: baths, theaters, a few small temples, an arena, and constantly flowing fountains, and they expanded into a district with garden houses.

In the former market area, they built the city's Forum as a precinct wrapped by a two-story Doric colonnade. Along one long side they built a place for keeping the city's official weights and measures, a long storehouse, and a latrine, and on the other side the *comitium* for voting, a large assembly structure (for corporations?), two shrines honoring Roman emperors or their families, and a market where the colonnade in front of shops was elevated to the Corinthian order. On the far short end, they built three small public buildings, and at the other, a temple atop whatever had preceded it that was typical of thousands throughout their empire. Here a pair of arches flank the temple, both originally at the front as in the Forum of Caesar but now with one moved back as part of the precinct walls as in Rome's Forum of Augustus; its mate's move was most likely delayed by the demands of post-earthquake reconstruction.

The hexastyle Corinthian temple with brick fabric that was either stuccoed or veneered in stone was the Capitolium with the three cells of Rome's Capitoline gods, Juno, Jupiter, and Minerva. We show the altar or *rostrum* reached by narrow flanking stairs with broad axial stairs leading up to the three-bay deep

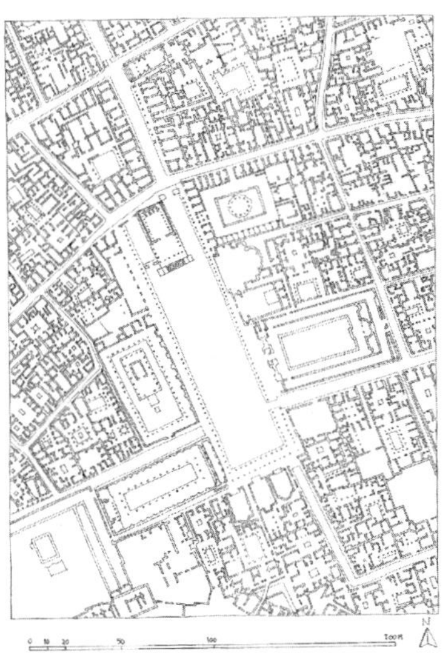

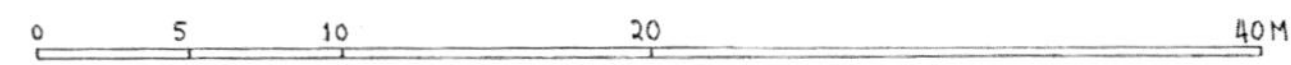

FIGURE 6.3 Temple of Jupiter, Pompeii, before 79.

pronaos. Its prominence and expressive character marks the gods' role in the social, political, and economic activities that were central to the Romans' life.

The instruction that Yahweh gave Solomon for the Temple as the only place where the Jews were to offer Him sacrifices survive in countless successors (Figure 6.4). Solomon brought Hiram the architect from Tyre in Lebanon to build the vast complex of palace, courts, and gates within an acropolis precinct variously named Zion, Moriah, and Temple Mount.[1]

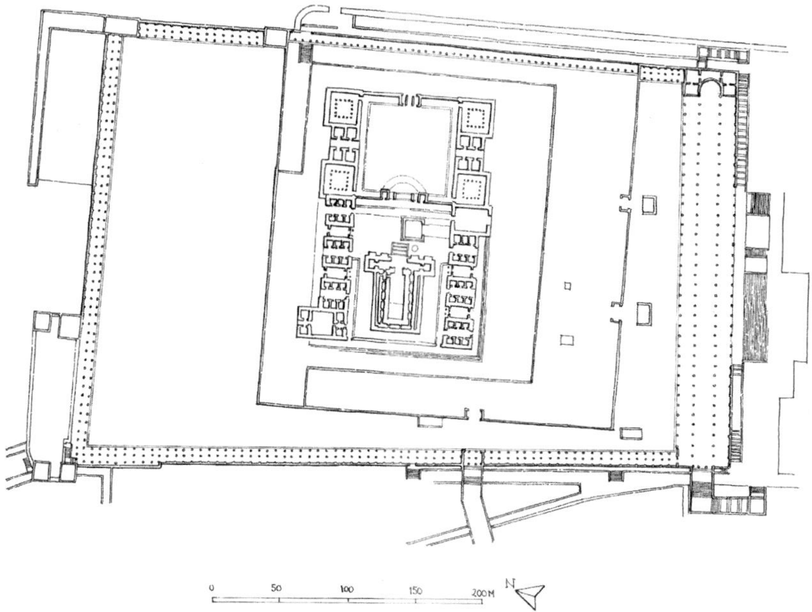

FIGURE 6.4 The Jewish House of the Lord (Solomon's Temple), Jerusalem, before 957 BCE; rebuilt 538 BCE. After Leon Rietmeyer.

The Temple proper was smaller than the later TEMPLE OF ATHENA (PARTHENON), IKTINOS AND CALLICRATES, ATHENS, 447–36 BCE. Built during seven years with stone and an interior of cedar and fir "overlaid with gold," "neither hammer nor axe nor any tool of iron [was] heard." Yahweh gave dimensions: a porch ten cubits deep with bronze columns eighteen cubits high named Jachin and Boaz with five-cubit capitals; a "House" 60 by 20 and 30 with narrow windows and a veil before the unlit Holy of Holies, a 20 cubit cube tholos with golden cherubims, altar, and various holy objects; only the High Priest entered it, and only once a year.

Twice sacked and reconstructed, in 586 BCE Nebuchadnezzar destroyed it and carried the Jews into their Babylonian Captivity.

Second temple, 538 BCE

After 25 years, Ezekiel prophesied the Temple's rebuilding, which occurred through the liberality of Cyrus, his successor Darius, and others, and without change except for doubling the height of the "House" to 60 cubits.

The Temple was in poor condition in 20 when the Roman governor Herod the Great began its restoration, but Titus destroyed it in 70 and carried its treasures to Rome; we see some in the reliefs of the **Arch of Titus, Rome, 81**.

In 130, Hadrian closed the Mount to Jews and built a great Temple of Jupiter; Constantine destroyed it in 325, another event that enhanced the Temple's mystical content for Abrahamic religions. Jews and some Christians await its rebuilding, while for Islam, the desolate Mount is one of its three most holy sites and marked by a tholos, the DOME OF THE ROCK, RAJA'IBN HAYWEH and YAZID IBN SALAM, 687.

Judaism and Islam retain the Biblical prohibition of "graven images," but Christian doctrine believes the prohibition was lifted when, during the Crucifixion, the Temple veil "was rent in twain from the top to the bottom" letting God's Holy Light dispel the darkness, making salvation accessible to humankind through the Church. The Temple's configuration and sometimes its proportions assumed mystical content in the transition from secular to sacred with the "House" becoming the nave where celebrants assemble, and the Holy of Holies becoming the choir or altar chancel, often a tholos, for Eucharistic celebrations and veneration of the Real Presence of Christ. We can see this in the **Sistine Chapel, Baccio Pontelli, Rome, 1477–80**, the papal palatine chapel (Figure 6.5).

After giving legal status to Christianity in 313, Constantine built this major basilical church in the imperial Lateran residential precinct. He reformed and expanded the small city of Byzantium to make a new Rome, transferring the imperial capital there that, according to a document proven fraudulent in the

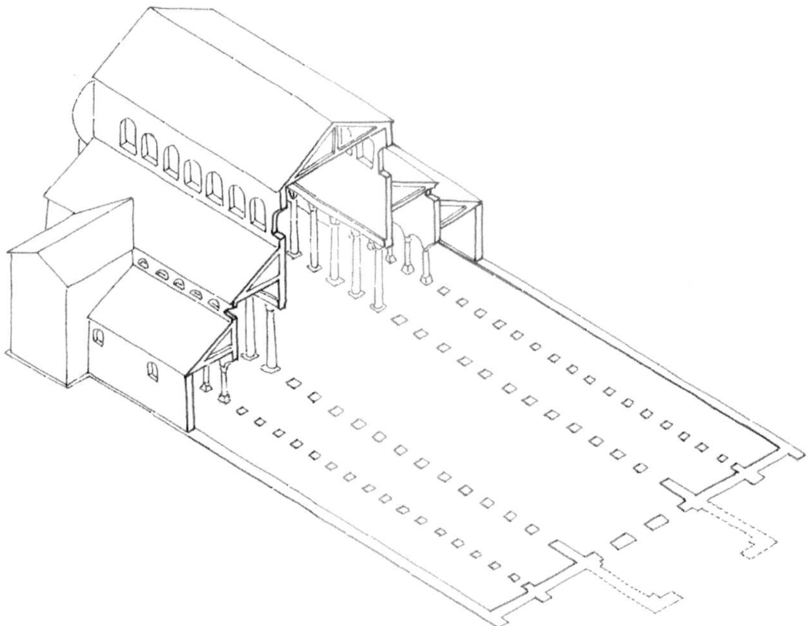

FIGURE 6.5 San Giovanni in Laterano, Rome, Italy, dedicated 324.

15th c., left old Rome to the Latin Church. With Saint Peter's tomb it became the seat of the Bishop of Rome who is the Pope. In 1929 it became one of several places in Rome that were given extraterritorial status within Italy.

We show only the original basilica without its atrium, baptistery, adjoining palace, monastic complex, and Holy Stairs. Occupying the highest rank among all churches and hence its title archbasilica, little of its original fabric survives. An earthquake in 897 and Rome's continued decline were costly. Impressive now are the notable 1234 cloister, grand transepts added shortly before the papacy's 1309 removal to is Babylonian Captivity Avignon, the altar ciborium from 1369, the refurbished **Nave, Francesco Borromini, 1646–49**, and the imposing **Façade, Alessandro Galilei, 1733–35**.

Its configuration elongates a typical Roman basilica to produce an emphatical longitudinally running from a plain entrance to a rich apse. The nave's five-aisle interior has colonnades and a clerestory with 15 large, colorful columns on each side of the nave with an aisle beyond formed by an arcade with 22 smaller green columns whose soffits had mosaics. Curtains probably isolated the catechumens (the not yet baptized) in the outer aisles with seven golden altars and finished with mosaics. Lighting the entire interior were more than a hundred gold and silver chandeliers and nearly as many candelabras.

The east ends hemispherical apse, loaded with gold, rich marbles, and mosaics could hold the hieratic assembly of 200 or more clerics arrayed as we see in the splendid mosaic of **Santa Prudenziana, 4th c., Rome**. A rood screen, apparently a double row of columns that alluded to the Temple's rent veil, probably separated them from the thousands assembled beneath the nave's open timber roof. Overlaid with silver, the screen carried solid silver statues with Christ the Teacher and His Apostles facing the congregation and the resurrected Christ and four angles facing the clergy. Flanking the altar small chambers projected on each side, perhaps for receiving gifts.

A few well-preserved, much-smaller Early Christian churches in Rome suggest its original splendor. For centuries down to the present day the configuration and expressive character of this "Mother Church" has been the model for columnar churches in variations of five, three, and single-aisle churches, with and without transepts, and with varying degrees of decoration (Figure 6.6).

When it was the capital of the Western Roman Empire, Aurelius Ambrosius (c. 340–97) was the Christian provincial governor. After he reconciled a major theological dispute, the Emperor responded to popular acclaim by making the future saint the Bishop. In 387, he baptized the convert, Augustine of Hippo, and as bishop he built four churches, among them this one.

The original construction has been extensively rebuilt, including repairs to the east end after World War II, but original fabric survives in the lower parts of the elevated presbytery and choir with its semicircular seating. Major alterations occurred in the Carolingian period, and it was an important imperial site. The nave's side aisles were extended beside the apse, ending in chapels.

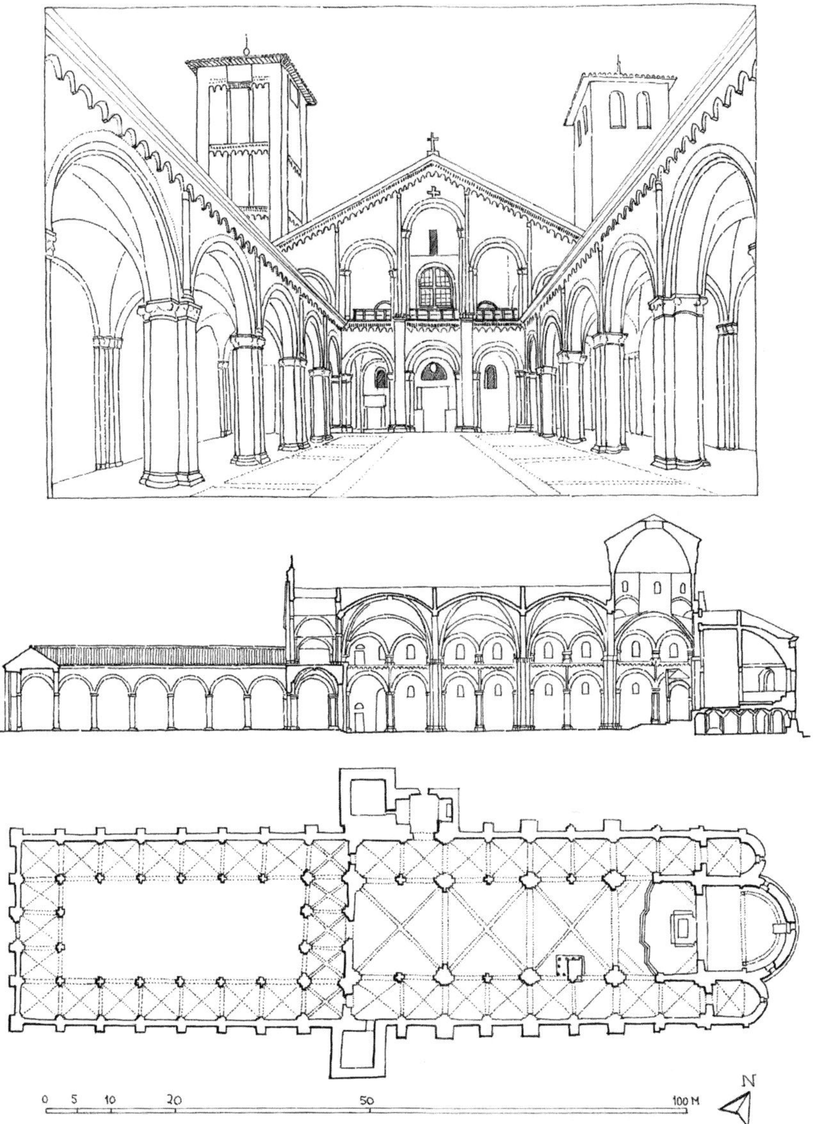

FIGURE 6.6 Sant'Ambrogio, Milan, 824–1144.

The apse's hemispherical dome was given a mosaic *Pantocrator attended by angles and saints* (now much restored). The 5 × 7 bay atrium (corner bays counted twice) was added. Surrounded by arcades with compound piers and colonnettes for the vaults' ribs, it is entered through a single portal and gives entry to the church for each of its five aisles; it served the catechumens. And the larger of the two campaniles, the Monks' Tower, was built by one of the two monastic communities housed here. The other, the Canon's tower from 1144, was made taller in the 19th c. A new altar and ciborium followed, celebrating the Ottonian Empire.

In 1080, a new presbytery was begun, a square bay framed by arches carrying squinches, a drum, and an eight bay domical vault within a two-story arcaded octagon with conical roof. The present nave's original fabric includes reworking begun in 1128; eventually, in 1140, it included ogive-ribbed vaults reached by colonettes along compound piers; its three bays call to mind the much larger **Basilica of Maxentius and Constantine, Rome, 307–12ff**. This vaulting is often cited in discussions of pre-Gothic rib vaulting. Above each two-story bay in the side aisles is a gallery with ribless vaults on compound piers, each bay a quarter the size of a nave bay.

This constantly amended and enlarged church's interior is stone and plaster with some brick, while the exterior is brick with some stone, both served by abundant tie rods. The five arches in the west wall beneath a pitched roof, like walls and their segments elsewhere, end in a corbel course, with the three beyond the atrium providing the composition for the picture-image of the UCLA campus (Figure 6.7).

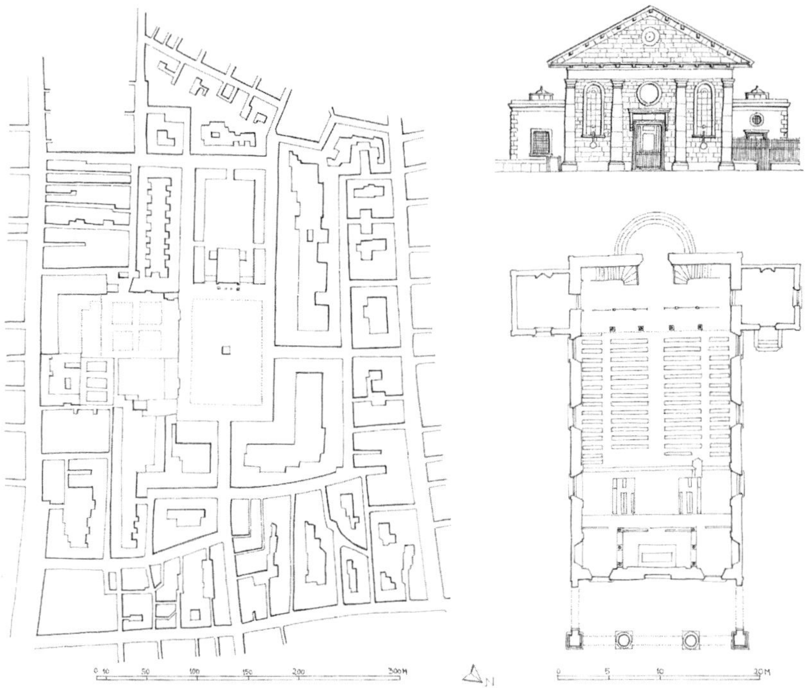

FIGURE 6.7 Saint Paul's Covent Garden, Inigo Jones, London, England, 1631–35.

England's first ex novo post-Reformation church, with the initiation of Francis Russell, the Puritanically inclined 4th Earl of Bedford, had Inigo Jones build England's first ex novo post-Reformation church. Bedford: Make it "not much better than a barn." Jones: "Then you shall have the handsomest barn in England." He included a market square and, "for persons of repute and quality," shops and dwellings.

Jones had twice visited Italy with special attention to Andrea Palladio. He introduced him to England, and his much-annotated copy of the 1570 *Four Books on Architecture* survives. Here we see a clear example of perspectival urbanism that welds the neighborhood and classical elements into a loose but controlled order, and whose expressive character is in line with England's complex common-law relationships and social-political-religious order.

Jones designed his "barn" as a pedimented, brick and stucco temple with a pedimented porch facing the market square. Its Tuscan order was proper for a rugged, masculine saint. The "barn's" wooden entablature crosses a pair of broadly spaced stone columns and end piers as a mere beam carrying a thin wooden cornice and pediment rake with thin, extensively projecting mutules, repeated at the garden facade. The pronaos ends were three arched portals, replaced in 1876 with large, arched openings. This was intended as the principal entrance, but church authorities forced the plan's reversal.

The entire exterior, now brick except for the pronaos wall, may have been veneered in stone or been stuccoed with stone details and the quoins that we see today. The enclosed yard entered from the market through portals replaced the originally intended entry. Flanking the entrance are low, square vestry rooms. Large, arched windows flooded light to the interior. A 1795 fire produced extensive reconstruction inside, including galleries all around for the first time but subsequently reduced to one as a choir and organ loft opposite the chancel. The chancel, always elevated but earlier not this high, has a simple altar rail, pulpit, reredos where the central entrance was to be, and communion table. The original belfry was not replaced.

Small dwellings faced out from the churchyard's enclosure, but Jones lined the long market square with arcaded row houses except across the Earl's garden. Behind its Portland stone arcade were shops, and above was a brick facade with stuccoed pilaster strips rising through a piano nobile, then through an upper story, finally ending in a pitched roof with dormers. This configuration of repetitive facades was familiar in Dutch and French dwellings (SEE PLACE ROYALE (NOW PLACE DES VOSGES), PARIS, 1605–12) but novel among London's wattle and dub and gable-front, peak-roofed streets. Streets enter the square from beside the churchyard and through midpoint gaps in a short side and one long one.

Everything except the church and its yard has been rebuilt, and even there, the steps leading to the market porch have been reduced to one. The square, originally enlivened by the usual ramshackle market structures and activities, is still a bustling center of activity with a large, permanent market hall (Figure 6.8).

James Gibbs' (1682–1754) first proposal for replacing the dilapidated church here was a domed tholos terminating in a temple, characteristic of the previous generation's characteristic of the free-wheeling manner found in Wren's parish churches, but church officials required a less expensive design. He drew on the familiar English single-tower configuration but enriched with the classicism he learned working with Carlo Fontana for five years in Rome.

Its interior, white and touched with gold has, a four-bay nave with another deeper bay for the chancel and an organ loft above the vestibule. Thin, Corinthian columns rise from the pew boxes carrying galleries halfway up and reaching dosseret capitals that carry the vault and the nave arcade opening to the galleries. The vault is richly articulated by large fields with low intersections

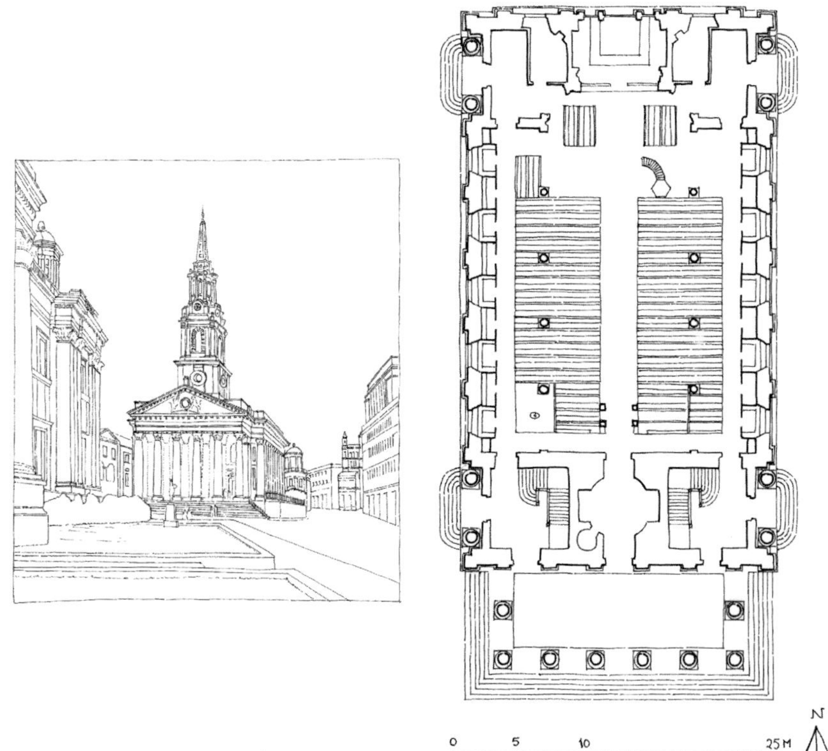

FIGURE 6.8 Saint Martin-in-the-Fields, James Gibbs, London, England, 1721–24.

from the galleries. These galleries have sail vaults carried on pilasters on the outer wall between large windows running from pew boxes to arch. The chancel's pulpit is close to the pews, and it holds server's stalls, altar, Palladian window, vestibules, and shielded entrance areas for the side entrances. In the front, the vestibule includes the tower's massive base and the gallery stairs for side entrances that, here as toward the back, have distyle in antis Corinthian columns.

Beneath this ashlar block is a capacious, vaulted crypt. The stone box is beneath a pitched roof with pilasters along its muscular sides that define bays holding windows framed with projecting sills, alternating projecting framing blocks (a so-called Gibbs surround), and prominent keystones. They reach an entablature with a balustrade that dies in the pediment of the hexastyle Corinthian temple front with a two-bay pronaos. The impressive tower was derived ultimately from those at **Saint Paul's Cathedral, Wren, London, 1675**, rising in triplets, the first one square, another octagonal, and the third tapering to a ball and cross.

In a 1728 book, Gibbs published this building, other buildings, and the orders. Its presence became an important element in Trafalgar Square's development began in 1826. It became a popular a model in North American, sometimes only slightly simplified, as at **Saint Michael's, Charleston, S.C., 1752–71**, but more often more abbreviated.

Variation 2: the palatine chapel

A palatine chapel was attached to a royal residence.

In 794, before Pope Leo III crowned him in Rome as a New Constantine, Charlemagne (748–814) had Odo of Metz (742–814) begin an ambitious new palace within a 1 × 3 walled precinct where ancient Romans had enjoyed a hot spring. As it had for his ancient predecessors, it served as a base while pursuing activities of the Carolingian Empire to the north and east. His regia's basilical council hall was like the nearby **Constantinian Basilica, Trier, c. 310**, and it was connected to this palatine chapel, **Figure 6.9**, by 100 Carolingian foot long gallery over the ancient *decumanus*.

The chapel's model was **San Vitale, Ravenna, 526–47**, the palatine chapel whose decoration stressed the eastern Emperor Theodosius' sacred legitimacy. Charlemagne and his successors stressed the Augustinian doctrine about the Latin emperor's role in the City of Man to host and protect the Church as the City of God. Much altered down to the present, we show its original setting in the palace precinct with the regia, gallery, and chapel, with the detailed plan's light tracing showing later additions.

The chapel's sixteen-sided perimeter originally stretched 144 Carolingian feet, the dimension in cubits of the Heavenly City described in the Apocalypse. The content of the interior's octagonal, domed tholos was heightened in 1165–70 when Emperor Frederick I Barbarossa installed the chandelier portraying

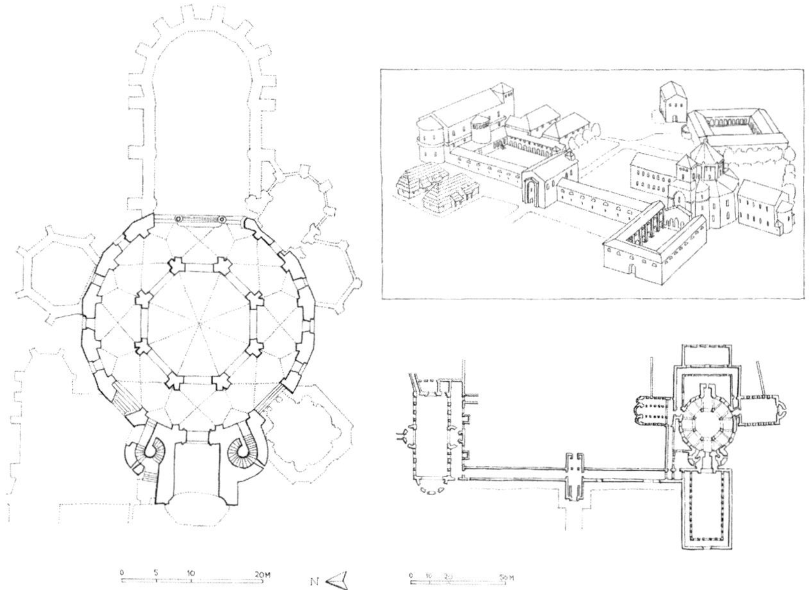

FIGURE 6.9 Palatine Chapel, Aachen, now Germany, 794–804.

the Heavenly Jerusalem. In the tall dome's cloister vault we now see a replica of the original mosaic with the enthroned Christ triumphant, evangelists, and 24 elders of the Apocalypse against a gold background. The tholos' lowest story is a cross-vaulted circuit beyond a stout, pier arcade, all with alternating-color voussoirs, a scheme repeated in the very tall upper story carried up into the cloister vault dome. The upper level's arched openings are divided into two registers, both with three-bay screens like those in Ravenna, but flat, and the lower one arcaded. The original bronze rails survive here. The columns, like the interior's booked marble veneering, are spolia, some claimed to be from Ravenna and Rome.

The *Westwerk* entrance includes paired stair towers leading to the galleries. There, opposite the apse, is the imperial throne, brought from the CHURCH OF THE HOLY SEPULCHRE, JERUSALEM, 326–35.

The exterior was originally stuccoed in imperial red. The body of Charlemagne, canonized in 1215, now resides with a golden casket installed in the glass-walled choir built in 1355 to replace the original small apse. This extension's expressive character is that of the great reliquary-shrine, the SAINTE CHAPELLE, PARIS, 1238 (Figure 6.10).

Louis IX (1214–70), crowned king at age twelve, governed from the Île de la Cité in Paris. He died during his second Crusade to the Holy Land. He had already begun this palatine chapel as a repository for the Crown of Thorns that

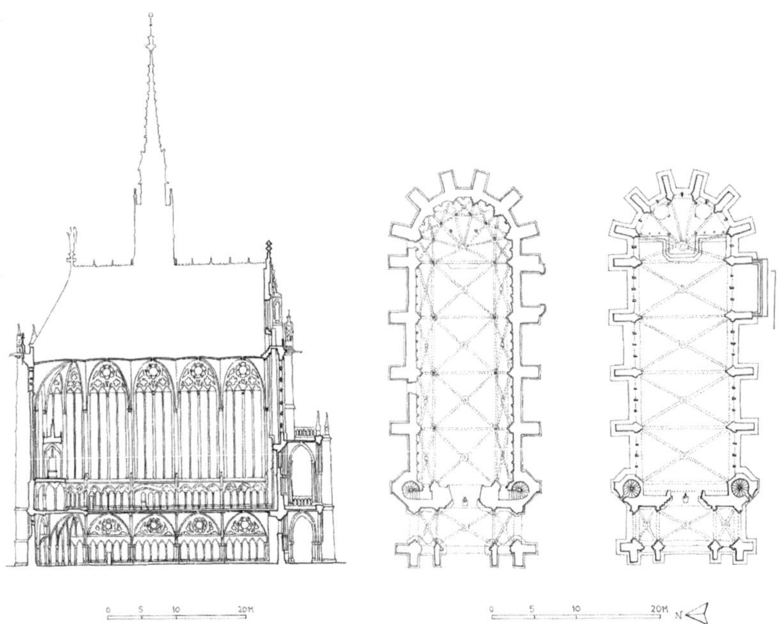

FIGURE 6.10 Sainte Chapelle, Paris, France, 1238–48.

the Byzantine Empire transferred to him for paying the Venetians its pawn. It was installed with other relics the famous stained-glass shell whose expressive character is that of a reliquary and whose windows affirm the French royalty as God's chosen governors. Reached from the palace by the long, upper-level *Galerie Mercière*, servants worshipped in its crypt, and the relics were accessible for public veneration on special occasions.

The configuration, membrature, and decoration draw on French experience gained for example in building cathedrals such as OUR LADY OF CHARTRES, CHARTRES, 1134–1260. Like Charlemagne's PALATINE CHAPEL, AACHEN, 794–804, it makes the Heavenly Jerusalem present on earth. The two stair-tower vestibule opens into a four-bay nave and a seven-bay radiating apse and ciborium. The thinnest possible colonnettes carry quadripartite ribbed vaults rising to great heights and painted with the king's blue and gold ornamentation. The stunning glass walls' decorative program moves from John the Baptist to the Resurrection with Old Testament history illustrating exemplary acts of kings and queens, culminating closest to the entrance with Louis installing the relics in Paris.

Its heavily buttressed, plain exterior, the palace's only substantive survivor, makes clear its two levels beneath a steeply pitched roof and fleche that formerly competed for dominance in the Parisian skyline with **Notre Dame Cathedral, Paris, 1163–1250**, the relic's post-Revolution home (Figure 6.11).

FIGURE 6.11 Royal Chapel, Jules Hardouin-Mansart, Versailles, France, 1689–1710.

The crown prince's late arrival in Louis XIII's marriage led Louis XIV (1638–1715) to be called Louis le Dieudonné or Gift of God. The king's involvement in religion increased over his long reign during, which continuous construction activity at Versailles, and in 1682, he made his official seat of government. This chapel, the chateau's fifth, towers above it as did the SAINTE CHAPELLE, PARIS, 1238–48 above Louis IX's on the Île de la Cité.

The interior's interior configuration evokes both that predecessor and the normative elevation of a canonic cathedral. Its low, lower pier arcade carries a very tall colonnaded gallery whose entablature supports the clerestory whose windows whose cross vaults cut into the barrel vault and whose fictive ribs obscured by the elaborate decoration suggest quadripartite vault. That scene, *God the Father in His Glory*, is joined by *The Descent of the Holy Ghost* above the altar and Louis le Dieudonné in the royal tribune. In the gallery's flat ceilings are similarly intensely colored portrayals of the concordance of Old and New Testament common in palatine chapels. They stand out against the lustrous white interior that contrasts with the colored interiors elsewhere in the chateau. Our view is from the gallery's royal tribune above where the courtiers would cluster and opposite the altar, a position like Charlemagne's in the PALATINE CHAPEL, AACHEN, 794–804.

The gallery's five bays of richly ornamented, fluted Corinthian columns gather and attach to a pier before swinging through the three bays of the semicircular apse. The richly gilded altar is placed in the apse three steps above the geometrically organized marble floor, with the organ above in the gallery.

Placed next to the *cour d'honneur*, the exterior's height rises well above the horizontal chateau with a low basement with small windows followed by the gallery level's four, tall, arched windows alternating with pilasters swinging up into buttresses stabilizing the clearstory and its tall, pitched, decorated roof with pilasters bunched and doubled before sweeping around the apse with projecting, paired of pilasters.

Note

1 The architect of that name is not to be confused with King Hiram of Tyre who provided the famed wood from the Cedars of Lebanon.

7

THE THEATER

The ***theater*** serves joining with others in imagining options in knowing, doing, or making something, normally with a half-circular disposition.

Autocrats use ritualized ceremonials to legitimate their power. When democracy began to take root in ancient Greece and individuals began to take responsibility for their actions, theater emerged as a surrogate to provide moral instruction. Festivals for Dionysus, theater's god, became formalized in Athens in the 6th c. BC, with three genres emerging, drama with epic actions of men and gods, comedy for displaying human interactions, and satyr depicting the affairs of rustics. Only males performed, at first with one and later a few more actors, who changed personae by changing masks along with up to fifteen singers and dancers and more for comedies. Stage apparatus was also developed to allow actors to appear to fly, and props were included for satires.

Greece's natural topography allowed theaters to be nestled and cut into hillsides and scaled in proportion to the population they were to serve. Seating occupied a *cavea* spanning slightly more than a half-circle with special seats in the front for important people. The *orchestra*, a circular area, is where the performance occurred with a shallow rectangular stage beyond it.

In the 5th c. BCE, a curtain called the *skene*, or scene, began to be placed behind the stage. Later superseded by a permanent backdrop, this backdrop eventually reached two stories with acting in front. Suggesting a nobleman's residence, the area for the performance in front was called the *proscenium*. In some theaters, arched entrances for the audience and actors connected the *cavea* and *skene*. We show a conjectural reconstruction based on ancient foundations.

In the Peloponnese and among Greece's largest, this theater was associated with the ancient world's celebrated healing center, the *Asclepeion*.

DOI: 10.4324/9780429506260-10

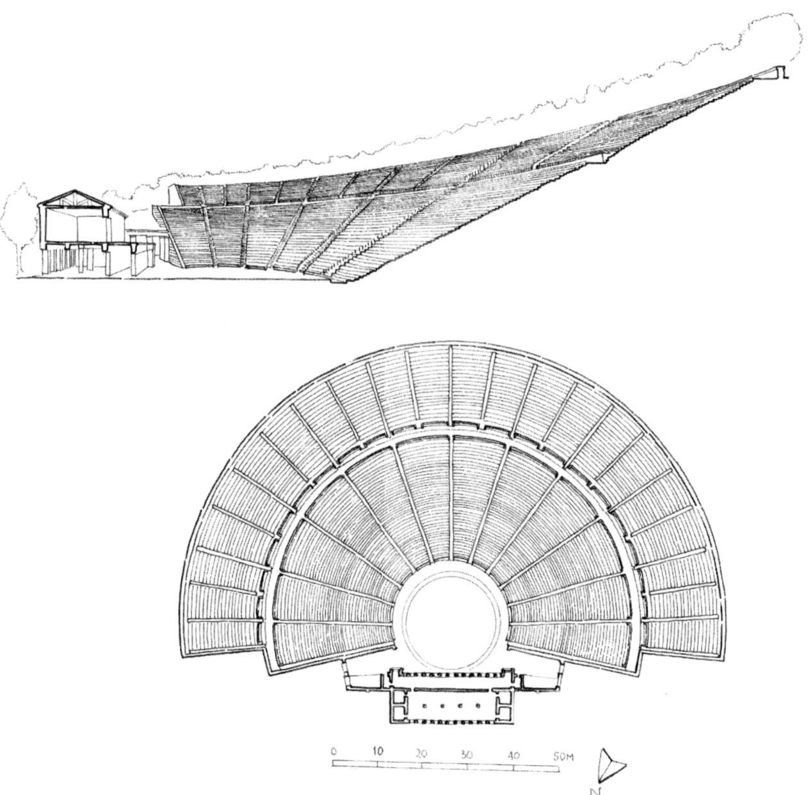

FIGURE 7.1 Theater, Epidaurus, Greece, 340 BCE.

The Romans expanded it to hold perhaps 12,000 or 14,000 without compromising its unsurpassed acoustics. It was put back in use in 1938 (Figure 7.1).

Figure 7.2. The Romans loved spectacle, but during the republic, only temporary theaters were permitted inside the *limes* of Rome's *pomerium*. Using subterfuge, Pompey the Great (106–48 BCE) built one of the grandest permanent theaters within those limits by ensconcing it within an enormous precinct sacred to Venus Victrix. The theater's configuration followed the Greek pattern: *cavea, proscaenium, scaenae frons, cavea,* but it was built upon the flat ground, which included *vomitoria* for access and egress. And uniquely here a temple for Venus at the top of the *cavea* was included to justify its intramural presence.

The extraordinary precinct was illustrate provided further justification: a garden surrounded by a portico with galleries and shrines displaying some of Pompey's war booty, and opposite the theater a meeting hall or *Curia Pompeiana* where the Senate often met; Julius Caesar would be assassinated there. Roman theaters hosted song festivals and rhetorical contests as well as Greek dramas, but Roman productions were more often, slapstick or bawdy entertainment

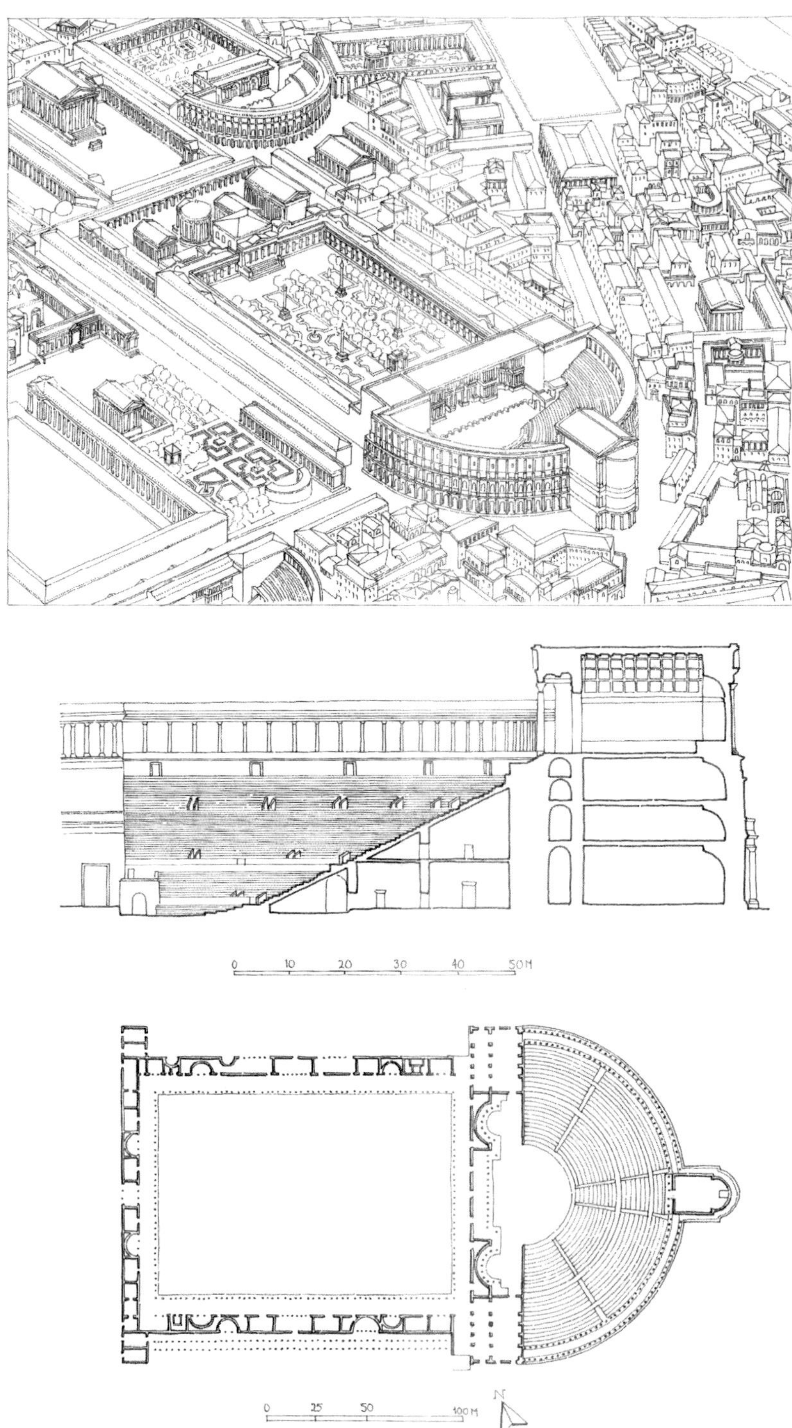

FIGURE 7.2 Theater of Pompey, Rome, Italy, 61–55 BCE. After Gilles Chaillet.

and even gladiatorial contests with wild animals. After 600 years of service, Pompey's great civic center gradually fell to ruin and was buried beneath modern Rome where, it is estimated, Tiber floods deposited a foot of soil a century on ancient Rome.

Romans usually sited theaters on flat ground with wood or combinations of brick, concrete, and stone for construction. Their membrature's expressive character placed the theater among the upper ranks of public buildings. Many survive in a ruined state. Largely intact and still in use is the 6,000-seat **theater, Mérida, Spain, 16 BCE** with a two-story Corinthian scaenae *frons*. The well-preserved exteriors of portions of the *cavea* and *scaenae frons* of the **Theatre of Marcellus, Rome, inaugurated by Augustus, 12 BCE** display the fornix motif in the canonic Doric, Ionic, and Corinthian sequence. Two variations in the plan were also popular: two *cavea* facing one another made an amphitheater such as the FLAVIAN AMPHITHEATRE (COLOSSEUM), ROME, 70–80, and two separated by long rows of seats for races made a *circus*, the basis for the Piazza Navona in Rome (Figure 7.3).

The name of this amphitheater, the largest in the Roman world, came from a long-lost colossal bronze statue of Nero whose **Domus Aurea** preceded it

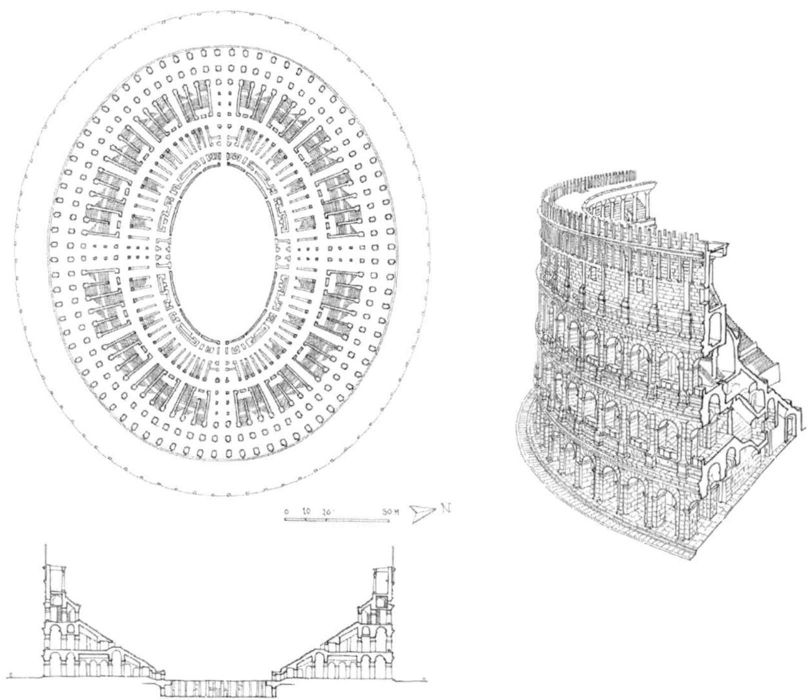

FIGURE 7.3 Flavian Amphitheatre (Colosseum), Rome, Italy, 70–80. Section-perspective. After Julien Guadet.

here. Into the 5th c., it presented dramatic displays of humankind in confrontations with nature and with one another. These ritualized confrontations now are in boxing arenas, football stadiums, soccer pitches, and baseball diamonds.

In seating its 50,000 or more spectators the ordered hierarchy of ancient Rome's authoritative classes was displayed. Each class entered through special tunnels and passages that prevented contact with others, and the location and accommodations for each were appropriate to its class: the emperor and Vestal Virgins in luxurious seats nearest to the arena, then seats for senators, then knights (*equites*), then common citizens (*plebs*), and finally, standing farthest away, the poor, women, and slaves.

The 83 by 48 m floor of the oval arena could be flooded for reenacting important naval battles, but not after it received a two-story complex beneath planks and sand for other entertainments. It was equipped with machines for lifting men, animals, and artificial mounds, trees, and buildings into the arena, and connected by tunnels to nearby gladiators' barracks, training facility (*ludus magnus*), armory (*armamentarium*), machine storage (*summum choragium*), and hospice (*sanitarium*).

The fabric of brick, concrete, and tufa has an 80-bay, four-story exterior with the fornix motif (*fornices*) in the first three stories. In each bay the piers, the three-quarter columns, and the arch and entablature used complex travertine blocks are structural pieces that run clear through. Statues of divinities occupied the second and third level arches. Here as at the **Theatre of Marcellus, Rome, 12 BCE**, they occupy the canonic order: Doric, Ionic, and Corinthian. High atop is a high attic whose bays used Corinthian pilasters between windows and bronze shields. In each bay, three brackets supported ships' masts that projected through the cornice, each one corresponding to a bollard eighteen meters beyond the exterior, where navel crews anchored the ropes of the giant shade awning (*velarium*).

An earthquake in 1349 collapsed the southern end, and more fabric disappeared well into the 18th c. through people living in it and quarrying fabric, for example for the BASILICA OF SAINT PETER, VATICAN, 1506–1614ff. Recent restorations have made more of it visitable and even usable for events (Figure 7.4).

In arid climates, people often sink wells deep into the earth and collect water from drenching rains. In India, there are as many as 100,000 such constructions. Called stepwells or *baori*, some date back to 2500BCE. A few are circular, some are long, many are square. During the Raj, the British found them unsanitary and replaced many with modern facilities. This *baori*, one of the largest and best preserved, survives as a water source and tourist attraction in this small town.

Apparently built in the 9th c. or perhaps the 8th c., It penetrates the earth's surface with a surrounding perimeter wall with defensive corner towers. Inside is a walkway sheltered by a columnar arcade with occasional piers. Descending from it are 3,500 steps, each one made from a single block mortared in place within masonry composed of various sized blocks. On three sides of a square,

FIGURE 7.4 Chand Baori stepwell, Abhaneri, Rajastan, India, 9th c.

they traverse 13 stories or 100 feet, while on the fourth, north side at various levels steps connect with a series of rooms and platforms connected to a temple breaching the walls. In the 18th c., this side was apparently rebuilt, and perhaps the *baori* proper was restored and enlarged.

Like other important Indian buildings, the order here has the bulbous bases and capitals (barely discernable in our drawing) and ornamented arches and spandrels, while the colonnade is slightly simplified with its slightly pointed segmental arches carried on octagonal columns with capitals like the bases, but inverted. From within, it suggests a theater ready for dramaturgy, perhaps related to the temple, perhaps associated with a nearby temple now devoted to the Harshat Mata but perhaps originally a Vaishnava shrine.

The expressive character comes from its fitness for its purpose and from its fourth wall's similarity to other Indian structures. That aside, it is like any city's public area where, as a late medieval European author observed, "the condition of man in this world can be observed" (or here more likely the condition of the women who come to fetch the water; Figure 7.5).

Antiquity's role in the post-medieval centuries extended to recovering ancient drama with the **Teatro Olimpico, Andrea Palladio, Vicenza, 1580, completed by Vincenzo Scamozzi**, an important site. Plush royal or ducal theaters upped the ante, with the court in Naples in 1737 introducing the common *parti* seen here.

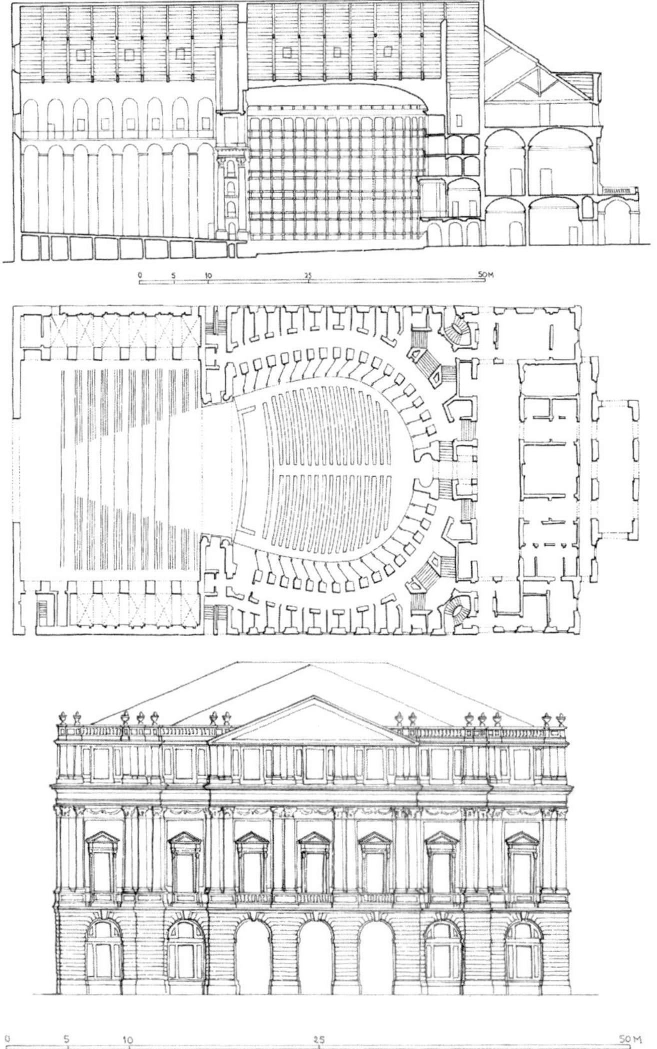

FIGURE 7.5 Teatro all Scala, Giuseppe Piermarini, Milan, Italy, 1776–78.

In 1773 Giuseppe Piermarini (1734–1808) moved from a career in Naples and Caserta to Milan, where Empress Maria Theresa (r. 1740–80) wanted here rebuilt archducal **Royal Palace, Milan, 1773** to have an expressive character appropriate to her enlightened governing. A 1776 fire destroyed its court theater, but the proposed small replacement would deprive 90 courtiers and wealthy Milanese of their boxes, and they persuaded the archduke to build a new, much enlarged opera house.

Santa Maria alla Scala standing well beyond the Duomo (see GALLERIA VITTORIO EMANUELE II, MILAN, 1865) was razed for its site but remembered in its name. Its interior had four tiers of boxes, many with anterooms and with one tier between the forestage's Corinthian half columns. This common parti always compromised stage views from some boxes, but it served the other important role of displaying their occupants. Two galleries above them were behind a colonnade aligned with the boxes' separations. The orchestra level entered from beneath the two-story archducal box raised the total standees to 3,000 standees, but reduced after the seats we show were installed in 1907.

The century's maxim "Early curly later straighter" is fulfilled inside by sparse low relief decorative sculpture on the boxes' fascia and the suppressed domical ceiling's coffers. Externally, its "straighter" expressive character shows up in the ground floor's fictive horizontal drafting and plain upper floors. A 1 × 3 bay arched entrance portico shelters arriving carriages. The piano nobile has three central bays defined by paired half columns, diluted to paired pilasters on the two flanking bays with the outer one slightly recessed. An attic story's stunted pilasters support a pediment above the center with a silhouette of balustrades with urns elsewhere. The side façade dilutes this scheme, and a grand pyramidal roof covers the house, truncated over the stage.

This parti, used for 150 years, was rarely this austere nor were the productions they housed more elaborate. Two qualities always set LA SCALA apart: its exceptionally large stage and its superb acoustics for every person in the house (Figure 7.6).

Buried within the large building are the nearly 2,000 seats in a horseshoe plan theater with three tiers of boxes with anterooms, an *orchestra* with fixed seats on a raked floor, and two raked-floor galleries. The stage is deeper than the house, with a farther extension available beyond in the storied Foyer de la Danse and salons where patrons could mingle with dancers. Its many technical innovations include a huge attic above the house with a gas fire and flue producing a chimney effect for ventilation.

Charles Garnier, the competition winner who taught at the École des Beaux-Arts, was assisted by other Beaux-Arts architects and students, which included Americans. The École's design method led to an exterior configuration that exhibits the principal interior volumes, with the theater's dome-like covering in front of the fly gallery's pitched roof. A bulge with a low dome on one side is a half-round *porte cochère* approached by long ramps (not shown) for the emperor's carriage, the one on the other side holds a restaurant. Within the cavernous interior are administrative facilities, music libraries, and rehearsal facilities.

The highly ornamented membrature and surfaces inside and out celebrate the arts and produce an imperial expressive character of extravagant opulence. It exhibits the pride the French took in their past, with the front appearing as an enriched version of the **East Front of the Louvre, Claude Perrault, 1667**, and the **Galerie des Glaces, Jules Hardouin-Mansart and Charles LeBrun, Versailles, 1678**, recalled in the *Grand Foyer* preceding the chamber for the central stair and side stair galleries, places calculated to allow their uses to be

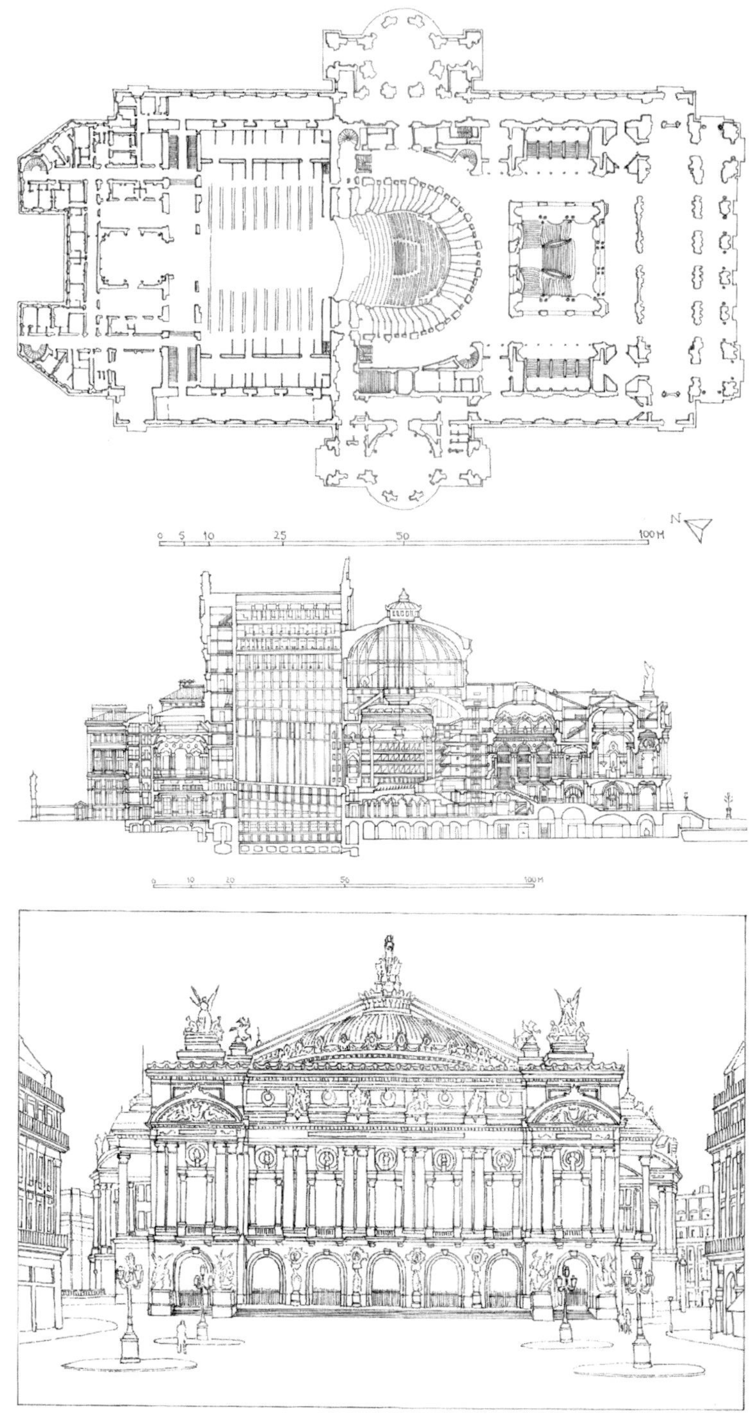

FIGURE 7.6 Opéra, Charles Garnier, Paris, France, 1861–75.

seen. Columns, usually Composite, are ubiquitous, paired in the façade's piano nobile trabeation, again in pairs beneath the segmental pediments of the façade's end pavilions, and yet again in their repetition on the sides where the wall recovers the primacy it enjoys in French buildings. Limestone fabric is joined by colorful marbles, with sculpture and ornament celebrating all the arts.

This notable monument epitomizes the École des Beaux-Arts' ability to produce prominent, stand-alone buildings that properly occupy prime locations within the system of **Boulevards, Baron Haussmann, Paris, 1854–70**, that were restructuring Paris. Now called the Palais Garnier, it continues to offer opera and ballet performances while joined by the **Opéra Bastille, Carlos Ott, 1984** with 700 more seats, no boxes, but a miscellany of steeply raked rear and side galleries (Figure 7.7).

Richard Wagner (1813–83) revolutionized opera with music as the vehicle for drama rather than drama as a vehicle for music. Using a self-financed construction, eventually aided by King Ludwig II of Bavaria, he introduced his "music dramas" in this theater design counterpart, cribbing from Gottfried Semper that went back to **Frederick Gilly, sketches for a national theater in Berlin, c. 1799**.

Sited it in the woods with only Wagner's works to be performed here, its brick exterior alludes to medieval wattle-and-daub construction. The house is beneath a semicircular sloping roof with a monitor, and the stage flies are beyond, within a temple-like pedimented enclosure. Corner elements hold stairways.

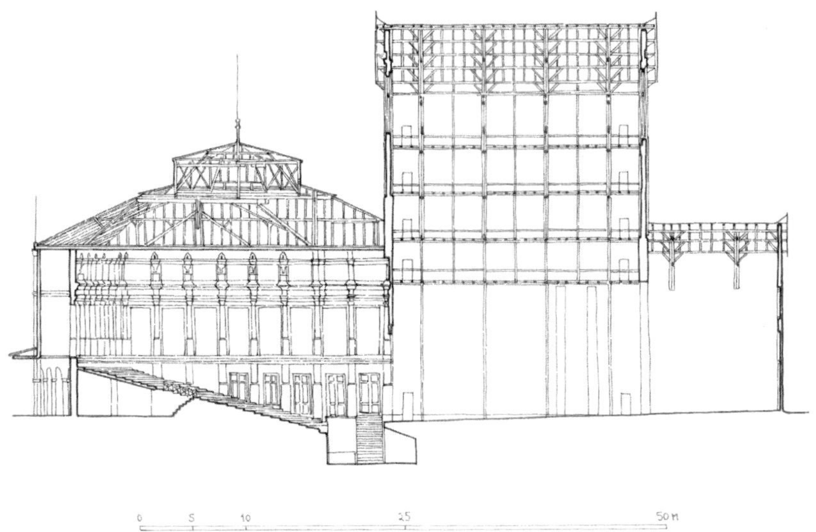

FIGURE 7.7 Festspielhaus, Richard Wagner, Bayreuth, Germany, 1872–76.

Various entrances in front and sides lead to the 1925 seats. Those in the main body of semicircular sweeps that recall an ancient Greek *cavea* are entered along their sides from vestibules between walls, each fronted by a single column. Those at the back of the house in the loge's boxes, including the royal box, and two tiers of galleries have separate entrances from the side elements. The interior focuses totally on the stage with nothing to distract attention. Two prosceniums frame the stage, a doubling intended to enhance the drama's mystical quality. The orchestra occupies a reverse rake under the stage with a hood making it invisible to the audience, further focusing full attention on the stage, a device that inhibits communication between it and the singers. To benefit the acoustics the interior is timber.

Many of Wagner's ideas were pushed farther in the project for **Totaltheater, Walter Gropius, Dessau, 1927–29**. Modified, Wagner's configuration was used in **Radio City Music Hall, Edward Durell Stone and Donald Deskey, New York City, 1931** within ROCKEFELLER CENTER, RAYMOND HOOD, HARVEY WILEY CORBETT, AND OTHERS, NEW YORK CITY, 1930–40.

8

THE REGIA

The ***regia*** protects authority with an idea-form of a square doughnut or some variation of it and falls into two categories, public and domestic.

Variation 1: the public regia

Priene is a double rarity: a city built by a tyrant to be governed democratically, and a master planned Greek city built ex novo (Figure 8.1). The tyrant Mausolus (377–353) (the great tomb he built would give great tombs their name), a renegade from the Achaemenid Empire, engaged the population of a city whose deep-water port was silting up to replace it with a new port, and this city, even before its completion, was occupied by the Persians. After they left, the city with a population of about 6,000 was completed with assistance from Alexander the Great (356–323). It prospered until silting afflicted their new port, and now far from the sea, it gradually became desolate.

In our plan of the city center, we show four closely related buildings in precincts in the gridded city's upland: a temple to Athena that Alexander dedicated, a theater, the agora with the market and a temple precinct, and the BOULEUTERION. It is stone with a timber roof, and with its tiers of seats occupying three sides focused on an altar, with our view from the speaker's dais on the fourth. In this public regia the members of the executive council or *boule* held deliberations and made decisions governing the city. Its neighbor was the *prytaneon*, a tholos where the executive magistrate kept the city's eternal flame and executed the laws. These two buildings open to the peristyle that fronts shops and steps, raising them above the similarly equipped agora they face.

A Greek *boule* exercised authority over moral issues concerning the common good, an activity that had grown out of Greek drama performed in theaters

DOI: 10.4324/9780429506260-11

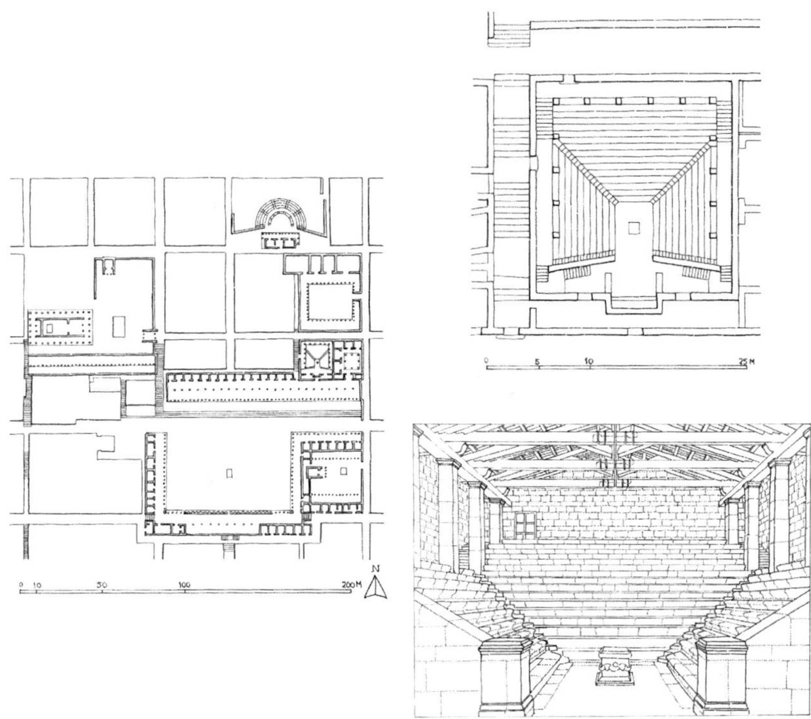

FIGURE 8.1 Bouleterion, Priene, in Turkey, 310BCE? 350BCE?

such as the nearly contemporaneous THEATER, EPIDAURUS, 340 BC whose *parti* was fitted into this public regia. Priene's democracy followed the model Solon had introduced sometime around 584 BCE in Athens, the largest Greek city by far, with a *demos* of perhaps 60,000. About a tenth of them formed the *ecclesia* (citizens empowered to participate in governing) that assembled on a theater-shaped hill, the Pnyx. The constant reshuffling of its democratic constitution prevented its engaging in long-term non-religious public-works projects. Hellenistic tyrants provided the stability, as Priene shows.

The Florentines built this garrison town to defend themselves from Arezzo after recently winning their liberty frontrunners overlords. In their plan they followed what they thought was Roman practice with towered walls and gates enclosing a rectangle within a grid defining four blocks proportioned 4 ½ × 1. Cross streets were aimed at towers, and major streets led to a broad, three-block-wide central piazza. In its midst they placed this building, fronting on the longest central road and produced in three campaigns (Figure 8.2).

First came the Florentine governor's large hall and stubby tower, doubtless crenellated, surrounded by a loggia's 2 × 5 segmental arch arcade carried on octagonal columns. Florence assured is security from Arezzo by conquering

FIGURE 8.2 Palazzo Pretorio (also known as Palazzo d'Arnolfo), San Giovanni Valdarno, Italy, 1296 et seq.

it in 1384, and in the first decade of the '400, it enclosed the side arcades and, in the front, added a two-story, two-bay loggia that repeated the motif of the original arcade and trabeation; its lower level was for the presence of a magisterial official. The building, now projecting beyond the cross-street's building frontages, immediately began collecting emblems and coats of arms. A final campaign in 1553 completed it with a reconfigured interior and a heightened, crenellated tower with a bell. The central corpus was also enlarged with the older two-story addition reproduced on the back and the entire body widened with a 6 × 4 loggia, with octagonal columns and piers turning the corners, and an enclosed upper story left unenclosed on the back.

The first phase is traditionally attributed to Florence's architect, Arnolfo di Cambio; its tectonics throughout is distinctly Tuscan, with local stone for structural members and stuccoed rubble walls finished to a level that places this public regia's status below that of its superior, **Palazzo Vecchio, Arnolfo di Cambio, Florence, 1299** (Figure 8.3).

Cities in northern Italy that gained increasing self-government liberty in the late 12th c. built a public regia for their governing assemblies. Called a *broletto*, it typically dominated the principal piazza with a great hall above a hypostyle market and was surrounded by a two-story loggia. Important examples are the **Broletto, Como, 1215**, and the earlier and larger **Palazzo della Ragione, Padua, 1172**.

Padua's rival Vicenza joined two regias and a campanile in 1441 to build its splendid *broletto* above a hypostyle market athwart the ancient *cardo*, with ship-building technology used to vault its great column-free hall. In 1481–94, its

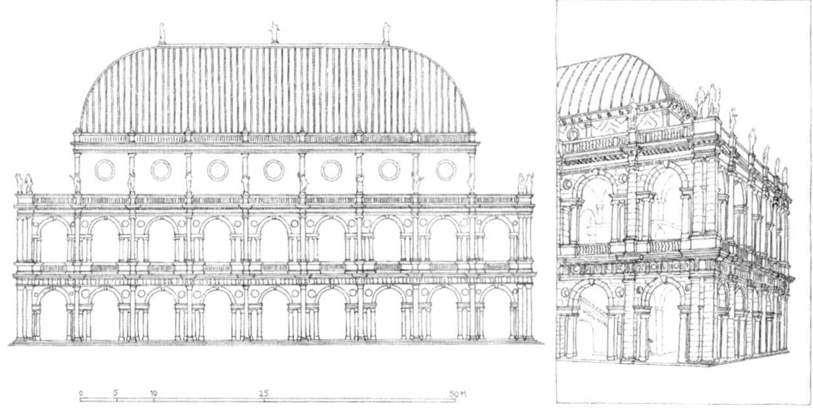

FIGURE 8.3 Basilica with loggia, Andrea Palladio, Vicenza, Italy, 1549.

surrounding two-story arcaded loggia was built, but two years after completion later a major portion collapsed, leaving behind the stairs up to the hall.

After consulting various architects about a replacement, the city chose the Padua-born local architect Andrea Palladio (1508–80). Begun in 1549, its vigorous membrature evoked ancient Rome, and earned it the name basilica, recalling the public regias where ancient citizens exercised authority. He wrapped the surviving building with two stories of a modern adaptation of the ancient fornix motif that had been introduced in the **Vatican Palace, Donato Bramante, 1506–14** with three different names: Palladiana, Veneziana for its prominence there, and Serliana after Sebastiano Serlio who had placed it among ancient and modern motifs and buildings in Book IV of his popular treatise in 1537.

Here each bay in a two-story assemblage with a pair of columns, Ionic above Tuscan and one behind the other, with sleeves at their bases. They support a slab finished as an entablature whose other end dies in a pier with two, low-relief pilasters on its reentry face. The arch has a simple profile and a mask on the keystones. Each bay is framed with half columns rising to a *ressault*, the Ionic entablature with a pulvinated frieze, the Doric with alternating triglyphs with bull sculls, and metopes with patera. These engaged orders are doubled at the corners, a widening that reduces the lintel slabs' span. An open roundel occupies each haunch except at the corners where it is blind at the Doric level and excised in the Ionic. In the balustraded silhouette, a block is above each smaller order carrying the arches, and above each engaged column a prominent *ressault* carries a statue with three at the corner.

Inside this wrapper are brick cross vaults on both stories, the original stair to the hall, and major portions of the original facade whose bays' irregular spacing is obscured by the just noticeable, varying spans of Palladio's lintels (Figure 8.4).

FIGURE 8.4 Modern Capitoline, Michelangelo, Rome, Italy, 1538ff. After Antoine Lafréry and Paul Letarouilly. (a) Perspective and (b) urban plan.

Since 1303 the Senator, a duke-like papal appointee, governed from the Palazzo del Senatore on the Capitoline Hill. With corner towers, crenellations, council hall, and campanile, it presented the expressive character of a ducal stronghold. Nicholas V (1447–55), a Tuscan, strengthened the papacy's role in Rome's government and administration, and he improved their facilities on the Capitoline. For the *conservatori*, representatives of the commune's *rioni* (wards, or districts), he built the **Palazzo dei Conservatori** with a council hall, offices in an attic, and below, places for the various guilds within an arcaded loggia.

The '500 popes' emphasis on the Church's imperial foundations included its suzerainty over Rome. In 1536 Pope Paul III (1534–49) Farnese, a Roman, had Michelangelo (1475–1564) launch the project illustrated in the **Etienne Dupérac etching, Paul Letarouilly's Edifices de Rome moderne**, and our drawing, completed finally when Mussolini installed the planned pavement.

Michelangelo moved the bronze equestrian statue of Marcus Aurelius, misidentified as Constantine and therefore preserved at the Lateran, into a new oval piazza. Its long axis would eventually extend to point on the processional route between the Vatican and SAN GIOVANNI IN LATERANO, 324 where the Jesuits would build **Il Gesú, Vignola, with Giacomo della Porta façade, 1568–80**.

His plan made the Palazzo del Senatore more emphatically ducal. Giant travertine Corinthian pilasters and strip frames define seven stuccoed bays above a deeply drafted travertine basement; the greater projection of the outermost bays suggest towers, and like the center bay they are slightly wider. They hold tall windows with alternating pediments, the *piano superiore's* slightly smaller (simpler square windows were built). The silhouette's balustrade carries small statues. The campanile is centered (lightning conveniently destroyed its off-enter predecessor), and a double-ramp stair shelters two ancient river gods, the Tiber and Nile, and reaches a baldachin (never built) for the Senator presided over public meetings.

Michelangelo's plan also completely transformed the Palazzo dei Conservatori. The original arcade columns were replaced by (enclosed within?) travertine piers with giant Corinthian pilasters on high pedestals and standing proud of the seven bays' strip-framed brick walls. The upper floor's Ionic columnar tabernacle windows have baluster sills and broken segmental pediments (the larger, central one is not Michelangelo's). The trabeated portico presents a vivid demonstration of masonry tectonics: on each bay's front, a simplified entablature is carried by in antis columns with garlanded Ionic capitals. On the interior brick wall, their mates are partially embedded within shallow, travertine niches, and the piers flanking them run forward as a stone beam to complete the support for the square bay's shallow-domed ceiling.

Completing the piazza is a replication, the Palazzo Nuovo, set against the hill crowned by the city's parish church, the Franciscan **Santa Maria in Ara Coeli, 1249**.

The Capitoline may be read as a normative piazza-block-garden with Rome as the piazza, then the block, and finally the Forum as the garden. Another plausible reading occurs as one moves up the sloping cordonata. The Palazzo del Senatore first appears as a two-story structure, seemingly a municipal building like the Palazzo dei Conservatori, until it reveals its full, ducal character. Finally, Dupérac's view presents the Capitoline as a hinge between modern and ancient Rome. From here in modern Rome through the gaps on the left, we see the ancient Forum and on the right the palatine. But in fact, those sites are visible only from inside the gaps or from within the respective loggias on either side of the piazza (Figure 8.5).

When Governor Thomas Jefferson (1743–1826) moved the state capital to Richmond, the James River's highest point for seagoing navigation, he modified the commercial town's grid to make a commanding Capitol Square. In his life-long fascination with temples, he saw embodied a geometric simplicity and proportionality between the variety of parts in the membrature and again with the configuration. He knew that the beautiful and the justice that its serves have common origins in nature, and he found the beautiful in architecture to reside in two geometric forms, the cubic exemplified in the **Maison Carrée, Nîmes, 4–7**, and the spherical seen in the PANTHEON, ROME, 117–26, his model for the **Library, University of Virginia, Charlottesville, 1817–26**.

After suggesting temple forms for Virginia's government buildings, he departed to serve as envoy in France and others began the state's capitol as a temple. After a year abroad, he was asked in August 1784 for a design to replace it. He promised his friend James Madison, it would come "from the best morsel of antient (sic.) architecture now remaining. It has obtained the approbation of fifteen or sixteen centuries, and is therefore preferable to any design which

FIGURE 8.5 Virginia Capitol, Thomas Jefferson, Richmond, U.S.A., 1785–98. After Henry Latrobe.

might be newly contrived ... It will be superior in beauty to any thing [sic.] in America, and not inferior to any thing in the world."

In a January 1786 letter to Madison when he sent the plaster model (now displayed in the Capitol) based on the Maison Carrée, he wrote, "its object is to improve the taste of my countrymen, to increase their reputation, to reconcile them to the respect of the world, and procure them its praise." Here taste meant sensitivity to beauty and not mere preference or fashion. The building's original prominence is clear in our view based on a Benjamin Latrobe watercolor.

Fourteen months passed before he saw the ancient temple in person. He knew it through Andrea Palladio's valued treatise, and the recent publication by Charles-Louis Clérisseau, who helped him make the model. Richmond's brick-and-stucco building differs from the plaster model, for example, pilasters are placed between the windows on the sides and back. Differences between both and the ancient building in Nîmes are greater: Ionic, not Corinthian; two-bay pronaos, not three; side entrances and fenestration on two stories plus basement added; and greatly enlarged dimensions overall. Inside it serves the functions of government (we show the lower floor), with chambers for two legislative bodies, governor's office, stairs, General Court room, and in a central, double-height square, a tholos with a dome extending into the attic where Jean-Antoine Houdon's statue of George Washington would be installed in 1796.

The building remains in use. In 1904–06, at the height of the restored role for the classical in America's civil architecture, a consortium of Virginia architects built recessed wings holding larger legislative chambers connected through the former side entrances. It also installed slightly enlarged columns, new matching capitals, and, finally, the temple's broad, front steps (Figure 8.6).

New York's third city hall originally dominated the common at Manhattan's northern edge, but now it seems a small gem in a park among neighboring giants that include the **Brooklyn Bridge, John Augustus Roebling, 1869–83**; the **Municipal Building, McKim Mead, and White, 1907–14**; and other structures built to serve the city after the 1898 consolidation of five, formerly independent municipalities. Today we see its 1950s renovation with limestone and granite replacing the original brownstone base and marble corpus.

Its design has deep roots in France. Joseph-François Magnin (1758–?), a 1793 arrival from France via Saint-Domingue and protégé of Alexander Hamilton, was city surveyor when he bested others including Benjamin Henry Latrobe in competing for this job. He joined John McComb, Jr. (1763–1853), a builder, in constructing it.

The five-part facade on its two stories beneath a balustraded silhouette recalls the corner towers and defensible central entrance of its public regia forebears. The trabeated central portico's Ionic columns are doubled at its ends, as are the engaged Corinthians above. The slightly projecting central five bays behind it have large, arched windows separated by single engaged columns.

Following modern French classical tradition, the central section is diluted for the pavilions projecting two bays and again for the hyphens. The facades facing

FIGURE 8.6 City Hall, Mangin, and McComb, New York, U.S.A., 1802–12.

the park on the other side are diluted slightly farther than their front's counterparts. Above, a square lantern with arched windows and a pair of composite columns set diagonally on each corner concludes with a base for a dome and a statue of Justice as a finial. The windows throughout, many with lintels, are multi-pane double-hung, and the wall has horizontal drafting below the arch-springs.

Inside is Magnin's impressive Rotunda with a double-curved stair leading up to a gallery where widely spaced composite columns carry a shallow coffered dome and glazed oculus. It gives entry to the subsequently remodeled oblong, low vaulted Council Chamber with an observers' mezzanine (Figure 8.7).

In 1895 fire gutted the Rotunda that Thomas Jefferson designed for the library of the University of Virginia. It also destroyed the post-Jefferson classroom

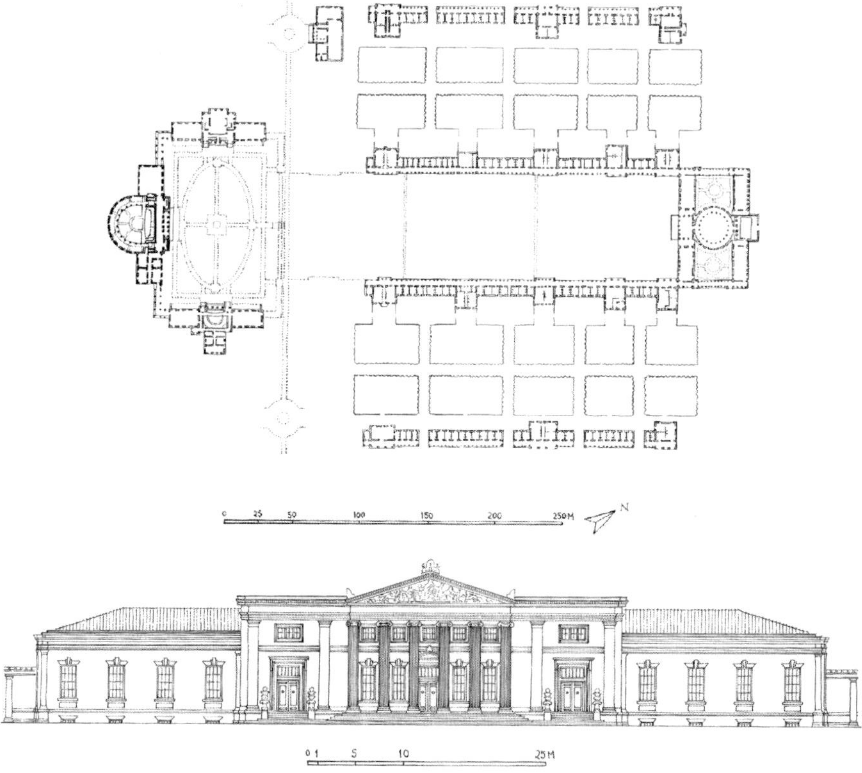

FIGURE 8.7 Cabell, Rouss, and McIntire Halls, Stanford White, University of Virginia, Charlottesville, 1895. After McKim, Mead, and White.

building attached to the Rotunda's rear. Undamaged were the colonnades with student rooms and the ten pavilions for professors stretching down the Lawn descending slowly to the open end.

Stanford White of McKim, Mead, and White was immediately hired to rebuild the Rotunda and replace the lost facilities. He replaced the timber dome with a tile dome, rebuilt the interior as two rather than three stories (subsequently restored to its original configuration), added a temple front and stairs on the back, and built quadrants on the sides. A faculty committee required that the new classrooms and an auditorium be at the Lawn's open end, still an unpopular decision. To mitigate the intrusion be broke the program into three parts with a central building and two more, all nestled into the sloping ground. To connect them and retain the view from the Lawn into the distant regions, he connected his parts with a columned trellis pergola.

The central, Cabell Hall holds 1,500 in a richly articulated and colorful auditorium covered by a shallow, skylit semi-dome. Most of its seats are reached by descending from a semicircular colonnade with four loge sweeps and three in a balcony behind it. Entrance is through a forward projection of the building's central mass where a hexastyle Ionic temple front has a low raking cornice set within flankers holding ancillary rooms. The lobby's attic windows' sills rest on a string course, while the temple front's entablature extends to top the flankers framed by a pilaster and, like the portal, have low attic windows. Next out and well back are wings with four windows with lintels with white keystones defining bays topped by a full entablature at the level of the attic windowsills' string course. The areas below grade receive light from front light wells and a lower story in the back where the upper, back facade has paired pilasters following the auditorium's curve above a rusticated stone, fenestrated base.

Two flankers farther apart than Jefferson's colonnades, one for science labs and one with classrooms, are smaller than the central building, and each has a dilution of its facade with unimportant differences between the two. The temple front is reduced to four columns standing in antis to a shallow depth with entrance through doors in the flanking, slightly recessed bays framed by pilasters; as at the central building, there are also similar, more deeply recessed wings.

Here again, sloping ground allows highly visible rear facades that are further dilutions. They also provide light for the rusticated lower story, as do light wells in front.

White was a worthy match for the inventive amateur Jefferson, but he was also likely responsible for changing what is thought to be the commonwealth's traditional architecture palette. His brick and white membrature differs from Jefferson's original palette whose brick-and-stucco columns were sand-dashed with buff sandstone here, at MONTICELLO, JEFFERSON, CHARLOTTESVILLE, 1768–1826, and at **Poplar Forest, Jefferson, near Lynchburg, 1814–26** where the sandstone columns were also originally unpainted and have been restored as such (Figure 8.8).

Prussian King Friedrich Wilhelm III, like other monarchs, opened his collections to the people. In this regia by Karl Friedrich Schinkel (1781–1841), ancient art could exert its authority in modern art. He and the landscape architect Peter Joseph Lenné gave it a central site with the Spree Canal along one side, the Protestant Cathedral on the other (later replaced), and the Royal Palace across a large parade ground that in 1825 Lenné would replace with a public garden, the Lustgarten. This was the first museum on what would be developed as the Museuminsel, a short distance away from the austere, Greek **Guard House, Schinkel, 1816**, and a block south of the BAUAKADAMIE, KARL FRIEDRICK SCHINKEL, BERLIN, 1832–36.

Germany's claims at this time for beginnings in ancient Greece set that nation apart from the Romanism in France and England, and Schinkel asserted this with a Greek-derived apparatus of forms and motifs for this regia displaying ancient art. Its front is a civic stoa with 18 fluted Ionic columns and entablature with an eagle above each column. From a distance is visible a central square projection with Horse Tamers at each corner, and down the sides and across the back between immured corner piers are windows on sharp moldings.

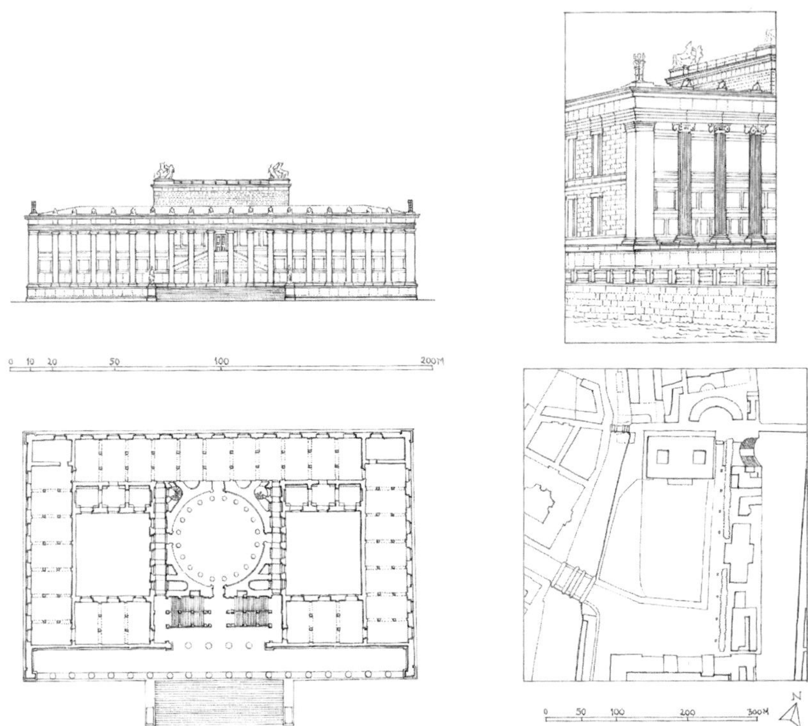

FIGURE 8.8 Altes Museum, Karl Friedrich Schinkel, Berlin, Germany, 1823–28.

Broad stairs span seven intercolumniations, with four columns in antis in the stoa's interior wall with frescoed marble panels. The vestibule within gives direct entrance to the tholos and the surrounding galleries with square light courts. The vestibule's pairs of parallel stairs give access to an upper vestibule offering a splendid view across the city and to the second-story galleries and a walkway with shallow niches around the tholos. Carrying the walkway is a colonnade with 20 unfluted Corinthian columns under a dome rising through four tiers of coffers to the oculus evoking the Roman Pantheon (Figure 8.9).

A block south of the Lustgarten and the ALTES MUSEUM, KARL FRIEDRICH SCHINKEL, BERLIN, 1823–28 and across the Spree Canal from the Royal Palace, Schinkel built a hypostyle serving as a state-sponsored regia. It incorporates what he found on his wide-ranging 1826 tour of Manchester and elsewhere in industrial Britain that rendered nugatory his 1803–04 Italian sojourn. Its war-damaged fabric was wantonly destroyed in 1961; its reconstruction is now underway.

The building's purpose was to provide instruction for the construction of low-status buildings in the state's modernization. It is quite properly elevated

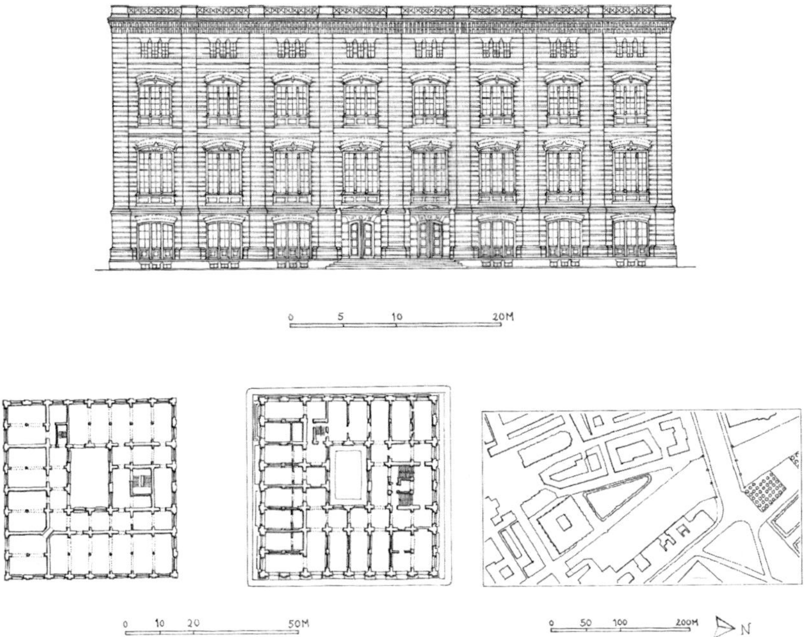

FIGURE 8.9 Bauakademie, Karl Friedrich Schinkel, Berlin, Germany, 1832–36.

above mere utility, with its central Berlin location and its exterior's expressive character based on, but disciplining, traditional construction.

Eight bays square with a light court, commercial shops on the ground floor were followed with three more of different heights, first the tallest, then a slightly lower one, and finally an attic story. The brick facades included thin, glazed purple tiles. Projecting piers rose as if pilasters above the ground floor with tiles on their faces describing vertical rectangles on each floor and squares in between; the piers interrupted terra cotta string courses. Tiles also drew horizontal lines within the brick walls. Segmental arched windows were on the second and third floors, and on all three thin, iron-framed triplet windows were set within terra cotta frames, with terra cotta reliefs showing busy workmen below the sills in the middle two floors. The attic windows lacked frames and heads. The silhouette's open metalwork stood on a molded-brick free-style cornice.

The double bays for the entrance had bronze doors and terra cotta relief panels celebrating the history and art of building. The generous stairs inside fed the school, the offices of the state's building authority that Schinkel headed, and his family residence. There are also several innovative tectonic elements. Some floors were carried on low brick vaults tied by iron beams springing from brick walls. In others, cast iron Tuscan columns carried ferrous arches supporting ferrous floors.

An unmistakable allusion to this building as obsolete was the Modernist six-story didactic **Concrete Office Building, Ludwig Mies van der Rohe, 1923** project (Figure 8.10).

Libraries are regias protecting the authority of learning. Earlier libraries isolated within monasteries and palaces were usually richly decorated and ornamented. This one, whose collection dates back to 831, was built as a public library, an instrument for public education. Its name comes from its location in the university district and to honor Sainte-Geneviève, the city's patron saint who saved Paris, Roman Lutetia, from the barbarians in the 5th c.

High windows in a long room usually provided the necessary light, as at the **Laurentian Library, Michelangelo, Florence, 1525–71** and **Vatican Library, Domenico Fontana, 1585–90**. The *parti* used here is similar but with auxiliary gas light extending the hours until ten at night. We see it later in **Boston Public Library, McKim, Mead, and White, 1888–95**; **Doe Memorial Library, John Galen Howard, University of California, Berkeley, 1911**; and a version using a medieval membrature, the **Suzzallo Library, University of Washington, Carl F. Gould, Seattle, 1926**. An alternative *parti*, or minimal diagram from which the plan is generated, here as an instance of the idea-type diagram, is seen at **Indianapolis Public Library, Paul Cret, 1914**.

Two stories with 19 bays under a pitched roof, its plane ashlar basement has a single central arched entrance and small arched windows and garlanded belt course below a march of arches ending in corner piers. The upper half is glazed, and each lower portion holds panels with 820 authors' names, originally picked out in red.

The entrance hall, three bays wide and four deep, has fluted piers and a flat ceiling carried on ferrous metal filigree arches. The walls have authors' busts below woodland scenes. In the flanking rooms are rare books and offices on one side and book stacks on the other.

A rear stair hall extrusion leads up to the impressive, long, reading room. Ceiled with a pair of longitudinal plaster vaults, they bear on filigree cast iron arches springing from cast iron columns on high stone piers. Originally, bookshelves followed down the room's center between parallel, long reading tables. In 1928 those shelves and lowest along the walls were removed and the tables set crosswise, increasing the seating from 400 to 720. The upper levels of shelves and those within the broad window alcoves remain accessible by catwalks. Steam radiators along the outer walls and between the central piers heated the room.

Innovative, its display of books inside and out remained the principal content of its expressive character (Figure 8.11).

The walled city of Djenné (a.k.a. Jenne), resettled in about 1,000, is the last green city encountered on the trade routes leading into the Sahara through Timbuktu. The library of Timbuktu's Sankoré Madrasah (School) has as many as 700,000 manuscripts that preserve ancient pagan and subsequent Muslim learning.

Djenné, which annually becomes an island when the Niger River and a tributary flood, prospered after the 14th c. when Europeans began exploiting Africa's

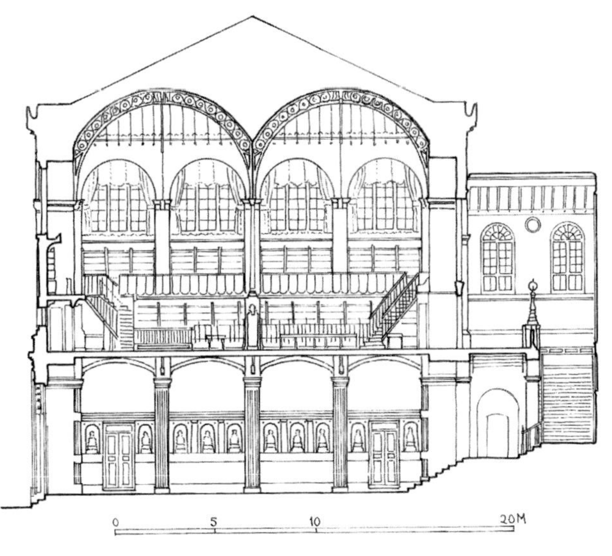

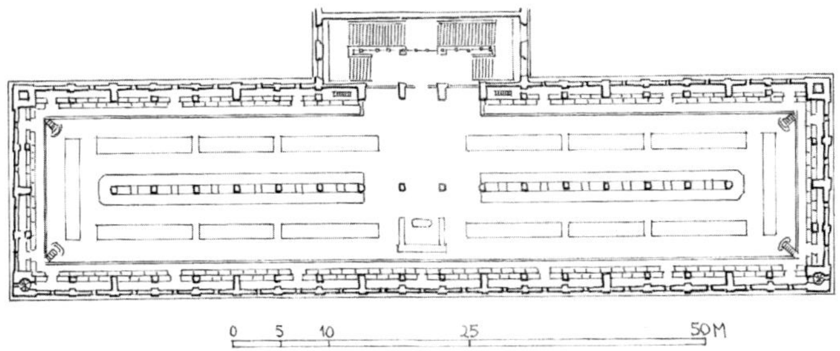

FIGURE 8.10 Bibliothèque Sainte-Geneviève, Henri Labrouste, Paris, France, 183850. (a) Plan and section and (b) perspective.

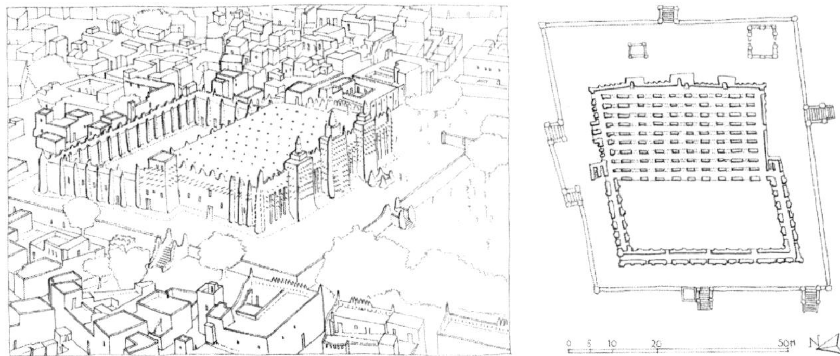

FIGURE 8.11 Grand Mosque, Djenné, Mali, 13th c.; 1906.

gold, salt, slaves, and other trade goods, but its decline followed the Portuguese opening of coastal trade routes. In the late 19th c., the French gained control of the region, and in 1906 the restoration of this mosque was undertaken. It followed its 13th-century plan but elevated 3 m within a 75 m square walled precinct nearly equally divided between a courtyard and a rectangular hypostyle prayer hall that can hold 3,000 people. The hall is lit by small windows in opposite walls, and its flat roof is built of rodier-palm (Borassus aethiopum) wood supported by 90 rectangular piers, each slightly different, carried on pointed arches with ceramic pots in the roof that can be opened for ventilation. The ratio of structure to void is nearly equal, with meter-thick walls built with sun-dried bricks (adobe) with tapered exteriors preserving the interior's cool air. The eastern, *qibla* wall facing the market has three towers crowned with tapering pinnacles, the central, taller one holding the *mihrab* and the other a *minibar* for Friday sermons. At the junction of the prayer hall and courtyard rises a simpler tower with stairs to the roof.

Said to be the largest mud building in the world, like the city's other buildings it requires constant maintenance. Bundles of rodier-palm wood poles projecting 60 cm serve as decoration, and they facilitate the day-long replastering festival, the Crépissage de la Grande Mosquée, each April held in anticipation of the exterior's assault by the substantial downpours between mid-July and December. The women supply the water, young boys playing in the mud stir the mixture, and teams of men compete for prestigious prizes while working above (Figure 8.12).

Jože Plečnik (1872–1957) worked in the seam between Eastern Slavic regions and the Romans' Europe, with many notable urban and architectural projects in his native Ljubljana.

While part of Otto Wagner's academy and circle in Vienna between 1894 and 1900, he traveled in France and Italy and concluded, "Everything here [in Italy] that is old is incredibly beautiful and everything that is new there [in Vienna] seems so mediocre."[1]

In 1895 an earthquake destroyed a much-valued Baroque ducal court and its library, and in 1930 he began plans for its site with objections by Modernists,

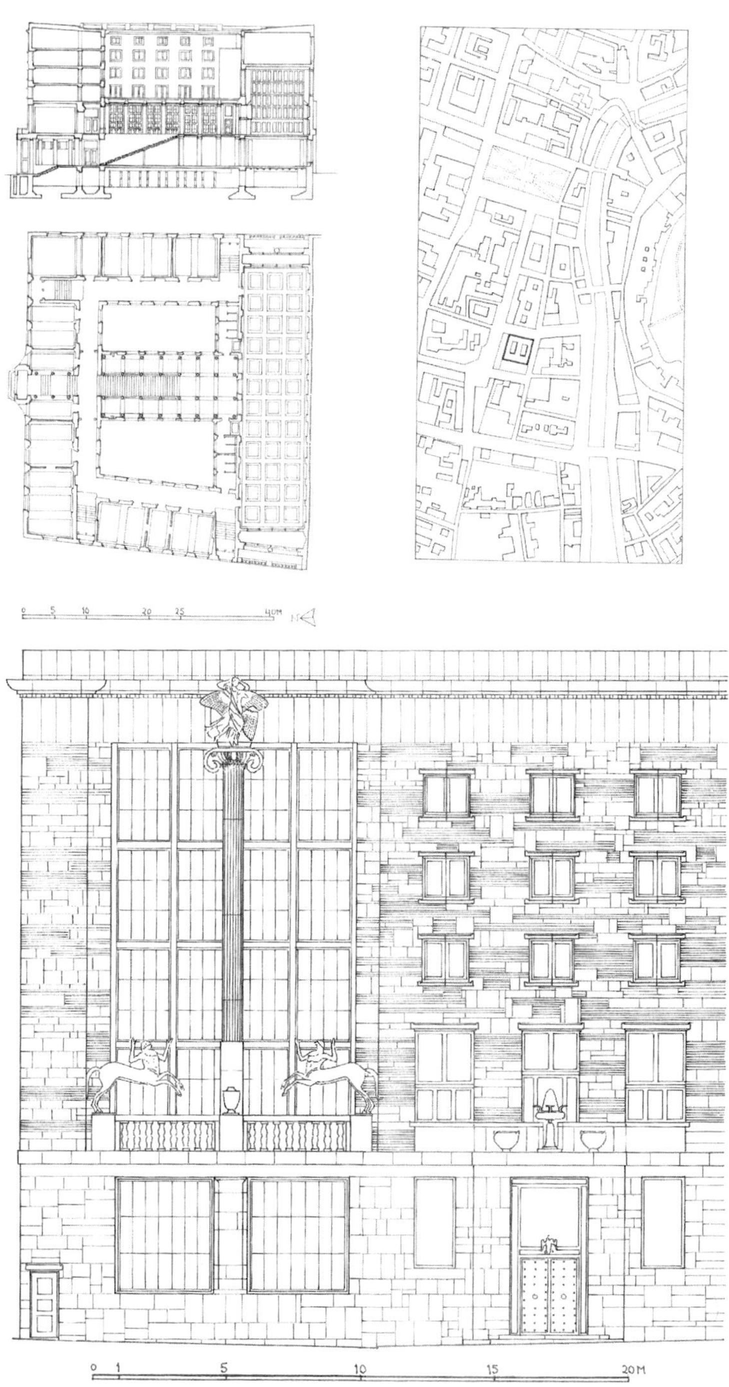

FIGURE 8.12 National and University Library, Jože Plečnik, Ljubljana, Slovenia, 1930. After Alberto Ferlenga and Sergio Polano.

neighbors, and national and university administrators delaying construction until 1936. He used some of its stone for the membrature and ornament to produce a rugged monumentality that is both regional and ancient while also producing the expressive character of a major institution holding the university reading room and classrooms.

A quadrangular block, its ground floor's facade is random limestone ashlar with some blocks rusticated. The four stories above are predominantly in brick, but include stone, again some rusticated, with a high, plain stone cap and cornice with Greek roof tiles with antefixes below a low parapet. The small windows in the three uppermost stories with book storage project in a slight V, windows in the next register down are larger, and larger again on the ground floor. Our drawing shows the deep recession of the reading room's end wall behind a balustraded front. Within, a central, single, thin, fluted stone column rises to an inventive Ionic capital (the sculpture we show there and below was never added). A wall of equal length beyond what we show lacks windows, but they reappear on the front with a simple, jutting entrance.

The vestibule reveals broad stairs within a generous, full-height, 7 × 3 bay hypostyle hall with light flooding in from flanking air courts. At the piano nobile level are 32 Doric columns of dark, polished, Podpeč marble, unfluted, multi-drum, baseless, and with cushion echinuses along both sides of a corridor and carrying the wooden ceiling's smooth, polished trabeation. On the sides at the stairs within the intercolumniations and doubling as bench and railing are smooth stone slabs, each carried on a slim, Aeolian order between fat, fluted Doric columns.

The reading room is the building's climax. Unlike departures from convention such as **Gunner Asplund's Stockholm Public Library, 1920–28**, it reworks the much-used *parti* of BIBLIOTÈQUE SAINTE-GENEVIÈVE, HENRI LABROUSTE, PARIS, 1838. Light floods in from both end walls' windows and from the long walls' center. Books in closed cabinets line the lower level, and open shelves above are reached by catwalks suspended from cast iron piping with bronze fittings and a transverse aisle through the room, yet another instance of Plečnik's unceasing inventiveness.

Variation 2: the domestic regia

In an autocracy, the autocrat's residence becomes the model for subordinates. In a perfect democracy, everyone resides in a regia except monks, college students, justly convicted prisoners, etc., who occupy dwellings, but social and economic conditions prevent this perfection.

Before the 15th c, a domestic regia constituted a precinct, but after precincts dissolved it was often aligned axially with a piazza or street with a garden behind (Figure 8.13).

Cities in ancient Greece and Rome were filled with party wall masonry and timber dwellings, the larger ones with rooms around an atrium, often with a shop in front. The larger ones for people with authority were therefore

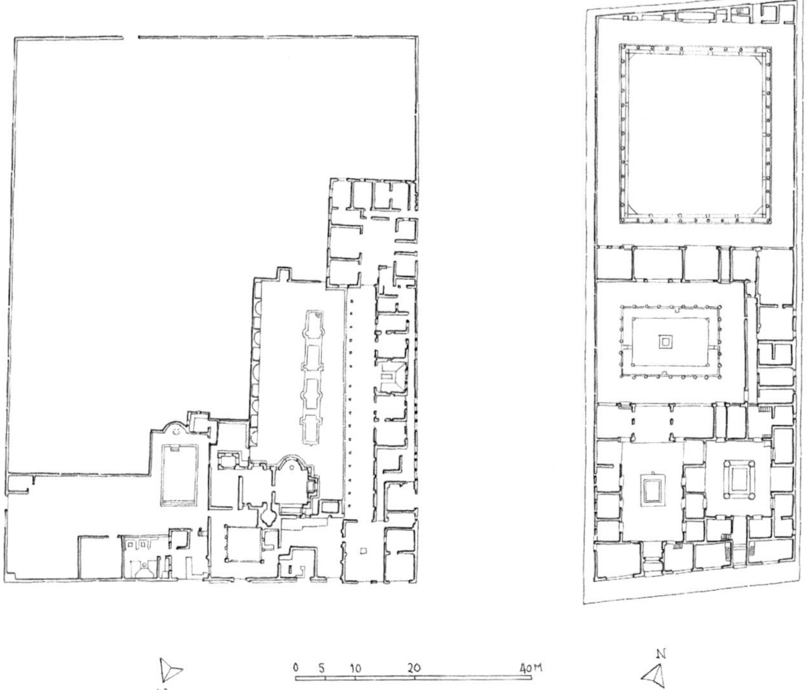

FIGURE 8.13 The Italic Atrium House, Pompeii, before, 79.

domestic regias. Vitruvius discussed them in Book VI, explaining how to get the greatest advantage from the sun, stressing dimensional proportionality in the parts and the whole, and the necessity that the decorum be proper for the proprietor's status. He explained that people "only moderately well off" do not need magnificent vestibules, *tabulina* and *atria*" open to public access because "they fulfill their social obligation by canvassing others for patronage rather than by being canvassed." (VI, v, 1: Schofield, trans.). He distinguishes five kinds of vestibules (*atria*), normally unroofed to catch rainwater, and mentions that beyond it, the *tabulinum* opens to the peristyle with an east-facing *triclinium* for dining and then a garden that might supply vegetables and fruits. The *lararium* (shrine for the household *lares* and *penates*) was normally in the *tabulinum* or atrium. Women, children, and slaves were in secluded wings (*alae*), often with upper-story rooms; they emerged after the men had left on their civic rounds. Street fronts, usually flanked by shops, were never pretentious, some in Pompeii, famously, buried in ash in 79, have an entrance (*fauces*) with a mosaic floor showing a chained guard dog and others with "Greetings" (HAVE) seen here.

The city's pre-Roman builders had laid out blocks (*insulae*) of dwellings on parcels having common frontages and depths, but after 80 BCE it became a

Roman city, and the wealthy began expanding their parcels by nibbling into their neighbor's dwellings. We show one of Pompeii's domestic regias, the most sumptuously decorated and largest, the **House of the Faun** near the Forum, named for the bronze faun found there, as was the famous **Alexander Mosaic**, now in the National Archaeological Museum in Naples. It had two *atria*, both with *alae*, two gardens, one of them very large, two entrances, and four shops.

The other, the **Praedia of Julia Felix** *en route* to the entertainment district, was a reworking from the earthquake of 62. Its female owner offered "the Venus Bath fitted for the well-to-do, shops with living quarters over the shops, apartments on the second floor…."[2] The bath had small cool, tepid, and hot chambers and even a small outdoor pool overlooking a garden and orchard. At the side street's corner were shops offering food and drink, and along that street and extending to a small atrium house with its own entrance was a long wing with slaves' quarters. A frescoed peristyle with thin, white, marble Corinthian pillars faced a garden, with three entertainment rooms in its center. The middle held a blue, barrel-vaulted, richly decorated *triclinium* where water trickling down a back-wall fountain before running into a garden basin crossed by three bridges. On the garden's far side echoing the peristyle were alternating rounded and rectangular niches. Leisure luxury indeed! (Figure 8.14).

The Forbidden City housed the autocratic empire's officials, and this ceremonial throne hall dominated it and Beijing. It was built in 1421 when the emperor of the Ming dynasty (1368–1642) moved the Middle Kingdom's capital from Nanjing to Beijing. The micro and macro design reproduced the form of heaven, just as its five predecessors had, with the city's million residents placed according to their class in three rectangular walled and gated precincts along a mile-long axis culminating here.

This HALL is on the cosmic axis on the first and largest of connected, three-level platforms. It suffered seven fires before the Qing Dynasty (1642–1912) rebuilt it in 1695. The absence of large trees forced its reduction by a third, but its distribution of 11 × 5 bays outside and 9 × 3 inside remained. The interior's ceiling and membrature inside and out are intensely colored with red (luck, happiness, joy) and gold (royalty, power, prosperity). The traditional bracket systems using earthquake-resistant timber tectonics, developed when the Greeks were working out the orders in stone trabeation, is largely hidden here except in instances where it supports eaves or ceiling.

The membrature rises from very low, round, stone bases reproducing stylized clouds. The bays have different widths but identical membrature with beams keyed into the shafts above brackets. Separate hipped roofs with flared eaves cover the outer, lower ambulatory, and the higher, inner one over the throne's site. Its ridge with very large dragons at each end is 100 feet above the pavement. All eight eaves have processions with a messenger leading ten celestial creatures and a dragon protecting the rear.

Three ramped stairs, the central one reserved for the emperor, lead up to the throne on the elevated, white jade platform. Looking south beyond the

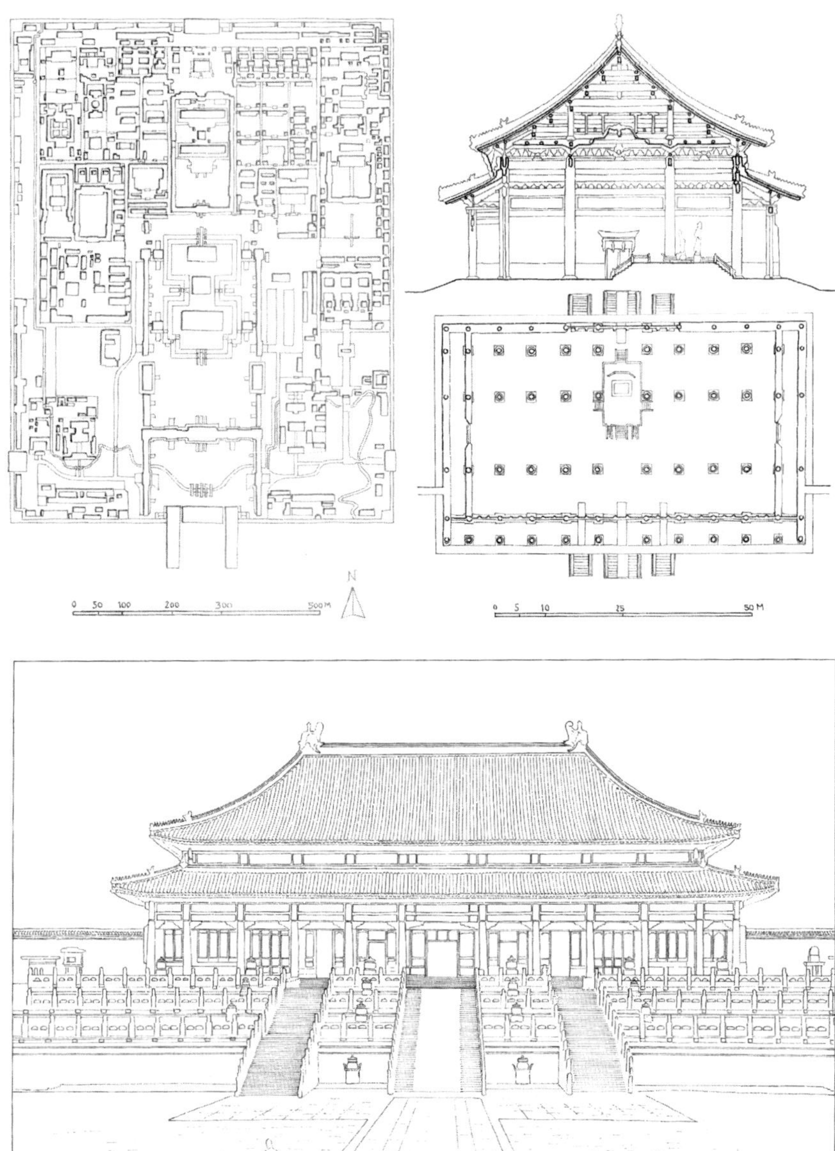

FIGURE 8.14 Hall of Supreme Harmony Beijing, China, 1421; 1695. (a) Urban plan, (b) plan section, and (c) perspective.

prostrated court officials he could see into the city and nation where, as the Son of Heaven, he exercised the Mandate of Heaven to maintain harmony between Heaven, the land, and the people. His tholos-like dais is accompanied by dragons, unicorns, turtle cranes, and braziers, and above it twisting dragons protect the emperor and play with huge Xuanyuan Jing pearl (Figure 8.15a, b).

The palace Cosimo de Medici built is the prototypical Italian domestic regia with a distinctly Florentine expressive character derived from its predecessors and innovations that its successor will incorporate.

An earlier example is the **Palazzo Davizzi (later Davanzati), 2nd half, 14th c.**, that, like many later Florentine palaces, incorporates fabric from earlier tower-residences that the Florentine republic later outlawed. Its expressive character follows that of the public regia, the **Palazzo Vecchio, Florence, 1299ff**, but one story higher (the loggia on top is from the '500) and without the tower and cancellations emblematic of government's authority (cf. PALAZZO PRETORIO, SAN GIOVANNI VALDARNO, 1296). Each upper story has five aligned windows rising above the legally mandated 1 × 3 loggia that follows the ceremonial **Loggia dei Lanzi, Florence, 1376–82**, but with drafted masonry differentiating its public role from the private residence.

When Cosimo dei Medici, the banker and first among equals controlling Florence's government, returned in 1433 from a year's exile in Venice, the story goes that he had Filippo Brunelleschi design a palace, but fearful of an envious reaction, he delayed construction until 1444, with Michelozzo as architect.

Is parentage is in the Palazzo Davanzati and Palazzo Vecchio with an open, rusticated 1 × 3 loggia for a ground floor front and two more stories with aligned bifore windows on belt courses. Each of its floors is lower than those of the two predecessors, with regular drafting carved into the piano nobile ashlar followed by smooth ashlar above. A massive cornice scaled relative to the building's mass with suggestions of classical detailing completes the height. In the square plan (ours is of the piano nobile), a generous 3 × 3 cortile was accessible from the loggia (closed in 1517 by Michelangelo with other changes following, including its two-bay extension after 1659, not shown). The bifore windows align but not with the ground floor openings, and its generous 3 × 3 cortile is accessible through the (now closed) loggia. Above the cortile arcade, sgraffito supplies garlands and Medici emblems. On the piano, nobile sgraffito provides ashlar around bifore windows. And on the top floor, open trabeation has columns aligned with the lower solids. All of this is carefully marshaled as if within a regular, gridded cube.

Beyond the cortile is a 1 × 3 loggia open to a garden, while outside, the crenellated walls with heavy rustication at the corner but sgraffito between it and the palazzo's ground floor, all perhaps to suggest it is a paradise garden. For public festivities, the family assembled in the garden, retainers in the cortile, and the general public outside in the streets where, on regular days, they and Medici clients could find respite on the bench along the façade.

Is Brunelleschi's design visible here? Certainly, the role of perspective is. The palazzo's configuration, proportioning, and membrature can be read as

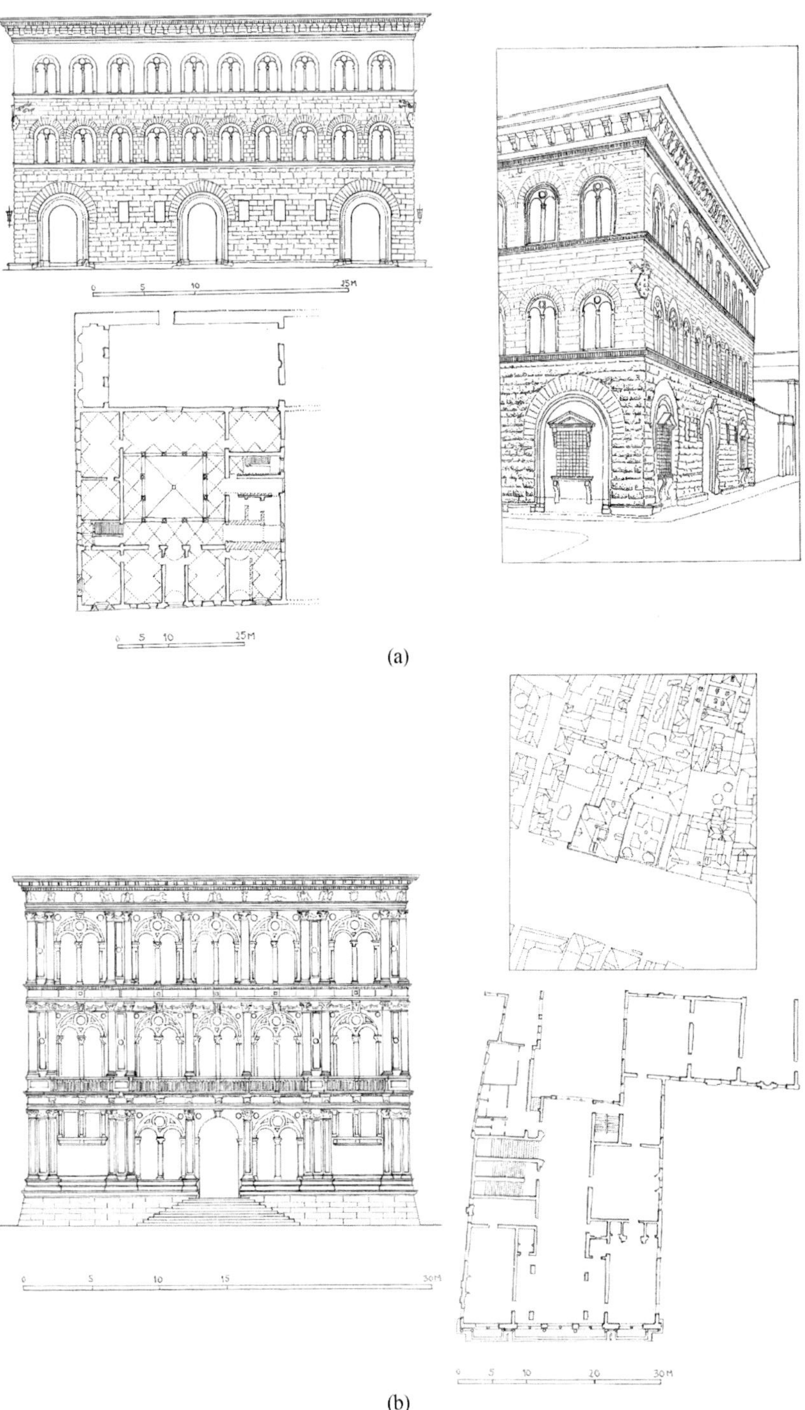

FIGURE 8.15 (a) Palazzo Medici, Michelozzo di Bartolomeo, Florence, 1444 and (b) Cà Loredan-Vendramin (Aka, Calergi; Venice Casino), Mauro Codussi, Venice, Italy, 1481–1509.

an ordered whole that nonetheless distinguishes between public and private portions. It also exploits its urban site where a street jog provides an impressive view from the Piazza del Duomo and stands in for the missing part of the normative piazza-block-garden urban configuration. And obviously, Medici arms were conspicuous on both corners (Figure 8.16).

Founded by refugees from the spent Roman Empire, Venice became rich by trading in the Byzantine world. After the Turks conquered Constantinople in 1453, the Serenissima reoriented its foreign and commercial policies toward Italy and Europe, a turn marked by building the **Arsenale Entrance Arch, Antonio Gambello, c. 1460**, modeled on ancient Roman triumphal arches but with distinctly Byzantine capitals, perhaps spolia.

The LOREDAN-VEBDREMIN PALACE by Mauro Codussi (1440–1504) on the Grand Canal also marks the turn. The A-B-A conventional Venetian configuration provided a wide B bay for business and great halls above, but its facade points not to Byzantium but to Italy. It uses the usual Istrian stone with colorful veneering including roundels sliced from ancient porphyry columns, but the elaborate membrature of the windows with bifores within arches draws on the classical apparatus of forms. So too in the nearly free-standing Corinthian trabeation framing the A bays and reduced to a single element in the B bays. The commercial ground floor dilutes this membrature and provides secure A bays. Its plan is typical of Venetian domestic regias with no cortile, the thinnest possible walls on piles, the side walls are left plain, and entrances from the canal and from the landward garden (Figure 8.16).

Domestic regias honor decorum by diluting the designs of political, social, or economic superiors. Bramante's **Vatican Palace** work for Julius II (1503–13) contained the normative ideal of piazza-block-garden sequence introduced at PALAZZO MEDICI, MICHELOZZO DI BARTOLOMMEO, FLORENCE, 1444—piazza; extant palace with **Cortile di San Damaso, with Raphael, 1509**; and garden **Cortile del Belvedere, 1505**; all shorn of crenellations and towers. It was the model for this cardinal's palace, a conspicuous fixture in modern Rome and now the French Embassy. It served as an aspirational model when new purposes for buildings were being developed, for example for the **Reform Club, Sir Charles Barry, London, 1837–41** and **University Club, Mead, McKim, Mead, and White, New York, 1899** where five-stories look like three.

The same year Cardinal Alessandro Farnese began it, Pope Leo X Medici (1513–21) began a huge, Romanized version of the family's Florentine palace that lesser architects in the '600 completed as the **Palazzo Madama**, now the Italian Senate.

Pope Alexander VI Borgia (1492–1503) had created Alessandro cardinal, age 25, in 1493 as a favor to the father of his favorite mistress, Giulia, Alessandro's sister. He began this family palace near the slum area where its rise had begun. After becoming Pope as Paul III (1534–49), he had Sangallo expand the palace, and he had Michelangelo take over after Sangallo died. Meanwhile, he was expanding the family's ducal possessions where his successors would build the PALAZZO FARNESE, CAPRAROLA, VIGNOLA, 1559.

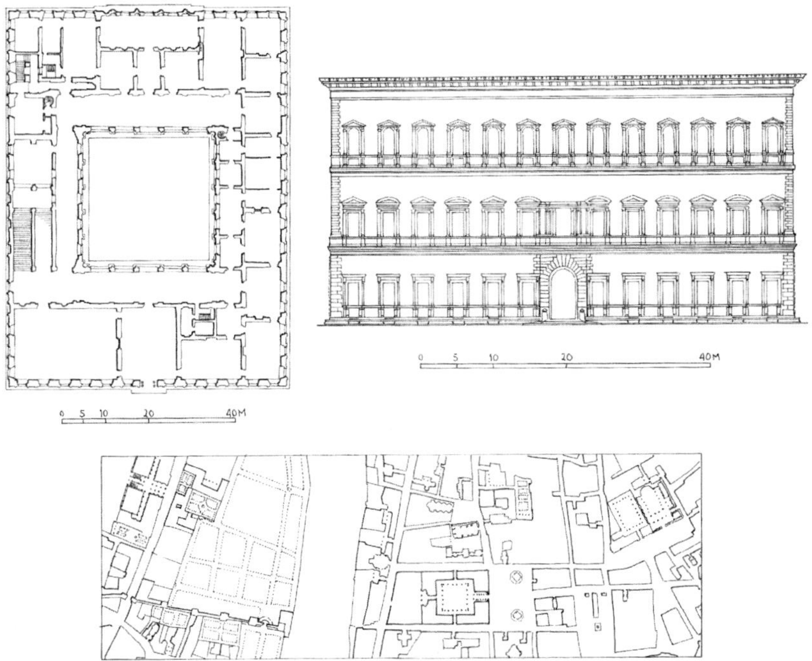

FIGURE 8.16 Palazzo Farnese, Antonio da Sangallo, 1516; Michelangelo, 1546, Rome, Italy.

The façade's ground floor has windows with lintels in dark brick masonry walls with yellow Roman brick above and travertine membrature used throughout. The piano nobile windows have alternating pedimented tabernacles, the corner quoins and central portal surrounds are rusticated, and the string courses firm. Six columns along flanking aisles with niches sustain the entrance's barrel vault. Michelangelo's top floor abbreviates Ionic tabernacle windows. They break the pediments, reduce the entablature to a thin molding contrasting with the pulvinated fragment above each column, and push the windows' arches through the thin molding. He increased the distance up to his massive cornice with darker brick describing curious, incomplete chevrons (not shown). And he enlarged the central piano nobile window with two green columns below a huge papal Farnese coat-of-arms (not shown).

The 5 × 5 cortile, again brick and travertine, has Sangallo's canonically sober membrature. An open arcade of Doric fornixes has piers capitals doubled in the enlargement. Above are pedimented, Ionic tabernacle windows beneath a frieze with garlands and masks. In contrast, Michelangelo's top floor has a mezzanine zone with windows (some blind) and pedestals sustaining engaged piers with pilasters that reach the cornice with *ressaults*. Sculpted blocks carry oversized segmental pediments well above their frames.

Our plan shows the piano nobile where grand stairs lead up to a double-height room followed across the front by a sequence of ever-smaller rooms.

An earlier design would have opened the cortile's rear with a piano nobile level of three fornix bays. Bridging the Tiber River (not done, and not shown) would have connected to the garden of the **Villa Farnesina, Baldassare Peruzzi's, 1505–11**. Instead, only the top floor of Vignola's three-story, three-bay completion connects, and only visually.

Our urban plan also shows its extension in the other direction where, as at the MODERN CAPITOLINE, 1538, Michelangelo projected its dominance into Rome. Not laid was his waffle paving (not shown) that extended the facade's bay spacing across a piazza that the Farnese acquired, cleared, and gave to the city. Across it, the palace's axis extends to a street made to cross the end of the Campo dei Fiori and reach the processional route from the Vatican to San Giovanni in Laterano; a jog would have taken it to Piazza Navona (Figure 8.17).

At the terminus of a rising straight street dominating the land he had acquired in 1504, Cardinal Alessandro Farnese, later Pope Paul III, in 1515–30 had Antonio da Sangallo and Baldassare Peruzzi built a moated, pentagonal fortification beyond a large plaza. In 1559, his grandson Cardinal Alessandro had Vignola (1507–73), who had been tutored by Michelangelo and in 1563 would write a still standard book on the five canonic orders, begin its conversion into a ducal regia.

Our section includes the level below the pentagon's cortile into which Vignola fitted a two-story circular peristyle from tufa using a rare Italian instance of three-dimensional arches. Based on the Belvedere motif (aka *rythmische travée*) introduced at the **Cortile del Belvedere, Bramante, Vatican, 1503ff**, it places a narrow bay with a niche between fornixes; its ground level is astylar and deeply drafted, its piano nobile level with engaged Ionic orders includes *ressaults* and ends in a balustrade that obscures the upper floors. In one of the pentagon's front bulwarks, Vignola fitted the circular ramp like Bramante's at the Belvedere whose annular vault uses paired columns that at the Doric level has triglyphs alternating with Farnese lilies. On a rear bulwark on the entrance axis, he added a low tower. The interior is lavishly frescoed.

Entry beyond the dry moat is between a pair of front bulwarks into the lower regions. The entrance facade of the canonic, three-story palace has six tufa, tabernacle windows and rusticated arched portal with Doric capitals carved out to hold the entablature, all in a field of drafted light-toned masonry like the stone used above. The seven bays above are recessed slightly behind bulwarks, with the piano nobile holding six Ionic pilasters flanking an open arcaded loggia (now glassed in) with a partially buried pilaster and segmental pedimented windows. In the brick and Corinthian trabeated top story, the projecting bays are again framed with rustication while pilasters with strip frames define seven bays with smaller windows above and below the larger trabeated windows, all beneath the large cornice.

FIGURE 8.17 Palazzo Farnese, Jacopo Barozzi da Vignola, Caprarola, Italy, 1559–73.

Enclosed orthogonal gardens are beyond each rear face, and farther away in the woods, an axial water chain terminates at flaking grottos after beginning at a casino facing another orthogonal garden. As at other cardinalate villas in the region (e.g., **Barberini**, **Gambera, d'Este**), the expressive character presents man's control over water, earth, and flora, the counterpart of the palace's that exhibits the proprietor's authority over his subjects. The **Casino, Giacomo del Duca, 1584–86**, a reworking of **Villa Chigi (Farnesina), Peruzzi, 1506–10, Rome**, at the head of the water chain is an often-used model varied for buildings of all sorts (Figure 8.18).

FIGURE 8.18 "Le paradis d'Anet", Philippe de l'Orme, now in Paris, 1547–52.

When the French invaded Italy in 1494 they encountered the new classical architecture based on free-standing classical orders, and they soon adapted it to their wall-based traditions within their fortified chateaux. The **Château of Chambord, Domenico da Cortona (c. 1465–1549) (possibly along with Leonardo da Vinci), 1519–47**, that Francis I (r. 1515–47) built, with a square plan and squat walls, had moved only a little away from the traditional five-part front with a central entrance, corner towers, and connecting hyphens.

The chateau at Anet that Henry II (r. 1547–59) had Philibert de l'Orme (1514–70) build for his chief mistress, Dianne de Poitiers, reveals his attention to architecture in his years in Rome between 1533 and 1536. Much was plundered during the Revolution, but what survives and was well illustrated in his 1567 treatise attest to Philibert's inventiveness in working Italian examples into traditional French compositions.

Our drawing presents the frontispiece that became the source of innumerable variations in five-part facades. Now displayed in the École des Beaux-Arts courtyard in Paris, its three stories of paired canonical orders rise from pedestals, stand free of the wall, and are connected by entablatures that retreat to the wall. Between the Doric pair is a portal with lintels. A niche is between the fluted Ionic columns, and the pair is separated by a window with lintels. Between the fluted, richly ornamented Corinthians is a now empty arched bay in an ornamented wall.

Surviving on site is the entrance to the court, a free interpretation of an ancient triumphal arch gate structure not unlike the interior of the entrance he saw at PALAZZO FARNESE, ANTONIO DA SANGALLO, ROME, 1516 where the side portals lack exterior entrances as they do here. An arch above the entrance frames a tympanum with a replica of Benvenuto Cellini's bronze, recumbent *Nymph of Anet*, and on top is a pair of hunting dogs braying at a stag.

Also on the site is the chapel, a tiny, exuberant variation on the PANTHEON, HADRIAN WITH APOLLODORUS OF DAMASCUS?, ROME, 117–26 and the TEMPIETTO DI SAN PIETRO IN MONTORIO, BRAMANTE, ROME, 1502? 1505–06?, that will be an important model in France The circular tholos encloses a Greek cross that on three faces pushing the exterior walls into bulges while the diagonal axes push through the wall into niches or sacristies. Above the three-dimensional arches and pendentives rise a dome with swirling coffers and a tall, columnar lantern whose plan makes the floor pattern (Figure 8.19).

As Louis XIII's Superintendent of Finances, René de Longueil (1596–1677) had virtually unlimited funds for François Mansart (1598–1666). Profligate in using them, he produced this small, stone, inimitable, and beautifully crafted country house just outside Paris.

The earlier fortified chateau assembly has by now been reconfigured with their revised parts strung along an axis. Louis XIII often hunted foxes in the forest of Germain-en-Laye, and Longueil, hoping to have him visit, had Mansart place an enticing entrance arrangement 900 meters away with an axial allée cut through the forest (the present-day Avenue Albine and Avenue du Général Leclerc).

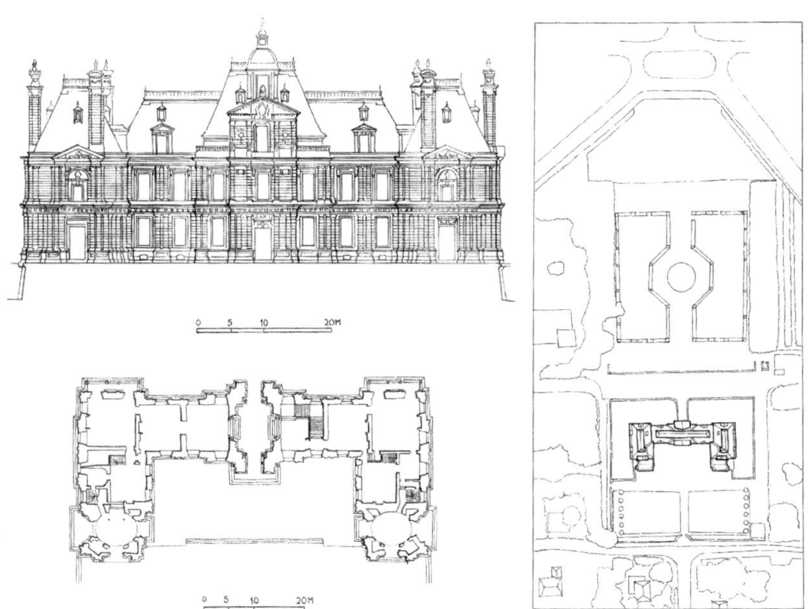

FIGURE 8.19 Château Maison-Lafitte, François Mansart, Paris, France, 1642–51.

Similar features terminated a 400-meter cross axis (now Avenue Egle) 300 m away from the gate of the *maison's* broad *avant-cour* where our plan begins with trees where the stables and orangery were.

The *corps-de-logis* within the *cour d'honneur* begins with a three-part frontispiece under a truncated hipped roof containing a low bell tower and sequence of square domes. Riffing on the prototype of PHILIBERT DE L'ORME, "LE PARADIS D'ANET," ANET, 1547–52, its paired orders appear on receding levels. The Doric pairs are closely spaced pilasters on a slight central protrusion. Beside it, solitary fluted columns back at the wall stand beneath the outer columns of the free-standing fluted Ionic pair with *pot de feu* before the top level where Corinthian pilasters carry a broken pediment. On these levels the entablature recedes, and the wall's farther recession holds openings.

The end pavilions, separated by gaps in the pitched roofs, become wings embracing the *cour d'honneur.* The Doric level projects beyond the Ionic level and holds entrances to the *corps de logis*. Both use paired pilasters, the Ionic one carrying a pediment. Sarcophagus-topped chimneys rise through their steeply pitched roofs. In the three-bay hyphens the outer pilasters of the pairs are buried; each central pair is below a pedimented dormer followed by a tiny dormer, a composition also seen in the two-bay reentrant facades.

More variations are in the garden facade (not shown) behind a broad sweep of stairs over the dry moat that extends along the sides. Its frontispiece's Doric level is all pilasters, and the free-standing Ionics support the free-standing Corinthians directly. The end pavilions have four free-standing fluted Doric columns and Ionic pilasters framing windows and narrowing in the center, with a niche at the Ionic level and Corinthian tabernacle dormer, and then a tiny dormer in the roof's hip. The three-bay hyphens, only slightly recessed, repeat this rhythm with pilasters and an *oeil-de-boeuf* dormer and tiny dormer. The side facades compress the articulation. A tunnel beneath the garden brought supplies into the basement.

The interior, equally meticulously articulated and ornamented, has a square, flat-vaulted entrance vestibule with massive *poché* framing a rectangle. In each corner, free-standing fluted Doric columns carry a low entablature and coved oval dome and oculus. A complex, domed stair hall adjoins it (Figure 8.20).

Nicolas Fouquet (1615–80), Superintendent of Finances for Lois XIV, spent lavishly to impress the king. Paid for through peculation, he then spent his last nineteen years in prison. The king, who was always building, had Fouquet's team of Louis Le Vau (1612–70), landscape architect André le Nôtre, and painter Charles LeBrun engulf the **Chateau, Philibert Le Roy, Versailles, 1631**, the brick-and-stone hunting lodge his farther had built, with an impressive character exhibiting an even more expansive display of royal control over the land and its inhabitants.

For this stone building and extensive gardens on reclaimed marsh land, Fouquet cleared three villages and laid three long avenues converging on the

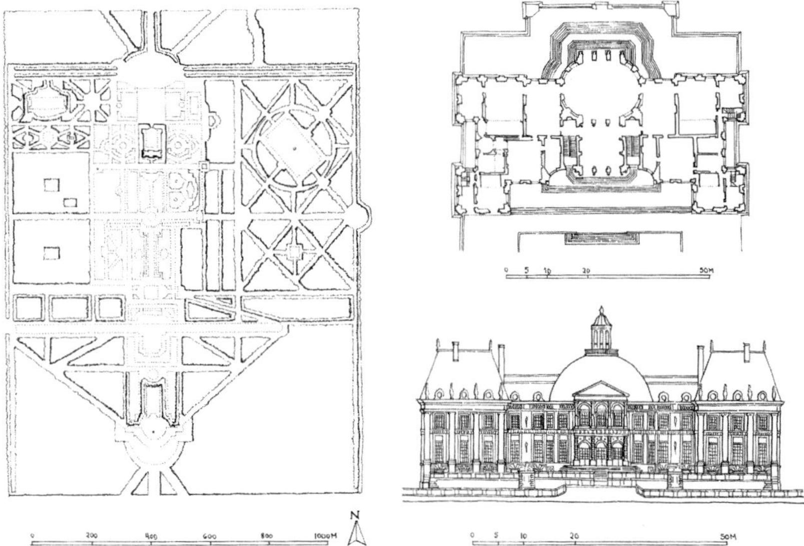

FIGURE 8.20 Château Vaux-le-Vicomte, Louis Le Vau, Moulon, France, 1657–61.

patte-d'oie before the stables and *cour d'honneur.* A balustraded parapet surrounds the *corps-de-logis* on a moated platform with the bulk of its innovative two-pile interior evident in the four corner pavilions with steep roofs and swelling central dome and lantern.

The front (not shown) has pavilions with a pediment above three giant Ionic pilasters set before the horizontally drafted walls used throughout. They reach the center's tetrastyle temple front with one-bay hyphens, with the lower story within recessed quadrant curves. We show the garden facade with its four giant Ionic pilasters on the end pavilions and brief hyphens reaching the center's dramatic salon's swelling oval whose dome and lantern crown the mass. Attached to its center is a two-story affair with are four free-standing rusticated Doric columns with statues above, and above are three recessed Ionic pilaster fornixes beneath a pediment.

The elaborate stair and dry moat's narrow bridge led to the gardens; only the central portion shown stippled on our plan survives. Viewed from the *corps*, the foreshortening of irregular parts make them appear regular, while in the garden itself various features such as the basin and the cascade filling it are playfully reveled only upon closely approaching them (Figure 8.21).

When the wealthy began building town houses in the 17th c. in Paris, they used stone rather than the brick and stone of Henry IV's PLACE ROYALE (NOW PLACE DES VOSGES), JACQUES II ANDROUET DU CERCEAU, or SOLOMON DE BROSSE, or both?, PARIS, 1605–12. Louis Le Vau had broached the typical *hôtel particulier* that compressed the typical country chateaux when sites were made available on the Isle Saint-Louis after 1614, but

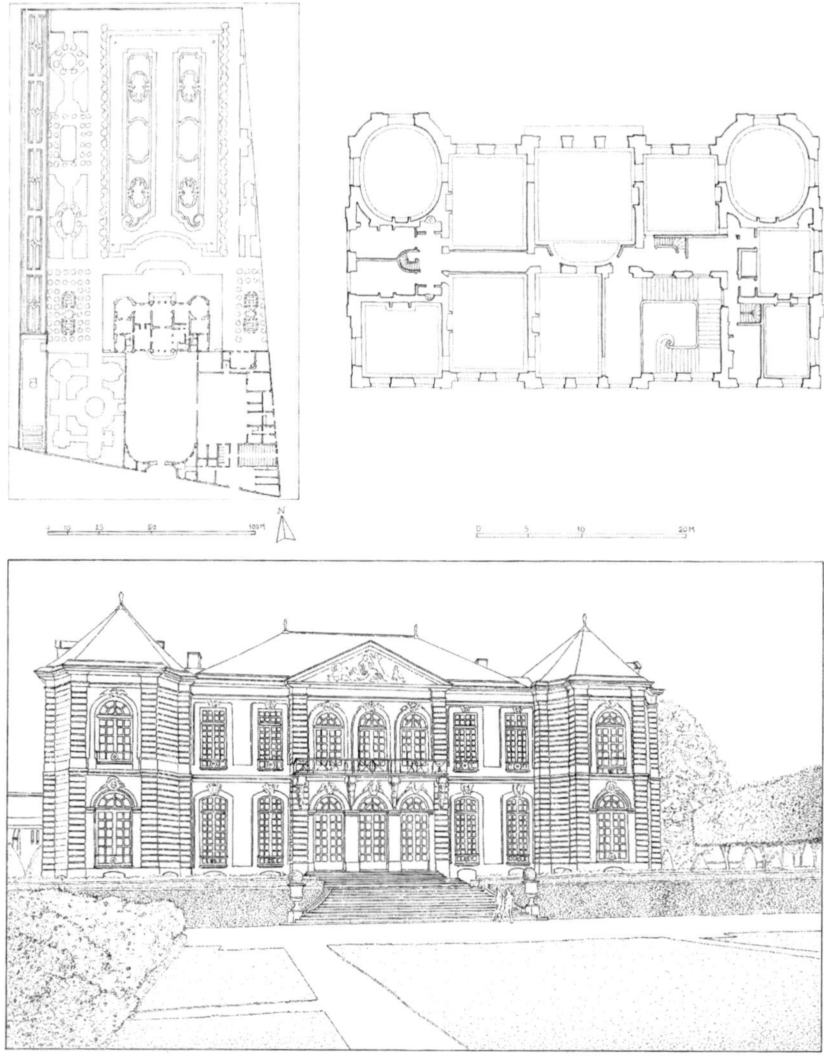

FIGURE 8.21 Hôtel Peyrenc-de-Moras (now Hôtel Biron and Rodin Museum) Jean Aubert, Paris, France, 1727–32. (a) Plan and (b) perspective.

those larger sites were later available only on the city's fringes. This example, built by a wealthy financier, is even more expansive with side gardens rather than party walls on its sides.

Walled along the street, a concave area before the arched entrance gate leads into a deeper than usual court. Originally low walls of the stable yard and garden, neither now extant, met the *corps-de-logis* pavilions at the midpoint. This front facade with two nearly equally high stories has a central pavilion framed, like the end pavilions, with banded corner plasters lacking capitals, the lower ones crossed by the mid-level stringcourse and those above by the thin architrave of the building's cornice. A pediment rises above the central three bays holding arched openings. The windows in the pavilions and hyphens, both with two bays, have segmental heads on the lower stories and flat arches above. Like the center's upper windows, they have unmolded surrounds, and like all the openings they have enlarged decorative keystones. Hipped roofs cover the center block and pavilions with a single semicircular dormer in each pavilion roof.

On the block's sides, the central section projects slightly, and a dormer is above each of the four windows.

We show the garden side where the end pavilions hold elliptical rooms on both floors. They appear beneath truncated pyramidal roofs as truncated octagons with the pilasters' banding extending across the brief curved walls. The front's fenestration is repeated except for using a semicircular window head on the singular window on both end pavilion levels. A second-story balcony is carried cross the center on large corbels, and that center's pediment contains relief sculpture. Broad stairs lead from the terrace down to the garden.

Inside, the ground floor vestibule opens to the stair hall. Unfortunately, only fragments survive of the Rococo wooden wall treatment with delicate sculpting and a few painted overdoors, the complement to the exterior's spare refinement (Figure 8.22).

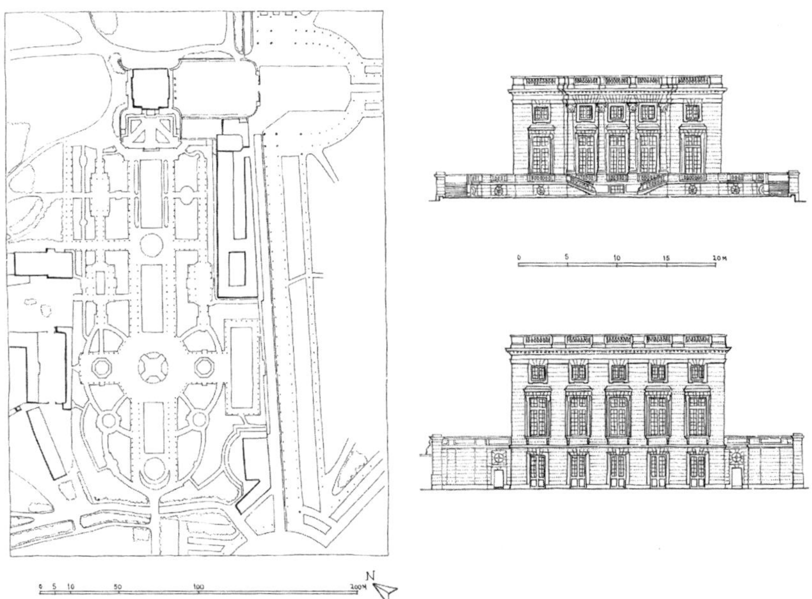

FIGURE 8.22 Le Petit Trianon, Ange-Jacques Gabriel, Versailles, France, 1761–73.

The Petit Trianon, a small retiring house for Louis XV's mistresses, was later enjoyed by Louis XVI's Queen, Marie Antoinette. This three-story, five-bay cubic regia by Ange-Jacques Gabriel (1698–1782) is the ultimate graceful refinement of membrature based on the wall with applied trabeation and immersion in a landscape.

Our lower elevation shows the south facade reached by a long axis through the gardens to a *cour d'honneur* with convex quadrant corners inflecting toward the five equal entrances. Horizontal drafting defines alternate courses becoming the jambs and swerving to make voussoirs for the flat-arch portals. The astylar western face is at this lower level. The other two faces are two stories with terraces and steps connecting the gardens and the piano nobile; we show the western face.

Three facades put three bays on a plane standing proud with an additional fillet along the edges, all embellished with four fluted Corinthian orders, ¾ columns on the facade we show, and pilasters elsewhere. The tall piano nobile windows have thin sills and eared, thin frames below an architrave, and a pulvinated frieze on the outer bays.

An attic holds smaller, square, simply framed windows. Above is a full entablature with a three-fascia architrave, high frieze, and cornice below a balustrade silhouette with blocks marking the bay divisions (Figure 8.23).

The Potala Palace complex is perched at 3,700 m on a high plateau with majestic mountain ranges to the North and South. The religious and administrative capital of Tibet since the 17th c., Lhasa (abode of great spirits or Lhas) is marked by two salient natural landmarks: Marpori hill, or the Red hill, upon which the Potala Palace complex was built, and Chakpori hill, with the city's Medical College that the fifth Dalaï Lama founded in 1696. This was the winter palace for successive Dalaï Lamas until the present fourteenth Dalaï Lama fled to India after the Chinese invasion of 1959. Damage from that year has been restored.

The fifth Dalaï Lama built it in 1696 facing south from the full length of Marpori hill, among some of the country's most noteworthy architectural monuments such as the Norbulingka palace and the Jokhang Monastery. Named after mount Potalaka, the mythical abode of the great Bodhisattva Avalokiteshvara in the waters south of India, the complex has two of the original cave/chapels—ostensibly built by Songtsen Gampo the 33rd king of Tibet in the 7th c., and one of the figures credited with introducing Buddhism to the country.

The Potala's thirteen or more stories are reached by four long external stepped ramps, one leading to the central White Palace's outer court and vast Assembly Hall to the East, another to the dominant, central, quadrangular, and properly named Red Palace to the west, with its Assembly Hall and auxiliary halls that contain richly painted and ornamented votive chapels. More than 1,000 rooms with richly polychromatic paintings serve Buddhist spirituality, and with thousands of shrines, statues, murals, and more than one hundred

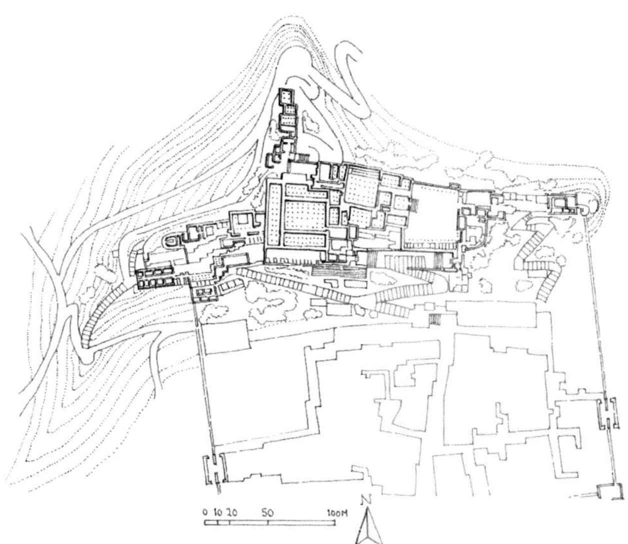

FIGURE 8.23 Potala Palace, Lhasa, Tibet, 1645–94.

thousand volumes, manuscripts, painted scrolls, and other precious artifacts under roof. A series of roof terraces offer views of the remarkable landscape and the Shöl, the old walled town below with terraces, red and orange buildings, and gilded roofs over the tombs of past Dalaï Lamas, the whole boldly standing out against the enclosing sky.

The palace's striking expressive character comes from its simple grandeur dominating the clustered arrangement of tower-buildings of different heights and dimensions, walls, and stair ramps and its gilded, flared-eave roofs, amplified by the considerable solidity evidenced by the dominance of solids over voids in the inward-sloping walls, some five meters thick at the foot of the hill, with horizontal bands of cornices tying together the layers of windows. In itself, it forms a fortified "hill" above the Shöl with its complex of civic and religious buildings. Its definite directionality merges it with an imposing hill overlooking an expansive plain, a quality it shares with other monumental complexes such as the **Mortuary Chapel of Mentuhotep II, c. Deir-el-Bahri, c. 2065 BCE** and **Temple of Hatshepsut, Senmut, Thebes, Egypt, 1520 BCE**; the **Asclepeion in Kos, Epidaurus**, and elsewhere in Greece; the **Sanctuary of Fortuna Primigenia, Palestrina, c. 120BCE**; or even the **Victor Emmanuel II Monument, Giuseppe Sacconi, Rome, 1885–1911** (Figure 8.24).

Two of England's greatest achievements in architecture are here. One is Cardinal Wolsey's large palace that master mason Henry Redman (d. 1528) began in 1515. It used the *parti* for fortresses, monasteries, and Oxford colleges, with its Great Gate at the Thames and a Base Court for the Cardinal. Following his downfall in 1528, Henry VIII (r. 1509–47) added the smaller, gated Clock Court and hammer-beam Great Hall with stained glass.

The other followed the "Glorious Revolution" when William III and Mary II asked Sir Christopher Wren (1632–1723) to produce a palace rivaling Louis XIV's **Château of Versailles, Louis Le Vau et al, 1661**. Only partially realized, we show its plan in a darker tone. Beyond Henry's palace, he placed the quadratic Fountain Court with the Long Gallery (Cartoon Gallery) with the King's Staircase in a Clock Court corner.

Along the Fountain Court's entry side is the two-story Communication Gallery added to Henry's fabric. The other three court facades have stone and brick bays used inside and out. A Portland stone pier arcade before a vaulted portico is followed by very tall brick walls with very tall multi-light, pedimented piano nobile sash windows, then a floor with a circular window within a square stone surround carved to represent a lion's skin and foliage-wreath, a fourth floor with square windows with eared architraves on a strong course, and a cornice and baluster silhouette.

These bays have different assemblies on different exterior facades. Not shown is the facade facing the Thames across the King's Privy Garden. Its five-part articulation holds the lowest floor in buff stone with segmental windows and piano nobile windows lacking pediments. Its three central bays in white Portland stone have story-high drafted pedestals beside portals and below engaged Corinthian columns. Two flanking windows have pediments, and the middle window is topped with drapery, trumpets, scepters, and crown. The four-bay end pavilions with brick-and-stone quoins project. The seven-bay hyphens replace the center's round

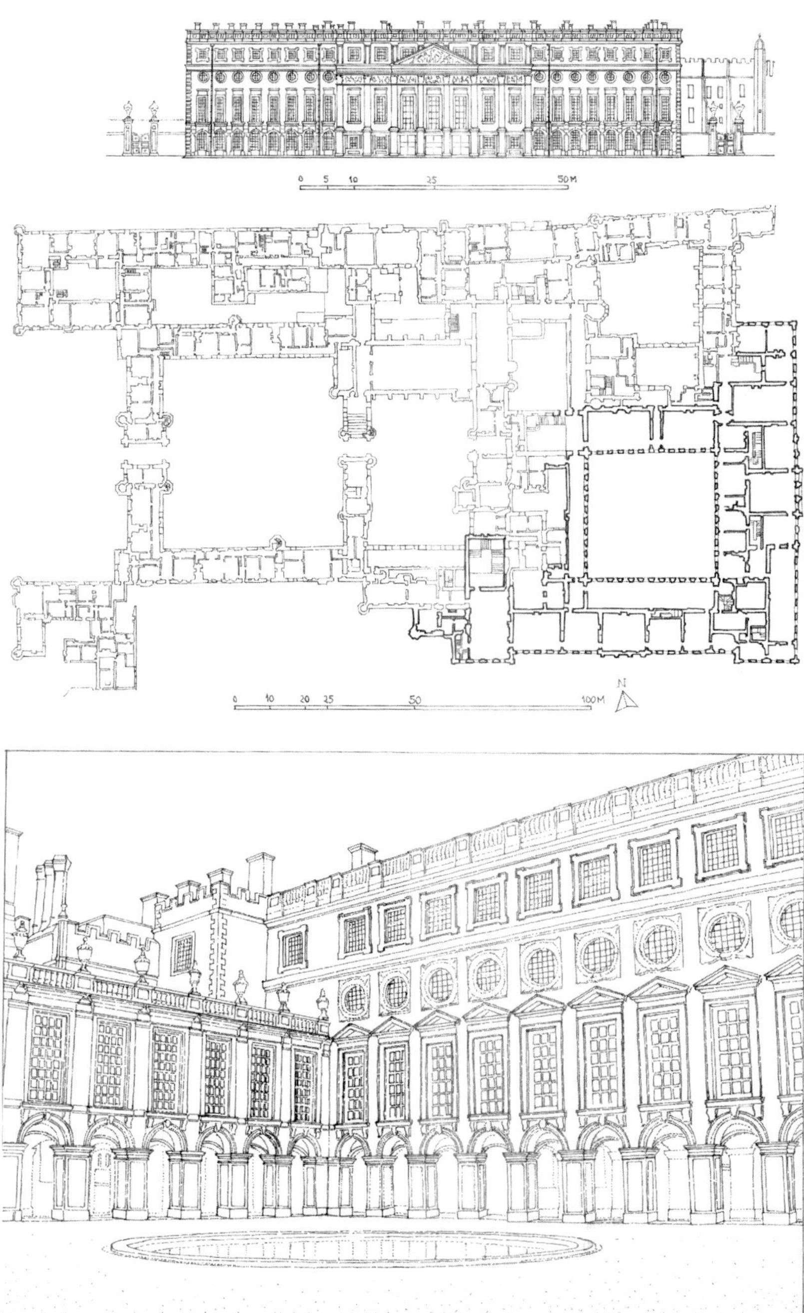

FIGURE 8.24 Hampton Court Palace, Henry Redman, 1515–40; Sir Christopher Wren, 1689, London, England.

windows with swags beside the center window's enriched pediment. An orangery (not shown) was built stretching from this wing beside the Tudor construction.

Our separate drawing shows the Fountain Court interior looking toward the Queen's wing with two-story and three-story variations of the basic facade articulation.

Above our plan, we show the exterior facade of the Queen's wing with its two piles of rooms visible from a loop in the Thames. Rather than end pavilions, it has a dominating seven-bay stone center with an engaged, richly decorated tetrastyle temple front with fluted Corinthian half columns that become pilasters on its flanks, all carried on drafted pedestals. The eight bays on each side repeat the usual articulation. It faces a *patte-d'oie* with axes extending to the garden's limits that, like the axes in the King's gardens, honored English land ownership unlike André LeNôtre's Tuileries and Versailles axes reaching across France.

George I (r. 1714–27) completed the work that became the basis for innumerable "Georgian houses" in Britain and America large and small, and still being built (Figure 8.25).

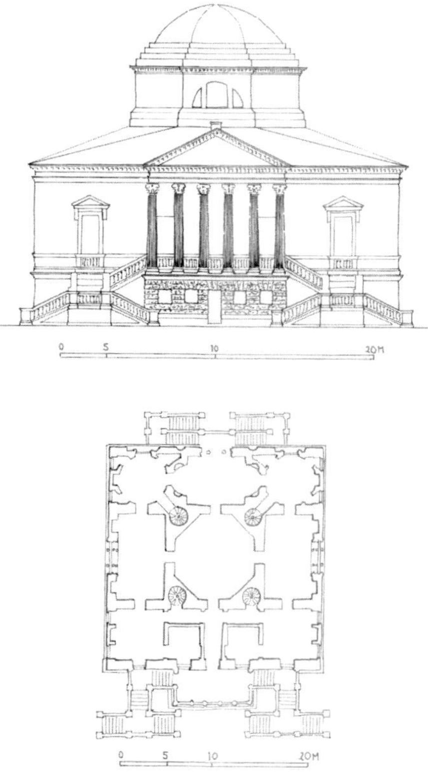

FIGURE 8.25 Chiswick, Lord Burlington and William Kent, London, England, 1727–29.

On three Grand Tours between 1714 and 1719 Richard Boyle, 3rd Earl of Burlington (1694–1753), saw ancient Roman architecture through Andrea Palladio's eyes. Back home, he collected Palladio's drawings, reinvigorated Inigo Jones' Palladianism, sponsored Isaac Ware's 1738 translation of Palladio's treatise, and in a 65-acre preserve built this essay in the classical based on **Villa Rotonda, Palladio, Vicenza, c. 1566–70** with attention to **Rocca Pisana, Vincenzo Scamozzi, Lonigo (near Vicenza), 1575–7**.

Brick with Portland stone facing, the building fills a 21 m cube. The basement portal leads directly to the garden, and a pair of double stairs lead into the sides of the two-bay pronaos of the hexastyle fluted Corinthian temple front on a drafted, vermiculated basement. A pair of pedimented windows complete the front. The temple's entablature extends below the low-pitched hipped roof that rises into an octagonal drum with a thermal window on each cardinal axis and an octagonal dome with four Pantheon-like steps.

The basement extends as vermiculated lateral walls. Behind them, each side facade has a lower level with pairs of small, unframed windows flanked by a small portal below a single Palladiana on a belt course with pairs of unframed windows on each side. Four truncated obelisk chimneys project above the cornice. The garden side's basement portal is beneath the main floor stair landing and three Palladiana, each set within an arched recess with a shallow unframed niche between.

The interior holds England's first "shaped rooms" around the central octagon with its coffered dome, all richly colored and gilded, with excellent pictures and sculpture. Stairs to the basement are in the *poché*.

William Kent (1685–1748), who had traveled briefly with Burlington in Italy, was, like Jones, an impresario of court masques and like Burlington an architect, but also a talented painter and furniture designer. Their garden here introduced the picturesque landscape garden that, named an English Garden, quickly replaced geometric parterres. Calculated to suggest a painting of ancient Roman vistas, it invited wondering along curvy paths through boskets, meadows, plants, and ponds with occasional follies called "fabriques" that included here a miniature Ionic version of the Pantheon and a bridge and statues honoring Palladio and Jones (Figure 8.26).

Thomas Coke, 1st Earl of Leicester (1697–1759), indulged in a Grand Tour during 1712–18 where he crossed paths with Lord Burlington and William Kent with whom he later worked in building this very large building. He sketched out ideas for his estate, and, after recovering from the bath he took in the 1720 South Sea Bubble, began its construction in 1734 with the involvement of the local builder Matthew Brettingham. Kent's extensive gardens are no longer extant.

Earlier English versions of plans with hollow squares with five-part front facades are plentiful: **Longleat, Wiltshire, Robert Smythson, 1567–79;** the Palladianism of **Wilton House with its addition by Inigo Jones, Wiltshire,**

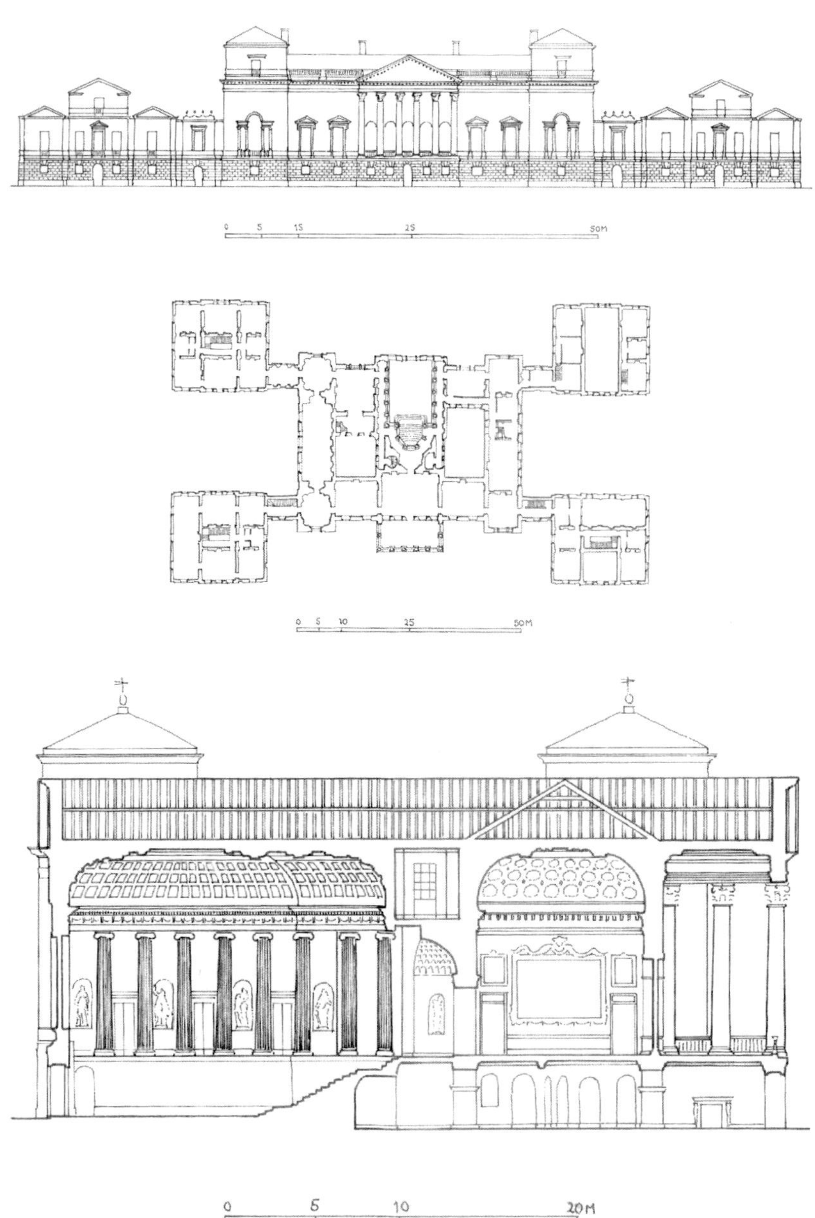

FIGURE 8.26 Holkham Hall, Thomas Coke, William Kent, Lord Burlington, near Norfolk, England, 1734.

c. 1636; and nearby **Blickling Hall, Norfolk, 1616**. This larger building is rendered in specially made yellow brick to evoke ancient Rome, and it uses a rusticated basement and abundant motifs from England's rising Palladianism.

Its plan throws large, cubic masses off each corner connected by short hyphens, each with a single window. We show the garden side facing south with its outlying blocks having a three-part compressed configuration with a central pitched roof kept lower than that of the central block, and with a slightly projecting side bay and a single window. A hexastyle Corinthian temple dominates the central block of the front's five-part composition. Its pavilions have a Palladiana at the piano nobile level, then extend up to a single window above the cornice, and end with a pyramidal roof. Two pedimented windows are in each hyphen connecting to the temple front.

The entrance front (not shown) is uncluttered by stables or other outbuildings. Its central, five-part bulk features a run of Palladianas within arched reveals in each part with the five-parts with the central one flanked by pedimented windows. The outbuildings repeat the garden facade, but with pedimented windows. The ground floor rusticated entrance was added in 1847.

That entrance facade's lack of display enhances the experience upon encountering the spectacular column-lined "Marble Hall;" sectional and plan drawings do not capture it. Apparently, Coke's design, its fluted Staffordshire alabaster Ionics with Scamozzi capitals, rising from the piano nobile level to an entablature with ornamented profiles and a frieze with putti and fruit garlands, is ceiled above with a complex, coffered plaster vault. The stairs narrow as they ascend, with a visitor finding double-height rooms along the garden front. Along the west side is the family's residence with a suite of shaped rooms; all these large rooms, lit by a pair of light courts, serve social activities and display Coke's impressive art collection, since dispersed (Figure 8.27).

This large plantation house is a much larger and more elaborate version of what realtors call Georgian that continues to be built in America. Its configuration and composition are seen in the larger **Governor's Mansion, Williamsburg, 1706**, now known in its 1931 reconstruction. A smaller, simpler version is the noteworthy **George Wythe House, Williamsburg, 1754–56**.

It occupies the planation mentioned in 1616 and bought in 1688 by the immigrant William Byrd, whose family and descendants would play important roles in Virginia politics well into the 20th c. Its builder might have been William Byrd II (1674–1744), Virginia born but educated in England from age seven. Admitted to the bar, a member of the Royal Society, and Virginia's representative in England, again in Virginia in 1705 he assembled one of the largest libraries in the colonies. He founded Richmond on his land in 1737 and named it for the similarities in the view down the James River to the view from London's Richmond down the Thames. A notorious philanderer and gambler, he treated his slaves abominably and left large debts. His son William Byrd III

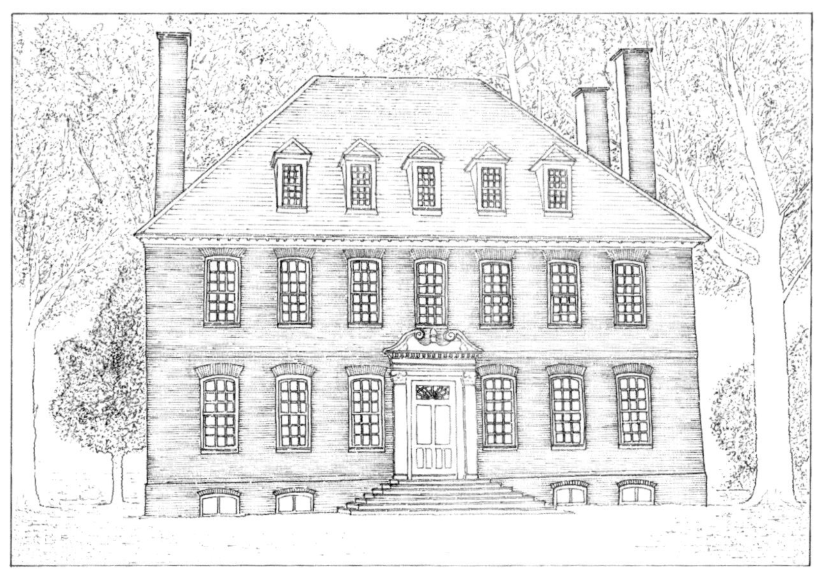

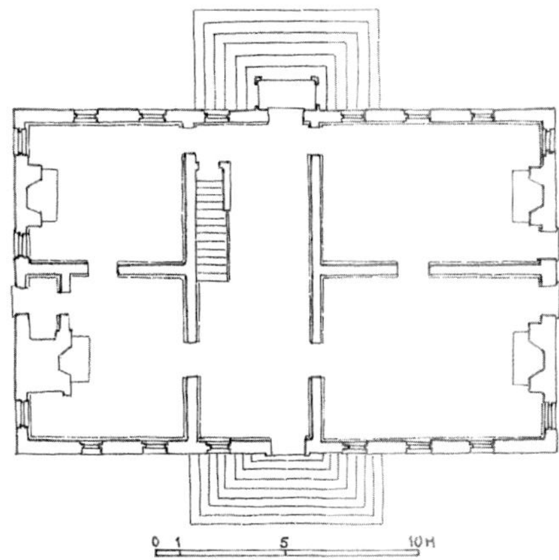

FIGURE 8.27 Westover, William Byrd III, James City County, Virginia, U.S.A., c. 1750.

(1728–77), the more likely builder, squandered his inheritance on it, incurred large gambling debts, and died a suicide.

Westover is an impressively large, two-story, Flemish bond brick box stretched to seven bays with a hipped slate roof up to a ridge with chimney pairs flanking a dormer window on the sides. Hyphens (not shown) from c. 1900 connect to brick outbuildings, only one of which is original. Also gone are the numerous outbuildings and the scattered, farm-like settlements of the plantation's many slaves.

The nine-over-nine double-hung windows under segmental arched heads have smaller panes on the second floor and even smaller ones in the attic's pedimented dormers, thereby stressing the ground floor. A thin, rubbed-brick string course separates the two stories. The principal, riverside has five dormers, the landside four, with pyramidal stairs allowing a shallow cellar. The land side's entrance frame is relatively simple with Corinthian pilasters under a segmental pediment. The river side's sports a robust, Corinthian pilaster tabernacle frame with a pulvinated frieze and goose-necked pediment built from Portland stone. Like the doors and mantelpieces, all following a 1734 English pattern book, it was most likely imported from England. The plan has a central hall with one side occupied by the stairs set at the land side's end and aligned with windows front and back, which makes the rooms on opposite sides unequal in size (Figure 8.28).

On a 5,000-acre plantation on the frontier acquired through inheritance and marriage, Thomas Jefferson (1743–1826) tinkered with this residence up to his death. He used local brick, rough stone, wood, and stucco tectonics. We show the main floor's final form.

Enamored of Palladio when a student, his first sketches showed semicircular quadrants ending in pavilions. Revised plans squared them with octagonal pavilions (never built) at their turns and ending in rectangular pavilions; he was living in one in 1770. Underneath the house and open to sloping land to

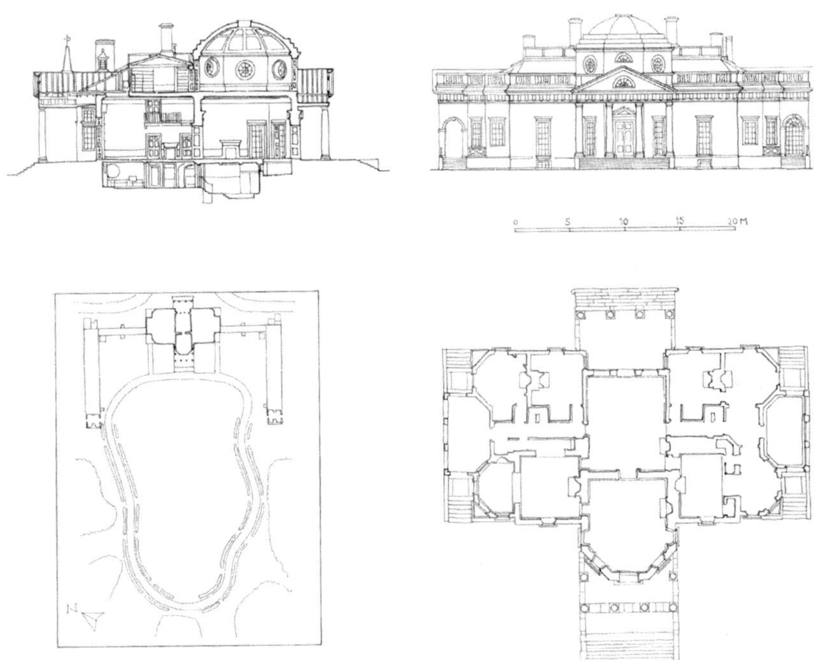

FIGURE 8.28 Monticello, Thomas Jefferson, near Charlottesville, Virginia, U.S.A., 1768–1826.

the west are kitchens and workrooms with stables, and along the terraces of the falling southern slope were slave quarters, workshops, and gardens.

His first construction had an east-facing entrance with superimposed tetrastyle orders, Doric below the pedimented Ionic, with an entrance hall flanked by rooms, the northern one for dining with a tearoom in a half octagon, the southern one his bedroom and half octagon study. Hidden stairs led to a low second floor.

Returning in 1789 after nearly five years in Paris, he began the present enlargement. Relocated and still unseen stairs reached additions to the warren of small upper-story rooms. Beyond the entrance hall, he added a large hall, half octagon, and temple front. On the sides he added rooms with half octagons and porches, on the north for guests, on the south for his library and study with a glazed greenhouse between the half octagons; both sides had access to the walkway above the galleries' wings.

The **Hôtel de Salm, Pierre Rousseau, Paris, 1782–87** suggested Monticello's manipulation of the upper-story rooms and balustrade to make the building appear as a single story. The entrance now became a tetrastyla Tuscan temple front with buff-colored drums, and another faced the garden. Above it he placed an octagonal dome using Philibert de l'Orme's tectonics, with round windows in its low drum for a children's playroom; here is the image on the U.S. 5 cent piece reverse.

Movement through the building carries charged meaning. The green-floored entrance hall displayed artifacts of natural and earlier human history in America; the next room had paintings and sculptures where friends and family gathered for polite conversation and music. Outside, the surface within the temple front leading to the garden was turf with steps down to where a romantic planting scheme (with an intended tower) ran out to the hills beyond.

Jefferson wrote that "kings, hereditary nobles, and priests" take the "earnings of the laboring people ... to maintain their privileged order in splendor and idleness, to fascinate the eyes of the people, and excite in them an (sic.) humble adoration and submission, as to an order of superior beings."[3] Monticello is the republican response built by a Virginia gentleman and twice president who used slave labor in a nation offering "the blessings of liberty for ourselves and our posterity" on the land of natives and claimed from wilderness (Figure 8.29).

We show the first of three residences, each different, that Charles Bulfinch (1763–1844) built for a wealthy, prominent lawyer and Federalist politician. Restored to its 1801 appearance in 1960, it displays richly colored interior and period furnishing on tours.

Its hipped roof covers a five-bay, three-story, Flemish bond brick box. The original entrance, now restored, to the original with side lights and fanlight within an arched reveal. A Palladian window is on the highest, middle floor of the central hall plan, with a lower ground floor and a very low (6-foot) third floor with a central fanlight.

Windowsills, jack arches, and thin, flush string courses are stone, doubling as windowsills on the third floor. The six over six double-hung windows sit close to the exterior. We show a conjectural reconstruction of the stable lost, with the cellar, when the street was proposed for widening in 1925 with the building moved back 42 feet to the site of two demolished rowhouses.

The building possesses a greater crispness and sparseness in the carefully wrought classical detailing compared to the other buildings from the early years of the new republic. Bulfinch had followed his physician father to Boston Latin School and Harvard, and between 1785 and 1788 visited

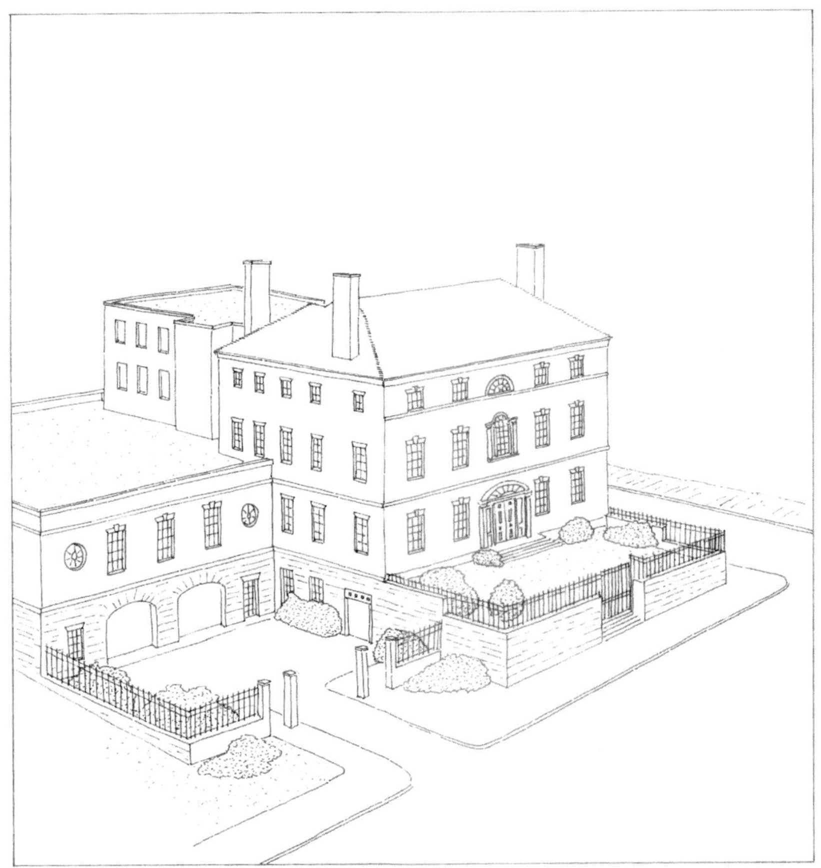

FIGURE 8.29 Harrison Gray Otis House, Charles Bulfinch, Boston, Massachusetts, U.S.A., 1795–96.

Rome, spent a long time in London where John Soane, James Wyatt, Robert Mylne, and Robert Adam were active, and visited Thomas Jefferson in Paris. After returning, he was considered the first American professionally trained architect and had several important commissions including the **Massachusetts State House, Boston, 1787; construction in 1795–97**, with a clear dependence on **Somerset House, William Chambers, London, 1776**, the headquarters of the British Navy. In 1818 President James Monroe appointed him to succeed Benjamin Henry Latrobe, who had resigned as architect of the burned and still incomplete **U.S. Capitol**, completing it with wings, the western (Mall side) portico, and dome (later replaced) (; Figure 8.30).

As the nation matured, the importance of family life increased with prosperity, and improved transportation made a free-standing suburban domestic regia within the grasp of many. Typically its expressive character followed local trends, for example, "Georgian" brick boxes on the east coast, stuccoed collections of rooms and patios in the southwest, and the ubiquitous brick or wood "American four-square" that was often prefabricated, available by mail order, and erected on site. Eventually the "California bungalow" gained command as the suburban, rambling, one-story "Ranch burger."

This winter residence of a Cincinnati soap manufacturer is a superlative "bungalow." Charles Sumner Greene (1868–1957) and Henry Mather Greene (1870–1954), themselves from Ohio, had studied woodworking in St. Louis, completed a two-year course in architecture at MIT, and worked in several Boston architectural firms before opening their office in Pasadena in 1894. It incorporates what other wealthy families had been building as summer "cottages" in elite, distant towns on Cape Cod and in Bar Harbor: wooden construction with open plans enclosed with shingle. Midwesterners used railroad Pullmans to escape winter in balmy Pasadena.

A large two-story interior with an attic and basement, it follows the previous generation's open planning innovations, but with lower ceiling heights that, like its generous vertical windows, project the interior outward. Its broad central stair hall opens to a den and a spacious living room across from a dining room with three interior sides. Sleeping porches were favorites in this period; three of the five bedrooms have them, one above the open area under the entrance veranda in our view, and two above patios, all with overhangs of the broad, low-pitched roofs.

The dark green-brown shingle walls interlace with wooden tectonic pieces and elements in the rich brown tones of exotic woods for railings, posts, trusses, purlins, rafters, and eaves that continue inside where the woodwork exhibits the craftsmanship of the "Arts and Craft Movement" and the newly established contact with Japan. The smooth, rounded shapes use pegs to cinch the tectonic pieces and elements. Textiles and other interior accoutrements include custom crafted electric light fixtures, decorative window glass, fireplace surrounds with art tiles and carved wood, and the architects' furniture.

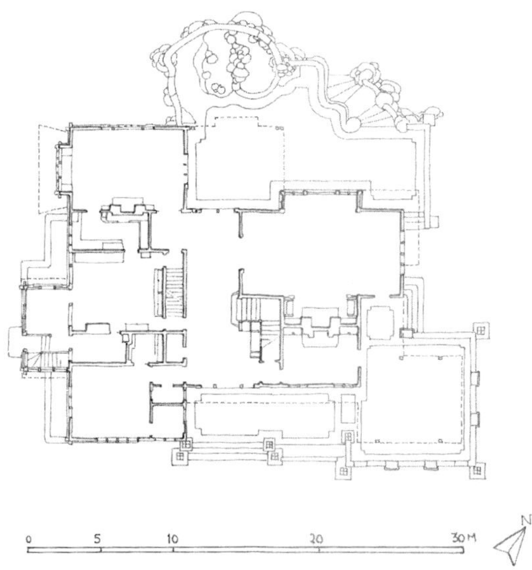

FIGURE 8.30 Gamble House, Greene and Greene, Pasadena, California, U.S.A., 1908–09.

Brick-and-stone porches and terraces carefully nestle the building into the landscape that includes swaths of grass, bushes, slopes, and water features that are easily accessible physically and visually from the interior. A separate garage, a California sine qua non, is now a bookstore (Figure 8.31).

The grandest apartment building in Chicago with the city's ten grandest apartments provided a prized views of Lake Michigan over the intervening

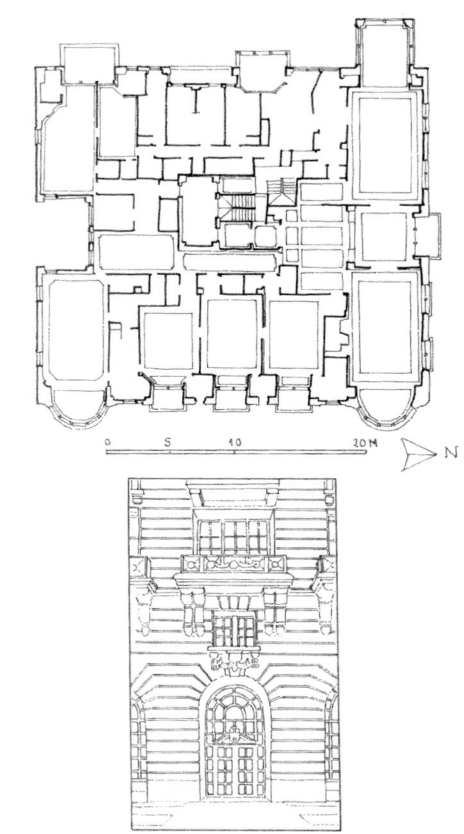

FIGURE 8.31 550 North State Parkway, Benjamin Marshall, Chicago, U.S.A., 1911.

mansions. Tall, Modernist apartment buildings would eventually block some, but the views from the principal rooms northward into Lincoln Park remain. Those three grand rooms, salon, foyer, and dining room, stretched 110 feet before reaching the west-end's glazed *orangerie*, a much-prized feature in wintery Chicago's luxury regias. Three lake-facing bedrooms have balconies, while the final one, the size of the salon, equals that of the grand salon. Fully a quarter of the 8,000-square-foot apartments was devoted to service and maids' rooms along interior lot lines.

The building's expressive character evokes French luxury, from the original rental plans labeled in French to the exterior's French tectonics, with horizontal drafting and subdued ornamentation rendered in white terra cotta, glazed as a defense against turning black from Chicago's air. As in regias in America but not France, it is framed by open landscaping reduced to thin strips and small trees.

Marshall (1874–1944), born into Chicago's wealthy commercial elite, abandoned his budding career in clothing design after visiting the World's Columbian Exposition held near his home. Following his apprenticeship with a local architect, he took as his partner Charles Fox, a veteran of Holabird and Roche's firm, and designed hundreds of buildings including theaters from New York to Los Angeles, country clubs, residences, hotels, commercial buildings, and even churches and a national chain of "quick eateries." His practice survived the 1903 fire that killed 602 in his **Iroquois Theater, Chicago, 1900**. He often had a financial interest in the buildings, as he did with 1550. His Chicago buildings, especially his regias, were the ne plus ultra, while his entrainments at his studio residence were legendary. Portraits of Augustus Saint Gaudens, Stanford White, and Daniel H. Burnham frescoed on the front facade of his studio residence (1927; razed) greeted guests who found a stage and an interior tropical garden-swimming pool where the bathing suits he offered his invited chorus girls turned transparent; the Duke of Windsor was among his guests. Two of his Chicago hotels, the **Blackstone, 1910**, and the **Drake, 1919**, remain Chicago's finest hostelries. The apartments in 1550 have been subdivided into condominiums, but interiors and exteriors are largely intact (Figure 8.32).

In *Modern Architecture* (four editions between 1896 and 1914), Otto Wagner (1841–1918) and his many buildings were a makeweight against excess as he tutored the rising generation of Vienna's avant-garde. Retaining the role of decorum in architecture as a civic art, he pushed for extensive immersion in the best works of the past and new roles for modern materials within architecture as an art of self-expression.

He built the predecessor **First Wagner Villa, Vienna, 1886** for himself in the suburbs, honoring the conventional configuration of a winged box with

FIGURE 8.32 Second Wagner Villa, Otto Wagner, Vienna, Austria, 1912.

Ionic columns across its porch, reached by double-ramp stairs, with unconventional colorful surfaces and surface ornament.

This SECOND WAGNER VILLA, a suburban summertime essay planned in 1905 and simplified when built, stresses the configurations' cubic character largely void of membrature. The 1905 servants' quarters in a high fenestrated basement with random ashlar became horizontal drafting in 1912. Entrance is through double valve doors with stained-glass upper sections set deep into a portal beneath a sunken, square mosaic panel with Pallas Athena by the

Succession artist Leopold Forstner. Inside, a straight flight of stairs leads up to the main floor's stair hall.

Here beside the stair hall is a single, large room. Across its front are seven tall, evenly spaced windows, repeated but smaller on the second floor, with two added above the entrance. The building's top is a projecting, simple cornice and parapet. Beyond the stair hall projects a three-bay portico with a terraced top reached by the separate stairs leads up to the bedrooms and down to the garden and tree canopy.

Its rather joyful expressive character resides in the crisp, white, cubic mass of reinforced concrete, one of several new materials such as aluminum found here, and glazed blue tile rectangles. These frame the portal, edge the main floor windows, rise at the corners stressing their sharpness, form a belt course along the wall's lower portion, and run up the loggia's columns where they stop short of the tops as if suggesting columns diluted nearly out of existence (Figure 8.33).

Although industry has increasingly gained command of construction, in most societies dwellings are still produced by a do-it-yourself vernacular, often offering mere protection. To enable self-built dwellings to serve their residents nobly and well, Hassam Fathy (1900–89) devoted study to traditional materials and their use in his native Egypt. He illustrated this project in his *Architecture for the Poor* (revised 1976) demonstrating how comfort can be obtained by using recovered vernacular building techniques and local materials requiring few specialized skills and benefiting from nature's light and ventilation. In Phase I, this residence was a modest studio with a small sleeping room and a loggia looking out to a papyrus and date palm grove.

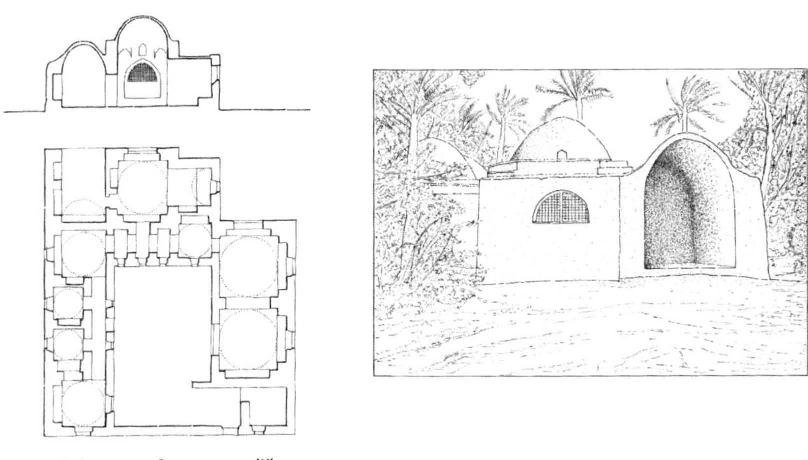

FIGURE 8.33 Sa'id House I and II, Hassan Fathy, Cairo, Egypt, 1942–45.

Thick, mud brick walls carry a catenary dome on squinches over the studio, and vaults cover the other two areas, none of them requiring support during construction. Phase II followed three years later, with the square doughnut shown here repeating the original studio module six times in three different sizes for studios and domestic uses with slots for access along three sides of a courtyard entered through a gate on the fourth side. Here vernacular simplicity participates with the art of architecture that for many millennia have produced an expressive character that here is a dwelling but also a regia for an artist in command of his circumstances (Figure 8.34).

This "cabin in the words" is perhaps pound-for-pound the most famous building in the world. Ludwig Mies van der Rohe (1886–1969) built it as a weekend retreat in a 60-acre (24-hectare) wooded tract next to the Fox River for Edith Farnsworth, a single Chicago nephrologist.

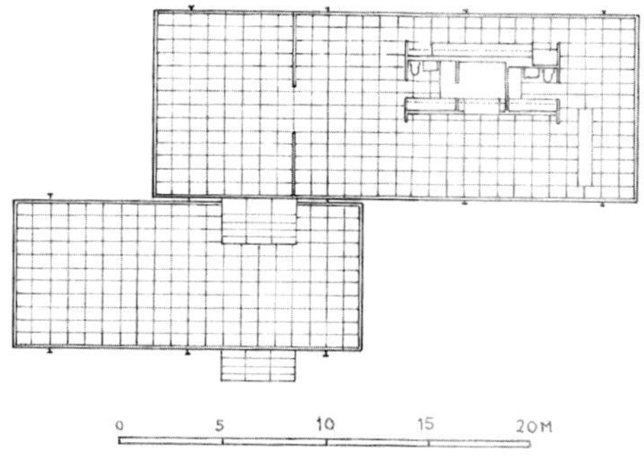

FIGURE 8.34 Farnsworth House, Ludwig Mies van der Rohe, Plano, Illinois, U.S.A., 1946–51.

Its craftsmanship and proportions using the minimalist membrature of white-painted steel, travertine paving squares, and plate glass were intended to produce the beauty and expressive character of the Modernist age. Circumvallating steel beams on three levels define a terrace one meter above the ground, a main volume 1.6 m above grade slipping beyond it, and a flat roof. Pavers document the proportion: along its long sides, fourteen pavers separate the four steel H sections welded to the beams as posts located two in from the corners and eight apart. The main volume, 28 long, gives eight to the porch (formerly screened). Inside, a wood veneered unit largely shy of the ceiling, encloses toilet and kitchen utilities, with open areas for sleeping, dining, relaxing, and entertaining.

In the tradition of follies, this one is radically innovative. With its minimalist art of building, it claims to be architecture that breaks from distinctions between public and private and interior and exterior, hovering completely isolated from anything else, whether urban, rural, or "natural." With its configuration and composition having no definitive beginning, middle, and end, it severs connections with architectural conventions that make metaphoric and humane connections, as in birth, maturity, and death in human life, the human figure's feet, trunk, and head, and the base, shaft, and bloom of a tree evoking to *natura naturans*.

Revolutionary but not reformatory, it is merely anti-traditional, occupying a germinal moment in Modernism's program of rejecting the past and pointing to a future whose moments quickly become a past. In van der Rohe's own work it stands between his Friedrichstrasse high-rise proposal from 1921 mentioned in BAUAKADAMIE, KARL FRIEDRICK SCHINKEL, BERLIN, 1832–36 and his FEDERAL CENTER, CHICAGO, 1958–74. This expressive character isolates architecture within a domain where technology is supreme, not only in architecture but in every aspect of humankind's purposes that architecture serves and expresses. With no value in the past and no goal for the future, it licenses the many variations of Modernism that eschew connections between the world we build and the world we live in as a people united in communities to assist one another in the pursuit of happiness.

Notes

1 Peter Krečič, *Plečnik: The Complete Works* (New York: Whitney Library of Design, 1993), 18–19.
2 Frances Bernstein, "Pompeiian Women," in *The World of Pompeii*, eds. John J. Dobbins and Pedar W. Foss (London and New York: Routledge, 2007), 529.
3 TJ to Justice William Johnson, Monticello, June 12, 1823.

9

THE DWELLING

The ***dwelling*** shelters or protects the survival of those whose authority is strictly curtailed or largely limited.

Dwellings generally are built with vernacular construction in great numbers providing the background for urbanism. Until recent centuries, they were normally clustered within a walled, multi-family precinct with animals and other necessities of life and communal activities within an interior courtyard. Something similar survives today, without the precinct-enclosing wall, for example in Italian hill towns with dwellings above shops along the roadway and in Hong Kong with tall residential pencil-towers surrounding a large courtyard with shops and public restaurants patronized by the residents.

In Europe after the 14th c. Black Death ended and prosperity increased, larger dwellings were constructed as timber or masonry versions of rural castles along irregular street alignments with overhangs and bay windows. On the continent, as population densities increased in a country's few metropolitan centers, multi-story apartment buildings developed with the modern form having a single entrance under the surveillance of a porter with economic standing of dwellers in inverse ratio to the height of their unit above the ground.

In rural districts and throughout England the dwelling was often a cottage on the grounds of a manor with the cottager owing a fee in service or rent but with use of a small garden. They were often clustered with others in villages, and many surviving today, with access to land reserved for common use. In the 17th c. in England and Holland, rural districts began to drain workers at a rapidly increasing rate to urban factories, and common lands were enclosed and reserved for feudal overlords. Displaced cottagers found minimal accommodations in dwellings ganged with a ground floor door and window and two windows on the one or two floors above, each with two rooms, and a wing in

DOI: 10.4324/9780429506260-12

the back for a kitchen. Each one was heated with a coal grate; a cesspit was next to the street, and water was carried from a neighborhood hydrant.

Most of North America's tidal wave of immigrants came from rural villages and brought their familiar practices with them, but by the mid-20th c. prosperity had moved their descendants into "Ranch burgers," single-story domestic regias in five-to-an-acre automobile suburbs.

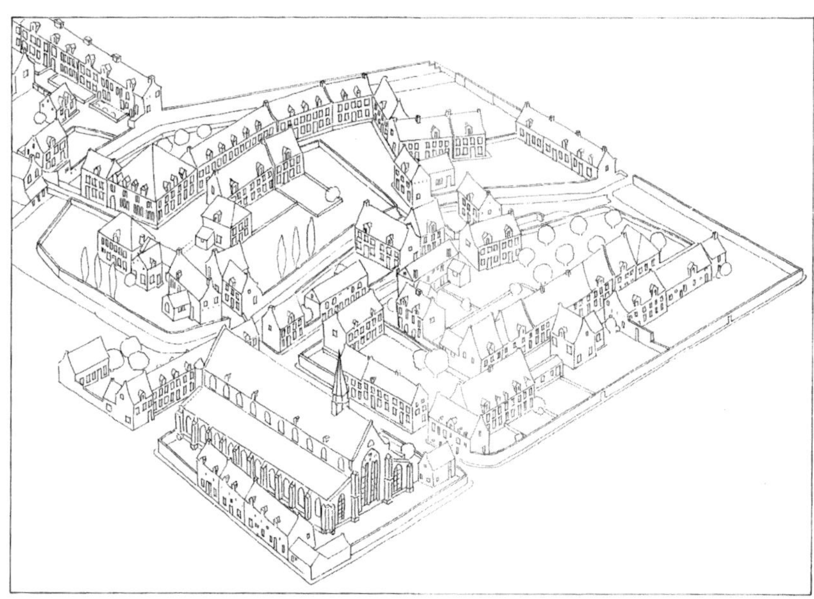

FIGURE 9.1 Groot Begijnhof, Leuven, Belgium, 13th–19th c. After Raymond Lemaire.

Individuals dedicated to religious life followed the Rule of Saint Benedict written in 516 that demanded poverty, chastity, and obedience within communities dedicated to a communal life. Variations adapted it to different circumstances, and many continue to guide life in religious communities.

In the Low Countries in the 13th c. communities developed for unmarried laywomen devoted to the Christian life who would engage in educating, doing fine needlework, etc. Named a Beguine (origins uncertain), she pledged to live chastely with others, set apart from the world but open during the day, and with freedom to leave the community when she wished.

This béguinage flourished in Leuven in the middle decades of the 17th c., with 360 residents living in nearly 100 simple vernacular cottages holding 300 apartments, some from the 16th c. Most are party wall structures strewn along lanes. They exhibit earlier timber and masonry vernacular construction, with openings frame in stone-framed, usually with two stories with few windows on the ground floor to assure privacy and an attic with dormers. A miniature walled city of 7 ½ acres with watercourses and ample open areas, it included a church from 1305ff (one of its priests became Pope Hadrian VI) and a hospital. With the order's decline and in the wake of the French Revolution, it became a municipal poorhouse. After its physical rehabilitation beginning in 1964, it has served the Catholic University of Leuven (Figure 9.1).

Cairo has always been an important center of trade within the Mediterranean basin (Figure 9.2). This recently restored Wikalat or caravanserai holds vertically organized apartments in its upper three stories, while elsewhere within a complex were an emporium, school, tax office, and exchange. Near the Al-Azhar University founded in 970 and attached to it across a street (not shown here), it was a religious center and intended mausoleum for its builder whose name it carries, the Mameluke Sultan Qansuh al Gouri (r. 1501–16).

Its closed street facade (not shown) with alternating color ashlar has a recessed entrance within an ornate portal concluding in colorful *muqarnas* in three different sizes. The second-floor windows are small and barred with none below them. Grouped in threes in the upper three stories below an overhang are windows grouped with wooden awning shutters on two floors followed on the top floor by *mashrabiyyas*, projecting wooden balconies enclosed by elaborate latticework and supported by brackets. Sometimes known as "harem windows," they have three-paneled subdivisions with operable awning shutters providing ventilation, comfort, and privacy for women residents.

The interior's rectangular court is surrounded by a pointed arch arcade with octagonal piers and facilities for pack animals and merchandise beneath a mezzanine's wooden walkway open to shops and other business facilities. On the third and fourth floors, the triplets of windows are nearly co-planar with the solid walls, producing a window-to-wall composition of expressive solidity and heavy austerity, alleviated by the mezzanine's latticed railings and fifth-floor *mashrabiyyas*. A colorful, tiled fountain is centered in the courtyard (Figure 9.3).

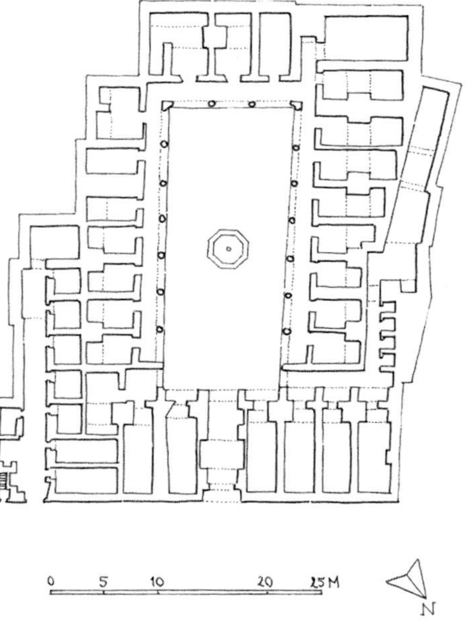

FIGURE 9.2 Wikalat al Ghouri, Cairo, Egypt, 1504–05.

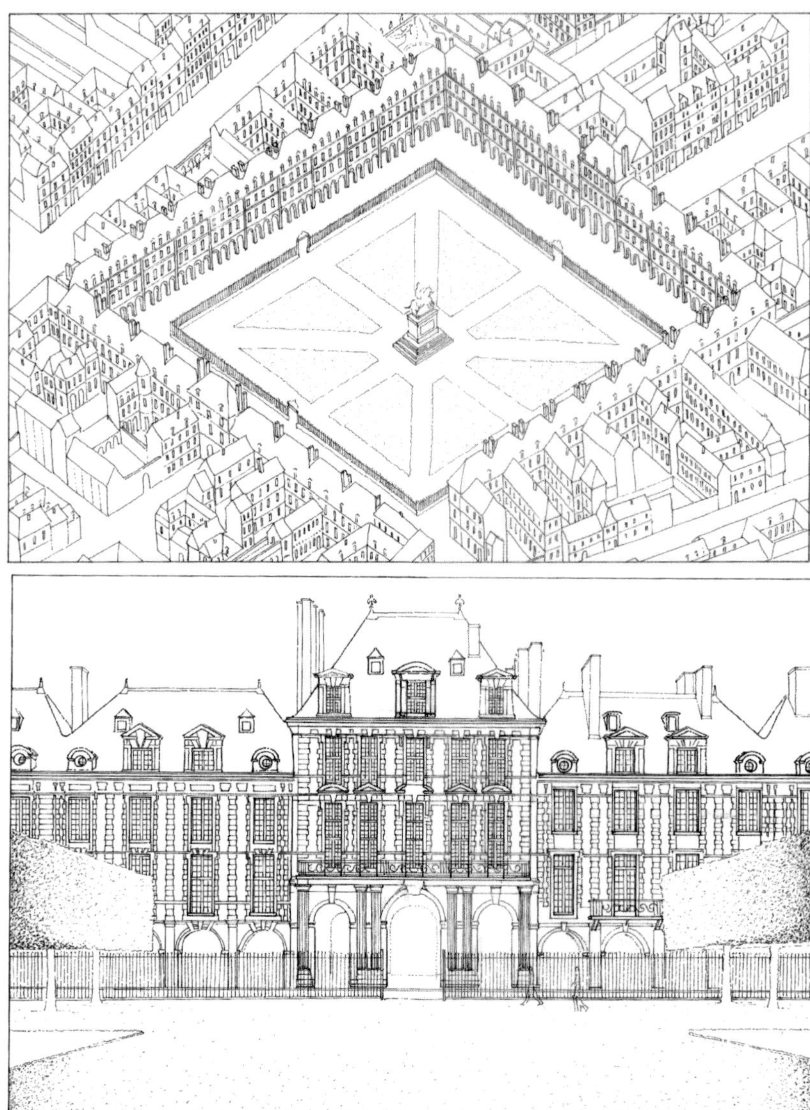

FIGURE 9.3 Place Royale (now Place des Vosges), Jacques Androuet du Cerceau, or Solomon de Brosse, or both? Paris, France, 1605–12. (a) Aerial, and (b) elevation.

Henry IV provided the first places in a modern city intended to ease the lives of residents. One was the completion of the **Pont Neuf, 1605**, begun in 1578 and integral to the soon-to-come **Place Dauphine**, discussed in Part I. The bridge eased cross-river traffic, uniting the city's two sides and giving Parisians places to view the city and meet and mingle. This first *place*, the first in a modern city, as another.

Its site was a jousting ground where, in 1605, he sponsored constructing a factory to produce silk fabric fashionable among the wealthy, being supplied by China and, more recently, Vigevano, in Italy. A brick and stone vaulted arcade ran before shops below two lofty stories for manufacturing and an attic for workers' dwellings. Later that year he expanded it with three connected wings enclosing the field to accommodate merchants, craftsmen, and tradesmen, whom noblemen and others with wealth would eventually replace. Above the arcades' Tuscan pilasters on each pier's face are uniform facades following the expressive character of the period's better dwellings. Tall 8 × 8 casement windows on the two upper floors were set in brick walls, and limestone structural elements sketched out supports for pitched, slate roofs above richly topped dormers; roof hips defined each of the several pavilions in each wing.

Henry's Royal Architects were probably involved: Jacques II Androuet du Cerceau (1550–1614) whose part of the **Louvre** was subsequently destroyed, and his kinsman Solomon de Brosse (1571–1626), architect of the **Luxembourg Palace, Paris, 1615–24**. In the wing opposite the factory, a royal pavilion was centered. Its larger vertical and horizontal bays and elevation above a street by three arches, the central one larger and pilasters flanking them, representing a triumphal arch. In 1607 Henry had the factory replaced by the fourth wing with a similar central pavilion called the queen's pavilion.

Today the square, with an equestrian statue from 1639 of Louis XIII in ancient Roman garb, offers not jousts and royal ceremonials but a carefully manicured lawn and pollarded trees with fine goods and food available in the arcades' shops (Figure 9.4).

England's increased prosperity enabled titled landowners to build Palladian villas in the green countryside and the merely prosperous to dwell in domestic regias clustered as genteel row houses. At Bath, Georgian England's toniest social scene with England's only hot spring, they could lease a temporary residence and hob-nob in activities where Richard "Beau" Nash was Master of Ceremonies between 1704 and 1761.

English taste shifted to preferences for Italian models due to their Grand Tour to Italy, what they read in books, and the Palladianism of CHISWICK, LORD BURLINGTON AND WILLIAM KENT, LONDON, 1727–29. In Bath, Italian architecture was adapted to English row house configurations with continuous facades.

Particularly proficient were the developer-architects John Wood (1704–54) and his son John (1728–82) who used the luscious creamy Bath stone for facades. In London, they built dwellings, and in Bath and elsewhere, more and several other important buildings. The elder Wood also wrote an eccentric treatise on architecture. As speculative builders working largely outside Bath's corporate limits, they laid out streets and squares, providing individual buyers with a facade and custom dwellings behind three or sometimes four or five uniform bays. Shops among Bath's high-class terraced dwellings being

FIGURE 9.4 The Circus and the Crescent, John Wood the Elder and Wood the Younger, Bath, England, 1754; 1767.

out of the question, they were collected in the central area and on PULTNEY BRIDGE, ROBERT ADAM, BATH, 1770–74, just beyond our urban plan.

The Rome-themed CIRCUS from 1754 to 1768 used the Colosseum's exterior for a three-story facade with paired columns arranged in the canonic Doric, Ionic, Corinthian sequence facing inward in a circle. Entered through three gaps, the inner circle originally had water for horses and a garden. An astylar connecting street ran to the CRESCENT (shown here) from 1767 to 1774, with 30 units with back gardens and strung in a graceful curve at the brow of a low rise with lawn stretching down to a ha-ha with a park beyond. Its solid base supported solitary engaged Ionic orders with a cornice and balustrade paired only for one entrance in the center and for the corners of the terminal boxes that have five bays with a central entrance. We show a three-bay dwelling unit's plan with the ground floor on the left entered directly from street level above its basement area with a fifth floor (not shown) in a recessed, dormered attic (Figure 9.5).

This building, a project of the Istituto per i Case Popolari (Institute for public housing), was central in the new town of Garbatella, Lido di Ostia, near

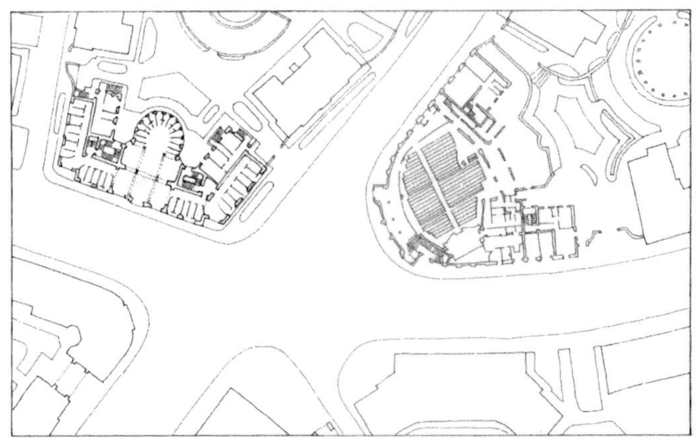

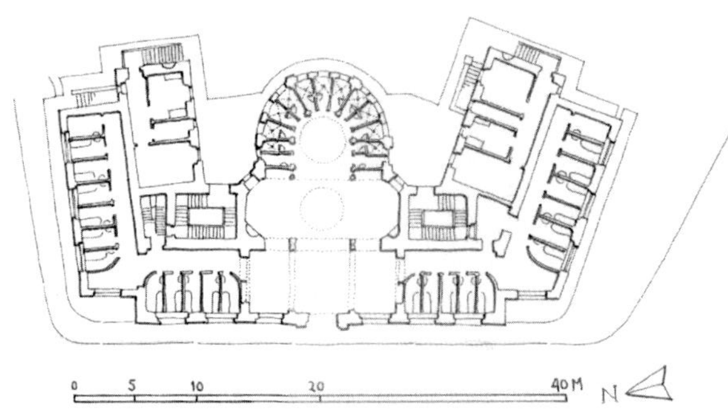

FIGURE 9.5 Stabilimento Bagni (a project of the Istituto per i case popolari) Innocenzo Sabbatini, Garbatella, Italy, 1926–27. (a) Plans and (b) elevation.

Rome. Here Innocenzo Sabbatini demonstrated invention within precedent that exemplified a modern traditional regionalism that is much more substantive, and quite different from other, contemporaneous developments that tend toward a vulgarized and whimsical *barocchetto romano*. His work connects modern work with ancient and subsequent developments in Italy's modern traditional regionalism.

Garbatella was the second of several government projects for citizens of modest means. A kilometer south of Rome's Porta San Paolo, Massimo Piacentini, and Gustavo Giovannoni, followed English **Garden City** models in subdividing its 26 hectares (64 acres) into 62 *lotti* (land parcels) with buildings allocated to several different architects. Our plan shows the confluence of streets at Piazza Bartolomeo Romano with Sabbatini's *Cinema Teatro* and, in our detailed plan and elevation, the building built as one of the era's public baths and public social centers (now the Moby Dick Bibliotheca e Hub Culturale) seen here in an earlier scheme altered slightly when built. Its elevation clearly displays its three layers with public baths (*bagni pubblici*) and exercise areas and a mezzanine (*taverna e cenacolo*), then three floors of apartments, and finally a hall with three prominent, front-facing thermal windows.

Sabbatini drew on Guido Calza's *Le origini latine dell'abitazione moderna* (The Latin Origins of Modern Dwelling; 1923) that included Italo Gismondi's able reconstruction of a Roman insula, the **House of Diana, Ostia Antica**, which, with its extant ruins, provided a model for this combination of commerce, housing, and leisure. He modified the original courtyard insula on a gridded site to fit this angled C-shaped urban site, retaining the large, ground floor entrance hall but projecting a single-story hemicycle into the court. For the main block, he elevated the model's squat and heavy proportions without diminishing the solid character, retaining on the front the exposed brick of the original's prominent, projecting cavetto that here carries a balcony above the sweeping and solid arcuation of the ground floor and mezzanine. Above in the modern fabric are the stuccoed floors with a higher ratio of wall to openings than the lower levels.

10

THE SHOP

The ***shop*** serves sustaining life. It accommodates production and commerce and sometimes public offices. Shops benefit through proximity with other shops. A shop is often combined with a dwelling and included in a hypostyle discussed in Chapters 5 and 7 (Figure 10.1).

Shops in ancient Rome were often collected into a precinct called a *macellum*, for example at the **Forum, Pompeii, before 79**. Here in the capital, we find them integrated into Emperor Trajan's great complex, the **Forum of Trajan, Apollodorus of Damascus, 106–13**, with its Temple, Basilica Ulpia, libraries, and Column of Trajan. The Forum's sides extended into exedras with semicircular collections of shops for official business, and others were reached by ramps leading up to more shops on the Quirinal Hill. A cross-vaulted chamber there holds ten shops, each with a mezzanine dwelling (*cenacolo*), and more in an exterior, open-air upper level. The typical individual shop's configuration is enduring, as we see in the four shops at **Palazzo Caprini, Bramante, Rome, c. 1510** (destroyed), where Raphael lived after 1517. Similar shops lined streets and followed them across watercourses as in Ponte Vecchio, Florence, the Rialto Bridge, Venice, and PULTNEY BRIDGE, ROBERT ADAM, BATH, 1770–74 (Figure 10.2).

Abbas I (1572–1629), the Safavid Shah of Persia, quelled civil strife, expelled foreign threats, and in 1598 moved the capital from Qazvin to Isfahan, an Islamic capital friendly to ethnic and religious diversity. The city flourished through his revitalization, with a more rectangular plan, the renewed FRIDAY (JAMEH; MASJID-I-JAMI) MOSQUE, 771, and a new city square and market in our plan.

The new square is the immense **Meidan-i-Shah** (king's field or square) or **Naqsh-e Jahan Square** (Image of the World square) 500 m × 170 m, lined

DOI: 10.4324/9780429506260-13

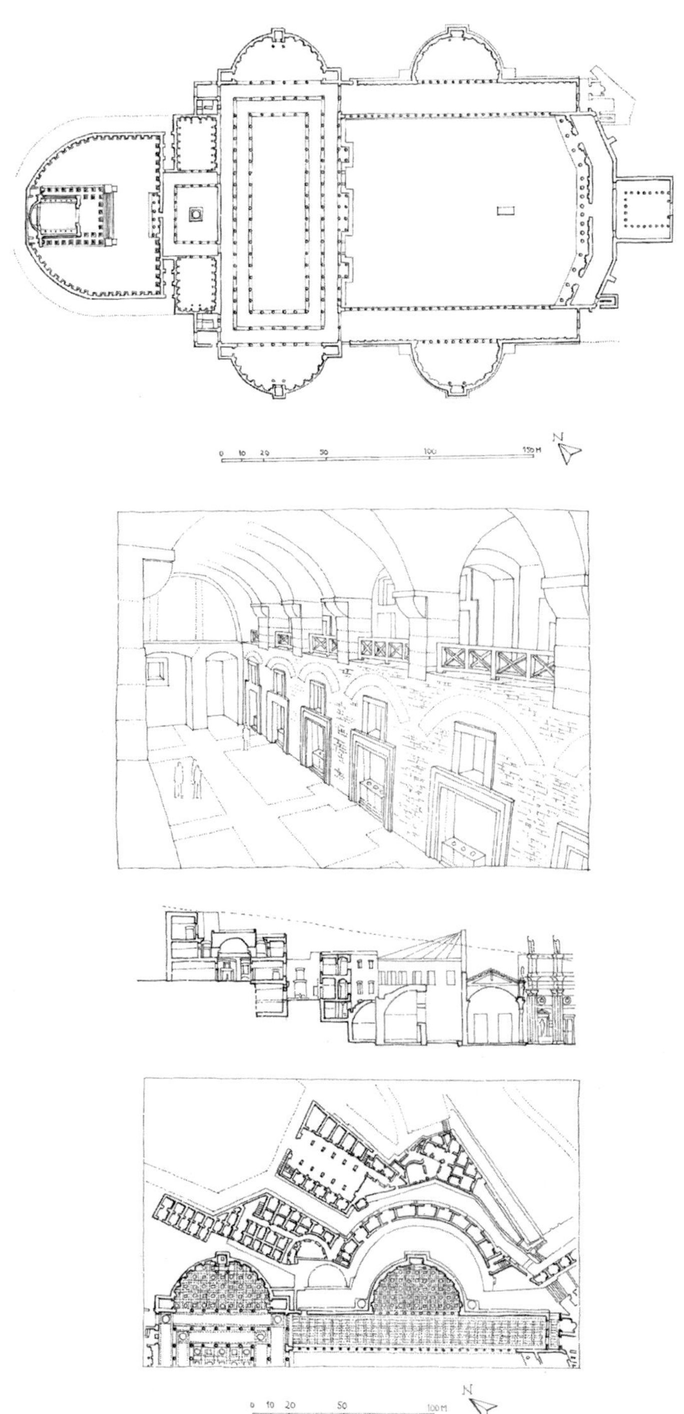

FIGURE 10.1 Trajan's Market at Trajan's Forum, Apollodorus of Damascus, Rome, Italy, 106–13, plan, section, and perspective.

FIGURE 10.2 Grand Bazaar, Isfahan, Iran, 1598ff.

with two-story arcades with shops and dwellings and elaborate, polychromatic fronts of civic monuments on each of three sides: the Shah's Mosque on the south, the Mosque of Shaikh Lotfallah, a revered wise scholar on a long side, and the other long side with the Palace of Ali Qapu. From its elevated terrace, the Shah could watch polo games, military exercises, parades, and a range of commercial activities in small, demountable tents and within large caravans.

At the narrow end of the **Meidan-i-Shah** the colorful and commanding **Qeysarie Gate** (its third story now removed) set within an exedra leads into the GRAND BAZAAR (Persian: enclosed market; the gate's name is often given to the bazaar) composed of streets and squares. We show only a small portion of the total that runs for two kilometers or more to the old city's walls with twists and turns through the urban fabric, uniting the old city with the **Meidan-i-Shah**. Serving as the dorsal spine for the city's pedestrian circulation and movement of goods, along it are caravanserais like the WIKALAT AL GHOURI, CAIRO, 1504–05, madrasas (Arabic: schools), mosques, and *hammams* (Arabic: baths).

The bazaar includes sections from the 11th to the 17th c. along streets or galleries lined by souks (shops), usually with mezzanines for offices or storage beneath cupolas. Goods spill freely into the route vying for the visual and olfactory attention of buyers whose lively hustle and bustle stimulate supply and demand. The expressive character is a synthesis of the profusion of objects, materials, and colors seeking buyers contrasting with the arcades' architectural character with simple geometric patterns of the brick or plaster domical cupolas and their oculus rising without capitals from pointed arches every five to seven meters. Wider than most of Isfahan's narrow streets and traversing the dark and cool gallery, the experience upon exiting into the explosion of light in the massive expanse of the **Meidan-i-Shah** can be likened to arriving at Piazza San Marco having traversed the narrow and labyrinthine streets of Venice, a trading partner in the west (Figure 10.3).

This bridge was built to connect a new suburban development with Bath, where Britain's only hot spring had become a popular spa when Augustan Britain

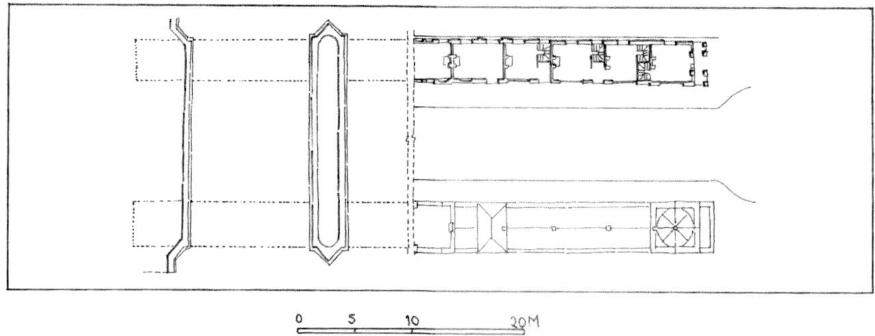

FIGURE 10.3 Pulteney Bridge, Robert Adam, Bath, England, 1770–74.

became fascinated with ancient Rome whose occupiers had also enjoyed its warm waters. The aspiring middle-class owned or rented dwellings in THE CIRCUS AND THE CRESCENT, JOHN WOOD THE ELDER and WOOD THE YOUNGER, BATH, 1754; 1767, and the Pulteney family planned an expansion across the River Avon. Bristol architect Thomas Palty designed a bridge to replace the ferry, and Robert Adam (1728–92), with an eye on Andrea Palladio, rejected Rialto Bridge for Venice, broadening Palty's roadbed with shops and built it with the region's honey-colored Bath stone. It has suffered repeatedly over time, but it has been largely restored and continues to carry vehicular traffic, including busses.

Both infrastructure and amenity, its shops, addressing the increased demand for luxury goods, benefitted from the availability of glass for shop windows. Built with eleven shops "fit for any genteel business" on each side, the center and end shops are the largest. On the well restored exterior south facade (we show it), a central shop has a very subdued five-part facade with a pediment above a Tuscan Palladiana within a reveal. Above Tuscan pilasters the terminal pavilions have pediments, attics, and octagonal domes. Roundels in the haunches of the three arches provide light and air for the shopkeepers' storage areas below the roadway. The present street facade is a much-simplified version of the south exterior facade with 6 over 6 double-hung windows serving the mezzanine shopkeepers' dwellings (Figure 10.4).

The GALERIE VIVIENNE by François-Jean Delannoy (1755–1835) is the darker-toned L embedded within a three-story block filled with the Galerie Colbert in 1826. These and various successors were built to serve rising middle-class affluence.

Their predecessors in Paris included the **Galerie de Bois, 1786**, explicitly modeled on mid-Eastern markets such as the GRAND BAZAAR, ISFAHAN, 1589 when it was built within the **Palais Royal, Jacques Lemercier,**

FIGURE 10.4 Galerie Vivienne, François-Jean Delannoy, Paris, 1823.

1633; Victor Louis, Paris, 1781. That Galerie would be replaced by **Shops, Pierre-François-Léonard Fontaine, 1829** that, like the Galerie Colbert, also followed the model of the GALERIE VIVIENNE.

Its two stories of dwellings above the *passage* following the L for 176 m between major entrances on two important streets. The entrance to the leg is flanked by restaurants. After its first dozen or so shops, the *passage* narrows between two large shops before entering a rotunda with a glazed domical roof. This opens to a narrower, longer *passage* reaching a square corner with shops and entry to the other foot. Near its street entrance a rich, curving stair rises to the upper stories. In both stretches, the shops are beneath a pitched iron and glass roof. Low relief sculptures of ancient goddesses and other ancient motifs reflect the popularity of Pompeii's discovery and the architect's three student years in Rome. The richly decorated mosaic pavement is coordinated with the pilasters separating the shops. Gas heat and illumination extended the hours of opening.

Shops within the **Boulevards, Baron Haussmann, Paris, 1854–70** and the development of department stores led to the Galerie's decline, but in recent decades skillful management and the quality of the architecture have restored its vitality (Figure 10.5).

The largest of Italy's many glass-covered 19th c. shopping arcades, e.g., the **Galleria Principe, Nicola Breglia and Giovanni de Novalis, Naples, 1873** and the larger **Galleria Umberto, Emanuele Rocco, Naples, 1887**, this great social center features an octagonal crossing and central dome more than twice the span of its four broad arms. Like them, it is glazed within an expressive ferrous tectonic structure above stone and stucco surfaces and a mosaic floor. The decorative scheme's program celebrates Italy's unification. The ground floor shops are high with mezzanines in their arches. Pilasters rise above the arcade's piers through the piano nobile with specialty shops and offices to a definitive cornice followed by low stories that seem to augment the height of the glazed vaults and dome.

This structure offers refuge from Lombardy's lamentable, wet winters, and constituted a major intervention in the cramped city. The shorter arms reach the commercial blocks. Not shown is the entrance from the Piazza del Duomo into the longer, central arm, a tall, two-story triumphal arch scaled to complement the Duomo. Indentations flank it, and three-story business blocks extend with a continuous arcaded ground floor. The galleria's plan cranks to allow a triumphal arch entrance to face the Piazza della Scala where Luca Beltrami's 1888–92 replication of **Palazzo Marino, Galeazzo Alessi, 1557–63**, for the City Hall faces the TEATRO ALLA SCALA, GIUSEPPE PIERMARINI, 1776–78 (Figure 10.6).

Several of Chicago's movers and shakers had Almerin Hotchkiss, a noted rural cemetery designer, lay out a town on 1,200 acres of lake-front land connected by rail 27 miles north. He placed very large home sites along winding

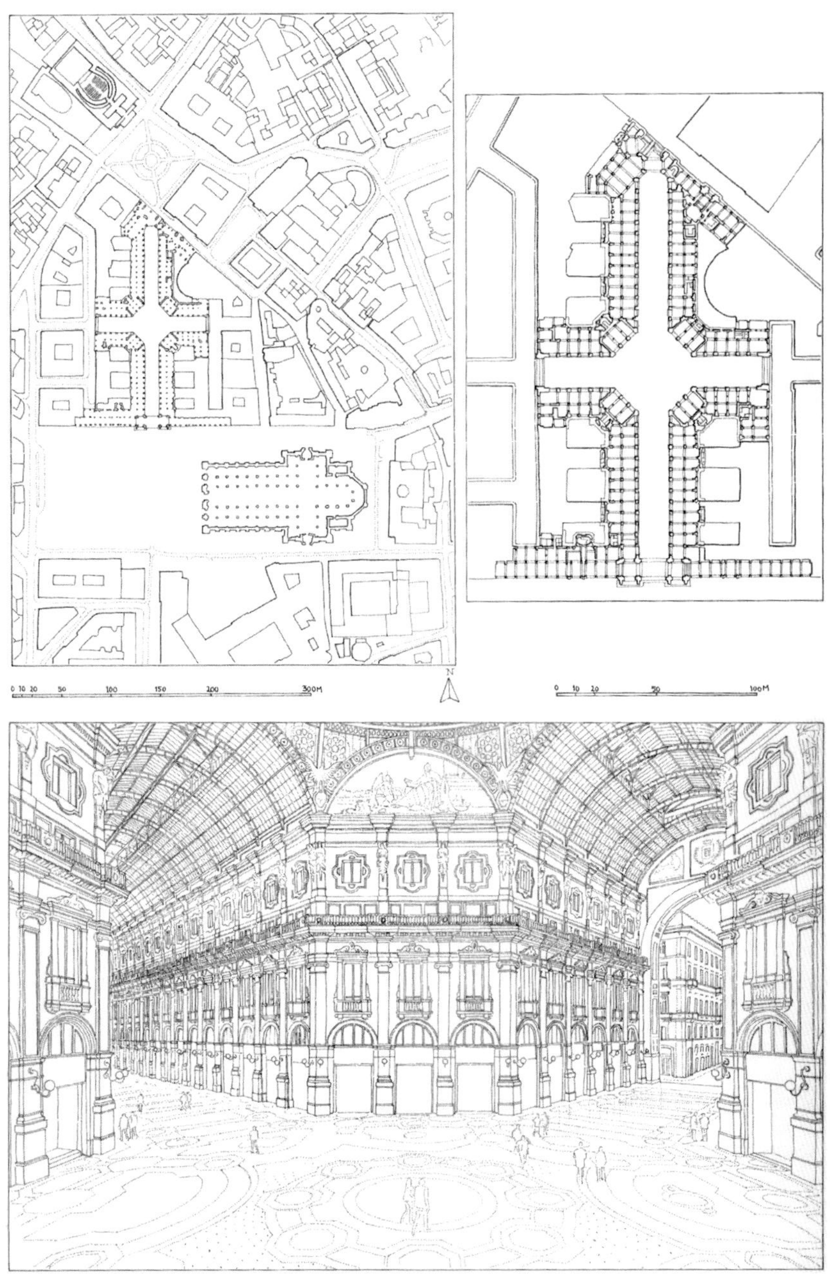

FIGURE 10.5 Galleria Vittorio Emanuele II, Giuseppe Mengoni, Milan, Italy, 1865–67. (a) Urban and detailed plans and (b) interior perspective.

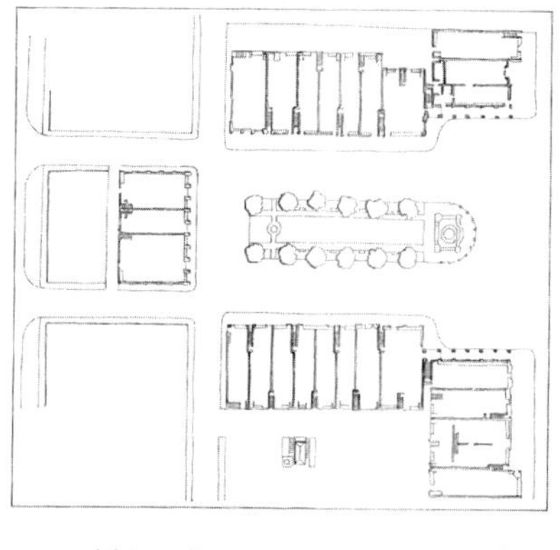

FIGURE 10.6 Market Square, Howard van Doren Shaw, Lake Forest, Illinois, U.S.A., 1912–16. (a) Plan and (b) perspective.

roads within the hilly terrain and included a small, gridded area opposite the railroad station as a site for workers' dwellings. Ramshackle shops grew opposite the station, but with the advent of the automobile Owen Aldis, a broker and manager involved in Chicago's early tall commercial buildings and who had a second home here swept them away for this shopping center.

Another local resident, the talented and admired Howard van Doren Shaw (1869–1926), used the brick, stone, and half-timber vernacular of English, German, and other villages that shared its expressive character with many of the local estates that he and others had designed. It faced the station and the road with wings facing one another across a broad, deep, landscaped U with an octagonal fountain between parking slots (originally parallel, now diagonal). In the wings, he placed groups of shops below apartments with gables and dormers. Colonnades in front of the foremost shops end at doglegs marked by towers, different on each side, before continuing further. At the U's bottom a two-story hypostyle with giant orders stands in for a tithe barn, originally holding a bank and a Marshall Field's outpost; a recreation center and clubhouse were eventually added beyond.

11

THE HYPOSTYLE

The hypostyle accommodates gatherings of various sorts, being a field of columns or piers supporting a roof. A workhouse of construction, its tectonic order rather than its purpose dominates its configuration, but with the art of architecture, it could be invested with the proper decor, although in the modern era this has become of less interest to its builders (Figure 11.1).

This great hypostyle stands on a platform built in 519 BCE by Persian Darius the Great (r. 522–486 BCE) in a ceremonial center he had founded distant from the population centers of the Achaemenid Empire. Darius lost to the Greeks in the Battle of Marathon in 490 BCE, but a decade later his son Xerxes (r. 486–465 BCE) returned and destroyed Athens and its temples on the Acropolis. On that platform, he began this 68 m × 68 m building to serve primarily as a ceremony hall; his son Artaxerxes (r. 465–425 BCE) completed it. To avenge Greek defeats Alexander the Great destroyed it in 330 BCE.

Here in the center's second-largest building, upper right in our plan, subjects and subject nations showed their submission. Its 10 × 10 grid of one-meter-diameter columns ran up 11.3 m from a high base with floral motifs, through shafts with layers of a rolled motif drums, and reached distinctive capitals, some the heads of kneeling animals, usually bulls or lions but also men, griffins, and eagles. They are placed back-to-back with the main beams set in a recession between the animals' heads to support the flat cedar roof; there is no evidence of a clerestory.

Extensive limestone surfaces are filled with low relief portrayals, formerly intensely colored, of courtiers, musicians, soldiers, etc., and of subject nations presenting their tribute to the king, all in full court dress, with trimmed beards framed with lotus flower friezes. The door jambs present the king battling lions and other great, even mythical, animals, or animals fighting among themselves,

DOI: 10.4324/9780429506260-14

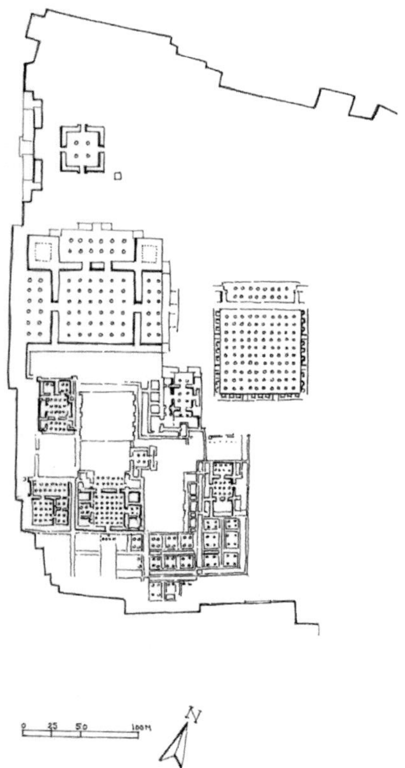

FIGURE 11.1 Throne Hall of 100 Columns, Persepolis, Iran, 518–460 BCE.

with a lion (the sun) defeating a bull (the moon) each spring to usher in the new year. Beyond the vestibule's double row of columns, two enormous bulls are followed by the great hall. Leaving the intense outside light and entering this vast, tenebrous interior surely enhanced the display of subject nations' tribute and the ceremonies' mystery (Figure 11.2).

As Rome's population expanded so did its appetites and the land needed to sate them. The sea lanes leading from Carthage's captured lands and Spain's grain fields and olive groves fed into the Tiber River's mouth at Ostia. In 193 BCE, with provisioning overwhelmed and inefficient, two family members holding the office of *aedile* entered a bid for higher office by building this utilitarian hypostyle commemorated with their family name.

A huge structure with an unpretentious, utilitarian expressive character, it covered a rectangle 487 × 60 m with 294 piers carrying parallel arches. The arches supported vaults covering 8.3 m aisles running from the river through three bays. In successive aisle bays, the horizontal vault was elevated to follow the ground's slope, producing gaps between successive vaults that were left open for light and air. Six aisles 50 bays long paralleling the river intersected

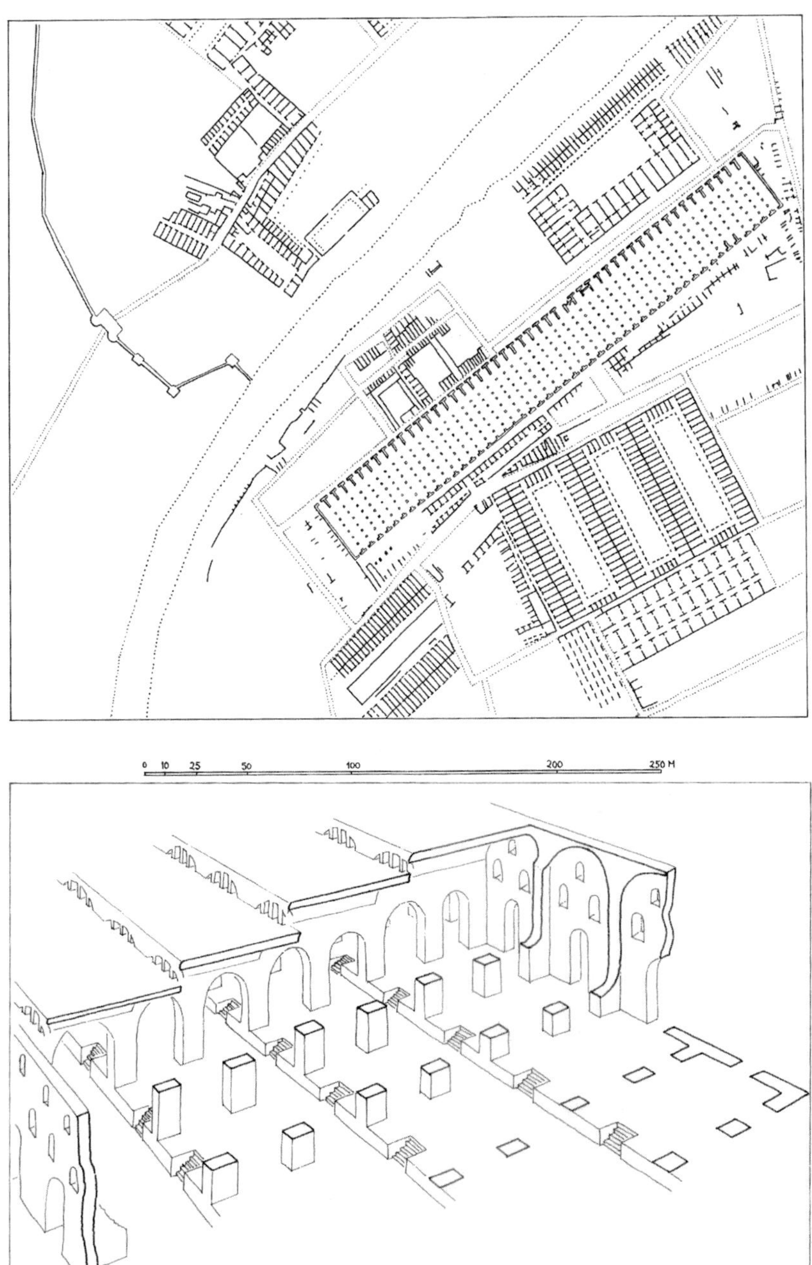

FIGURE 11.2 Porticus Aemilia, Rome, Italy, 193 BCE. (a) Plan and (b) section.

them; a seventh nearest the river with deeper bays interfaced with the emporium where all manner of goods were unloaded and distributed.

This arched, vaulted hypostyle constructed with small, irregular stones bonded in cement slurry is the earliest known public use of what would become the common basic·material and membrature for innumerable later buildings. Modified and adapted, this familiar membrature served a wide variety of purposes from basilicas to porticos, palaces, theaters, circuses, amphitheaters, etc.

With Rome's decline, the building suffered through disuse, with some of its original fabric and later restorations surviving in extant buildings and mere fragments in the district that it and its ancillary buildings dominated. Some of the emporium has recently been disinterred, but the most prominent evidence of the work done there is the nearby 49 m high mountain of discarded olive oil pots (Figure 11.3).

This hypostyle hall, larger than an American football field, occupied the largest platform in the crowded ancient Roman Forum. Julius Caesar removed other buildings, including a basilica, to clear the site for this building that his adoptive son Augustus finished and named after him. Buildings press upon it on three sides, and its narrow end is approached at the base of the Capitoline. It suffered serious damage from time to time, but its important uses and central location assured its restoration or preservation until the 5th c. when its marble began to feed lime kilns and on into the 15th c. when the remaining pieces were used in new palaces.

A hypostyle often serves several functions, and its design can be worked out to give them the expressive character usually suitable for the most important

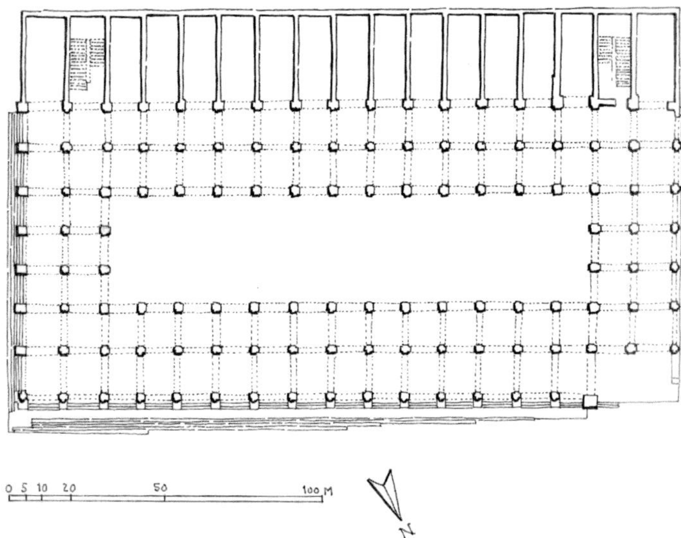

FIGURE 11.3 Basilica Giulia, Rome, Italy, 54 BCE.

one. This basilica's principal purpose was to serve the law, which was signaled by its similarity to Sulla's recently completed, nearby **Tabularium, 78–72 BCE**. There judgments were archived; here they were handed down.

The 3 × 13 bay central 82 × 18 m open, roofed area was surrounded by two aisles of two stories of fornixes (brick interiors and Carrara facings) carrying concrete vaults that were among Rome's early examples. On the side away from the Forum the fifth aisle of shops serving commerce, offices, and gatherings opened into the basilica and stairs giving access to the galleries. Along the outside of most of the basilica's length ran three steps providing a little prominence for its impressive fornix facades. Internally the upper gallery offered a clear view down into the central area's polychromatic geometric marble pavement, roofed with trusses and lit by a high clearstory. Like other basilicas, it could be divided into smaller areas, in this case, four. Today only scruffy remnants remain (Figure 11.4).

This Great Mosque is Islam's oldest extant mosque and model for many others. It replaced a large Roman Temple of Jupiter that Theodosius had converted into a Byzantine Christian church; its outline is dotted in our plan. After 634 when the Umayyads had conquered Syria, Christians and Muslims alternated using it. In 661, Damascus was made the capital, and the Umayyad Caliph Al-Walid I (r. 705–15) ordered this mosque to replace the church. He included a place for Christian worship within it, and the Byzantine Emperor supplied mosaic workmen and materials for its elaborate paradise ornamentation, some of which survives despite centuries of hard use and many restorations.

It occupies a large, 170 × 100 m walled precinct encased within the sprawling, tight-knit fabric of ancient Damascus, and it includes a courtyard (*harem*) and prayer hall. After the successor Abbasid dynasty assumed power in 750 and moved the capital to Bagdad, the local governor added two free-standing structures to the courtyard's ablution fountain, in 780 the open, so-called "Dome of the clock," and the domed, octagonal treasury, 789, with mosaic facades carried on stout, baseless Corinthian columns.

Three courtyard sides have two-story semicircular arcades built with much spolia, with columns and an occasional pier on the lower floor, and above each support a pier above the columns and two arches between. On both floors along the short ends, the galleries give access to rooms serving various administrative, judicial, and educational functions, and to pilgrims' lodging.

The prayer hall occupies nearly half of the precinct. Three aisles deep and 22 seemingly endless bays wide, its membrature includes 40 reused monolithic Corinthian columns and impost blocks carrying plane, slightly horseshoe-shaped arches. Above them, another, lower arcade with two arches above every bay below carries a pitched, open timber roof. In one intercolumniation there is a domed, tholos Shrine of the Head of John the Baptist, venerated in both faiths, found there in the 6th c. The north wall, poorly restored, has a shrine to Mohammad's grandson Husayn son of Ali (626–80); in a small garden outside the precinct's northwest corner is a mausoleum to Saladin (r. 1174–93).

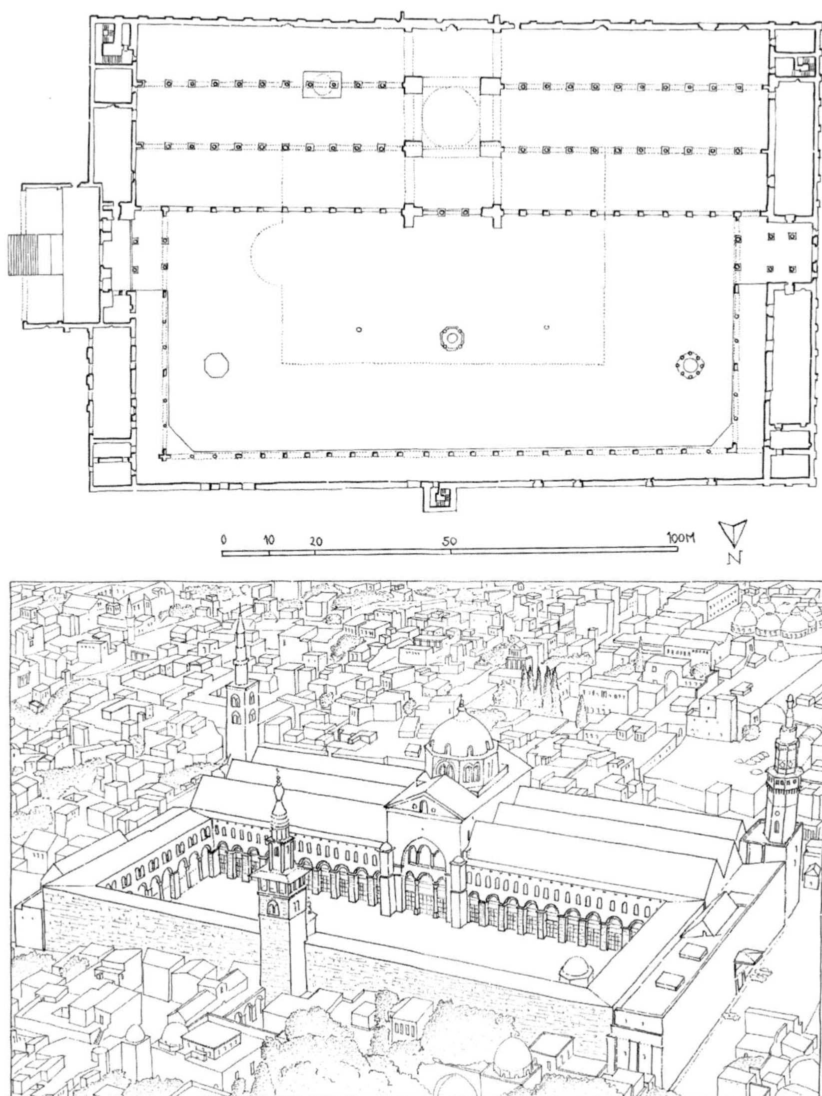

FIGURE 11.4 Great Mosque (Umayyad), Damascus, Syria, plan, 706–15. (a) Plan and (b) aerial.

A central area of three square, arched bays intersects these long aisles. Massive piers ornamented with marble intarsia support the arches. The required *qibla* wall and the hall's grandest *mihrab* among many others are here. The central bay's original, octagonal wooden drum and dome was replaced in 1893 with a stone, octagonal, squinched dome.

The prayer hall's courtyard façade has a triple-arched portal under an arch with its own triplet of windows below a pediment, all framed by massive side piers; very little of its present mosaic ornamentation is original. An axis from the main entrance with one of Islam's first minarets leads through the ablution fountain to the *mihrab*. Two minarets on the far corners are also very early but often repaired, one of them named the minaret of Jesus following the Muslim belief that the Great Mosque is the place where Jesus will reappear at the End of Days (Figure 11.5).

This sprawling mosque reached its present state across nearly 1,300 years with the greatest activity when the city was the capital of an Islamic state. One revitalization occurred when, a kilometer away, the GRAND BAZAAR, ISFAHAN, IRAN, 1598 was built.

The oldest section, from 771, was built by the Umayyads as a 3 × 6 hypostyle leading to the *qibla* and *mihrab* in the south. In our plan, it is the southern protrusion with square bays; our interior view shows several of its bays, with cylindrical columns holding brick horseshoe arches and uncovered masonry, with each bay different and vaulted with squinch pendentives.

Later enlargements came in 840–1, 908–32, and, most notably, in 1086 by the Salijuq vizier (local governor) Nizamal al-Mulk, who added nearly 200 more domed or vaulted bays, some punching above the otherwise flat roof. He replaced the original hypostyle bays in front of the original *mihrab* with a domed tholos seen in our plan and like the one at the GREAT MOSQUE (UMAYYAD MOSQUE), DAMASCUS, 706–15. A tour-de-force of craftsmanship,

FIGURE 11.5 Friday Mosque (Masjid-I-Jami') Isfahan, Iran, 771ff.

its two piers and two half piers on each side with arches between them project colonnettes up to support the frames of niches acting as squinches. Farther up, broad *maqama*-like forms, unusually flattened, extend up to a circular spring line for the spherical dome with ribs controlling the brick structure and ornamented with parallel bands sweeping up the surface, white and in regular patterns (the order of heaven?). Steams of light enter through four narrow, rectangular windows in the intermediate zone, and two tiny windows reside in the dome. Later minarets reach a little higher than the dome's slightly pointed extrados. In 1088–89, Nizamal al-Mulk's successor built another dome at the opposite side but outside the mosque; tectonically ingenious, it uses squinches to circle the square.

Those domes survived the destructive fire sometime in 1120–21, and in the rebuilding, a great courtyard was carved out of the complex. Roughly 60 m × 70 m and entered through inconspicuous portals at various locations, it has two stories of piers carrying low, pointed arches with an *iwan* centered in each face. This high, vaulted area serves as an indented entrance porch beyond the arched opening, usually pointed, the high, flat front of each of them facing the courtyard rising high to dominate the city's skyline, a scheme that would become popular in Islamic architecture. The largest of the four leads directly into the *qibla* and *mihrab* under Nizamal al-Mulk's dome.

The mosque gained new prominence after 1598 when the Safavid dynasty made Isfahan its capital. Minarets were added to the southern *iwan*, and over time the elaborate tiers of *muqarnas* and mosaics inside and out were extensively ornamented, as were the courtyard's surfaces. Two ablution fountains and a pair of elevated prayer platforms were added there, along with additional fabric or adaptations for madrasas, library, treasury, and an additional mosque with its own entrance and larger bays in the northwest quadrant; the east and west *iwans* were also given *mihrabs*.

Today we see Islamic architecture's expressive character of the glimmering ornament with dark blue backgrounds for a wide range of motifs and *muqarnas* in domes and squinches. Particularly notable is the exquisite brickwork seen in the nude surfaces, and the tectonic role given to ribs in displays of the indispensable contribution of the art of building's materials to the art of architecture (Figure 11.6).

Before Charles Martel stopped them from entering France in 732, the North African Moors had begun in 711 to construct a mosque in Córdoba, where they would remain until 1236. They shared it with Visigothic Christians until 785 when they began replacing it with this mosque modeled on the Umayyad GREAT MOSQUE, DAMASCUS, 706–15, and growing to a walled precinct 180 m × 130 m.

In the first structure (upper right in our plan) shafts, capitals, and other spolia gathered from far and wide were crafted into horseshoe arches (Visigoth invention?), with alternating white and red voussoirs producing eleven aisles

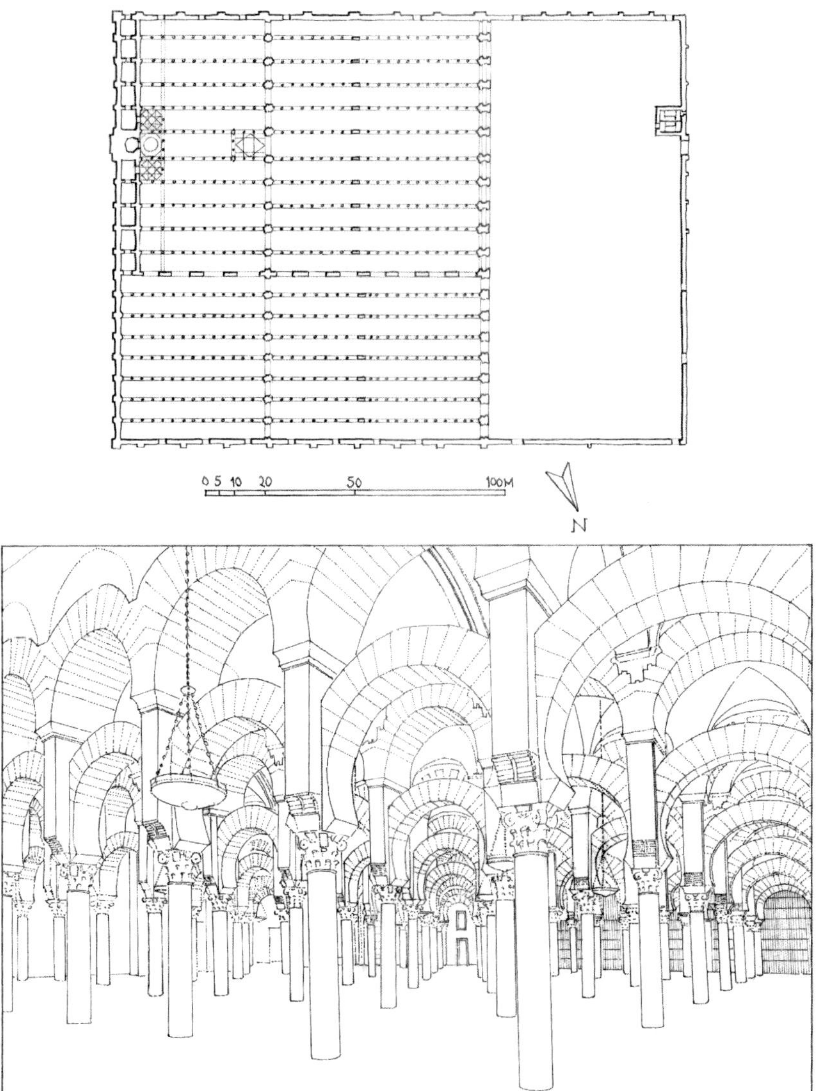

FIGURE 11.6 Mosque at Córdoba, Spain, 785ff.

with a horseshoe-arched entrances from the garden, a wider center aisle, and the *qibla* twelve bays away. Two tiers of arches, horseshoe below and semicircular above, with broader soffits and carried by piers, probably spolia, rested on the columns below to provide added height for the flat ceiling below a hipped roof over each aisle. Enlargements began in 833, with aisles moving the *qibla* another eight bays to the south (to the left in our plan) with three skylights at the juncture. The courtyard's enlargement began in 951, with a minaret at its main entrance. Another expansion in 961–6, again to the south, added another twelve bays with four skylights, a bay at the junction rising into an eight-ribbed dome, and farther along, the relocated *qibla* with a spectacular new *mihrab.* Horseshoe-arched, framed with calligraphy, and topped with a low, trilobe arcade, it is ornamented with gold and colorful mosaic encrustation, perhaps donated by the Byzantine Emperor. Before the *mihrab* is a tholos whose octagonal frame provides support for gold-encrusted, intersecting, semicircular arches running to alternate corners and crowned with a pointed-rib dome. Similar but less ornamented elements for the caliph and courtiers are in the bays flanking it. Their membrature involves spectacular lower arches with five lobes carrying a horseshoe arch with another five-lobe arch split in two inserted between them. Topography prevented further expansion to the south, so in 987, expansion went east with eight full-length aisles parallel to the existing ones with more skylights, with the courtyard expanded to match.

The courtyard, entered through several horseshoe arch portals, some of them decorated with colorful masonry, takes up about a third of the precinct with a cistern for ablutions and irrigating its palm and citrus trees. The arcade open to the prayer hall was eventually walled.

Our plan predates the post-Reconquista adaptation for Christian usage with its major insertion of a temple-tholos that occupies four bays of nine aisles athwart the axis leading to the *mihrab.* Begun in 1523 by architect Hernán Ruiz with later work by others until 1766, its interior includes nave, chapels, altars, and entrances in the courtyard loggias, incorporating undisturbed mosque fabric. Its presence outside is broadcast by flying buttresses, a tall, pitched-roofed nave, and an octagonal, pyramidal crossing higher than the one over the tholos at the *mihrab.* Completing the transformation was the minaret's encasement, which had begun in 1593 (Figure 11.7).

Open loggia hypostyles often served as markets, often under public regias as at the BASILICA, ANDREA PALLADIO, VICENZA, 1546 and PALAZZO PRETORIO, SAN GIOVANNI VALDARNO, 1296. **Orsanmichele, Florence, 1337** was a hypostyle grain market below the hall where the guilds managed the grain supply to assure its availability during shortages, drought, and sieges and to control its price. After a painting of the Madonna in the open loggia worked a miracle, it was enclosed and made into an oratory in 1380.

This free-standing hypostyle loggia built to market luxury goods was designed by the court architect of Duke Cosimo I de Medici. It stands on the point where the ancient Roman cardo entered the ancient city and steps away from the medieval city's addition of the Palazzo Vecchio.

Four bays by three, the longer side parallels the main street at grade. Twenty Composite columns carry broad, blank arches and sail vaults above tie rods below an unseen, four-pitch, tile roof. Large piers equipped with sculpture niches on their exterior faces stand outside and just shy of the columns at the corners with thinner, blank piers along both short ends. That unconventional treatment

FIGURE 11.7 Mercato Nuovo, Giovanni Battista del Tasso, Florence, Italy, 1547–51.

elevates its status above a mere market hall and is typical of that period's style, as is the uncanonical entablature: a very thin two-fascia architrave followed by a tall blank frieze and concluding in a thin cornice; note also the scroll modillions acting as keystones and piers and columns in the spandrels.

The eight niches were ready for statues like those at earlier Florentine public loggias. Orsanmichele had fourteen sculpture niches holding statues of the guilds' patron saints. The civic ceremonial, 1 × 3 **Loggia dei Lanzi, 1356** included small statues of the cardinal and theological virtues in the arch spandrels and frieze. Here, however, only three hold statues, from the 19th c. and honoring Renaissance Florentines (Figure 11.8).

Ferrous metals had been given hidden roles in the art of building or as tie rods left unobserved in the architecture. Here was iron's great coming-out party in what has become an icon in the Modernist canon. Construction is in command, and architecture plays no role, in a dramatic building that served a program that traditional means and design could not, and one that itself was new only in the elephantine size of the event and the conditions it had to satisfy: to provide a venue for a vast international exposition of manufactured goods built quickly and inexpensively, be only a six-month resident in London's Hyde Park, and not disturb a single tree on the site.

Hundreds of designs were offered, but only the one that the gardener and greenhouse builder Joseph Paxton had developed for greenhouse construction satisfied all the conditions. Industry could produce the thousands of cast iron, wood, and glass pieces that were required, and cheap, unskilled labor using specially built machines could quickly assemble them into repetitive, trabeated

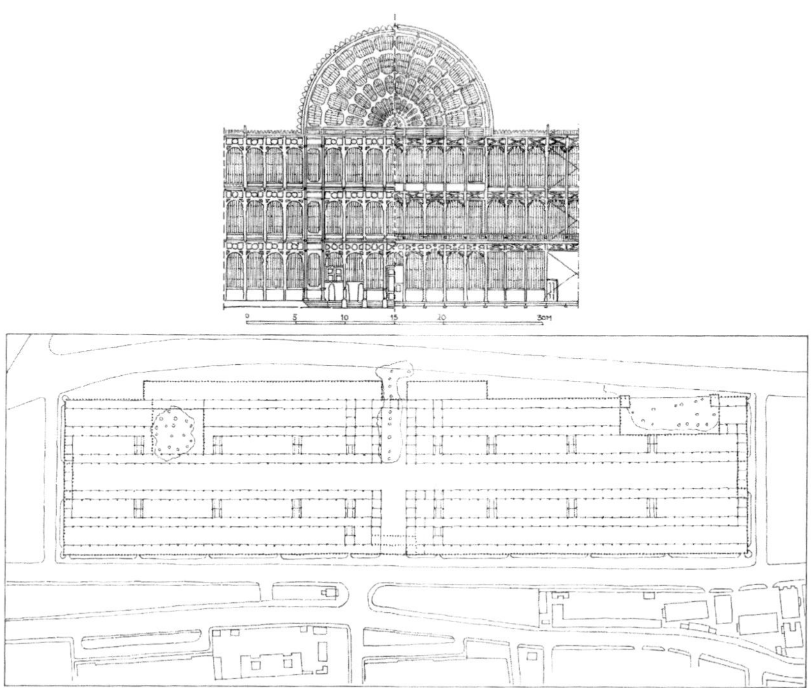

FIGURE 11.8 Crystal Palace, Joseph Paxton, London, England, 1851.

bays 24 feet (7.3 m) square and install the acres of glass for walls and roof that gave it its popular name. Ridge-and-furrow roofs drained rain out through the columns, and canvas protected the contents from the sun. Enlarged bays accommodated larger exhibits, and the configuration skirted two clumps of trees and put another under a great laminated wood-trussed cross vault 128 feet (39 m) high that bisected the simple plan. A similar vault ran through the main concourse's 1851 feet (564 m), the year of the event, and like it rose through two layers of two galleries separated by 72 feet (22 m) rising above the ground.

Often overlooked is the role of Owen Jones (1809–74), who supervised the installation of exhibits from throughout the world and gave the building color. He had studied the newly discovered polychromy in ancient works, and he had been deeply moved by the **Alhambra, Granada, 13th–14th cs**. He had the building painted with alternating stripes of red, yellow, and blue separated by stripes of white that led to giving a larger role to color in architecture.

The building's novelty and the exposition's popularity and success—six million visited it—led to variations for fairs in New York, Chicago, and elsewhere. This building was disassembled and rebuilt, enlarged, elsewhere in London where it served as an exposition and museum venue until its contents burned in 1936 and destroyed it (Figure 11.9).

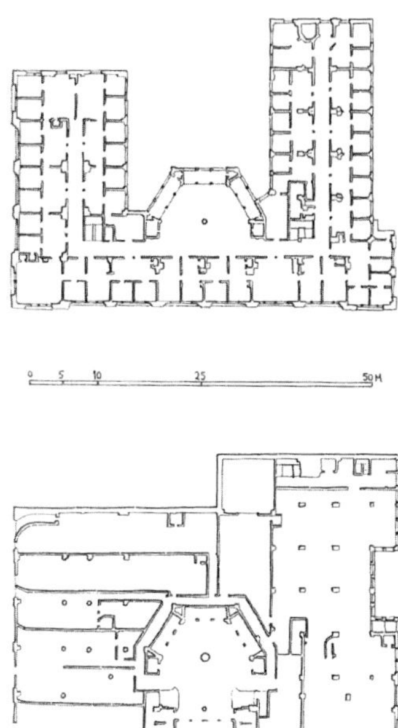

FIGURE 11.9 Marquette Building, John Holabird, Martin Roche, Chicago, Illinois, U.S.A., 1893–95.

Chicago rose from trading post in 1837 to the first world city founded during the commercial age. It was nearly destroyed by fire in 1871; it recovered; and as it prepared for the **World's Columbian Exposition, Daniel H. Burnham, et al, Chicago, 1893** the commercial center, squeezed into a muddy area between two branches of the Chicago River and Lake Michigan, was becoming seriously overcrowded. Railyards now blocked its southern expansion with an elevated transit system in 1891 further constricting it. The only place to go was up, but three massive masonry buildings demonstrated the high foundation costs involved: the **Monadnock Block, John Holabird and John Wellborn Root, 1884–91**; the **Marshall Field Wholesale Store, Henry Hobson Richardson, 1886** (not extant); and the voluminous **Chicago Auditorium Building (now Roosevelt University), Louis Henry Sullivan and Dankmar Adler, 1887–88**. Two of these buildings survive, but a person now walks slightly down when entering them. Machine-compressed brick ("sewer brick") gave the Monadnock, a commercial office building, additional rentable space with swelling oriel bays following its rise for seventeen stories up tapering walls that never encountered a molding or ornament. Here was an "honest" (as per John Ruskin) expressive character with an internal ferrous metal framework providing lateral stability and holding elevators, corridors, and stairs, with light filtering in from glassed-in offices.

Anticipating building height restrictions, developers rushed to obtain building permits at the old, 220-foot height. Advances in foundation and steel technology allowed them to build steel-framed, terra cotta-clad commercial blocks later cataloged as "Chicago School Buildings," among them the MARQUETTE BUILDING, a hypostyle with double-loaded corridors. (The shortener street wing in the plan was filled in 1905 as shown in the drawing.)

It deserves an exalted place within the classicism that gained the world's admiration for America's tall buildings that had earned the **Flatiron Building, Daniel H. Burnham, New York, 1901–02** fame and star billing atop Banister Fletcher's "Tree of Architecture." These and others illustrate the absorption of traditional design with invention serving new functions and using new technology while retaining an undeniable connection with the classical tradition, for example, the PALAZZO FARNESE, ROME, ANTONIO DA SANGALLO, 1516; MICHELANGELO, 1546, here heightened with a stretched middle, an increased window to wall ratio, corner bays suggesting quoining but using horizontal drafting popular in 17th and 18th c. French *hôtel particulier,* and a cornice (now restored) scaled to the building's mass. Inside, the richly decorated double-height elevator lobby retains the second level's parapet decorated by Tiffany featuring the expedition of Père Marquette, the first Europeans to overwinter in Chicago. The marble vestibule was originally entered through a three-column in antis propylaea (subsequently removed for subway construction) that, like banks ranking next higher among civil purposes, elevated the civil purpose of the functions it served.

Similarly inventive within traditional classical compositions but carried much farther was the **Schlesinger & Meyer Store, Louis Sullivan, 1899–1904; restored 2006–09,** with elaborately decorated shop window frames displaying fashions for the sporting set below nine stories of wide, light-admitting windows within simply incised white terra cotta up to a recessed story where his inventive columns hold a thin, projecting cornice.

It, the **Flatiron**, and the MARQUETTE BUILDING enjoy iconic status in historicist histories of architecture as examples of styles that Modernism must replace. Sigfried Giedion called the MARQUETTE BUILDING "exceptionally well-proportioned, imposing in its simplicity and its wide expanse of 'Chicago windows'," a comment he illustrated with a cropped photograph erasing its classicism and from an angle that obscured the propylaea (Figure 11.10).

In New York City, the Pennsylvania Railroad's impressive metropolitan station stood iceberg-like above tracks and platforms. Access through tunnels beneath the rivers east and west of Manhattan forced the substitution of steam locomotives with electrical traction, for example, since the 1930s in Washington, D.C., which allowed for the station's below-grade operation and platforms. The exterior of Charles Follen McKim's masterpiece rose above its five-story neighbors with a pink granite mass occupying two city blocks.

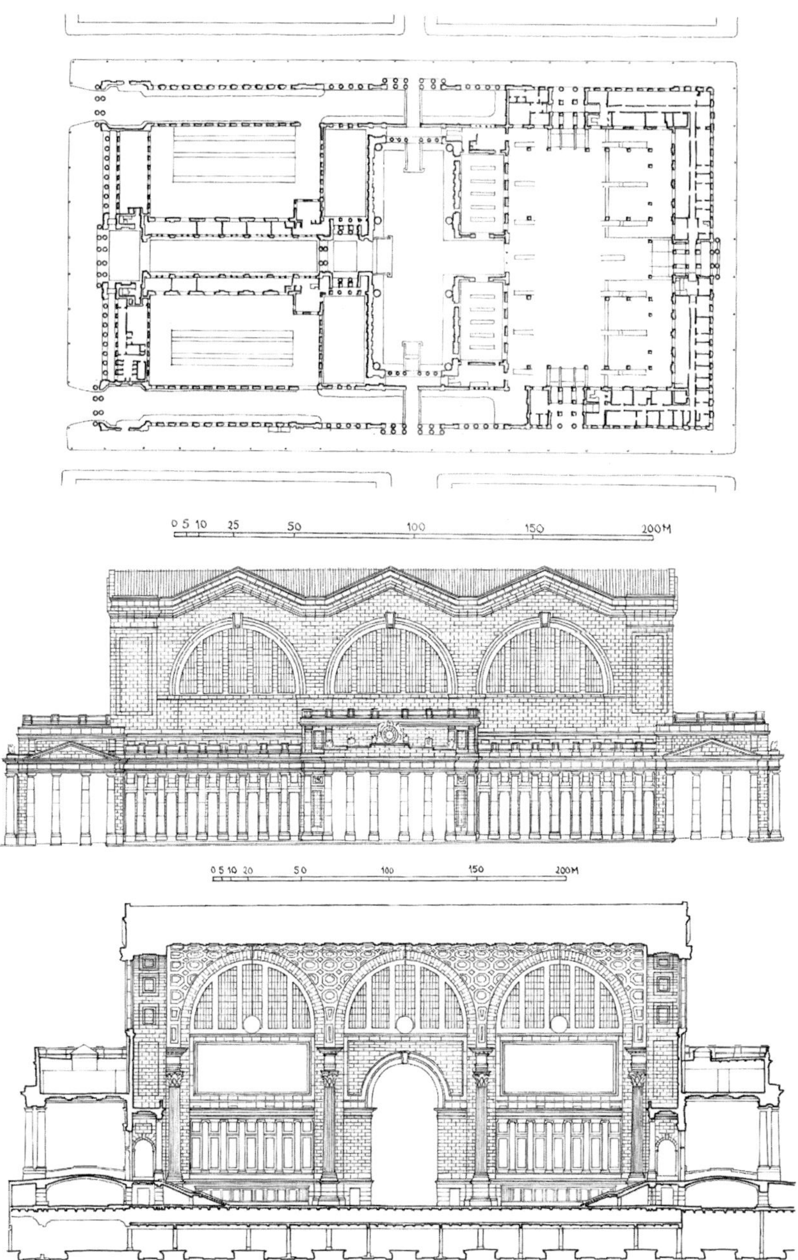

FIGURE 11.10 Pennsylvania Station, McKim, Mead, and White, New York, U.S.A., 1901–10. (a) Plan and (b) elevation and section.

Its broad, five-part front façade had a hexastyle propylaea with eagles flanking a clock before an attic, end pavilions with tetrastyle temple fronts, and connecting hyphens, each with eight pink Tennessee marble unfluted columns, Doric on bases here as elsewhere. Each side dilutes this scheme with a tetrastyle propylaea at midpoint below a high, looming enclosure with a peaked gable and five-pane thermal window, a motif repeated in triplicate along the long enclosure's sides paralleling the front.

Beneath that enclosure, the general waiting room is based on the caldarium of the **Baths of Caracalla, Rome, 212**. It is reached after a long shopping arcade over an open court ventilating the tracks. A cross-vaulted vestibule opens to stairs descending beneath a grand arch. Side entrances offer entrance directly from vehicle ramps that enter through the front's end bays and descend along the exterior's sides, and by pedestrians who find stairs at the end of the bridge over that ramp.

Within this magnificent hall massive, fluted, Corinthian columns support three great coffered cross vaults rising 150 feet and lit by those great thermal windows. Lunch and dining rooms are on the entrance side, and separate men's and women's waiting rooms on the other flanking its broad access to the concourse where stairs lead down to eleven train platforms and 21 tracks beneath glass floors.

The hypostyle's steel frame was encased within the fictive membrature of travertine, plaster, and terra cotta with the concourse's glazing held within exposed steel reproducing vault shapes. Here we find an expressive character for the place where the city meets the railroad and a counterpart to the great vaulted hall that passengers passed through on their way to the great machines that carry people to and from distant places. That hall, the crown jewel of the hypostyle, was based on the great hall in an ancient hypostyle bath that survived to be adapted into **Santa Maria degli Angeli, Michelangelo, Rome, 1563**.

The hypostyle was barbarically destroyed in 1963, and the air rights sold for development, giving a major boost to the preservation movement. The facilities for continued operations below have received deserved condemnation, and they have recently been supplemented by the Moynihan Train Hall within the reconstructed interior of the former **Farley Post Office, McKim, Mead, and White, 1908** surviving immediately east of the station.

Figure 11.11 (same as Figure 4.7). At ROCKEFELLER CENTER, RAYMOND HOOD, HARVEY WI-LEY CORBETT, AND OTHERS, NEW YORK CITY, 1931, **Radio City Music Hall, Edward Durell Stone and Donald Deskey, 1931–32** (see plan in our drawing) came first with a spectacular golden interior holding 5,960 spectators for stage shows and films. Occupying the northwest corner of the original six-block development, a 31-story building rises above its entrance lobby. In 1936 an unsuccessful retail center was modified to become the Center's most familiar and public element. In a block on the eastern edge (right on our plan) is the sunken plaza surrounded by convenient places for viewing and used as an ice rink in the winter, an open-air dining plaza

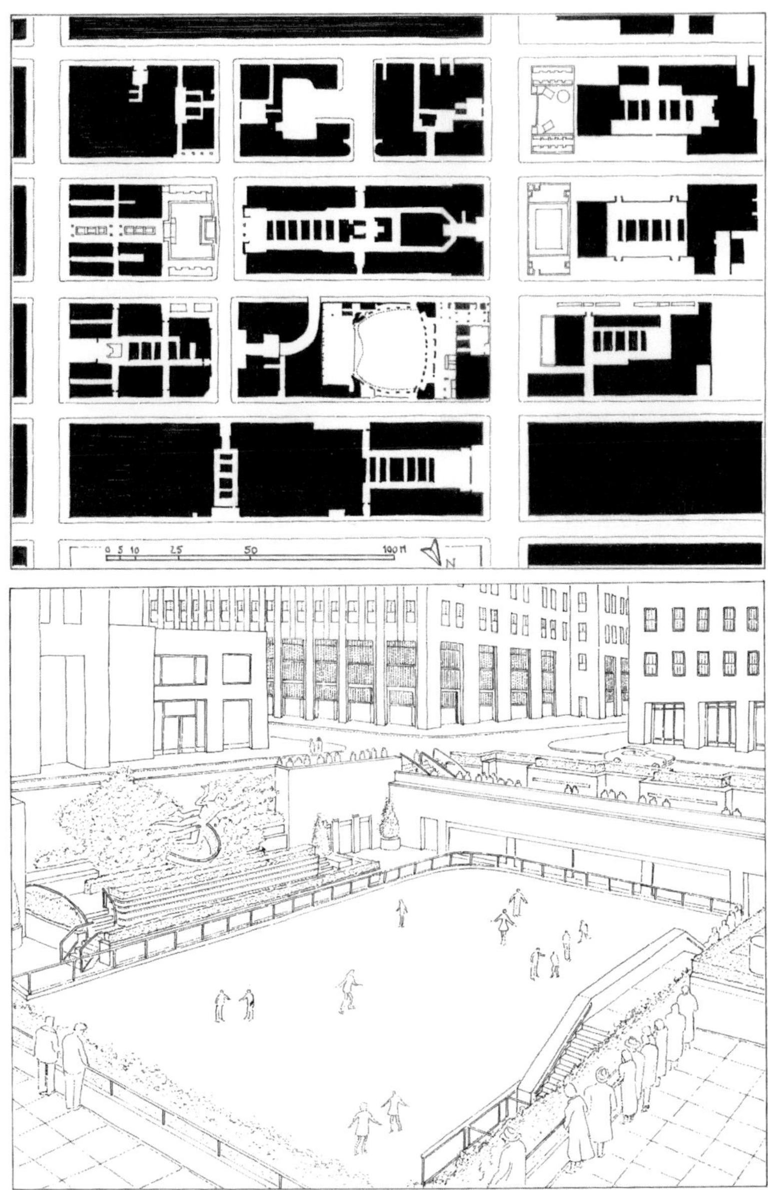

FIGURE 11.11 Rockefeller Center, Raymond Hood, Harvey Wiley Corbett, and others, New York, U.S.A., 1931. (See also figure 4.7, Rockefeller Center Rink.) Six thin Manhattan blocks, formerly the site of Columbia University, were involved in the Rockefeller family's first real estate investments. After a projected new Metropolitan Opera House ran afoul of the 1929 Depression, attention shifted to serving new industries involved in radio, film, television, publications, and air travel, with development occurring piecemeal according to opportunities, and guided by a traditional image of the modern commercial city.

in other seasons, and between Thanksgiving and New Year's the setting for a decorated Christmas tree sized in scale with the site. Access from fashionable Fifth Avenue across from **Saint Patrick's Cathedral, John Renwick, Jr., 1858** is via a through-block, 60-foot-wide pedestrian Promenade or Channel Gardens, with plantings sloping downward between two 7-story buildings with shop windows for high-end goods, the British Empire Building and La Maison Française. Seen from it and prominent as a backdrop between a pair of bulkier, slightly lower buildings is the short side of the 70-story **RCA Building** slab, the Center's tallest, with Paul Manship's *Prometheus* statue (1934) at its base.

Nearly every one of the fourteen buildings in the original six-block area has a different height, between 6 and 70 stories. The areas between the north-south Avenues constitute a largely car-free pedestrian zone. The buildings meet the sidewalks, many are enriched with sculpture, and along the side streets are trees. These factors produce a sense of enclosure that is reinforced by the similarity of the lower stories to one another, making the differences in height hardly noticeable except from a distance, where their collection into an identifiable entity comes from their limestone facades rising unbroken between tiers of metal-framed windows or set on flat setbacks responding to zoning regulations.

Our plan includes the tier of blocks built west and north of the Center has been expanded after World War II. Their buildings are alien, lacking limestone skins, standing back from the streets, satisfying the new zoning codes that replaced setbacks with plazas, embodying the expressive character of Modernism, and, in typical New York fashion, being derided as "the boxes the first buildings came in." (Figure 11.12).

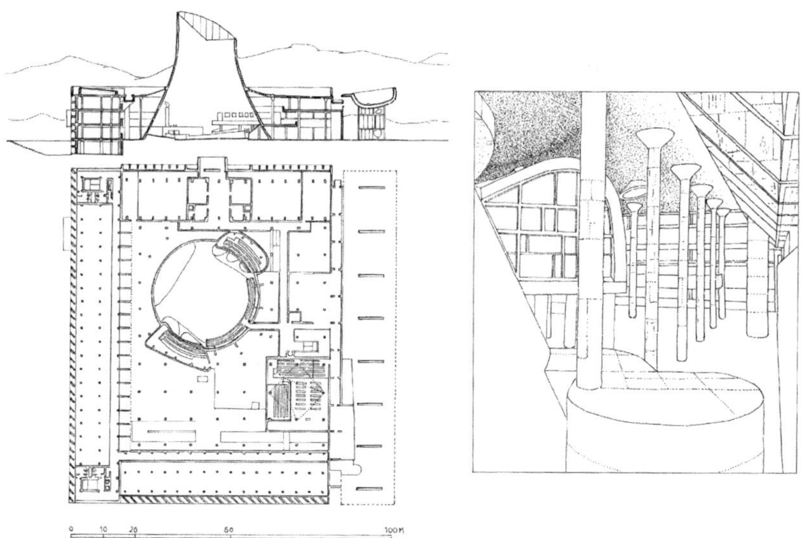

FIGURE 11.12 Palace of Assembly, Le Corbusier, Chandigarh, India, 1951–62.

This Modernist monument serves the unicameral legislature of a new Punjab state formed after Britain's 1947 departure and India's sanguinary separation from Pakistan. At the foot of the Himalayas, Oxford-educated Indian Prime Minister Jawaharlal Nehru (b. 1889; r. 1947–64) founded Chandigarh as its capital; it now has more than a million residents. This new city was designed according to the **CIAM "Charter of Athens," 1933** and, like its buildings, was intended to have a distinctly anti-traditional expressive character to represent this new nation's future. The gridded plan of Albert Meyer, planner, and Maciej Nowicki, architect, passed to Charles-Édouard Jeanneret (1887–1965) (Le Corbusier) after Nowicki's death. He added a nearly 1 × 3 km appendix for its three principal government buildings with one, the governor's palace, never built.

Le Corbusier had pioneered designs using concrete, a low-technology material appealing to developing countries. He popularized the **Dom-ino, 1914–15**, a simple concrete floor-frame-roof configuration that could be enclosed with simple materials such as concrete blocks. It is now a ubiquitous vernacular: stacked, it makes a tall building; spread out, it makes a hypostyle; and elaborated, it can make government building such as these.

They illustrate his maxim, "architecture is the masterly, correct and magnificent play of masses brought together in light." The PALACE OF ASSEMBLY has four such masses. One is the four-story, nearly square enclosure capped by a high, flat extension and balconies with angled sides and *brises-soleil* defending against the sun. The second is the building's fourth side where, beyond a water basin (visible in plan and section here), the entrance and colorful entry door are deep within a long canopy consisting of a curved, upward swooping bib supported on eight thin fins suggesting a propylaeon. The other two masses project above the roof. One is shown in dotted lines in the plan but not in our section: a three-sided pyramidal form signaling the presence of council rooms inside. The other, and most conspicuous, is an adaptation of an industrial cooling tower using a hyperbolic curve rotated about a central axis with a slant-cut top. Its top can be reached by a catwalk on an open framework truss from a small, rectangular, equally high shaft, not shown in our drawing.

Beneath that conspicuous topping is the theater-shaped legislative chamber below tiers for spectators and service rooms. The saucer dome giving way to sides leading up to this blue top have amoebae shapes against red and yellow backgrounds that, along with other elements, add vibrant color displays relieving expanses of bare concrete. Surrounding the chamber is a grid of thin, circular columns with flaring cone capitals making possible the interior's free plan, triple-height vestibule with ample circulation around the chamber, and walkways looking into the court.

Far across the long plaza over a carpark is the **Palace of Justice, 1953**, a lower, simplified version of the Palace of Assembly. In the other direction behind and away from the legislature is the eight-story, 254 m long **Secretariat Building, 1953**, whose parentage is his **Unité d' Habitation** in **Marseilles, Berlin, and elsewhere, 1947–52** (Figure 11.13).

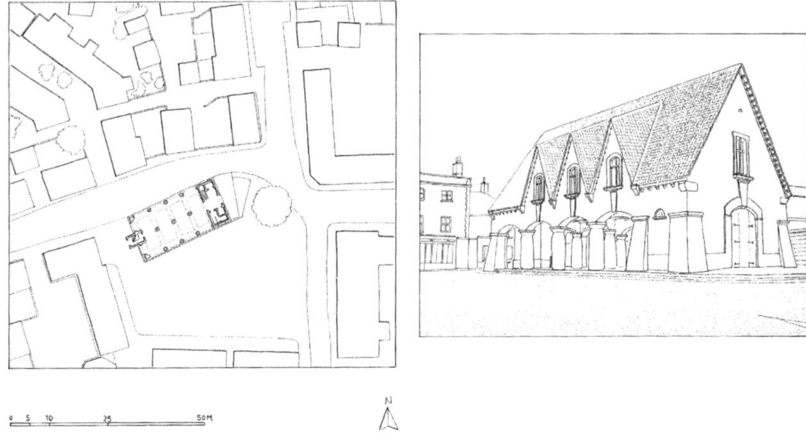

FIGURE 11.13 Brownsword Market Hall, John Simpson, Poundbury, England, 2000.

From Italy to England, people often gather at a centrally located hypostyle market beneath a large hall used for important occasions. This example in Poundbury is for the resident of the project sponsored by Charles, Prince of Wales, and guided by Léon Krier. It, the town plan, and the buildings by builders and architects draw on local traditions embodying New Urbanism.

The model for its configuration and membrature was **Market Hall, Tetbury, 1655** (with later alterations). Both have robust Doric columns on the perimeter and through the long center, with robust piers at the corners completing Tetbury's 2 × 8 hypostyle and Poundbury's 2 × 5. In the pair of bays at one end, the columns are replaced by piers like those on the corners to frame the enclosure for the hall's entrance and for access and service facilities. An emergency exit with corner piers is attached to the other end. The hall's interior has open, timber cedar framing that exploits the spatial potential of the dormers. Natural light enters through steep-pitched dormers above the central three bays on each side.

The lower story's unfluted baseless Doric columns have an exaggerated stoutness even greater than those at the ancient so-called **Basilica, Paestum, c. 550 BCE**, that became popular around 1,800 after that site's publication and the period's Egyptomania popularized Egyptian pylons seen in the corner pylons. The columns carry low segmental arches supporting exposed wooden beams for the hall's floor. The dormers stop short of the steeply pitched roof's ridge, all with brown tile roofing and corbels at the main roof's eave line. The end wall window and dormers are set in buff-colored, rendered walls and have frames and exaggerated keystones in brown stone connecting the arches to the windowsills.

INDEX